Stripes, Nails, Thorns, and The Blood

By

Dr. Bree M. Keyton, Th.D., D.C.E.

Black Forest Press
San Diego, California
September, 2002

Second Edition

Stripes, Nails, Thorns, and The Blood

By

Dr. Bree M. Keyton, Th.D., D.C.E.

PUBLISHED IN THE UNITED STATES OF AMERICA
BY
BLACK FOREST PRESS
P.O. Box 6342
Chula Vista, CA 91909-6342

Scripture references are *King James Version* and *Strong's Exhaustive Concordance*, unless otherwise specified.

First Publishing Quadrilogy Publishing © 1997
Words and Lyrics by Bree Keyton © 1977 All rights reserved.
Cover Art by M & N Design Company, Monica Nagy
New Revised Version of *Strips, Nails, Thorns, and The Blood* 2002
Segen Books and Black Forest Press 2002

Printed in the United States of America
Library of Congress
Cataloging-in-Publication

ISBN: 1-58275-076-9

Stripes, Nails, Thorns, and The Blood

Overview

Part One: *THORNS*
*Significance of the thorns
*What we gain by Jesus' crown of thorns
*How to resist attacks against the mind

Part Two: *NAILS*
*What was accomplished by the nails
*Breaking demonic strongholds
*How to receive deliverance
*Spiritual warfare—dealing decisively with the enemy
*Understanding the enemy
*Detailed account of the spirit realm
*The armor of God—function of each piece of armor revealed
*Tough questions answered—myths dispelled
*Complete listing and explanation of demonic strongholds

Part Three: *THE BLOOD*
*The significance of Jesus' blood
*Jesus' passion—reveals significance of each moment
*Event by event exegesis from Gethsemane to the resurrection
*Analysis of Isaiah 53

Part Four: *STRIPES*
*The significance of the stripes
*Complete listing of healing scriptures
*How to receive and maintain your healing
*Walking in divine health
*How to heal the sick
*Perplexing healing questions answered

Table of Contents

Table Of Contents For: *THORNS*

Table Of Contents For: *NAILS*

Table Of Contents For: *THE BLOOD*

Table Of Contents For: *STRIPES*

Foreword

An absolutely amazing personal testimony which shares the power of the Holy Spirit and the healing and anointing of the Lord, as manifested through the person of Dr. Bree Keyton through her faithful and committed service to God. Each page is filled with golden nuggets of information which help the reader in his or her quest for deliverance. Hope is given for suffering lives that have been troubled with the spirit of Jezebel for long and short periods of time, by sharing living examples of persecutions overcome that were transcended into holy victories of glory for Yahshua our Messiah.

Dr. Keyton displays her dedicated courage and fervent desire to see the devil's captives set free by praying for the healing of the sick, hurting, and broken-hearted. These tasks have been a true joy and challenge every step of her way, as God continues to be victorious. The Lord provides Dr. Keyton with comfort and assurance, as He renders His perpetual godly assistance and divine intervention in her ministry. This book is awesome and rich in illustration and direction; *Stripes, Nails, Thorns, and The Blood* is one of the best biblical references, and perhaps the most useful available for study, healing and learning, in the Christian book market today, for utterly detailing the spiritual warfare in which we are constantly consumed and the daily struggle against it. Herein, the answers and explanations for perplexing questions are answered intelligently and sensibly.

Every Christian, new or old in the faith, needs to have this book in his or her arsenal of spiritual weapons. Christians need to be militarily equipped with the word of God and the knowledge of how to properly and effectively defend against satan and his demons. Dr. Keyton speaks about demonic strongholds and how to identify the enemy. Is this important? Yes, it is, and so is recognizing demonic spirits, the councils of hell and the chains of bondage existing in today's world. We learn about the role of an intercessor, family and generational curses, bitter-root judgments, inner vows and soul ties and we become aware of many types of spirits spreading their deadly venom amongst mankind. Spirits like that of suicide, death, fear, anxiety, confusion and rejection. We learn where they come from, what makes them strong and what makes us so vulnerable. In fact, we simply learn how to cope with the forces of evil which cause us ominous affliction, pain and sorrow.

Read this book for knowledge and enlightenment. Read this book for preparation and awareness. Read this book to discover meaningful ways to glorify and magnify the power of the Lord Jesus Christ.

Dahk Knox, Ph.D., Ed.D., D.Sc.
Publisher, Author, Retired Professor,
Dean and Vice-President of Academic Affairs

Introduction

The first time I was asked to give my testimony on TV, my pastor's wife cautioned me not to disclose anything that wasn't "nice." She contended that people would be turned off. I discovered, over time, that giving my testimony is not so much about sharing every detail each time, as it is about imparting the right details as the Holy Spirit leads and breathes on it.

One time I might be led to share about Jezebel, or healing, another time, deliverance, the occult, depression, rock and roll, abortion, persecution, or bitter-root judgments, etc. Each time, as I learned to be led by the Spirit, He would bring people who needed a specific touch from the LORD. As I saw lives profoundly changed by the anointing, and the LORD used me as a catalyst to break strongholds, I lost the desire to be a man-pleaser, and fervently desired to be a God-pleaser.

Being transparent with my testimony and helping others receive deliverance has been my delight: finding that my failures and victories help others break through, a privilege. When people feel isolated in their problems and are embarrassed to seek help, the devil has a field day. This book will be used, I pray, to heal the sick, the hurting, the broken-hearted, bring deliverance to the captives, and to teach God's people to walk in victory.

In May of 1993, YHWH gave me a vision of Yahshua Messiah (Jesus Christ) receiving His stripes before He went to the cross. It was a horrible, bloody vision that shook me to my foundation. The sight of Yahshua Messiah's blood and flesh being ripped and flayed, pieces of skin and blood exploding everywhere, was more than I could bear. YHWH spoke to me and told me to write a song and He would heal His people. I wrote a song with thirty-nine whip cracks in it, and YHWH has been faithful to heal His people. I debuted it at a crusade two weeks later and many were healed that night.

The next day I was praising and worshiping my Father for His faithfulness, when He gave me the directive to write the songs *"Nails"* and *"Thorns."* I said, "LORD, what do the nails and thorns represent?" The subsequent three-year journey to find the answer to this question was fraught with prayer, fasting, waiting, and YHWH's divine influence working patience in my heart.

I received all of the Quadrilogy, *Stripes, Nails, Thorns and The Blood*, through revelation. Throughout this time I praised YHWH for His comfort and assurance, and the aid and assistance He constantly ministered to me. Many people have been healed and delivered through the anointing on these songs after hearing them on the radio and TV, at my concerts and from listening to the CD. My husband likes to listen to it routinely while driving, to get free from daily oppressions that attempt to attach themselves to all of us. I recommend using these powerfully anointed songs and this book as a springboard to deliverance.

Writing this book, with the fervent desire to see the captives set free, has been a joy and a challenge. It is such a privilege to uncover the truths of Biblical healing and deliverance, so YHWH's people may walk in victory, marching together to defeat the enemy of our souls.

Since there are many gods, I have decided to make frequent use of *our* God's Name, YHWH (pronounced Yahweh). Also, I love to call Jesus by His given Hebrew name, Yahshua (some spell this Yeshua), the Messiah. In the movie *"Chariots of Fire,"* the missionary Eric Liddell, an Olympic athlete, told his wife when she wanted him to give up running and go with her to China, "God made me fast! When I run, I feel His pleasure!"

I must tell you that when I speak Jesus' true Hebrew name, Yahshua, *I feel His pleasure!*

Part One

THORNS

The crown of thorns
precedes the crown of glory

Thorns

from the *Heart & Soul Surrender* CD   Quadrilogy Publishing 1997
Lyrics by Bree Keyton

The crown of thorns *(Mark 15:17)* **that Jesus wore was an attack on the soulish realm; mind, will, emotions, imagination and memory, where the** *real* **battles take place. Thorns represent the hindrances, evil circumstances, and cares of this life.** *(Matthew 13:22)* **He could never lean His head to rest from the unrelenting pain as the thorns bit into His flesh. He suffered this to provide us rest from the ceaseless attacks of Satan against our souls** *(1 Peter 4:12)*, **through leaning on Christ and His protection against the fiery darts of the wicked one.** *(Ephesians 6:16)*

Thorns and thistles were part of the curse, and a sign of our sin. *(Genesis 3:11-18)* **But He Who knew no sin became sin for us, that we might have eternal life.** *(2 Corinthians 5:21)* **He bore the curse on His own head, that we might have the mind of Christ.** *(1 Corinthians 2:16)* **Blood from the thorn's wounds fell on the ground to cleanse it and deliver us from the curse.**

The first Adam was condemned to labor among the thorns and thistles to bring forth a harvest. *(Genesis 3:17)* **The last Adam wore the thorns and a robe of purple** *(John 19:2)* **that stood for purple thistles, to bring forth a harvest of souls.** *(Mark 15:17)* **Jesus gave us the weapons of our warfare. They are not carnal, but mighty through God to the pulling down of strongholds, casting down imaginations, and every high thing that exalts itself against the knowledge of God, bringing into captivity every thought to the obedience of Christ.** *(2 Corinthians 10:4-5; Ephesians 6)*

His thorns became our helmet of salvation. *(Ephesians 6:17)*

The crown of thorns precedes the crown of glory. *(1 Peter 5:4)*

Chapter One
Thorns: A Metaphor For Sin

Thorns illustrate and symbolize sin: Under the beauty of the rose, lurks the pain and ugliness of a thorn. As thorns pierce inwardly (Jesus' side was pierced), they draw blood (He shed His blood for us), they make holes (holes left in Jesus' hands and feet), and can shred flesh (the scourging shredded His flesh): Thorns became a metaphor for sin and punishment. As we meditate on what Jesus endured for us, our love blooms and flourishes. Jesus is the "Lily" and "the Rose" *(Song of Solomon 2:1)*, Who took the thorns for us on His head, and set us free from the damaged, wounded memories that Satan uses to torment us. He bore the curse in His own body. *(Galatians 3:13)*

The curse of the thorns

The "Crown of Thorns" was a constant, painful reminder to Jesus that He wore, for us, the chastisement of our peace. It was probably intended to mock the crown of laurel leaves that Caesar and other officials wore whenever they returned in victory; the purple robe was a noble symbol as He bore our sins and carried our sorrows, which the soldiers put on Him to mock His claim of deity. The curse, that after the perfection of Eden we should toil on ground that brings forth thorns and thistles, was unwittingly fulfilled through the soldiers' cruelty. Thorns tear the flesh, as His flesh was torn for us. *(Genesis 3:17-18)*

Thorns: the place of the skull

Jesus was crucified at Golgotha, which means place of the skull. This was no accident. The skull is where we must be crucified daily, allowing God to mold us into His image. Because of the fall, there is a curse against our minds. Jesus redeemed our minds, so that now we have the mind of Christ. *(1 Corinthians 2:16)* Messiah's mind is not our mind until He fully owns us, and we cannot become fully His, until we do what He told us to do.

Jesus' helmet was the crown of thorns, but He gave *us* the helmet of salvation *(Ephesians 6:17)* to war against the enemy, a weapon *proven in battle* through His victorious resurrection, to protect our minds from the constant bombardment in our thought lives. As we allow ourselves to be conformed to Christ's image through renewing our *minds*, we can wear this helmet, trusting in the perfectly fitted armor, because we know the One Who *proved* it. He demonstrated to us that it works.

Pulling down strongholds

How can this be possible? Because Jesus was tempted just as we are, yet without sin. *(Hebrews 4:15)* The evil desires of our carnal flesh *can* be harnessed. How? Because the weapons Jesus gave us are *not* carnal. They have been tried in fires of affliction, so extreme that you and I can only imagine them. He wore the crown of thorns on His head so that we can pull down strongholds, the desires of carnal flesh that exalt themselves against the knowledge of God. *(1 Corinthians 10:4-5)* His thorns become our helmet of salvation. *(Ephesians 6)* Some day we will wear a crown of glory. *(1 Peter 5:4)*

Sin personified

Sin is personified beginning in Genesis 4:7.

> *...if thou doest not well, sin LIETH at the door. And unto thee shall be his desire, and thou shalt rule over him.*

The word LIETH *(Strong's 7257, rabats)* means to crouch or hide on all four legs like a recumbent animal. This is a vivid picture of how the devil lies in wait to pounce on us as we open the portal to sin through our own acts of disobedience. *The Amplified Bible* is illuminating on this scripture:

> *...if you do not do well, sin crouches at your door; its desire is for you, and you must master it. (Genesis 4:7)*

Sin was crouching at Cain's door just as it is crouching at our doors. He failed the temptation, displeasing YHWH by failing to offer a blood sacrifice. Instead, he followed his own willful desires by offering grain. God saw this and warned Cain, but his desire for revenge was greater than his desire to please and obey God. Jesus mastered sin by successfully resisting temptation and defeating the devil on the cross, that we, too, could master sin in Jesus' Name, take up our crosses and follow the true Messiah.

Chapter Two
Attacks Against the Mind

The mind is focal point of attack

The mind, being the focal point of Satan's attack on us, becomes high ground in the battle against Satan. When ancient pagan peoples worshipped their gods, they worshipped on high ground, called high places or groves. Satan wants to attack our high places (our minds). Satan is a constant aggressor and bombards us daily, perhaps hundreds of times a day, with thoughts of unclean origin: thoughts shot into our midst from Satan's arsenal are most accurately defined as propaganda. They are just like the propaganda of modern warfare. Their goal is to demoralize the victim by any method possible. Lies and half-truths are propagated, and if you receive these lies then the battle is lost, your homeland defeated. Demons are often assigned to speak the same lie in a person's mind several times a day for a whole lifetime. It is necessary to launch a resistance that is equally persistent.

Personal attacks

Other tactics used by Satan's army are personal attacks against you to demoralize or take the wind out of your sails through shame and guilt over both past and recent sins. Even if you have repented of the sin, Satan is frequently successful at reminding you of your unworthiness and causing you to hang your head and agree with him that all is lost and hope is gone. The result is a warrior with his defenses down, vulnerable to the next round of attack.

Mixing truth with lies

Another effective mode of attack is that the enemy mixes truth with lies to confuse us. Con artists, thieves and opportunists of all kinds have employed this tactic for personal gain for thousands of years, ever since Adam and Eve's expulsion from the garden. The father of lies became our father the moment the first Adam yielded to temptation and sin. If one lie of the enemy is accepted, others will follow. It is even better for demons if they can coerce their victims into speaking lies out of their own mouths, such as judgments against others, and lies, rumors, anger and false blame. Negativity attracts demons because it can be used as a wedge to divide and conquer. Negativity engenders bitterness, offense, hatred, blame and feeds hurts and wounds. Demons of the same name can easily attach themselves to each negative, sinful emotion that we allow to gain a foothold, and make it worse. All praise to our Messiah for coming to deliver us from the deceiver. Satan's only weapon now is *deception*. He goes about *as* a roaring lion, seeking whom he may devour.

Spiritual warfare

The devil remains a powerful force to deal with for those who are not born again, and those who do not employ spiritual warfare. (Much more on this subject in the *Nails* section of this book.) Jesus' nails, thorns, stripes, His blood and His death were endured for our sakes to set us free. Do not delay in receiving Jesus Christ as your Savior today. The attacks against your thoughts are Satan's bullets, an enemy tactic to demoralize and destroy you. Evil thoughts will come, but this is not sin. It only *becomes* sin when you *take* the thoughts, and let them have a place in your heart. Turning an evil thought over and over in your mind is a sign that spiritual warfare needs to take place against that thought and the demon who originated it. Demons love to attach themselves to a person's evil thoughts and stir up the emotions, energizing them. Put on the helmet of salvation right now! Resist the enemy by defeating him *before* he gains a foothold in your thought life. Apply the blood of Jesus to your mind daily, and bind scriptures to yourself for protection, deliverance and healing. Resist wicked thoughts and claim the victory in Jesus' Name.

Prayer for salvation

Jesus (Yahshua), I am a sinner, but I repent of all my sins right now in the Name of Yahshua the Messiah (Jesus the Christ of Nazareth). Please forgive me and wash me clean in the blood of the perfect Lamb Who died for me.

I believe You are the Son of God (YHWH) and that YHWH raised You from the dead. I speak these words with my mouth and I believe them in my heart.

> *If thou shalt confess with thy mouth the LORD Jesus, and shalt believe in thine heart that God hath raised Him from the dead, thou shalt be saved. For with the heart man believeth unto righteousness; and with the mouth confession is made unto salvation. (Romans 10:9)*

Now, by faith, I believe I am born again. I receive eternal life through my Savior, Jesus Christ. Thank you, Jesus, for saving me. Amen. Now, I choose to give my life to You and to live for You.

Part Two

Nails

The final unchangeable blows that bound Jesus to the cross

Nails

from the *Heart & Soul Surrender* CD   Quadrilogy Publishing 1997
Lyrics by Bree Keyton

Nails: the final, unchangeable blows that bound Jesus to the cross in excruciating agony. The sound of the hammer rang out as each stroke that pierced His hands and feet brought us closer to deliverance from the enemy of our souls. For we wrestle not against flesh and blood, but against principalities, against powers, against the rulers of the darkness of this world, against spiritual wickedness in high places. *(Ephesians 6:12)* For the Name of Jesus is far above every name that is named *(Philippians 2:9)*, not only in this world, but also in that which is to come *(Ephesians 1:21)*, and He has put all things under His feet. *(1 Corinthians 15:27)* Jesus said, I give unto you power to tread on serpents and scorpions, and over all the power of the enemy. *(Luke 10:19)*

Therefore, in the Name of Jesus Christ, according to the authority given the believer in Luke 10:19, I bind Satan, the strong man *(Matthew 12:29)*, and I command the principalities, powers, mights and dominions to be loosed from all their assignments against <u>you</u>! In the Name of Jesus Christ of Nazareth:

PRINCIPALITY	*POWER*	*MIGHT*	*DOMINION*		*SINS*
I CAST OUT A SPIRIT OF:					
error	antichrist	heaviness	rejection		idolatry
(1 John 4:6)	*(1 John 4:3)*	*(Isaiah 63:1)*	*(Romans 1:28)*		*(Colossians 3:5)*
I CAST OUT A SPIRIT OF:					
slumber	whoredoms	gluttony	guilt	familiar spirit	unclean spirit
(Romans 8:11)	*(Hosea 4:12)*	*(Luke 21:34)*	*(James 2:10; Romans 3:19)*	*(2 Chronicles 33:6)*	*(Mark 1:23)*
I CAST OUT A SPIRIT OF:					
fear	bondage	anxiety	confusion		
(2 Timothy 1:7)	*(Romans 8:15)*	*(Psalm 55:3-6)*	*(Psalm 44:15; James 3:16)*		
I CAST OUT:					
a perverse spirit	a deaf & dumb spirit	a slothful spirit	a spirit of defiance		
(Isaiah 19:14)	*(Mark 9:25)*	*(Proverbs 26:13-14)*	*(Zechariah 7:11-12)*		
unbelief	a stubborn spirit				
(Matthew 17:20)	*(1 Samuel 15:23)*				
I CAST OUT:					
a lying spirit	divination	exhibitionism	deception		seduction
(1 Kings 22:22)	*(Acts 16:16)*	*(Acts 16:17; 1 Kings 22:11)*	*(2 Timothy 3:13)*		*(1 Timothy 4:1)*
I CAST OUT:					
a haughty spirit	a spirit of blindness	a critical spirit	a spirit of strife		
(Proverbs 16:18)	*(Matthew 12:22; 2 Cor.4:4)*	*(Matthew 7:5; Proverbs 22:10)*	*(James 3:16; Philippians 2:3)*		
a spirit of racism	pride	a religious spirit			
(Proverbs 26:21)	*(Psalm 73:6; 1 John 2:16)*	*(James 1:26)*			
I CAST OUT:					
a spirit of envy	unforgiveness	jealousy	hate		murder
(Proverbs 27:4)	*(Hebrews 12:15)*	*(Numbers 5:14; Proverbs 6:34)*	*(1 John 3:15)*		*(John 8:44)*
revenge	bitterness				
(Romans 12:19; Leviticus 19:18)	*(Romans 3:14; Ephesians 4:31)*				

I CAST OUT:

a spirit of witchcraft   **infirmity**   **anger**   **control**
(Deuteronomy 18:10)   *(Luke 3:11)*   *(Colossians 3:8)*   *(Matthew 20:25-26; Ephesians 1:21)*

sorcery   **a Jezebel spirit**   **rebellion**
(Revelation 21:8; 18:23; Genesis 31:25-26)   *(Revelation 2:20)*   *(1 Samuel 15:23)*

I CAST OUT:

All other strongholds that protect and keep pain and lies in, and God's truth and deliverance out. *(2 Corinthians 10:4; Ezekiel 13:6; 2 Thessalonians 2:9; Luke 4:18)*

It is written in Ezra 9:8, *Now for a little space, grace hath been shown from the LORD our God, to leave us a remnant to escape, and give us a NAIL in His holy place, that our God may lighten our eyes, and give us a little reviving in our bondage.*

In Colossians 2:14, it is written, *Jesus blotted out the handwriting of ordinances,* (the devil's ammunition against us) *and NAILED it to the cross.*

Now I pray God your whole spirit, soul and body be preserved blameless at the coming of our LORD Jesus Christ. *(1 Thessalonians 5:23)*

Will you repent and give up your sin today?

God will NAIL it to the cross! (sound of hammer)

Chapter Three
The Nail

In Satanism and the occult, Satan has a code name: The Nail.[1] He is the nail that fixed Jesus' hands and feet to the cross, but it is our sins that bound Him there, and His love for us that kept Him there. Satan would not have stirred up the envy (the Sanhedrin), hatred (the Pharisees) and greed (Judas) necessary to bring the innocent Lamb of God to the cross if he had known what the result would be.

> ...*the hidden wisdom...none of the PRINCES of this world knew: for had they known it, they would not have crucified the LORD of glory. (1 Corinthians 2:7-8)*

Satan and fallen angels are referred to in Biblical texts as PRINCES or principalities. *(Daniel 10:13; John 12:31)* All fallen angels were not locked up in Genesis six. The Bible reveals this clearly in numerous places, including the previous reference in Daniel. So, who are the fallen angels and who are the demons? These questions will be answered later, but one thing must be established: demons are not fallen angels and fallen angels are not demons. Because the wiles and deceit of Satan precipitated the fall of mankind, we must study and prepare, so that we do not continue to fall prey to his traps. Satan no longer wanted to serve the true King of the Universe in heaven, thus he led a rebellion because he wanted to rule, taking one-third of the angels with him when he fell. *(Revelation 12:7)*

The matter of who Satan was is answered in Luke 10:18 when Yahshua (Jesus) stated that He saw Satan fall from heaven like lightening. Satan, a fallen angel, was once Lucifer, a covering cherub, who had musical instruments in his body, and was a leader of angelic hosts in heaven, who caused one-third of the angels to fall. *(Isaiah 14:11-12; Ezekiel 28:13)* We need not fear him because the Messiah made a show of him openly, triumphing over him, and utterly defeating him. *(Colossians 2:15)* Satan is a forceful personality who hates mankind because we have been redeemed (though it is an individual choice to accept this salvation) while he is doomed forever to the lake of fire. *(Revelation 20:15)* He has great wrath against us because he believes this is unjust punishment. He has set out to destroy YHWH's plan for mankind, and turn humans into his slaves.

Our job, as Christians, is to find the slaves of Satan and set the captives free. The first Christians cast out demons, and so should we. Following are some extra Biblical quotes from early historians concerning the early Christian's zeal:

"And now you (Roman Senate) can learn this from what is under your own observation. For numberless demoniacs throughout the whole world, and in your city, many of our Christian men exorcising them in the Name of Jesus Christ, Who was crucified under Pontius Pilate, have healed and do heal, rendering helpless and driving the demons out of men, though they could not be cured by all the other exorcists, and those who used incantations and drugs." [2]

"Let a person be brought before your tribunals; who is plainly under demonic possession. The wicked spirit, BIDDEN TO SPEAK by a follower of Christ, will readily make the truthful confession that he is a demon, as elsewhere he has falsely asserted that he is a god." [3]

"...the demons themselves confess concerning themselves, as often as they are driven by us (Christians) from bodies by the TORMENTS OF OUR WORDS and by the FIRES OF OUR PRAYER." [4]

"But these (demons), as long as there is peace among the people of God, flee from the righteous, and fear them; and when they seize upon the bodies of men, and house their souls, they are adjured by the Christians, and at the Name of the true God are put to flight. For when the demons hear of this Name they tremble, cry out, and assert that they are BRANDED AND BEATEN; and being asked who they are, whence they are come, and how they have insinuated themselves into a man, confess it. Thus, being tortured and excruciated by the power of the divine Name, they come out of the man." [5]

"The Christians expel evil spirits, and perform many cures, and foresee certain events, according to the will of the Logos." [6]

"...even to this day the demonized are sometimes exorcised in the Name of the living and true God and these spirits of error themselves confess that they are demons who also FORMERLY INSPIRED THESE WRITERS (Homer and Hesiod)." [7]

There is the story of Smith Wigglesworth in which Satan appeared to him when he was sleeping. He opened his eyes and said simply, "Oh, it's only you," and he rolled over and went back to sleep. This is an excellent re-action. The Bible says that one day we will look at Satan and be amazed at how little power he had: *...Is this the man that made the earth to tremble, that did shake kingdoms; That made the world as a wilderness and destroyed the cities thereof; that opened not the house of his prisoners? (Isaiah 14:16-17)* With that in mind, I would like to outline some information and strategies in the next chapter, to help you be a strong overcomer.

Chapter Four
Military Readiness

Why must we be in military readiness at all times? To stand against the WILES (strategies or schemes) of the devil. WILES (methodeia in Greek), is where we get the word "method," meaning the following or pursuing of orderly and technical procedures in the handling of a subject. *You are the subject.* Like the Terminator, the devil has no remorse, and he won't stop—*ever!* The terminator got knocked down but he kept getting back up. David cut off Goliath's head. Crowns are wrestled from the giants we conquer.

> *...be STRONG in the LORD, and in the power of His might. PUT ON THE WHOLE ARMOR OF GOD, that ye may be able to STAND against the WILES of the devil. (Ephesians 6:11)*

STRONG (*Strong's* 1743, endumamoo) in the above scripture means to empower, enable, increase in strength. We are to increase in strength as we stand (that is, take a stand) against the wiles of the devil. That is why we are commanded to put on the whole armor of God and then STAND. STAND is a military term that signifies to be in readiness.

> *Wherefore take unto you the whole armor of God, that ye may be able to WITHSTAND in the evil day. And having done (overcome) all, to STAND. STAND therefore... (Ephesians 6:13-14)*

Since God said the word STAND four times in three verses, it's time we paid attention to His command. God's blueprint for success:

1. Be strong! (In the LORD and His power)
2. Put on your armor! (His powerful armor)
3. Stand therefore! (Stand on the Word)

God has given us everything we need to stand against the enemy: The Word, the Name, the Blood and His armor.

> *Behold, I give unto you power to tread on serpents and scorpions, and over all the power of the enemy: and nothing shall by any means hurt you. (Luke 10:19)*

There would be no reason for STANDING in military readiness if there were no enemy, and no battle to be fought. The amazingly good news is that JESUS HAS ALREADY WON this battle.

> *And having SPOILED PRINCIPALITIES AND POWERS, HE MADE A SHOW OF THEM openly, TRIUMPHING over them in it. (Colossians 2:15)*

We never have to run away defeated. Jesus SPOILED (*Vine's*, apekduo) PRINCIPALITIES meaning to divest wholly oneself, strip off and unclothe. This is a graphic description of His victory over the powers of darkness. Our armor (which is really His armor, tried and tested) is greater than the enemy's armor, and we need not fear.

> *...For the weapons of our warfare are not carnal, but mighty through God to the pulling down of STRONGHOLDS... (2 Corinthians 10:4)*

These STRONGHOLDS will be the main subject of this section of the book. However, I wish to state that while we have a personal God Who loves us passionately, we also have a personal devil who hates us vehemently. He has designed a plan for our destruction to counteract God's plan for our victory. The minions of the enemy observe us continually, attempting to drag us away from the path of salvation through deception, temptation, intimidation. We must stay in a state of constant repentance, keeping our lives clean and free of sin, and live for what is being written about us in heaven.

In Ephesians 6:10-17, God states that we are wrestling against Satan's army, which is organized by rank into principalities, powers, rulers of the darkness of this world, and spiritual wickedness in high places. Your job is to resist! *(James 4:7) If you resist,* he will flee, but do not expect the devil to give up easily. He may flee, but he *will* return. Open up a small crack in your armor, and watch out! He is methodically pursuing you and your loved ones. The good news is that Jesus defeated the enemy and won the war. We, however, must continue to fight battles and skirmishes. In Jesus' Name we have the victory. The spirit of antichrist is in this world, but we are of God, and we are more than conquerors through Christ. *(Romans 8:37)*

Rank and file

Revelation 21:8: All the following have their part in the lake of fire and brimstone; which is the second death.
1. fearful
2. unbelieving
3. abominable (despising)
4. murderers
5. whoremongers
6. sorcerers
7. idolaters
8. liars

1 John 2:16: Temptations
1. lust of the flesh
2. lust of the eyes
3. pride of life---is not of the Father, but is of the world.

Above are listed sins of the flesh that so easily beset us, which are also useful tools of the devil. He turns our own lusts against us. If our conscience is clean we can easily hear from the Holy Spirit. Holy, qodesh in the Old Testament, means separation, set apart. The temptations of the world come from opening ourselves up to sin through our actions and thoughts, and listening to the lies of the evil one.

> *But every man is tempted, when he is drawn away OF HIS OWN LUST, and enticed. Then when lust hath conceived, it bringeth forth sin: and sin, when it is finished, bringeth forth death. (James 1:14-15)*

Our God desires that we would choose the path of salvation, putting aside all the filthiness of the flesh, that we may be conformed into the image of His dear Son. We, alone can make the choice to follow righteousness and true holiness without which no man will see God. *(Hebrews 12:14)*

> *...let us cleanse ourselves from all filthiness of the flesh and spirit, perfecting holiness in the fear of God. (2 Corinthians 7:1)*

> *...Be ye holy; for I Am holy. (1 Peter 1:16)*

> *...present your bodies a living sacrifice, holy acceptable unto God, which is your reasonable service. And be not CON-FORMED to this world: but be ye transformed by the renewing of your mind, that ye may prove what is that good, and acceptable, and perfect, will of God. (Romans 12:1-2)*

The word CONFORMED in the above scripture means *poured into* (the image of the Savior), molded and shaped like Him, transformed by the Word. The devil may come with his wiles and slippery, slimy seductions, BUT LET HIM FIND NO PLACE IN ME. *(Ephesians 4:27)* A demon's job is to convince an individual to take the words the demon speaks and speak them out of his own mouth, thereby cursing himself and others. Demons must have an entry point, either a legal right or an emotional or spiritual weakness to attach to.

Ephesians 1:21	*Ephesians 6:12*
1. principalities	1. principalities
2. powers	2. powers
3. mights	3. rulers of the darkness of this world
4. dominions	4. spiritual wickedness in high places

Notice the similarity between the two Ephesians' scriptures above. There is rank and file in Satan's kingdom. He runs it like an army, employing deceitful tactics to cause you to take his thoughts. There are eight main principalities named in Revelation 21:8, and they work through reasoning. [8] These evil spirits attack by planting thoughts in your mind, then persistently urge you to take them, and make them your own. Demons may harass an individual by speaking the same lies from birth, dozens of times a day, thousands of times over a lifetime. They build on weaknesses and compulsions, often entering a person before salvation, and staying afterward by moving out of the spirit where they are evicted upon salvation, into the soulish realm (mind, will, emotions, imagination and memory) or into the body. They use the victim's own thoughts and imaginations to lead him to conceive sin in his heart. That is why God's Word says we should be:

CASTING DOWN IMAGINATIONS, and every high thing that exalteth itself against the knowledge of God, and bringing into captivity every thought to the obedience of Christ. (2 Corinthians 10:5)

CASTING (*Strong's* 2507, kathaireo) meaning to lower with violence, demolish, destroy. This demonstrates that God wants you to deliberately slam down and crush every thought that is contrary to His Word. You must take your thought life captive, or the devil will.

Principalities: Chief rulers (want you to take their thoughts)

Principalities (*Strong's* 746, arche) means chief, first estate, rule, beginning. They conduct operations from the second heaven above the earth, where they set up command centers. The lower ranking demons come and go from there, cowering in hatred before the principalities, which are the ruling princes, the fallen angels. They are huge in stature and are well proportioned. They wear full armor, never knowing when they will be attacked by the angels of the LORD (YHWH). Some principalities rule over territories and stay in those areas to oversee operations on earth. Others come and go through portals in the earth.

Powers: Second in command (use thoughts already planted)

Powers (*Strong's* 1849, exousia) means mastery, force, superhuman, authority, strength. They move in once a sinful thought is conceived and the person *stops resisting*. The person has given them authority by receiving, speaking or acting on the thoughts. They work through the imagination and wreak havoc on a person's conscience. They expand the work of the principality and open a person up to more demonic influence, prompting compulsive and impulsive behaviors. There are eight main categories of powers, and they work through imaginations. [9] These powers can take many forms using the person's weaknesses and strengths against him. They oversee the carrying out of commands by principalities and formulate strategies of their own. They seek to inhabit humans. Those the powers rule, the mights and dominions, cower and obey their commands, but hate them and deeply resent following their orders.

Mights: Satan's enablers (stir up emotions and passions)—rulers of the darkness of this world

Mights (*Strong's* 1411, dunamis) means special *miraculous power*, strength, violence, ability. **Rulers of the darkness of this world** are the same as mights. Rulers (*Strong's* 2888, kosmokrator, from 2902, krateo) means world ruler, an epithet of Satan, to use strength, seize, take. Mights stir up the emotions and passions of sin, watering the sinful seed, compelling a person's emotions to justify sin with vain imaginations and uncontrollable lusts. When in this state a person no longer has resistance and can be drawn into lusts of the flesh, the lust of the eyes and the pride of life. The person becomes a victim of his own lusts. He has yielded to Satan's snare.

Then when lust hath conceived, it bringeth forth sin: and sin, when it is finished, bringeth forth death. (James 1:15)

Know ye not, that to whom ye yield yourselves servants to obey, his servants ye are to whom ye obey... (Romans 6:16)

No one starts out wanting to be the servant of sin, but when we open the door by not protecting our thought lives, this can be the result. Jesus stated:

Whosoever committeth sin is the servant of sin. (John 8:34)

Getting free from these demons means breaking our agreement with darkness. The victim becomes bound with the CORDS of their sin.

His own iniquities shall take the wicked himself, and he shall be holden with the CORDS of his sins. (Proverbs 5:22)

Mights sometimes take human form, appearing to children when they are in distress or feeling lonely, taking the form of "protector" (the actual name of a demon I cast out of a woman). If the child accepts the demon, it will stay until cast out. There are eight main categories of mights, and they work through emotions. [10]

Dominions: Assume control of subject—spiritual wickedness in high places—thrones

Dominions (*Strong's* 2963, kuriotes) means government, *mastery*, rulers. They come in when the other evil spirits obtain mastery [11] in some area, dominating and ruling the person, compelling him against his will, manifesting in sickness or disease, confusion, compulsions and addictions. Often, demon infested people are placed in powerful positions by Satan to further his kingdom, operating under his evil influence and doing his bidding. **Spiritual wickedness in high places** is essentially the same as dominions. The word spiritual (*Strong's* 4152, pneumatikos) means a demon spirit, religious, supernatural. Wickedness (*Strong's* 4189, poneria) means depravity, malice, iniquity. High (*Strong's* 2032, epouranios) means above the sky, celestial. **Thrones** (*Strong's* 2362, thronos) means a stately seat, a potentate. Some wicked spirits sit on thrones here on earth. *(Colossians 1:16)* They may rule through mastery of a person in a position of power that they inhabit, such as the Jezebel spirit does, or rule from a seat of mastery over other demons. The human heart is a throne room, from which Jesus (Yahshua) or a wicked spirit may reign. *(Colossians 1:16)* Each demon is an expert in its field and is uniquely qualified for its position. There are eight main categories of dominions, and they work through memory. [12]

Spiritual wickedness in high places means two things: your mind is a high place, as discussed in the *Thorns* section, and additionally these demons occupy people in high places of authority. From this position, they are able to manipulate commerce, politics, the world financial situation, control media, even start wars. One of my neighbors is so bound up that he has stopped eating. He smokes continually, is on a breathing machine, drinks beer without ceasing and can hardly walk. The only place he goes is the liquor store, where he staggers in with his oxygen tank. This man is under control of dominions. Demons of this lowest rank are hideous. They are horrifying to look upon, misshapen or slimy, sometimes appearing like frogs or other creatures. The man who designed the creature in the movie *Alien*, claims to have taken it from actual demons he has seen. A person will be compulsive and feel out of control while victim of these demons. They can be changlings (able to change appearance into a beautiful form in order to seduce their victims).

It is easy to see that the more a person opens himself up by yielding his will a piece at a time, the more power and control the demons have over him. A person who is progressing along this path will be more and more irrational, confused, harder to reach.

Following is a rubric of the various rank and file of demonic spirits. This chart is meant merely as a reference guide to help you identify the possible progression from principalities all the way through to the accompanying sins, demons or manifestations under that category. This is only a partial listing. Demonic spirits take the names of the sins they promote, and aid in energizing them. There can be crossover in every rank and category. Some demons can achieve the status of a higher order if they are successful in their operations, much like our own military.

Principality	Power	Might	Dominion	Sins (demons & manifestations in each category)
error	antichrist	heaviness	rejection	idolatry, theft, fraud, gambling, cheating, greed, grief over indebtedness, covetousness, selfishness, loneliness, darkness, child neglect
slumber	whoredoms	gluttony	guilt	fornication, adultery, lasciviousness, fetishism, overeating, excessive affections, low self-image, unclean, desire to conquer, vileness, homosexual, compulsive and impulsive sexual behavior, familiar spirits, anorexia, bulimia, shame, embarrassment, over-sensitivity, seducing spirits
fear	bondage	anxiety	confusion	fearful, fretting, worry, dread, terror, anxiety, unbelief, frustration, depression, defeat, anger, forgetfulness, inadequacy, worthlessness, perfectionism, insecurity, superstitious, instability, nervousness, rejection, shame, torment, cowardice, dismay, inhibitions, insanity, fear of death, self rejection, faithlessness
perverse	deaf & dumb	slothful	defiance	unbelief, argumentative, wastefulness, self-will, stubborn, refusal to hear, heresy, love of honor, procrastination, laziness, disputations, selfishness, twists scripture
lying	divination/python	exhibitionism	deception	lying, excessive exaggeration, cons money, cheats, gossip, slander, tale-bearing, deceitful, divination, false prophecy, love of self-image, performance, oriented, deceit, self-deception, back-biters, hypocrisy, boasting, detraction (disruption, confusion), darkness
haughtiness	blindness	critical	strife	despising, accuser, racism, pride, murder, rape, slander, scornfulness, arrogance, mocking, scoffing, violence, critical, contention, bad disposition, prejudice, self-righteousness, self-justification, religious spirit, hostile to virtue, condemnation, judgmental, fault-finding, vanity
envy	unforgiving	jealousy	hate	murder, grudges, unmerciful, malicious lies, bitterness, bad memories, betrayal, bitterness, loves revenge, rage, anger, plotting evil, cruelty, brooding on injustices, resentment, suicide, death, competition, insecurity, destruction, violence
witchcraft	infirmity	anger	control	witchcraft, sorcery, drunkenness, violence, murder, flattery, torment, tears, hypochondria, complaining, drug addiction, profanity, bribery, vandalism, cursing, murmuring, seduction, cunning manipulation, violence, bargaining, charm, rebellion, speaking against rulers, love of dominion, love of independence, craftiness, beguiling, enticing, tempting, leviathan, anger, rage, torture, bitterness, blasphemy, mockery, sickness, stubbornness, tears for manipulation [13]

The demonic rank and file is a highly orchestrated machine, but do not be fooled. The name of Jesus, the Messiah of Nazareth, is above any demon. The angels of YHWH (our God) are ALL very powerful. When you pray according to God's will, in the Name of Jesus, holy angels go into action, and demons must obey. When you cast them out, they must leave. Sometimes confusion will break out in the enemy camp as they rush frantically to escape, or whine and beg to stay. There may be tens of thousands of demons on earth with the same name, such as fear. Fear may be a principality, but it may be taking orders from an even higher ranking principality, or it may be a might, subject to a power.

Sins of the flesh, or weaknesses of the flesh are simply starting places for demons to gain a foothold. Any sin of the flesh is an open invitation to a demon (unforgiveness, offenses, unresolved hurts or wounds, self-pity, anger, rejection, low self-image, hatred, jealousy, bitterness, excessive grief, judgments against self or others, pornography, stealing, lying, cheating, shame and guilt, gossip, tale-bearing). Demons usually work in clusters. For example, death, destruction and darkness are powerful spirits that rarely work alone. Death often works with suicide and murder. Destruction works with violence, and darkness works with deceit, to control their victims. They can all work under any category.

Deliverance

True and lasting deliverance is often the culmination of other ministry work that has been done with the person. One is better off taking time, allowing deliverance to be a process. Casting out demons prematurely, before the rest of the job has been done, may result in the person being reinfested with demons. Demons may have a right to be in a person. What those rights are must be determined, dealt with and eliminated. When demons no longer have a legal right to stay, they must leave when they are cast out, and stay gone.

There is some disagreement over whether to simply engage in casting out demons, or do a great deal of initial work by eliminating the things demons are attached to first. Some deliverance ministers prefer to go through the great physical and emotional stress of casting out demons without dealing with the other "stuff" that allowed them in, in the first place. In a situation where there is not much time, this is necessary. However, if time for counseling is available, I believe it is better to weaken the demon's grip and right of access by dealing with the "stuff" they are attached to. Demons feed on and energize emotional hurts, wounds, unforgiveness, bitterness, generational curses, sin, fear, inner vows, soul ties, abuse (emotional or sexual), etc. When these things are eliminated, it is much easier to cast out demons, because there is no garbage they can cling to. [14] They will go much more quietly, with less effort and stress, both on the minister and the victim. Have a time, perhaps a whole session of discovery, in which the person reveals what is going on, any known generational sicknesses or curses, any involvement with the occult, any serious illnesses or physical constraints, alcohol, drug abuse, sexual sins, other known sins including abortion. The person must want deliverance, and have a strong desire to be free, or you will have a battle on your hands that is unnecessary.

One man, typical of some who come for deliverance, never wanted to talk about the real core issues. He was clearly uncomfortable, and dug his heels in every time we got close to deep and lingering childhood wounds. He would weasel out of admitting that he even had unresolved issues, or that he had shut other people out to protect his shame and guilt. He just wanted deliverance the easy way, without working on the deep problems that got him into that state in the first place. He thought my job was to cast out the demons, and his was to waltz away scot free. Because he would not cooperate, eventually I cast out the demons, but they came back. I believe this was a mistake. Recently, a man called me long distance demanding that I cast out his demons. He was impatient when I began to move in word of knowledge. I asked him about unforgiveness toward his father, and homosexuality. I talked to him about some deep hurts from childhood. Finally, he said, "Can't you just cast out my demons like you do on TV?" I told him that unless he forgave his father, it would not do any good to cast out his demons, for they would return. He hung up very upset, but I believe he would have been worse off, if I had done as he demanded. A minister can wear himself out trying to help people who resist inner healing, but demand deliverance. I do not recommend it. Every inch of ground must be fought for, and why cover the same territory again and again. The sin nature always wants the easy way out.

Begin by inviting the Holy Spirit to lead any session, and He will bring wisdom in how to proceed. Fast and pray before a deliverance session. Pray for discernment. Confess Jesus, the Christ of Nazareth (Yahshua Messiah), as LORD over the place. Take authority over all spirits troubling the property and command that they be exposed and cast out. In the Name of Jesus break any silver cords (witches spying through astro-travel), blind any watchers (spies that are wicked angels or people). Break all lines of communication between any demons and their superiors. Bind the blood of Jesus to the property and all the people involved, their families and property. Cut off all enemy routes into the place of deliverance. Command all demons to be deaf and blind to what goes on. Afterward, ask the Holy Spirit to heal any parts of the person torn or scarred by the demons, such as emotions, etc. Forbid any demonstrations such as vomiting or violence. If the person has problems during deliverance such as pain, fear, voices, confusion, sleepiness, ask them to tell you. Have the person pray for strength to overcome habits, addictions and sin, and renounce them. They need to pray and do all renouncing, breaking of curses and strongholds, and pray out loud. Forbid any retaliation from any demonic spirit against you, your family and your possessions, against the person being delivered, his family and possessions, and any others involved. Break the authority of any higher or lower wicked spirits, outside or inside the person, than the one being cast out, and forbid the others from bonding together. Forbid the demons from hearing your plans and from strategizing against them. [15] Bind false tongues and bind demonic forces to inactivity. Before a person can order a demon to leave, they must be born again, or they have no authority.

Even if the demon is cast out, the stronghold may remain, necessitating further ministry. [16] Cancel Satan's authority, breaking his power over the person. Smash strongholds, which are thick walls of deception constructed around a person's beliefs that prevent them getting free. The flesh becomes imprinted with these patterns like the grooves on a CD. Though the person may not believe it initially, he can be loosed from the structures the demons have built to protect their positions. Demons can cause the same problems and temptations from outside the person, that they caused when in residence in the person, tricking them into thinking they have not been delivered. I have seen this happen many times. A person will come for deliverance who is already delivered. They simply need to exercise their authority to stand. Have the person renounce and repent of any sins in his life before proceeding, and be sure to break any soul ties keeping him from being completely set free. I always have the person tell the wicked spirit they no longer want it, and command it to leave. Then, I command it to leave, reminding the demon that the person, themselves, told it to go. This is more effectual than simply evicting the demon myself, because the person's will is involved, and the demons certainly know the difference. Later, the person will have already practiced once or twice when the demon tries to return, and has a better chance of not being reinfested. Very few people receiving deliverance are really strong the first time they tell a demon to go, but as they practice, they will grow in faith and confidence. After the person has been loosed from demons, then I plead "The Blood" over them, and pray for healing in every area. I admonish them to fill their hearts with a liberal dose of the Word. Anywhere there are severed bitter-roots, soul ties, generational curses, etc., I seal it with the blood of Jesus (Yahshua Messiah). Encourage the person to repent and cleanse himself in the blood every day, from all filthiness of flesh and spirit. *(2 Corinthians 7:1)*

Study Questions: Chapter 4
1. How many pieces of armor did our God give us?
2. What are the three points in God's blueprint for success?
3. What are the four major ranks in Satan's army?
4. What do you think the LORD means by the "lust of the eyes?" *(1 John 2:16)*
5. By what process does Satan get us to take his thoughts? Explain in detail.
6. Where in the Bible can we find descriptions of God's armor?
7. What detail can you offer about each rank in Satan's army

Chapter Five
Picture of Total Love and Commitment

Significance of the nails

The powerful striking sound of the nails signifies total commitment, no turning back for Yahshua the Messiah. There is no turning back for *us* once we are committed to walking free in Jesus. The horror of what Jesus endured brought us victory from demonic strongholds that come against our lives. The (exousia) power we are capable of walking in is only limited by the amount of faith we are willing to exercise.

The nails used to impale Jesus to the cross were large spikes. As they pierced His hands and feet *(Psalm 22:16; John 20:25-29)* they were intended to help affect *our* deliverance all down through the ages. God, in His mercy, knew that people would need great assistance in being set free and remaining free from the strongholds of the enemy. NAILS symbolize the Word of God, vows and unchangeable covenant promises.

> *...he fastened it with NAILS (vows or covenant promises) that it should not be moved. (Isaiah 41:7)*

The nails affix Jesus' HANDS (which symbolize works, and guilt because of evil deeds) to the cross. [17]

> *Give them according to their deeds, and according to the wickedness of their HANDS... (Psalm 28:4)*

> *Their idols are silver and gold, the work of their HANDS... (Psalm 115:4)*

The guilt generated by evil deeds and weakness caused by shame, are the result of evil works. Nails affix Jesus' FEET (which symbolize a person's walk, the heart, offense, stubbornness, unbelief or error, one easily offended, sin) [18] to the cross. The *right side* represents natural things. The *left side* represents spiritual things. Jesus was pierced by a spear in the left side and blood ran out that cleanses us from our sin. The flow of His blood opened up a river of spiritual blessing that has never ceased, and His blood continually cleanses us from our sins.

One *possible* way to delineate right side (natural) from left side (spiritual) is a quick look at Revelations 21. *This is not meant to be definitive*, but simply a way of explanation.

> *But the FEARFUL, and UNBELIEVING, and the ABOMINABLE, and MURDERERS, and WHOREMONGERS, and SORCERERS, and IDOLATERS, and all LIARS, shall have their part in the lake which burneth with fire and brimstone: which is the second death. (Revelation 21:8)*

A. Right side = *natural things*
  1. Right hand
       a. lying
       b. abominable (*Strong's* 948, bdelusso) meaning to stink, be disgusted, detest, abhor, despise
  2. Right foot
       a. murder
       b. fornication
B. Left side = *spiritual things*
  3. Left hand
       a. idolatry
       b. unbelief
  4. Left foot
       a. fearful---opposite of faith
       b. sorcery

Most criminals were tied to the cross; only the most *violent* offenders were nailed.

> *...the kingdom of heaven suffereth VIOLENCE, and the VIOLENT take it by FORCE. (Matthew 11:12)*

Jesus was the most VIOLENT offender to the kingdom of darkness Who ever lived. Jesus took the nails in His hands and feet, that our feet could be shod with the preparation of the gospel of peace. *(Ephesians 6:15)* He brought peace and good will toward men *(Luke 2:14)*, and a lively hope for redemption.

The kingdom of heaven is FORCEFULLY advancing and FORCEFUL men lay hold of it. (Matthew 11:12, Weymouth version)

Palms vs. wrists

Though some scientists have tried to invalidate the Word of God by declaring that Jesus was nailed through the wrists, claiming that the palm will not hold a man's weight, it *is* possible to nail through the palm of the hand without breaking any bones. There are several sites where this is possible, and each of these is capable of supporting a person's weight, without danger of tearing through the flesh. These locations include the upper part of the palm, the ulnar (small finger) side of the wrist, and the radial (thumb) side of the wrist. The thenar furrow is located at the base of the thenar eminence muscles. These areas are capable of supporting hundreds of pounds. Research does support scripture, and debunks the notion that the wrists had to be used instead of the palms, at Jesus' crucifixion. [19]

Death by asphyxiation or by shock

Some very compelling evidence and various theories have come to light concerning our Savior's death. One scientist, due to his World War I and II observations, claims that Jesus succumbed by asphyxiation. When people were strung up by their hands, with feet off the ground, it only took six to ten minutes for them to die by asphyxiation. This is because they could not exhale without raising themselves up by their hands, and they quickly became exhausted and died. [20]

Another scientist used his medical students in experiments that suspended them with wrists above their heads. In a few minutes the pulse rate increased, blood pressure decreased, perspiration became shallow. He concluded that collapse from inability to breathe would occur in six minutes. [21] Clearly, this research, though well intentioned, could not be the answer. Jesus hung on the cross for several hours.

Another more likely theory was advanced in 1989 that involved volunteers hanging on a cross with arms at 60 and 70 degree angles. The subjects experienced leg cramps and chest rigidity between 10 and 20 minutes into the experiment, with profuse sweating at about six minutes. The heart rate increased, but there was no difficulty inhaling or exhaling. This contrasts with Barbet's theory that Jesus died from asphyxiation. [22]

A piece of evidence was found in a tomb at Jerusalem, of a man who was crucified in the early first century A.D., excavated in 1969.[23] Two bones were pinned together by a large iron nail. A wooden plaque less than one inch thick was attached to the bones by the nail. The right tibia was smashed as well, The investigative team concluded that the bones were smashed to hasten asphyxiation.[24] However, Zugibe's experiments negate this theory. He establishes that it is arm position, not leg position, that determines breathing ability.

Events leading up to death

Jesus was in terrible mental anguish in the Garden of Gethsemane. His sweat became like (as) great drops of blood. There have been actual medically documented cases of people sweating blood under great duress. Being scourged by the flagrum (or flagellum), a tool composed of strips of leather with pieces of metal and bone tied into it, exposed Jesus' nerve endings, muscles and skin, causing great trauma. As Jesus became exhausted, He would have experienced shivering, severe sweating, frequent seizures, hypovolemia (loss of fluid), and extreme thirst. Fluid would have begun to collect around His lungs from trauma. He was slapped and hit repeatedly. Thorns were placed on His head, assaulting the delicate nerve endings on His head. He probably entered a state of traumatic shock.[25]

On the way to Golgotha, water loss and shock worsened. When His hands were nailed to the cross with large, square iron nails, the probable damage to sensory branches known as the median nerve caused one of the most extreme agonies known to man. This was exacerbated by the nailing of His feet. Excruciating agony every time Jesus moved, the hours on the cross with the weight of the body on the nails, unrelenting pain in the chest wall from the scourging, with the hot sun beating down, would have caused hypovolemic shock. It is reasonable to state, from a medical viewpoint, that Jesus died from shock, brought on by heart failure, caused by exhaustion, pain and loss of blood. [26]

However, physical problems were not the only factors that played into His death on the cross. Otherwise, He might have died after the scourging. Yet, Jesus had a powerful reason to survive the overwhelming physical torture until He, by an act of His own will, gave up His life at the appointed, preordained hour. He had to fulfill the types and shadows of the feast of Passover, completely. Our Savior had accepted His role as a sacrificial lamb willingly, suffering unspeakable torture, pain and humiliation, to pay for the sins of billions of the sons of Adam, many of whom had not even been born yet. When His Father released Him to do so, Jesus finally gave up His life, surrendering totally to His death. What followed was uniquely His to do, and His journey into hell was quickly followed by victory over death and Satan. All Jesus' acts were previously and accurately prophesied, fulfilling all the types and shadows played out by Israel for over a millennia in the feast of Passover.

Passover fulfilled

The shadow pictures in the Passover feast had been practiced by the Israelites every year since they left Egypt, yet they had no idea that Yahshua was the Messiah sent to fulfill every part of the feast. On the 10th of Aviv, Yahshua told His disciples to find Him a donkey's colt. Early that morning the high priest left the Temple Mount and went to the sheepfolds of Bethlehem where the sacrificial animals are bred. The path through the north gate was lined with priests standing shoulder to shoulder, holding palm fronds, just as they always had. The high priest selected a perfect lamb and started back on the path toward Jerusalem, where the lamb would be inspected for four days to see if there was any fault in it. Yahshua, our high priest, approached the city from the other direction, arriving before the other high priest. His disciples began shouting, *Blessed be the King that cometh in the Name of the LORD. (Luke 19:38)* Thousands of the Levites, not being able to see all the way up the path, began shouting this same phrase, as they had always done. However, when they realized it was Yahshua, not the high priest, they angrily ordered Yahshua to quiet the disciples. Jesus corrected the Levites: *I tell you that, if these should hold their peace, the stones would immediately cry out. (Luke 19:40)*

At last, the true Passover Lamb, born in the sheepfolds of Bethlehem, entered the city where He was examined by the religious leaders for four days. Then, when Pilot finished examining Jesus, he said the exact words the high priest speaks when he has finished examining the Passover lamb, "I find no fault in Him."

On the cross, when Yahshua knew His appointed hour was come, so that the scripture might be fulfilled, He cried out, *I thirst. (John 19:28)* At that exact moment, on the Temple Mount, just before killing the lamb, the high priest always said, "I thirst." After he drank, he slit the throat of the lamb and caught the blood in a bowl. Then, he uttered the words, "It is finished." At that moment, Yahshua bowed His head and said, *It is finished. (John 19:30)* The ensuing earthquake rent the rocks and caused a crack in the ground next to the cross. Meanwhile, the high priest sprinkled the blood of the lamb on the altar. When the guard pierced Jesus' side, His blood flowed through the crack in the ground onto the mercy seat of the Ark of the Covenant, buried directly below almost six-hundred years before, by Jeremiah. The perfect blood of Yahshua fulfilled the law once for all.

Traditionally, the Passover lamb was killed on the afternoon of the 14th day of Aviv, and put in the oven before sundown, and so was Yahshua killed and put in the grave before sundown, when Passover begins. Just before Passover began, blood was placed on the doorpost that death and judgment would pass over the Hebrews. In His death He fulfilled the Feast of Unleavened Bread, which begins on Passover, for in the Messiah there was no leaven (sin). Yahshua's blood fell on the mercy seat to take away the sins of the world. He went to hell and conquered death, having taken our rightful punishment upon Himself. The Passover lamb was placed on a piece of wood in the shape of a cross, and when it was finished roasting, it was to be consumed completely, just as we are to utterly embrace all that our Savior accomplished for us. He rose from the dead, fulfilling the Feast of First Fruits. He was the first born of a new covenant, the first born from the dead (dead in sins).

The shame of the cross

The *shame* of the cross was worse than the *pain*. Paul calls the cross *"foolishness"* and a *"stumbling block."* *(1 Corinthians 1:18-25)* This is because the cross was used to humiliate. It was a public symbol of *indecency* and *obscenity*, intended to defame. The intention was to crush a man's spirit. This is why it was always done in a public place. Golgotha was at a crossroads, just outside the city gates, where everyone passing would see it. Roman law expressly forbid that a Roman citizen be crucified because of the extreme *stigma* and *offense* that the cross signified. In Greek romances, crucifixion was always circumvented in the end by the rescue of the hero. Pliny, the Younger, referred to Christianity as a "perverse and extravagant superstition," because it preached a crucified Messiah. A Savior who could be crucified was utter foolishness to the Greeks. The idea of a crucified Messiah was an oxymoron. **The Messiah should bear the image of victory**, a conquering king, *not* the horror and shame associated with the cross. [27]

Peter, the disciple, spoke vehemently against Jesus when He revealed His upcoming crucifixion, and he was severely rebuked. Thomas, too, refused to believe after the resurrection for this same reason. In the context of the stigma of the cross, it is not hard to understand why the disciples did not immediately believe when the women returned from the tomb announcing that Jesus had risen. Their culture was replete with people who wanted to take Judah back from the Romans. Clearly, they were looking for a Messiah who would come as a conquering hero, according to their culture's expectations.

This expectation is one of the reasons why Saul, a true legalist, was "breathing murderous threats," persecuting the early church to the death. *(Acts 22:4; 9:1)* The Jews insistence that Jesus be crucified was engineered to illicit the public's contempt and loathing for this Messiah. In Saul's view, YHWH had obviously cursed and rejected Yahshua as Messiah. Calling Him the Messiah was outrageous blasphemy to Saul! [28]

Cursed is everyone that hangeth on a tree. (Galatians 3:13)

Chapter Six
Why Talk About Demonic Strongholds?

We are in a war whether we acknowledge it or not. There would be no reason for standing in military readiness, as we are commanded to do in Ephesians 6, if there was no enemy and no danger of defeat. The battle is for the lives of our husbands and wives, our children and friends, our homes and churches, our nation and its cities, the lost, and for our eternal destiny. This is not a battle that we can ignore and have any legitimate hope that it will just go away. As long as we live in this flesh, temptations will come. We must learn to face them with courage and faith, and realize that Jesus has already won. Children from Christian homes are being snatched away by Satan in alarming numbers, and the divorce rate for Christians is currently at 60%, surpassing even the secular statistics. Once strong Christians, are falling away from the faith. Some are even turning to Judaism while turning their backs on Yahshua as the Messiah. We cannot expect to win this battle unless we learn to walk in the power (authority) of God. How can we expect to walk in victory, or help anyone else, if we don't even believe there is an enemy, or a battle raging around us.

When I ministered my testimony at a home for unwed mothers, a girl in residence there had been involved in witchcraft. She was shocked by what I told her, and though she had been in an occult group, she renounced all occult activity and was born again. She, like so many others, had been deceived by the desire for power, and a need to belong and be accepted by a group. Because she suffered from a spirit of rejection and low self-image, she was a ripe target for the occultists.

From the pulpit to the pit

Since I became a Christian, I have witnessed a large number of pastors fall from the pulpit to the pit in relatively short order. Some of them had large congregations, some were small, but all were powerful men of God who seemingly had it all. The first church I attended after being born again had a pastor who was caught in adultery several times, and molested little girls in the Christian school he ran. Another large church was shocked when their married pastor ran off with his secretary.

One famous evangelist was exposed because of his guilty conscience. A cop pulled him over after he swerved all over the road trying to conceal the porn in his back seat. Another famous preacher, who fell into sin, has since radically and publicly repented for his actions, and has more anointing now than ever. If we humble ourselves under the mighty hand of God, then He will exalt us in due season.

Identifying demons

There are essentially two ways to identify demons. The first is by character and the second is by actions. [29] Demons can be correctly identified by their works. We disarm the invasion of demonic forces by:

1. Repenting and breaking our covenant (agreement) with sin (darkness).
2. The person needing deliverance must confess Jesus as LORD before deliverance.
3. The person must order the demon to leave.
4. Closing the doors and resisting the devil.
5. Seal the person with The Blood of Jesus.

Satan's purpose, according to Jesus, is to steal, kill and destroy. *(John 10:10)* He is the ***enticer*** to sin. Ultimately, however, the Bible reveals that people are drawn away *by their own lusts*. When lust is conceived (connoting that we must receive and internalize it) it grows in us like rotten seed, defiling ourselves and others. Finally, it gives birth to sin, which ends in spiritual death. *(James 1:14-15)*

A. The ***tempter*** entices us by stirring up our imagination of the pleasures of sin. *(1 Thessalonians 3:5)* He knows where our fleshly weaknesses are and lays the ***snare of the fowler*** *(Psalm 91:3)* in areas where he already knows we struggle. *(1 Timothy 3:7; Psalm 91:3)* He gains access by ***seducing*** *(1 Timothy 4:1)* those who oppose themselves and are double-minded. *(2 Timothy 2:25-26; James 1:8)* In other words, when the spirit wars against the flesh, and the lust of the flesh is allowed to conceive, it produces sin. *(James 1:13-14)*

B. The ***accuser***, Satan, accuses, ***condemns*** *(1 Timothy 3:6)* and ***slanders*** us day and night. *(Revelation 12:10)* He even uses our own brothers and sisters in Christ to attack us through strife, tale-bearing, criticism, ridicule and ***envy***. *(Revelation 12:10-12; Luke 16:15)* The name Satan signifies the ***hater***, the ***accuser***, the ***adversary***. He is the ***enemy*** and the ***avenger*** (*Strong's* 5358, naqam), meaning begrudge, punish and take vengeance. *(Psalm 8:2; 44:16)*

C. The ***deceiver*** *(Genesis 3:13)* ***twists*** appearances through deception to make things look one way, when they are really another. *(Revelation 12:9)* He poses as an ***angel of light*** *(2 Corinthians 11:14)* to deceive all who have not trained themselves to try the spirits. He is the ***wicked one***. *(Ephesians 6:12)* The word wicked comes from the wick of a candle which is twisted deep within the candle to insure that it will burn. Satan twists us through the deceitfulness of sin to insure that we will burn with him in hell. *(Revelation 20:10; Hebrews 3:13)* He was a ***murderer*** from the beginning. *(John 8:44)* He is a ***beguiler*** *(2 Corinthians 11:3)* and very ***cunning***, a ***liar*** and the ***father of lies***. *(John 8:44)*

He is ***subtle*** (*Strong's* 6175, aruwm), which implies craftiness and cunning *(Genesis 3:1-5)*, and uses deception to bend us to his purpose. He is permitted to roam the earth and tempt us *if* we allow it. *(Matthew 12:43; 1 Peter 5:8; Job 1:7)* Just because temptation comes from Satan, this does not make us guilty of sin. He tempted the sinless Son of God. Jesus, our righteous King and Savior, came to redeem our hearts and souls from deceit. *(Psalm 72:14)* As the ***prince of the power of the air*** *(Ephesians 2:2)*, Satan ruthlessly attacks through our communications, twisting both what we say and what we hear. As the ***god of this world*** *(2 Corinthians 4:4)*, he blinds the minds of all who believe not, so that the light of the gospel of Christ does not shine on them.

D. The "heart" (kardia—Greek; leb—Hebrew) came to stand for man's entire mental and moral activity. It is regarded as the seat of emotions, moral nature and physical life, the sphere of divine influence, and it represents true character in relation to the inner or hidden man of the heart. *(1 Peter 3:4)* On the one hand, the heart can be desperately wicked and deceitful *(Jeremiah 17:9)*, and it's depravity defiles all our actions, and others around us. This is possible because its seat is at the center of the inward man. The devil puts wicked thoughts into our hearts *(John 13:2)* through the deceitfulness of sin, but we are admonished to resist the devil and make him flee. *(James 4:7)*

E. On the other hand, the LORD blesses the pure in heart *(Matthew 5:8)*, faith that comes from the heart *(Mark 11:23)*, and He blesses doing the will of God from our hearts. *(Ephesians 6:6)* He calls us to purify our hearts *(James 4:8)* that our hearts condemn us not. *(1 John 3:21)* God Himself tries our hearts *(1 Thessalonians 2:4)* and His peace will keep our hearts and minds through Yahshua Messiah (Jesus Christ). *(Philippians 4:7)*

F. The ***destroyer*** (***Apollyon***, Greek) is part of the character of the devil. *(Revelation 9:11)* He hates mankind because of his fierce envy toward us. God made man to:

1. Be in God's own likeness and image. *(Genesis 1:26)*
2. Have dominion over this world. *(Genesis 1:28)*
3. Have close fellowship with God. *(Genesis 3:9)*
4. Have authority to choose through free will. *(Genesis 2:17)*

After the fall, Satan had the power (was lord) over death. *(Hebrews 2:14)* But his victory was not the wonderful triumph he envisioned. He became ***Beelzebub*** (*Strong's* 954), the ***lord of the flies*** (lord of the dung hill), prince of the devils *(Mark.3:22)*, a long fall from the creature he once was. *(Ezekiel 28:13; Isaiah 14.11-17)* He drags human victims through his filth and slime drawing them ever deeper into his web of deception. He became an evil ***serpent*** that bites the unwary with deadly venom, and a ***great dragon*** that breathes fire to destroy the unwise. *(Revelation 12:9)* He became an ***oppressor*** that causes sickness *(Acts 10:38)* and the ***tormentor*** *(Matthew 8:6)* that brings depression and defeat. Jesus defeated him and gloriously destroyed the devil's power, brought it to naught, pulled it down by force and made it of no effect. He delivered us from the power of darkness, and translated us into the kingdom of His light. *(Colossians 1:13)*

A Savior reigns

Yahshua haMashiach (meaning Yah is our salvation, the Messiah), Jesus Christ *(Matthew 1:16)*, is our **Savior** *(Luke 1:47; 1 Timothy 1:1)*, our **Deliverer** *(Romans 11:26)*, our **Preserver**, **Purifier** *(Malachi 3:3)* and **Refiner**. *(Malachi 3:3)* He gives all **Life** *(John 11:25)* and breath to all things. He alone is the **Sustainer**, the **Living Water** *(John 4:10)* that preserves and purifies the church, His bride. *(Ephesians 5:23)* Words cannot convey the adoration I feel for this

Great Shepherd *(John 10:11)* Who loved me in my deepest sin, sought me out, laid down His life for me and saved me.

He is our **Advocate** *(1 John 2:1)* Who ever makes intercession for us. He has obtained a Name higher than any other name, **Faithful and True** *(Revelation 19:11)*; He is our **Wonderful, Counselor**, the **Mighty God**, the **Prince of Peace**. *(Isaiah 9:6)* He is our **Redeemer** *(Isaiah 59:20)* our **Ransom** *(1 Timothy 2:6)*, our **Righteousness** *(Jeremiah 23:6)*, our **Resurrection** *(John 11:25)*, our **Rock** *(Deuteronomy 32:15)*, He is the only **Way**. *(John 14:6)* He is our **Mediator** *(1 Timothy 2:5)*, our **Living Water** *(John 4:10)*, the **Light of the World** *(John 9:5)*, the **Faithful Witness**. *(Revelation 1:5)* He is the **Bread of Life** *(John 6:35)*, the **Bright Morning Star** *(Revelation 22:16)*, the **Bridegroom** *(Matthew 9:15)*, and the **Captain of our Salvation**. *(Joshua 5:14)* He is the **Author and Finisher** of our faith *(Hebrews 12:2)*, the **Branch** *(Zechariah 3:8)*, the **Rose of Sharon** and **Lily of the Valley** *(Song of Solomon 2:1)*, the **Anointed One**, the **Christ** *(Matthew 1:16)*, our **Beloved** *(Ephesians 1:6)*, our **High Priest** *(Hebrews 3:1)*, our **Judge** *(Acts 10:42)*, the **Lion of the Tribe of Judah** *(Revelation 5:5)*, the **Messiah** *(Daniel 9:25)*, the **Holy One of God** *(Mark 1:24)*, the **Lamb of God** *(John 1:29)*, **King of Kings** and **LORD of LORDS**. *(Revelation 19:16)* No devil will ever overcome Him. As He is, so are *we* in this world. *(1 John 4:17)*

Chapter Seven
Identifying the True Enemy

When the Spanish conquered the Mayan Indians in the 1500s, they were able to quickly accomplish their goal because the Mayan's thought the horse and rider were all the same creature. They had never seen horses, so they shot them with their arrows in great numbers, but the riders, who wore armor, jumped off and shot them with guns.[30] Ignorance of the enemies' devices and inferior fire power worked to their defeat. God's people are often defeated because of ignorance. *My people are destroyed for lack of knowledge. (Hosea 4:6)* In God's economy, ignorance is decidedly *not* bliss.

Do demons really exist?

In case you are a skeptic about the existence of demons, I will relate a story that occurred early in my Christian walk. My band and I were last to play at an outdoor city festival in Blue Springs, Missouri. No one knew we were a Christian band, because none of the other bands had been that day, and no announcement was made. We only had a few minutes to set up our equipment, and because of the time constraints, *we forgot to pray.* This is a serious mistake and it cost us dearly. Just before we began, people came boiling out of the penny arcade next to the stage. Two women and a man began hissing, spitting and cursing us. We started our music and they moved to the corner behind us, continuing to hiss and curse. Suddenly, in the middle of the second song, the two grandstands in front emptied and the people ran away, some as far as three blocks. During the next thirty minutes, my drummer, bass player and guitar player were beaten and punched in the stomach repeatedly by unseen forces (demons). There was a heavy attack against my husband and I, as well. Afterward, we discovered that the arcade was a stronghold of the enemy where drug dealing, prostitution and illegal liquor was sold. Though the Father redeemed the situation and we were able to lead some of the people to the LORD, I learned my lesson: Always pray before doing any kind of ministry. God, in His mercy, knew that in the future we would be in more dangerous circumstances, and that it would be best to learn this crucial lesson early.

A shocking vision of the battle

In a vision given to Rick Joyner, he saw a demonic army in divisions riding against a small army of true Christians, most of whom did not have on their full armor; most were wounded. The main assignment of the evil army was to cause division in every relationship. The most powerful divisions were pride, self-righteousness, respectability, selfish ambition, and unrighteous judgment. The largest division was jealousy. The leader of this army was the accuser of the brethren. The weapons carried by the horde were intimidation, accusation, gossip, slander, faultfinding, rejection, bitterness, impatience, unforgiveness and lust. The Christian prisoners had armor, but didn't use it, and were held captive by little demons of fear.

The shocking part of this vision was that this evil horde was riding on the backs of deceived Christians. These people were so deceived, that they thought they were being used by God. The demons urinated and defecated a repulsive slime on them that was pride and selfish ambition. They thought this was the anointing of the Holy Spirit. Vultures named depression vomited condemnation on the prisoners. If they fell, the other prisoners would begin stabbing them with their swords. They thought condemnation was truth from God, and that everything happening was from the LORD, so they accepted it, instead of fighting against the true enemy.

A battle was about to begin, but the true Christians were singing and feasting, and roaming from one camp to another. Even the ones who had armor, had very small shields of faith. When the trumpet blew for battle, most were quickly wounded (hurts, unforgiveness, bitterness, offenses), and when wounds were not covered, they were wounded again and again in the same place. Those hit with arrows of gossip and slander began to gossip and slander others. They were so angry, they allowed themselves to be carried away by the vultures. The wounded sat in unbelief and were easily carried away as well. When the true Christians fighting in God's army fired arrows of truth and hit the ones being ridden by demons, instead of waking them up to the truth, they became enraged and the demon riding them became much larger. Some true Christians began to pick up the enemies' arrows and shoot them back. This was a terrible mistake, for when a deceived Christian was hit by an arrow of accusation or slander, a demon of bitterness or rage would fly in and perch on that arrow. He would urinate and defecate his poison on them, until they began to change into the image of the demon themselves.[31]

This vision is a reflection of what is happening all around us in the spirit realm. The key is to learn to recognize and fight the *true* enemy, and stop fighting our brothers and sisters in Christ. It is imperative to wear the whole armor of God, and allow the shield of faith to grow. The battle cannot be won if it is fought on enemy ground. Fight only from God's holy mountain with *His* arrows of hope and truth and love.

Agreement with a demon?

You are a three part being, serving a God Who is three persons. You were made in His image. The level of agreement any part of you has with a demon is the level you will reflect in your spirit, soul or body. It is a question of taking back the ground the enemy occupies. If we yield territory to the enemy through sin, he takes it. Your flesh lusts and wars with your spirit. *(James 4:1; Galatians 5:16-17)* Your soul is the prize. The soul can be in agreement with the flesh *or* the spirit. If any two agree, then they have the majority *(Matthew 8:19)*, and a person's actions and words will reflect this agreement. This can work for the good or for evil.

Anyone can have a demon who wants one. A person possessed with demons is a prisoner of war. Satan is preying on both our weaknesses and strengths. In a born again believer, a demon can manifest in the soulish realm with physical manifestations, but NOT IN THE SPIRIT. God's Word admonishes us not to war after the flesh *(2 Corinthians 10:3)*, but to be transformed by the renewing of our minds through the Word of God. *(Romans 12:2)*

One of the Greek words for AGREEMENT (*Strong's* 4856, sumphoneo) is the word from which we derive symphony, means to be harmonious and in concord together. When we are in godly agreement, it is like a symphony to the LORD. When a person's spirit, soul and body are not in agreement, they will constantly struggle with confusion. Give up your right to self defense, self pity and self righteousness. This will kick the support from under many demons.

> *...if two of you shall AGREE on earth as touching any thing that they shall ask, it shall be done for them of My Father which is in heaven. (Matthew 18:19)*

God desires that His people work together like a SYMPHONY, so He provided us with the powerful prayer of AGREEMENT. This is why Satan fights so hard to bring disunity into marriages and relationships, weaving a web of offences, hurts and wounds. When we are in discord (asumphonos), it is like a cacophony of inharmonious sound. *(Acts 28:25)*

Can a Christian have a demon?

A devil cannot have a Christian, but a Christian *can* have a devil. A person can be possessed **with** devils, not **by** devils. Wherever there is unrepented sin, demons flock around. Sins of the flesh and soulish realm (mind, will, emotions, imagination, memory) draw demons like magnets. When temptations have worked in the past, demons bring continual badgering and enticement until the weakness is once again exploited. Everyone needs deliverance. Assume this. *Everyone* has pride, so that's a good place to start. Repent of self pride, self righteousness and self reliance.

> *...that which I do I allow not: for what I would, that do I not; but what I hate, that do I. (Romans 7:15)*

> *But I see another law in my members, warring against the law of my mind, and bringing me into captivity to the law of sin which is in my members. (Romans 7:23)*

It is really a question of ground. When ground is surrendered in the soulish realm through sin, a door is opened. Until one has personally cast devils out of Christians, and heard deep, demonic voices coming out of born again church members, it is easy to say that a Christian cannot have a devil. Only God, Himself, truly knows the heart of an individual, but it must be stated again that anyone can have a devil that wants one. Many Jews of Jesus' time were possessed **with** devils. This means that within the person there were devils. He cast them out with His Word, and we can cast them out the same way: **With His Word.**

> *When the even was come, they brought unto Him many that were possessed WITH devils: and He cast out the spirits WITH HIS WORD, and healed all that were sick… (Matthew 8:16)*

How can a demon live in the same place as the Holy Spirit?

The Holy Spirit abides in our *spirit*, but we are *three* part beings. We may have a demon operating in the flesh or the soulish realm that is wreaking havoc, such as a spirit of infirmity, confusion, fear, lust, doubt, unbelief, haughtiness, a religious spirit, etc. Some people say that if the Holy Spirit lives in you then you definitely cannot have a demon. Let me ask, "How can the Holy Spirit possibly live in unholy flesh?" If people were all cleaned up the second they were born again, then why are there so many Christians in adultery, fornication, pornography, fear, unbelief, envy, strife? Why do we need scriptures like the following?

> *And be not conformed to this world: but BE YE TRANSFORMED by the renewing of your mind... (Romans 12:2)*

> *...BE CONFORMED to the image of His Son... (Romans 8:28)*

> *And the very God of peace SANCTIFY YOU WHOLLY; and I pray God your WHOLE SPIRIT, SOUL AND BODY be preserved blameless unto the coming of our LORD Jesus Christ. (1 Thessalonians 5:23)*

> *For the Word of God is quick, and powerful, and sharper than any two-edged sword, piercing even to the DIVIDING ASUNDER OF SOUL AND SPIRIT, and of the joints and marrow, and is a discerner of the thoughts and intents of the heart. (Hebrews 4:12)*

Notice the spirit, soul and body are referred to separately. Being born again is the beginning of a *PROCESS* of being CONFORMED and TRANSFORMED into His image that can only begin at the rebirth of the spirit man. Otherwise, we would all be perfect creatures and amaze the world. Instead, Christians astound the world with how unholy (unsanctified and not set-apart) they behave and turn many away from the faith through their ungodly actions. The Holy Spirit is everywhere in the universe. Does this mean that there are no demons anywhere in the universe? Of course not! A demon's presence certainly cannot hurt the Holy Spirit.

> *From whence come wars and fightings among you?... even of your lusts that WAR IN YOUR MEMBERS? Ye lust, and have not: ye kill, and desire to have, and cannot obtain: ye fight and war, yet ye have not... (James 4:1-2)*

Notice that sin conceived manifests through WARRING IN OUR MEMBERS. The soul was against the spirit, the spirit against the flesh, the flesh against the soul. The word MEMBER (melos in Greek) means a limb or part of the body.

> *Mortify (put to death) therefore your MEMBERS which are upon the earth; fornication, uncleanness, inordinate affection, evil concupiscence, and covetousness, which is idolatry: for which things' sake the wrath of God cometh on the children of disobedience...put off all these; anger, wrath, malice, blasphemy, filthy communication...PUT OFF the old man...PUT ON the new man, which is renewed in KNOWLEDGE after the image of Him that created Him... (Colossians 3:5-10)*

There are things we are to PUT OFF and things we are to PUT ON, such as the KNOWLEDGE of our Messiah, by renewing our minds *(Romans 12:2)*, and putting on the whole armor of God. Otherwise, demons can infest the fleshly realm and the soulish realm. Ownership is really the issue. If we are children of the Most High, then we should KEEP HIS COMMANDMENTS. Whomever we YIELD ourselves to, we become his SERVANT.

> *Know ye not that to whom ye YIELD yourselves SERVANTS to obey, his servants ye are to whom ye obey; whether of sin unto death, or of obedience unto righteousness? (Romans 6:16)*

> *He that hath My commandments, and KEEPETH them, he it is that loveth Me... (John 14:21)*

Demons enter through sin, inheritance, unforgiveness, and by being invited. Yes, Christians can do all these things. Demons do not want to leave, so they step up their activities when they know they are about to be cast out. They will try to lie about the deliverance minister or even offer soulish (psychic) gifts. They will increase the fear of deliverance.[32]

Seeing angels and demons

If someone has the gift of discerning of spirits, they will see both angels and demons. Both are constantly active around us all the time. When I was a small child I used to sit in my stairwell and sing love songs to Jesus in an unknown language by the hour, weeping for joy. The angels would gather around me and worship. I wanted to serve Jesus with all my heart. I recall the first time I saw the angels who work with me when I minister. One went out among the crowd when I sang and played flute, the other when I spoke and prayed for people. Lots of people have told me they have seen an enormous angel who stands behind me, and ministers with me. When I wield my sword, he uses his sword in concert with me.

On a ministry trip, I was lodged at a bed and breakfast that featured an "angel" room. There were angels *everywhere*: numerous books stacked randomly of a New Age religious nature, picture albums, figurines, paintings, bedspread, etc. The room actually attracted demons posing as angels of light. We prayed for protection, pleaded the blood and took authority over the wicked spirits in the room. We slept peacefully. If you are troubled by dreams of a sexual nature, it is likely that you are being assaulted by demonic spirits that attack when you are most vulnerable. Fear not! It is important to wear your armor *(Ephesians 6:11-17)* at all times, especially the helmet of salvation, which will protect your dreams and thought life. Repent of any sin that could have opened a door to the enemy. Plead the blood of Jesus over your mind at all times and bind 2 Corinthians 10:4-5 to yourself. Ask the Father to send angels to guard your dreams.

The glory cloud

One of my band concerts was scheduled in a theater just over fifty miles outside Kansas City. I already knew the LORD was going to do great things, but that there would be a battle. On the way there, my husband jokingly said, "Wouldn't it be funny if the van broke down?" I looked at him in shock and rebuked the words, but it was too late. The van, loaded with all our equipment, broke down immediately in the middle of nowhere. I began praying for divine intervention. Suddenly, the rest of the band, who were supposed to take a different route, drove up right behind us. I got out and began firmly speaking words of faith that everyone could hear, so that they would not curse us with words of doubt and unbelief. I said, "I believe someone will show up and tow us to the concert. I believe they will fix our van and we will start on time, and many will be saved." Miraculously, the concert got started on time. *Faith moves the hand of God!!!*

The anointing was so strong as I sang and exhorted the people that I could barely stand. About halfway through I saw a bright misty light hovering all over the auditorium. Joy unspeakable filled my soul, for as I looked I saw that there were angelic beings, worshiping and **ministering with us**, as many people were saved and healed. Since that night I have seen the glory cloud several times. I praise my heavenly Father for His wonderful presence and deliverance.

Are they not all MINISTERING SPIRITS, sent forth to MINISTER FOR THEM who shall be heirs of salvation...How shall we escape, if we neglect so great salvation... (Hebrews 1:14; 2:3)

Chapter Eight
Fallen Angels, Mighty Men of Renown, Giants, Demons

The Nephilim and the Rephaim

It is imperative to establish who the Nephilim and the Rephaim are. Matthew 25:37 states, *But as the days of Noah were, so shall also the coming of the Son of man be.* What happened then is happening again, as we approach the end of this age. A man I know that does deliverance told me that he ministered to a woman with a human mother, a witch who conceived by having sex with an angel of light. The result was a beautiful young woman with dark hair and translucent skin. Her eyes have pupils like a goat—sideways slits. She always wears sunglasses to conceal them. According to her, there are many offspring from these unions, but often they are so grotesque that they are killed. Because she had revealed the truth of her origins, her mother was trying to have her assassinated.

Inordinate attention to angels, such as current movies and a rash of new books reflect, can lead to unhealthy affections. There have been a number of talk shows hosting people who claim to have had visitations from angels, and the New Agers appear to be positively obsessed with angels. No holy angel of the Most High God would do such a thing, but many fallen angels did. Those before the flood were locked in the bottomless pit for these wicked acts. In witchcraft and Satanism, having sex with angels or demons is called "drawing down the moon." This is depicted in numerous movies such as: *Rosemary's Baby* (a coven drugs Rosemary who conceives by the devil and bears his offspring), *Michael* (angel claiming to be Michael the archangel, with crude habits, has numerous sexual encounters), *Conan the Barbarian* (the barbarian almost has sex with a demon and destroys a snake cult), *City of Angels* (an angel "falls" from his heavenly position, has sex with a woman and runs off with her), *The Preacher's Wife* (an angel is sent to help a troubled marriage and falls in love with the wife, nearly stealing her away from her husband), *Angels In the Outfield* (an angel picks sides to help baseball team), *Meet Joe Black* (an angel has sex with a woman and enjoys many sensuous pleasures).

When a person has sex with a demon, the demon is called an incubus (male) or succubus (female). I was very surprised to bring up this subject at a meeting through a word of knowledge, and discover that several believers in the group had been repeatedly troubled, both in waking and in their dreams, by demons of seduction seeking a sexual encounter. Some had given in and I led them in repentance.

> *...the SONS OF GOD saw the daughters of men that they were fair; and they took them wives of all which they chose...There were GIANTS in the earth in those days; and also after that, when the SONS OF GOD came in unto the daughters of men, and they bare children to them, the same became MIGHTY MEN which were of old, men of renown. (Genesis 6:2-4)*

The word SONS OF GOD is "ben elohym" in Hebrew, meaning angels. GIANTS comes from the word Nephilim (*Strong's* 5303, nephily) meaning those who were cast down, giant, a feller, a bully, a tyrant. Notice that their offspring were MIGHTY MEN OF RENOWN, from the word Rephaim (*Strong's* 7497, Rapha) meaning giants. The word MIGHTY means giant, tyrant, warrior, strong. Notice that similar definitions are used for the giants and the mighty men, their offspring. The Nephilim and Rephaim demanded worship and were violent tyrants. Later, in scripture, Nimrod, king of Babylon, is described as a "mighty" hunter "before" (meaning against) the LORD. *(Genesis 10:9)* His mother and wife, Semiramis, who was queen of Babylon, may have also been a Rephaim. She set herself up as the first goddess to be worshipped, and her son as the sun god, Baal. They were building a tower to the heavens in Babylon to look for the return of the Nephilim. The Pharaohs claimed to have descended from the gods and Semiramis also demanded worship as having divine bloodlines. Could this be the source of myths in which people who were half man and half "god" were capable of mighty feats of strength? The fate of those "cast down" (fallen angels) is described in the following scripture. It is clear that their sin, in addition to siding with Lucifer against God, was fornication with women.

> *And the ANGELS (ben elohym) which kept not their first estate, but left their own habitation, He hath reserved in everlasting chains under darkness unto the judgment of the great day. Even as Sodom and Gomorrah, and the cities about them in like manner, GIVING THEMSELVES OVER TO FORNICATION, and GOING AFTER STRANGE FLESH, are set forth for an example, suffering the vengeance of eternal fire. (Jude 6-7)*

> *Now there was a day when the SONS OF GOD (ben elohym) came to present themselves before the LORD, and Satan came also among them. (Job 1:6)*

Again the word "ben elohym" is used for angels, referred to as the SONS OF GOD, appearing before the LORD. Some scholars say that the "sons of God" referred to in the above scriptures are really the godly offspring of Seth, Adam's son. However, could Seth's sons have appeared before the LORD with Satan? Could they have been the ones referred to in Jude 6? A careful look at emphasized words reveals that something unnatural was going on in Genesis 6. The pre-flood angels who mated with women were locked up in "outer darkness." Satan continued his activities after the flood. The true reason fallen angels wanted to impregnate women was to pollute the bloodline of Adam to keep our Savior from being born. *(Genesis 3:15)* Noah was a man who was PERFECT in his generations (bloodline), thus he and his family were chosen to be saved. *(Genesis 6:9)*

The Nephilim first descended to earth on Mt. Herman which is in Jordan.[33] Jared, father of Enoch, was so named because he was alive when it happened.[34] Jordan means "place of descent," and Jared means "low ground, descent, shall come down." Herman *(Strong's* 2768, chermown) means abrupt, make accursed, utterly destroy. The Nephilim produced offspring for perhaps 120 years. There may have been as many as six-million Rephaim offspring from these unions before the flood.[35] Zophim *(Strong's* 6839), meaning watchers, angels who fell, are the evil watchers, another name for Nephilim. *(Numbers 23:14)* The holy angels, also known as watchers *(Strong's* 5894, 'iyr), have biblical reference. *(Daniel 4:13, 17, 23)*

Some Rephaim, tribes of giants listed in the Bible, are the sons of Anak (ancestor of the people known as Anakim) *(Numbers 13:33)* who lived in Canaan at the exodus. Anak means "hero Baal." The Emim *(Strong's* 368) meaning terrors, were a Moabite race of giants. Og was king of the Rephaim on the east of Jordan, in Bashan. His bed of iron was 9X4 cubits, about 15 feet long. *(Deuteronomy 3:11)* The Zuzim or Zamzummim *(Strong's* 2162 and 2161) meaning to plot or plan in the bad sense, think evil, were also from Canaan. *(Deuteronomy 2:20)* Gath was a dwelling place of giants and home of Goliath and his brothers, on the sides of the plain of Philistia. *(2 Samuel 21:22)* Ancient Sumerian and Babylonian records mention giants, and refer to "the Annuna (descendents of Anak) gods of heaven and earth." [36] The Annunaki literally means "those who fell from heaven to earth." [37] Pagan peoples worshipped the goddess and the baalim (lords), a plural word for the star gods, fallen angels, Nephilim, hosts of heaven. *(1 Samuel 7:4; Deuteronomy 4:19)* The Philistines' and Ammonites' gods and goddess were embraced by the Israelites who also worshipped the Queen of Heaven (another name for Semiramis, Ashtoreth, Isis, Diana, Easter, etc). The same goddess had different names in every culture because the languages of all people were confounded at Babel. *(Judges 10:6; 1 Samuel 7:3)* At Babel, people were looking for the return of the star gods, thus they were building an observatory in the shape of a Ziggurat. [38] People still worship the goddess, even in America. I saw a large place of worship recently that had emblazoned on their building, "Mary, Queen of the Universe."

There is a place called Valley of Rephaim where David held several battles against the Philistines. A battle was fought at Ashtoreth-Karnaim (meaning star of the two horns) where giants had built a fortress to the goddess. *(Genesis 14:5)* Gilgal Rephaim, meaning circle of the giants, is in the Golan Heights, and exists to this day as five enormous, concentric circles thought to be about 5,000 years old, created with 37,000 tons of rock. This was part of Og's territory and thought to be built by giants, possibly to measure the solar solstice. Gibor, another name for giants, may be the root of the word Gilgal.

The deep, outer darkness, the bottomless pit

Essentially, "the deep," "outer darkness" and the "bottomless pit" are all the same thing. The wicked angels were delivered into chains of darkness, the bottomless pit which is a depthless, infernal abyss. The same word *(Strong's* 12, abussos) is used in Luke 8:31, but translated as the DEEP, a place the demons begged Jesus not to send them.

> *And they besought Him* (Jesus) *that He would not command them to go out into the DEEP. (Luke 8:31)*

> *…God spared not the angels that sinned…delivered them into CHAINS OF DARKNESS… (2 Peter 2:4)*

> *…angels which kept not their first estate…He hath reserved in everlasting chains under DARKNESS… (Jude 6)*

> *And he opened the BOTTOMLESS PIT. (Revelation 9:1, 2, 11; 11:7; 17:8; 20:1, 3)*

In the Old Testament the word used for the DEEP was tehowm, meaning an abyss. *(Genesis 1:2; 7:11; 8:2)* The word PIT *(Strong's* 5421, phrear) also means an abyss or prison. DARKNESS *(Strong's* 4655, skotos; or 2217, zophos) means gloom, blackness, obscurity, shadiness, mist, shrouding. Adding the word OUTER *(Strong's* 1857, exoteros), meaning exterior, to the word darkness, seals the meaning.

But the children of the kingdom shall be cast out into OUTER DARKNESS: there shall be weeping and gnashing of teeth. (Matthew 8:12; 22:13; 25:30)

This bottomless pit, outer darkness or the deep cannot be on earth. It must be in outer space, since the earth has nothing that is bottomless.

In Sodom and Gomorrah the people gave themselves over completely to fornication, and went after "strange" flesh (*Strong's* 2087, heteros) meaning "altered." *(Jude 7)* Altered flesh? What is that? In the account of Sodom's destruction, the angels entered Lot's house and the men of the city began demanding the angels come out and have sex with them. The angels had to smite them with blindness to stop them. *(Genesis 19:1-12)* It is possible that the people of Sodom were accustomed to having sex with angels?

The bottomless pit will be opened during the tribulation and horrible creatures will be released onto the earth. A star will fall from heaven, this will be Satan, accuser of the brethren, and he will have a key to open the pit, releasing wicked creatures. *(Revelation 9:1-2)* Jesus (Yahshua) said He saw Satan fall as lightening from heaven. *(Luke 10:18)* Later, in Revelation, the accuser is referred to as having been "cast down." This is the devil, coming with wrath and destruction, but he is already a defeated foe.

...the accuser of our brethren CAST DOWN, which accused them before our God day and night...Woe to the inhabiters of the earth...For the devil is come down unto you, having great wrath... (Revelation 12:10-12)

Chapter Nine
The Councils of Hell

Demons, under instruction from their superiors, implement a personal plan for each life. They work the plan, setting up TRIGGERS, until it is firmly in place, then they leave it alone to run without assistance. If their strategy is going according to plan, they really do not hang around. You are sinning and making wrong choices all by yourself. The demons that worked you over are busy working on another victim. They are only alerted by fervent, effectual, sincere prayer. *(James 5:16)* The minute you strategically pray in this way, breaking off a demonic attack, and begin breaking the strongholds that have been established through consistently yielding to sin and temptation in the soulish realm, a council is convened in hell. All the demons assigned to you begin formulating strategies for how to break you again, and regain the lost territory. First, they will attempt reentry on FAMILIAR levels. The following are possible scenario examples:

Plan A: If, for example, a stronghold in your life has been anger, and you have broken that attack off, sincerely repenting, loosing yourself from bondage to anger (the principality is a spirit of witchcraft) and casting it out, then the demons will work on known TRIGGERS to try to drag you back into sin and bondage: Perhaps your spouse, accusing you of a particular shortcoming, is one of your triggers; then the devil will immediately attack you through your spouse, stirring up your spouse using a lying spirit in whatever areas trigger them: such as resentment, bitterness, wounds, anger, etc./// **Alternate Plan A** scenario: If you are a smoker fervently desiring to quit, and you have taken the proper steps to be free: Demons will be sent in to work your TRIGGERS. If your triggers are anger, rebellion, stubbornness, self-pity (which can be triggered by an internal demand for self-medication and/or gratification), then your spouse or someone else will be sent to trigger you in your vulnerable areas.

Plan B: If this strategy fails, the devil will continue hammering on you with other faults through your spouse or others, or he will use circumstances to defeat you, until you respond in a way that cancels your prayers, and allows reentry of the stronghold. If you resist *consistently* in this area, plan C will be implemented.

Plan C: If Satan can't defeat you through attacks on your shortcomings or character (or other FAMILIAR triggers), and if your spouse is one who pouts (pouting is behavior used to control others), then he or she will move out, or move to the basement or couch, or refuse to talk, or leave for hours without saying why, or refuse to perform critical tasks, or yell at you, etc. Anything to drag you off your resolve to stand firm on the promises of God, and resist the devil. Difficult people or circumstances are an effective management tool Satan uses against you. Faltering in unbelief will defeat you if you do not stand firm.

You may be surprised by the extremes the devil is willing to go to, in order to keep control of territory he has previously managed. This territory is so FAMILIAR to you that responses are automatic. All wicked automatic responses must be viewed as strongholds, usually set up by the enemy at an early age. All TRIGGERS must be broken permanently, and covered by the blood of Jesus. Bathe yourself in prayer constantly and stand guard against the devil, for he is surely assigned to enslave you by going about as a roaring lion seeking whom he may devour, through your own weaknesses. *(1 Peter 5:8)* I must warn you that according to the Word, we are enslaved by our own lusts. *(James 1:14)* The devil will never give up in any area, until you declare yourself victorious, and with vigilance and determination walk it out in the strength of our God, YHWH Nissi, our conqueror. In time, Satan will concede defeat and leave you alone in any area where you consistently declare victory, and launch this specialized demon toward someone else who is more vulnerable in this area. Victory at last!

Fight, manifesting the fruit of the Spirit

Fight using the Word, manifesting the fruit of the Holy Spirit in your life. In the above scenario, use love and peace to defeat the enemy. The enemy is not your spouse or other people, and all the behavior modification techniques in the world won't help. The person in the first example needs deliverance from a spirit of anger and hate. Rage, cursing, rebellion, complaining, bitterness, murder and unforgiveness are some of the operations of this spirit.

Whosoever hateth his brother is a murderer: and ye know that no murderer hath eternal life abiding in him. (1 John 3:15)

...jealousy is the rage of a man... (Proverbs 6:34)

The spirit of anger uses bullets of accusing, harsh, lying words to bring destruction and break the victim's spirit, not just guns to kill the body. The ultimate weapon against the spirit of anger is repentance and humility, followed by forgiveness and loving your enemy, just the opposite of what the world teaches. These powerful tools work to pull the fangs right out of your own heart where wounds, revenge, bitterness, self-pity and jealousy have been festering, so that you may walk victoriously.

Cursing and complaining

CURSING is a manifestation of a spirit of anger.

> *As he loved CURSING, so let it come unto him...As he clothed himself with CURSING like as with his garment, so let it come unto his bowels like water, and like oil into his bones. Let it be unto him as the garment which covereth him and for a girdle wherewith he is girded continually. (Psalm 109:17-19)*

Have you ever noticed that people who curse become worse and worse, until they spike everything with profanity. Profanity, threats, accusations, hitting, sulking, not speaking, pouting, withdrawal, murmuring and complaining are manifestations of the spirit of anger. *Murmuring is witchcraft prayer.* Israel suffered repeatedly in the desert for this sin, referred to as MERIBAH (*Strong's* 4849), where the people CHODE (*Strong's* 7378, ruwb) with the LORD. *(Numbers 20:3)* CHODE means wrangle, hold a controversy, chide, complain, debate, strive, gripe, adversary, lay wait. It is of note that part of the meaning of this word is ADVERSARY LAYING WAIT. When we yield ourselves to the sin of anger, complaining and cursing, the adversary, Satan, is ready to spring on us. By entrapment he can now *use our own words* and actions against us, as we curse ourselves and others.

Unforgiveness

Unforgiveness is a pervasive sin. I was raised in a family that held grudges to the bitter end. If someone ever gave offense, it was never forgiven or allowed to rest. Before God dealt with me in this area, I would carry grudges and bitterness around like a weapon, using it as an excuse to be angry or hate someone, and even plot revenge. He showed me that if I didn't forgive others, then He couldn't forgive me. *(Matthew 6:14-15)* This was serious business. I had to let go of a lifetime of unforgiveness, wounds, offenses, but the LORD empowered me to forgive all offenders. I began to meditate for hours on Christ's betrayal and crucifixion, and His forgiveness of His enemies while He hung on the cross. In this light, it is impossible not to forgive others, love our enemies and even pray for them.

Step 1: Ask God to forgive you for carrying the offence.
Step 2: Give up your right, permanently, to hold offences, bitterness, and wounds.
Step 3: Forgive your offender(s).
Step 4: Admit your own part in the situation and ask God to forgive you for the sin of carrying a grudge.
   Even if you were a small child when the offence took place, you are still responsible for your
   own reaction to it. This removes any legitimate accusation the devil may have against *you*.
Step 5: Ask God to forgive your offender. (See the chapter on *Bitter-Root Judgments* for more on this subject.)

Same old devil

The devil uses the same strategies, whether it is an emotional or physical healing you need in any area such as: poverty, envy, strife, unbelief, rebellion, bitterness, fear, etc. His chief strategy is deception. If he can get you to give him dominion over any part of you through guilt, shame, deception, lies, etc., he will establish himself in that area.

How demons exit a body

Demons generally exit through the mouth. When I minister deliverance I often have to ask the person to keep silent. People want to talk or pray and this stops up their mouths so the demon cannot exit. One girl I ministered to had a tremendous number of demonic strongholds. In a deliverance that lasted several hours, she began burping and belching. This continued throughout our session together. She was gloriously set free, and has established a ministry for native Americans.

A hairy beast

Don't be surprised by strange events. Lester Sumrall started a church in the Philippines, but for two years only a handful of people came. May 12, 1953, a girl possessed with the principality that ruled over the

Philippines, was being covered by the local newspaper, *The Daily Mirror.* Lester was able to convince her doctor to let him minister deliverance to her. She was being bitten and attacked constantly by two black, hairy demons that only she could see, yet observers could see the bites and saliva mysteriously appear all over her body. Lester fasted, prayed and went to the prison to cast out the demons.

The first day he rebuked them until they quit biting her. He went home to *fast and pray again*. When he went back and cast them out the second day, they left but soon returned demanding the right to reenter her. They asserted that she was unclean. Lester made them leave again, and led the girl in a prayer of repentance. The demons returned again. This time they demanded reentry because they claimed she had not asked them to go, and that she wanted them. Again, Lester made them leave. This time he led her in a statement, demanding that they leave. He taught her to pray and how to resist the demons. He left the prison and they tried to return, but she fought in Jesus' Name. During this struggle she grabbed a handful of fur off one of the demons. When the doctor examined it, it was not human or from any known animal. After this, the whole of the Philippines was opened up to the gospel and Lester won thousands of souls for Jesus.[39]

Possession through pornography

Lester tells of a Christian woman, a Sunday school teacher, who came forward for prayer. A man's voice came out of her saying that she had been to a porno film and the demon had a right to enter her. She repented, told the demon she didn't want it, and it left.[40] Lester tells of another man who was a Christian missionary, but had become demonized and shut himself up in his darkened house for weeks. He went to the man's home, cast out the demons, and got him set free.

At one of my crusades, a girl of about fifteen, who was born again according to her parents and her pastor, fell down and began writhing and screaming. I knew by the Spirit that there was something in her room at home that was a point of contact for entry into her soulish realm. Perhaps it was a "charged" fetish, or an object left by a friend, or an ungodly CD. I cast the demon out and she was delivered instantly. At the same meeting, two other Christian women had identical attacks. They, too, were set free. Because this comes up a lot, people have argued with me about whether it is possible for a born again person to have a demon, and my response is that anyone can have a demon that wants one. If you open yourself up through sin in the soulish realm, a demon will believe it is his right to take that ground. The ground must be reclaimed through sincere repentance, telling the demon he is not wanted, and casting him out.

Possession through abortion

One story in evangelist Carlos Annacondia's book struck me. A woman who had been a born again believer for a long time was manifesting demons, and the counselors could not get her set free. Carlos had a word of knowledge about abortion, and when she repented of this sin she was set free.[41] A similar thing happened during several of my meetings. When women open themselves up to demonic attack through abortion, there will often be demonic manifestations when they attend meetings where deliverance is taking place. If there is no manifestation, yet they come up for prayer for something else, it may be unproductive until the strongholds of guilt, murder and abortion are dealt with.

Voodoo and possession

Annacondia tells of a person vomiting up pieces of snakes and frogs, and another vomiting up parts of liver and intestines during deliverance and healing. David Hogan, a missionary, tells of snakes coming out of one person's back and red ants literally coming out of the back of another person during deliverance. A pastor friend who visited Haiti says the voodoo priests exhibit great power and hate the Christians, continually sending zombies to harass them. They were forced to build thick walls around their living quarters because of the constant assault of these mindless, walking dead (mind control through demon possession, dead or undead). At death the priest doesn't bury them completely, but calls their bodies up to walk about and perform commands. Sometimes people are given a substance to drink that renders them helpless slaves of the shaman. In Central and South America these events are commonplace, while in the USA people don't even believe there is a devil. What deception!

Peter Pan syndrome

A woman came to my home for ministry a few years ago. She was very frail and thin. She wore a helpless expression and had a slight bowing in her back. As I began to minister to her, the LORD spoke the words "Peter

Pan" to me. She revealed that she had made an inner vow that she would never grow up due to an overbearing father. A spirit of deception entered her life. She never grew up and remained immature. As an adult she had developed an illness that would not allow her to metabolize many foods, and she was afraid to eat. Fear set in. She wanted to be free but had lost all perspective.

The spirit of deception had tormented her, coupled with a lying spirit, and a spirit of infirmity. She had helplessly accepted these spirits because of the mind-set of her inner vow, which was compelling her body to remain childlike and thin. I led her in prayer to break the inner vow, and loosed her from it. She repented and asked for forgiveness, forgave her father, and asked God to forgive him, as well.

Three years later I was ministering when a lovely woman came forward to greet me. She said, "Don't you know me?" I was delighted to see her healthy and vibrant. God had changed her life and set her free.

Deliverance notes

1. If a person is unable to speak for himself because he is demonized, and he has a glazed or distant look, is unable to participate, or is violent, take authority over the demon(s) in Jesus' Name.
2. Help the victim to recognize that he is in bondage. The person has a free will, and he must *choose* to be free. You can cast out the demon, but if the person wants the demon, it will come back and the person will be worse off than before.
3. The victim should speak out loud his desire to be free and tell the demon to go.
4. Now the person ministering has the right to rebuke and cast out the demon.
5. When people genuinely want to be free, and the things the demons are attached to are broken and repented of, deliverance happens quickly.
6. Only one person should be casting out demons at a time. This is because if several are rebuking the devil, then the authority is diluted, and it will not go.
7. If the person doing the deliverance gets tired, then he or she should *verbally* give the authority to another.
8. All others involved should apply prayer pressure and continue to lend prayer support with intercession throughout the deliverance.
9. After deliverance, lead the person to Jesus, repentance, and instruct him in how to fill his heart with scripture, how to resist the devil, and how to stand.
10. Bind the blood of Jesus to him and appropriate scriptures. Play worship music and praise the LORD for His deliverance. Teach the person to rejoice.

Study Questions: Chapter 5
1. What do hands symbolize in scripture?
2. What sins are represented by the hands?
3. What do the right and left sides represent?
4. Why do you think, scripturally speaking, it's important to include a section on palms vs. wrists?
5. What are your personal thoughts after reading about the suffering Jesus experienced?
6. How can the shame of the cross be worse than the pain?
7. Why was Paul so enraged against the early church?

Study Questions: Chapter 7
1. Give five names of the devil. Then, give five names of Jesus (Yahshua) that defeat them.
2. Why is it important, tactically speaking, to know your enemy?
3. Why does God give His people visions?
4. How does the Joyner vision affect you?
5. What is the difference between agreement with a demon and agreement with God?
6. How can your words get you into trouble?

Chapter Ten
Chains of Bondage

Areas of access and weakness

A spirit of bondage can gain access to a person through a number of avenues. Essentially, bondage to any spirit that has a foothold or stronghold in your life can manifest and gain access through unrepented sin. A spirit of fear often works as the main entryway. Fear of death brings a lifetime of bondage *(Hebrews 2:15)*, as does religious involvement with controlling churches or cults. Generational curses can bring bondage, as can bitter-root judgments, soul ties and inner vows. (See the chapter on *Bitter-Root Judgments*.) Once an addiction establishes a stronghold through various spirits and sins of the flesh such as gluttony, brings compulsions and uncontrollable lusts of the flesh, witchcraft, whoredoms, addiction to alcohol, drugs, food and eating disorders, cigarettes, compulsive behavior, pornography, etc., then a spirit of bondage gains access, establishes itself in the person under its control, and blinds the victim to what is going on. If a person under bondage fights to get free in one area, such as drug addiction, then the spirit will simply establish a stronghold in another area, such as food, drink or cigarette addiction, until this spirit is cast out. If a person has multiple addictions, this evil spirit may only relinquish one area of addiction at a time, battling every step of the way to retain control. The victim must renounce each area of addiction separately. Demons promise power, liberty, pleasure, even happiness, but the end is destruction.

> *While they promise them liberty, they themselves are the servants of corruption: for of whom a man is overcome, of the same is he brought in bondage. (2 Peter 2:19)*

Definition of addictions

Addictions begin because of a negative self-image caused by unforgiveness, abuse, rape, rejection, grief, shame or guilt. They can manifest because of generational curses, inner vows or bitter-root judgments. Addictions are:

1. A form of spiritual idolatry.
2. A barrier to God.
3. They demand attention and cause shame and guilt.
4. They prevent obedience to God.
5. They perpetuate sin.

Learning to hate the sin

Sometimes deliverance is a process that takes time. Some people actually want their addictions and enjoy them. Cigarettes are a particularly stubborn addiction that smokers enjoy so much, they really don't want to forsake *all* and follow the LORD. They must learn to hate the sin. Compulsive behaviors often have deep ties to bitter-root judgments and inner vows, anger or self-pity. These roots and vows must be uncovered in order to set the person free. Often, simply calling out the name of the drug itself and casting it out will be enough. A person addicted to cigarettes is really addicted to the nicotine in them. Many pagan religions have drugs and alcohol as part of their ceremonies. Origins of addictions to wine may be in Baal and Ashtoreth worship. Other names for Baal are Baccus and Dionysus, both known for drunken orgies. If a kind of liquor is named for a particular person, and someone is addicted to it, come against that name.

Hallucinogenic plants have devas (goddesses which are really demons, who rule over the kingdom of plants) behind their usage and addictions: marijuana, cocaine, opium, heroin, peyote, psilocybin, etc. Because nature was worshipped in ancient pagan religions, and in modern day witchcraft, the usage of plant derived drugs to elicit hallucinations for worshiping the goddesses are common. Apparently, practitioners can evoke the effect of a drug at will, without having to take it. Drugs are used to open the "third eye," ushering in divination and familiar spirits, whether or not the drug user has ever practiced witchcraft, they are still defiled by the occultic, consciousness-altering effects of drugs. [42]

An addictive personality goes from one obsessive behavior to another, and may have several addictions at the same time, including oral fixations with cigarettes or food, etc.. A demon will often attach itself to each behavior and sin with manifestations such as: bulimia, anorexia, self-pity, gluttony, anger, resentment, excessive spending, compulsions, self indulgence. One person I ministered to was addicted to drugs, alcohol, and cigarettes. First, with much encouragement, and threats by neighbors, he gave up the drugs. Next he gave up the alcohol, and finally the cigarettes. In his case, deliverance was a long process. Another person I ministered to was addicted to sex, gambling, overspending. When the spirit of bondage was cast out, he was delivered. A woman I ministered to, was addicted to sex, drugs, alcohol and had an eating disorder. It took several years but she is totally free and living a victorious life.

A smoker's tale

My husband, who used to smoke, tried to quit but couldn't seem to get the victory. I struggled with him in the flesh for years, but he stubbornly refused to quit. It was ruining his ministry through guilt and shame; of course he didn't want to face this. He couldn't fellowship with others because all he could think about was escaping somewhere and having a cigarette. My nagging made his resolve to smoke even stronger. One night I was on my knees in the living room praying and weeping before the LORD. I turned and saw a huge, black, oily, foul-smelling demon standing over the place where my husband sits. It was a spirit of nicotine. This spirit works with a spirit of gluttony and guilt, and brings the sin of compulsive behavior. Bondage then gains a foothold to keep the victim bound. Additionally, nicotine is a drug. The door was open for pharmakeia, witchcraft, rebellion, anger and control got involved. I saw all these manifestations at one time or another.

I was angry that it was in my home, and commanded it to leave, after binding up it's influence. Then I began to command it to loose my husband. I ordered the spirit to stay outside, and told it not to come in my house. I anointed my doorposts, his chair, pillow and desk with oil, praying constantly. When my husband came home that night he stood in the doorway looking bewildered. Finally, he wandered uncertainly to his seat. Things felt very different to him and he sat uneasily. Finally, he grumpily went to bed early, but he didn't smoke that night. I knew the battle wasn't over, however. The demon stood outside whining and begging to take back the ground. It would have been much easier to give in, because the battle got heavy over the next days and weeks. The difficulty was that my husband's will was involved, and he *liked* to smoke. There were a few displays of temper, but I continued to stand on Luke 10:19 for one month, fasting off and on, coming against the demonic strongholds several times a day. It is important to note that he continued to smoke throughout the month, but I knew the battle was the LORD's, and the victory was mine from the moment I first saw this demon.

Throughout this time I *never* brought up the subject to my husband because that would have activated stubbornness and rebellion. I just waited and prayed. After four weeks I noticed one day that he didn't light up. This became a week, then two. Finally, I casually mentioned that I hadn't seen him smoke for a while. He informed me that the LORD spoke to him and told him to quit, and he had obeyed. Praise YHWH, our God, for His strategies and timing! When we hold back the demonic strongholds through intercession until the person is strong enough to stand on their own, then breakthrough comes.

Manifestations of a spirit of bondage

1. Fears: *For ye have not received the spirit of BONDAGE again to FEAR... (Romans 8:15)*

2. Addictions, drugs, alcohol, cigarettes, food:

...for of whom a man is overcome, of the same is he brought in BONDAGE. (2 Peter 2:19)

3. Fear of death:

...that through death He might destroy him that had the power of DEATH, that is the devil; and deliver them who through FEAR OF DEATH were all their lifetime subject to BONDAGE. (Hebrews 2:14-15)

4. Captivity to sin:

...that they may recover themselves out of the SNARE of the devil, who are taken CAPTIVE by him at his will (2 Timothy 2:26)

...another law in my members, warring against the law of my mind, and bringing me into CAPTIVITY to the LAW OF SIN which is in my members. (Romans 7:23)

5. Cords of compulsive sin:

His own iniquities shall take the wicked himself, and he shall be holden with the CORDS OF HIS SINS. (Proverbs 5:22)

6. Servant of sin: The Gadarene demoniac of Luke 8:26-33 was a servant of sin, but he was gloriously set free.

...Whosoever committeth sin is the SERVANT OF SIN. (John 8:34)

Know ye not, that to whom YIELD YOURSELVES SERVANTS to obey, his servants ye are to whom ye obey... (Romans 6:16)

7. Bond of iniquity, bitterness:

For I perceive that thou art in the GALL OF BITTERNESS, and in the BOND OF INIQUITY. (Acts 8:23)

Stand fast

YHWH, our God, wants us to walk free of bondage. Some people serve God out of fear, and God is not pleased with that. Some are even avid soul winners, not out of love, but fear. He does not bind us up; that's the devil's work. Most bondages are because of what *we* allow; our own actions. If you are a smoker, get rid of all cigarettes; if an alcoholic, all liquor; if a drug or porn addict, clean out your house and destroy it all. Sometimes bondages come because of hexes and curses. First, make sure that you are born again. Then:

1. Repent for the sin of not trusting the LORD to set you free.
2. Repent for willful disobedience to the Word.
3. Repent for idolatry.
4. Break off every word curse spoken by you, or others against you. Break all generational curses.
5. Break off any cords or attacks by psychic power, soulish power, satanistic power, hexes and vexes.
6. Cut off all lines of communication access between yourself and this demon. Close each door through repentance, breaking off bitterness, judgments, inner vows. Seal each one with the blood of the Lamb.
7. Repent for allowing the strongman authority in your life and for giving it ground.
8. Forcefully tell it you don't want it, and insist that it leave. Raise your voice. To engage your human spirit, you must be vehement. An apathetic tone of voice tells the demon you don't mean business, and thus it may hide and pretend to leave, until the next opportunity to work you over by lying in your ear. If you yield to this spirit's lies again, you will be entrapped in a cycle of failure; quitting and restarting again. This invites guilt and shame.
9. Cast out a spirit of bondage, and any other specific spirits that may be present, such as familiar spirits, lying spirits, fear, idolatry, nicotine, etc.
10. Bind the blood of Yahshua Messiah (Jesus Christ) to yourself.
11. Resist the devil's temptation and deception whenever he returns.
12. Stand fast. Don't allow yourself to be sucked into the devil's lies and deception again.

STAND FAST therefore in the liberty wherewith Christ hath made us free, and BE NOT ENTANGLED AGAIN with the YOKE OF BONDAGE. (Galatians 5:1)

Chapter Eleven
The Role of an Intercessor

The oppressed, the tormented, the demonized, the psychotic

Oppression is from the outside. It manifests through temptations and deceptions. The tormented are people in whom the devil has gained a foothold, to one degree or another. The evil spirit works from within. This is not possession. The Syrophoenician's daughter was delivered from a demon that was inside her when Jesus cast it out. *(Mark 7:29)* Demonization is when the devil can get the person to throw themselves in the fire, foam at the mouth, step in front of trains, commit murder, destroy things, etc. They often remember these actions. The father in Mark 9:25 had a son who manifested demons in this way. The psychotic (insane) are people over whom the devil has complete control.[43] The Gadarene demoniac is an example of this last category. *(Mark 5:1)* He ran through the tombs, cutting himself and crying out, naked and with great strength of many demons, so that none could even chain him. If a person receiving deliverance faints or falls into a glazed state, bind the demon and command the person's human spirit to come back and take control over their body. The victim must choose to renounce his specific sins. Following that, the person receiving deliverance must order the spirit to go. Then the minister must rebuke the evil spirit, and use their authority in Jesus' Name to set the person free.[44]

Manifestations

1. Insanity: the eyes go weird or become like glass.
2. Occult: legs start trembling when calling them out.
3. Satanism: (practicing) stomach goes wild, or body may shiver up the spine.
4. Witchcraft: neck goes wild.
5. Under a curse: smell sulfur; break the curse and command devil to come out and not return.
6. Fornication: spirit of whoredoms; vibration on head or mind; lust.
7. Suicide: shivering; person's eyes become almost white; eyes start to shut or start flipping.
8. Lunatic or schizophrenic: eyes roll up or close eyes to prevent minister from seeing this.
9. Addiction: must first cast out strongman, spirit of bondage.[45]

One of the tasks of an intercessor is to hold back strongholds long enough to let God's light shine in, enabling the captives to be set free. The deliverance can be instant, or can occur over a period of time. A person who is oppressed needs to pray for wisdom. Those who are standing in the gap for an oppressed or possessed person need to pray and possibly fast for them, as well.

Esther the intercessor

In the book of Esther, after she was chosen, she spent twelve months purifying herself with oil and myrrh (speaks of death to self), and then sweet spices and balms (speaks of becoming totally permeated with the fragrance of the Holy Spirit). Then she went into the presence of the king. The oil created through the crushing of the berries and spices creates a fragrance on the altar, a sweet smelling smoke that hides us from God's wrath like a veil.[46] Esther fasted for breakthrough, for divine strategies, timing and for wisdom. Esther, who is a type of the bride of Christ, had an enemy, Hamon, who represented evil, She didn't ask for war the first day. Instead, as she waited upon the LORD, she fasted and prayed for strategy. She had a key: Intimacy with the "King," just as we have the key to our breakthrough. This only comes through time spent with the Father. She fell on her face before the King to plead for the lives of her people. Esther took a stand so that her seed could live. She interceded and strategized how to get Hamon out of the situation. She was willing to die to follow righteousness. *...if I perish, I perish. (Esther 4:16)* She got the victory and saved herself and her people, and so can you. I challenge you:

...who knoweth whether thou art come to the kingdom for such a time as this? (Esther 4:14)

Divine Ambush

As Esther moved in divine strategy by waiting on the LORD for His timing and intervention, she moved the battle to her territory, having banquets in her own house. She wisely operated in a realm she was familiar with.

This allowed God time to bring supernatural disruption to the king's sleep, which caused the king to look in the exact book, at the exact strategic time, on the exact page where deliverance for the Jews could begin. God effected a divine ambush for His enemy, Hamon.

The Chief Intercessor

Jesus is our Chief Intercessor. Every time the enemy accuses us, He defends us to the Father. He is faithful and just to forgive us our sins, when we choose to follow His direction to repent and forgive. He ever lives to make intercession for those who are heirs of salvation; unlike human prayer warriors. He never gets tired or gives up. He is full of perfect understanding and compassion, and He is our role model. Discouragement is not an option. It must be vigilantly resisted! We, as intercessors, must not look at the circumstances to rightly judge the situation. Unlike Jesus, we need sleep and food and must not neglect our bodies. We need to come out of the prayer closet from time to time and walk, see colors, enjoy the beauty of nature. Otherwise we are targets for a spirit of heaviness.

Evil is here, now. We want to break these strongholds off our lives. We need supernatural deliverance, divine strategies and intervention, but we must be willing to lay down our lives through intercession, fasting and waiting on the LORD.

Hope for fanatics

I once heard a prophet say that each time he sees a rebellious youth he says, "There goes another future prophet." If a person is a fervent servant of the devil and sin, rest assured, it is not too late to save them unless they have blasphemed the Holy Ghost *(Matthew 12:31)*, or committed the sin unto death. *(Hebrews 6:4-6)* If a person was fanatical at serving the devil, then they will be just as intense serving God. If they were deep in sin, they may seek holiness with even greater fervency, and their love for Jesus will be great.

> *Wherefore I say unto thee, her sins, which are many, are forgiven; for she loved much: but to whom little is forgiven, the same loveth little. (Luke 7:47)*

How do you know whether you have blasphemed the Holy Ghost, committed the unpardonable sin, committed the sin unto death?

> *For it is impossible for those who were once ENLIGHTENED, and have TASTED OF THE HEAVENLY GIFT, and were made PARTAKERS OF THE HOLY GHOST, and have TASTED THE GOOD WORD OF GOD, and the POWERS OF THE WORLD TO COME, if they shall fall away, to renew them again unto repentance, seeing they crucify to themselves the Son of God afresh, and put Him to an open shame. (Hebrews 6:4-6)*

1. Enlightened (conviction and knowledge of truth)
2. Tasted the heavenly gift (salvation)
3. Partakers of the Holy Ghost (filled with the Holy Spirit)
4. Tasted the good Word of God (solid strong meat of the Word)
5. Tasted the powers of the world to come (gifts of the Holy Spirit)

To commit the sin unto death, a person must be deep in the Word, having known Jesus as Savior, having received the strong meat of the Word, been filled with the Spirit, and operated in one or more gifts of the Spirit (healings, miracles, discerning of spirits, prophecy, word of knowledge, word of wisdom, tongues and interpretations, faith).

Shot in the head

Before I knew Jesus, someone stood in the gap for me through prayer and intercession that saved my life numerous times. I became a concert act and nightclub entertainer. One night a man came into the back of the Colony Steak House, a club in Kansas City where I was singing, and shot me in the head. It felt like a mule kicked me. I fell forward on the floor. The man escaped and was never caught. I was taken to a hospital where they dug the bullet out, washed the wound with salt water, x-rayed me and sent me home. Aside from a walloping headache and a lot of fear, I was fine. Prayer saved my life, and it will save yours.

Attacked with shotguns

One time I was praying fervently before a concert in a dangerous part of town, "Behold, LORD, You have given me and my band POWER to tread on serpents, and on scorpions, and over all the power of the enemy.

Nothing shall by any means hurt me or my band." *(Luke 10:19)* I always make the scriptures personal when I pray them. The word POWER (exousia) in that scripture means authority. As a born again believer, each of us has the authority to command the enemy to leave. We have the authority to break strongholds off ourselves and others. I was praying, at that very moment, "No weapon that is formed against me or my band shall prosper..." *(Isaiah 54:17)* Four men came down the street with shotguns and attacked and threatened the band. One man held a gun up to my drummer's head and could not pull the trigger. No harm came to anyone, and many people were saved that night during the concert.

When we put the sword of the Spirit, the only piece of our armor that is an offensive weapon, into action by speaking the Word out of our mouths, we can defeat the enemy. The sword of the Spirit, which is the Word of God, is far more powerful than the weapons of man. I always pray, "The weapons of my warfare are not carnal, but they are mighty through God for the pulling down of strongholds in my life. With these supernatural weapons God gave me, I cast down imaginations, fear and unbelief that raise their ugly heads in my thought life, and every high thing that exalts itself against the knowledge of God, and I bring into captivity every thought to the obedience of Christ." *(2 Corinthians 10:4-5)* Many of the attacks we encounter are against our minds.

I met Terry Mize a few years ago and had the privilege of ministering at his church in Tulsa. He is the author of *More Than Conquerors*, a book about God's supernatural protection. Once, he picked up a hitchhiker in Mexico who turned out to be a bandit, just escaped from prison. The bandit shot at Terry five times at point blank range, and all the bullets fell in the dirt at his feet. He defeated the enemy by the words he spoke with the anointing of God. All the bandit had was bullets. Terry had the Word of God.

Fight using the fruit of the Spirit
Some of the worst attacks I've ever faced have been from Christians. The LORD spoke to me while I was on the set of a TV show where I was a regular. He directed me to do a three-day seminar with two other well-known people. After some initial organizing, I gave the task to others. Opening night was a wonderful success, with a packed house and many salvations. I was standing in the crowded lobby when the designated organizer, a pastor in whose church I had ministered, rushed up to me with his assistant and began hurling insults at me, demanding that I back out of the program. A crowd gathered as I stood in shocked silence. I perceived that this unprovoked attack was from the enemy, so I calmly informed them that I could not quit since it was my obligation to obey my heavenly Father, first.

When I got home, I immediately forgave them and prayed for them. Then the phone began ringing and continued for hours. I didn't answer because I knew a wrong spirit was motivating the calls. When we fight using the fruit of the Spirit it indicates that we do exactly the opposite of what the devil and our flesh want to do. The victory lies in total submission to Jesus' authority, not to man, and certainly not to Satan's tactics. The next night I called this pastor up on stage and honored him for his hard work in organizing the seminar.

I ran into this pastor several years later. He approached me with tears in his eyes and said, "What I did to you was so terrible. I was wrong and immature, but God has really done a work in me. Can you ever forgive me?" I told him I had done so the very night it happened. He confessed that because of his hardened heart, mixed with pride, he had suffered for several years and lost his church and ministry. We hugged and cried together. To God be all the glory, for He alone could bring true reconciliation.

The power of praise
Praise is one of the most powerful weapons we have as Christians. It is also a tool of intercession. When we offer true praise to the LORD, the devil cannot stand it because it glorifies the one true God. Singing hallelujah (praise ye Yah) brings YHWH into our midst in His glory and presence. It is the keynote in the song of the great multitude in heaven *(Revelation 19:1-6)* at the end of this age. If you need deliverance, begin to praise our mighty God with your whole heart, and you will begin to sense His presence and power to set you free.

The power of fasting and humility
When we humble ourselves and pray, YHWH answers our prayers, but the prayers of the haughty, the proud, God resists. *(James 4:6)* Praying for nations or for individuals requires humility on the part of the petitioner, after which YHWH declares He will hear their prayers, forgive and heal their nation. *(2 Chronicles 7:14)*

The link between prayer and fasting is magnified in my own life. I am able to focus in a humbled and repentant state in a way that causes me to be more open to the Spirit. Fasting draws me closer and amplifies discernment, beginning with myself. Invariably, the Holy Spirit deals with things I need to fix in my own life, first. This can be painful, but is exceedingly rewarding. During a fast, I become increasingly alive to things of the Spirit, and dead to the lusts and leading of the flesh.

Failure to cast out demons is a tricky subject. Jesus admonished His disciples that some kinds of demons come out only by fasting and prayer. If a believer engages in very much deliverance, then fasting is an imperative part of their lives. By the way, it is possible to cast out demons, even if a person does not want them to go, but they will come back. Have you done the person a favor? No! They will be worse off, because the demon will come back with more of his friends to take up residence. I always have the person I'm ministering to declare that they *want* to be free, and tell the evil spirit that they *want* it to go. Then, it is much smoother casting it out, and it is less likely to regain entrance. Sin in the minister's life will cause the demon to refuse to go, and unrepented sin in the victim's life will leave ground the demon will have a right to reoccupy.

Boldness through the Messiah

Boldness and confidence are vibrant parts of our witness and stand for our Messiah. Doubt and unbelief will cause true boldness to leave. Boldness is not the enemy of humility. They work together. True humility through the Messiah will cause us to be pliable in the Father's hands, while sometimes having to take a stand against what people desire from us. I have had things demanded of me that I could not comply with, and I've taken a bold stand against, because my fear of the LORD is greater than my fear of man.

In Whom we have BOLDNESS and access with CONFIDENCE by the faith of Him. (Ephesians 3:12)

Herein is our love made perfect, that we may have BOLDNESS in the day of judgment: because as He is, so are we in this world. There is no fear in love; but perfect love casteth out fear: because fear hath torment. He that feareth is not made perfect in love. (1 John 4:17-18)

And this is the CONFIDENCE that we have in Him, that, if we ask any thing according to His will, He heareth us: And if we know that He hear us, whatsoever we ask, we know that we have the petitions that we desired of Him. (1 John 5:14-15)

We must believe that He is faithful Who promised. *(Hebrews 11:11)* Confidence and faith in God that He will do what He said He will do, produces boldness to witness and trust that His Word is true. Abraham received the promise of God because he trusted Him.

He STAGGERED NOT at the promise of God through unbelief; but was strong in faith, giving glory to God: And being fully persuaded that, what He had promised, He was able also to perform. (Romans 4:20-21)

If we understood the holiness of God we would never question His integrity.

In hope of eternal life, which God, that cannot lie, promised before the world began… (Titus 1:2)

If God was to lie, then everything He has built with His Word would collapse.

Chapter Twelve
Binding and Loosing

Binding

Binding and loosing are the KEYS OF THE KINGDOM.

> *And I will give unto thee the KEYS OF THE KINGDOM of heaven: and whatsoever thou shalt BIND on earth shall be bound in heaven: and whatsoever thou shalt LOOSE on earth shall be loosed in heaven. (Matthew 16:19)*

> *…Whatsoever ye shall BIND on earth shall be bound in heaven: and whatsoever ye shall LOOSE on earth shall be loosed in heaven. (Matthew 18:18)*

Binding and loosing are two of the most powerful tools we have on this earth. Jesus instructed us that whatever we bind or loose on earth, has *already* been bound or loosed in heaven. It is important to note that in the following scriptures from Proverbs, good things are BOUND *to* the individual. This is different than we've been taught, but is a powerful revelation. BIND (*Strong's* 7194, qashar) means to tie, confine, compact, join together, knit, stronger.

> *…forsake not the law of thy mother: BIND them continually upon thine heart, and tie them about thy neck. (Proverbs 3:3)*

> *Keep My commandments, and live…BIND them upon thy fingers, write them upon the table of thine heart. (Proverbs 6:21)*

Definition: Binding indicates a knitting or joining together to make stronger. BIND means to cause to stick together in a mass; tie or fasten tightly; constrict or cohere; be closely associated with; compel; order a person to do something; fasten, secure, attach, join, stick, fuse, mix, blend, combine; restrain; put in bonds.

There is another aspect to binding. In Mark 3:27 we are enjoined to BIND the strong man before we try to take his goods. When ministering deliverance, it is often critical to take authority over the demon (strongman) before beginning deliverance (entering his house) and casting him out (spoiling his goods). Once his operations are bound, the person can be loosed from the control of the evil spirit. BIND, in the following scripture (*Strong's* 1210, deo), means to be in bonds, knit, tie, wind.

> *No man can enter into a strong man's house, and spoil his goods, except he will first BIND the strong man; and then he will spoil his house. (Mark 3:27)*

Loosing

Strong's definition for loosing shows us that loosing is freedom *from* something; to get free from oppression. Notice that Jesus told the woman in Luke 13:12 that she was LOOSED from her infirmity. He didn't bind it *to* her, He loosed her *from* it. I've heard many people pray, loosing what they wanted to happen. This is not nearly as effectual as binding good things *to* ourselves, and loosing ourselves *from* bad things. Pray and meditate on these truths. One nugget like this could totally change the effectiveness of your prayer life. In the two scriptures following, LOOSE (*Strong's* 3089, luo) means break up, destroy, dissolve, melt, put off.

> *Whatsoever ye shall LOOSE on earth shall be loosed in heaven. (Matthew 16:19)*

> *Then the lord of that servant was moved with compassion, and LOOSED him, and forgave him the debt. (Matthew 18:27)*

> *For this purpose the Son of God was manifested, that He might DESTROY (undo, loose dissolve) the works of the devil. (1 John 3:8)*

> *And ought not this woman…be LOOSED from this bond on the Sabbath day? (Luke 13:16)*

Notice that Jesus came to LOOSE us from the works of the devil, in other words, to set us free.

Definition: LOOSE means no longer held by bonds or restraint; detached from its place, not held together, release, set free from constraint; untie, undo, discharge, freed; unshackled, unchained, detached; deliver, unbind, let go, release. The following scripture demonstrates the Hebrew word, pathach, which means put off, ungird, unstop, let go free, have vent.

> *Is not this the fast that I have chosen: to LOOSE the bands of wickedness, to undo the heavy burdens, and to let the oppressed go free, and that ye break every yoke? (Isaiah 58:6)*

Another word for LOOSE is (*Strong's* 630, apoluo) defined to mean to free fully, relieve, release, dismiss, let die, pardon, depart, dismiss, divorce, let go, send away, release, set at liberty. This application is seen in the following scriptures.

> *...Woman thou art LOOSED from thine infirmity. (Luke 13:12)*

We want to bind good things to ourselves, and loose bad things from ourselves. These are wonderful tools that will help every intercessor. You can hinder, cast out, restrain and resist the devil by correctly using the Word as a sword.

Chapter Thirteen
A Seared Conscience

What can be done for someone who has a SEARED (*Strong's* 2743, kauteriazo) conscience? This Greek word is where we derive the word cauterize, meaning to brand, to render insensitive, sear with a hot iron. *Vine's* defines the word seared or branded as burning with a branding iron, caustic, to mark by branding; apostates whose consciences are branded with the effects of their sin. To apostatize is to abandon one's religious convictions and principles, and defect from the faith.

> *Now the Spirit speaketh expressly, that in the latter times some shall depart from the faith, giving heed to seducing spirits, and doctrines of devils; Speaking lies in hypocrisy; having their conscience SEARED with a hot iron... (1 Timothy 4:2)*

Drop outs

I have encountered individuals over the years who were once considered Christians, but have dropped out for one reason or another. My mother used to sneer about the people who came to brush arbor or camp meetings she attended as a child. She was forever prejudiced against apparent radical conversions, because she observed derelicts who would run forward hollering and get saved. She would see them a week or a month later, right back where they were before, drunk in the street. She decided that all conversions were insincere and, therefore, she wanted no part of "religion." A young, intense pastor I knew, who had a small but devoted church, suddenly left his wife, abandoned the church, got in trouble with the law and ended up in jail. His wife was a wonderful, godly woman, his kids were great, the church was going well. What caused this apostasy? Another pastor set his heart on robbing the sheep from all the other churches in the area. He established church service at a time when no one else had service, and campaigned heavily to draw a crowd. He succeeded in part, but began to reap in other ways, through strife, and church splits. God wants his pastors to go after the lost, but He looks on the heart. If the intent is to rob others to build your own kingdom, then that is idolatry.

Deception

A spirit of deception uses its wiles to manipulate people into whatever worldly gain the person they are using lusts for: status, position, power, respect, money, material goods? This spirit works with a lying spirit and a spirit of defiance to justify and gain its diabolical ends. Deception then manipulates the defense and cover-up that follow. If only we could see that ungodly gain is really loss in God's economy.

A "Christian" businessman, who held prayer meetings before work each morning, began fraudulently taking money from his family, friends, employees, and other businesses, all the while claiming to be running a "Christian" business. When people realized what was happening and attempted to recover their funds, loans, equipment or paychecks, he began spreading malicious lies, discrediting them in order to maintain his own business. Missionary organizations sent boatloads of supplies to starving children, discovering later that it was rotting at the docks because he had pocketed the docking fees. Idolatry wedged its way into his heart. He obtained at least five million dollars through frauds and embezzlement. How can this happen to a man who once was a strong Christian, and conversely, how can so many Christians be deceived by one man?

Idolatry

The love of money (*Strong's* 5365, philarguria), which literally means "fondness for silver," is the root of all evil. *(1 Timothy 6:10)* The root of this Greek word (argos) means shining; the desire to know intimately, that which shines.[47] We are attracted to that which shines for us. Is it to have a big church, even if it involved manipulating the money (or people with money, or allowing them to manipulate you) and deceiving the sheep; is it to have millions of dollars, even if it has to be obtained fraudulently; is it to have a fancy car or house, even if it means living well beyond your means and getting into excessive debt; is it to succeed at your job, even if it means spreading gossip about another employee to gain an advantage? Satan's sin is detailed in the next scripture.

> *By the multitude of thy merchandise (possessions), they have filled the midst of thee with violence, and thou hast sinned...by the iniquity of thy traffic (trade). (Ezekiel 28:16, 18)*

Sin sears the conscience and hardens the heart to the things of God. Unrepented sin causes a separation from God and a guilty conscience. Then it's hard to pray. Soon the heart loses the ability to tell right from wrong, good from evil. A liar will no longer be able to tell when he is lying. Whatever serves his purpose *seems* like truth, and an acceptable means to an end.

Abortion and idolatry

If a person engages in sin, whether he is a Christian or not, it opens the door to the devil. In a crusade in Argentina, the counselors told Brother Annacondia that a woman in the deliverance tent had accepted the LORD some time ago and was attending church, but she was manifesting demons and shaking violently. Through a word of knowledge, it was discovered that she'd had an abortion. When she confessed and repented of this sin, she was delivered.[48] Abortion and idolatry sear the conscience and go hand in hand. Abortion becomes possible through a spirit of error and antichrist that manifest through the sin of idolatry. When people idolize their own selfish interests above those of their potential progeny, abortion and murder are the result, followed by guilt, shame, and a lifetime of bondage to Satan.

Simon the sorcerer was saved and baptized but was tempted by idolatry, the love of power and respect of men. He desired what the apostles had and even offered money for the gifts and anointing. He would have perished in sin had he not repented.

> *And when Simon saw that through laying on of the apostles' hands the Holy Ghost was given, he offered them money, Saying, Give me also this power, that on whomsoever I lay hands, he may receive the Holy Ghost. But Peter said unto him, Thy money perish with thee, because thou hast thought that the gift of God may be purchased with money. (Acts 8:13-24)*

It is interesting that the apostle who rebuked him was Peter who once had similar troubles of his own. Satan used Peter to try to stop the great work of the cross, and Jesus rebuked him for allowing this to happen.

> *But when He had turned about and looked on His disciples, He rebuked Peter, saying, Get thee behind Me, Satan: for thou savorest not the things that be of God, but the things that be of men. (Mark 8:33)*

Judas Iscariot, who had walked with Jesus, allowed demons to use him in greed, theft, and idolatry. Satan entered him and used him to betray the King of glory.

> *And when He had dipped the sop, He gave it to Judas Iscariot, the son of Simon. And after the sop Satan entered into him. (John 13:26-27)*

Greed

The spirits of greed and COVETOUSNESS are two of the major players in these end times as the world prepares to receive the antichrist. What causes Christians to allow their consciences to be seared with a hot iron? The biggest cause is IDOLATRY.

> *…no whoremonger, nor unclean person, nor COVETOUS man, who is an IDOLATER, hath any inheritance in the kingdom of Christ and of God…because of these things cometh the wrath of God upon the children of disobedience. Be not ye therefore partakers with them. (Ephesians 5:5-7)*

God is not pleased with idolatry. He shows us that idolaters will have no inheritance in His holy kingdom and instructs us not to partake with them.

> *Now the works of the flesh are manifest, which are these…IDOLATRY, WITCHCRAFT…they which do such things shall not inherit the kingdom of God. (Galatians 5:19-21)*

> *For the wrath of God is revealed from heaven against all ungodliness and unrighteousness of men, who hold the truth in unrighteousness…for God hath showed it unto them. (Romans 1:18-19)*

People who display such idolatrous greed as cited above may get "stuff" here on earth, but the really worthwhile things that our God has for us, (the "good stuff"), they will not partake of, unless they truly repent, submitting to the chastisement of the LORD, true repentance and humility, allowing God to come in and purify the heart.

> *…God resisteth the PROUD, but giveth grace to the HUMBLE. SUBMIT yourselves therefore to God. Resist the devil, and he will flee from you. Draw nigh to God, and He will draw nigh to you. Cleanse your hands, ye sinners; and purify your hearts, ye DOUBLE-MINDED…HUMBLE yourselves in the sight of the LORD, and He shall lift you up. (James 4:6-8, 10)*

> *PRIDE goeth before destruction, and a HAUGHTY spirit before a fall. Better it is to be of a HUMBLE spirit with the lowly, than to divide the spoil with the proud. (Proverbs 16:18-19)*

Getting free

If there are aspects of our lives not yielded to God, then we need to deal with them. Remember, you are a three-part being. Being born again means the Holy Spirit dwells in your spirit. That leaves the soul and body where the devil may try to gain access through sin. Unlike the devil, the Holy Spirit will not take areas we do not give Him. Give Him your fear, your rage, anger, lust, idolatry, pride, greed, covetousness. Problems result from open doors which *must* be shut. Deliverance is shutting doors.

1. Confess and repent.
2. Break specific strongholds in Jesus' Name.
3. Cast the spirit out.
4. Close all doors of access (sins that have made you vulnerable).
5. Bind appropriate scriptures to yourself.
6. Bind wisdom, knowledge, God's love and truth to yourself.
7. Bind your feet to the path of righteousness.

Study Questions: Chapter 13

1. Do you know someone who has a seared conscience? How do you know?
2. Will you set aside time to pray for this person for breakthrough? Then follow up by going to them at the leading of the Holy Spirit, and entreat them to repent. If they repent, then you have won a brother or sister back to the LORD.
3. Could you yourself have a seared conscience? Let the Holy Spirit search your heart.
4. When it comes to idolatry, what "shines" for you? Everyone has something they lift above the LORD. Let us desire to lay up treasure in heaven rather than on earth.

Chapter Fourteen
Evolution: Lies from the Pit

When I was in elementary school the teachers introduced evolution as a fact. You have all heard the diatribe: "Billions of years ago there was a big bang..." I was raised in a church, and had heard, "In the beginning, God..." Now I was being asked to make a paradigm shift to, "In the beginning, a big bang..." I began to question everything I had ever learned, including the existence of God. The devil's tactic: question everything. His first words in the garden were a question. His desire is to be God, but that job is already taken, so he is angry. Hitler got his ideas from his father, the devil, when he said, "If you say anything long enough, loud enough and often enough, people will believe it."

Evolution and the public school

If you have children in the public school, please study up on creationism and instruct them, so their belief in God will not be destroyed. I believe the earth is approximately six thousand years old, and here are some compelling reasons: First, if there really had been a big bang, then all planets and moons would spin the same way. However, Venus, Uranus and many moons spin backwards. Second, the sun is burning at the rate of five million tons per second and shrinking. If the earth is 6,000 years old there is no problem, but if the earth is billions of years old, then the sun would have been big enough to touch the earth. Third, the rings around Saturn are expanding and would have hit earth's atmosphere by now. Fourth, we are losing the moon at the rate of two inches per year. It couldn't be billions of years since the earth began, or the moon and earth would have been so close to each other that the earth's gravitational force would have pulled the moon into it, destroying both. Fifth, when the space program landed on the moon, they built special landing gear because they anticipated deep moon dust, consistent with the "billions of years" theory. The moon accumulates one inch of dust every ten thousand years. The dust was just over one-half inch thick at the time of their landing, which is consistent with the earth being six thousand years old. By the way, one of the evolutionist's favorite arguments for their theory is carbon dating, which doesn't actually work because of the increase in C-14 levels (too complicated to discuss here). Finally, the spin of the earth is slowing down. In 1990, 1992, 1994, 1996, 1998 and 2000 we added a leap second to our clocks. If earth was billions of years old, it would have been spinning too fast in the beginning, and everything would have flown wildly off the surface.

Nearly 300 legends collected from around the world, tell of a great flood about 4,400 years ago. The tremendous forces of the raging waters formed the mountains, the Grand Canyon and other wonders, not millions of years of erosion. The oldest living tree is 4,300 years old; the oldest coral reef is 4,200 years old. There would be *something* older if the world was billions of years old. Under the Lincoln memorial in Washington D.C., there are 50-inch stalactites. It didn't take "billions and billions" of years to form them as we've been told.[49]

Chapter Fifteen
Family and Generational Curses

I will now recount a story about our local public elementary school teaching witchcraft to the fifth graders. One of the parents (we'll call her Linda) I had alerted, asked me for prayer and help with her own situation. I went to her home and immediately sensed that it was infested with demons. Linda was trembling with fear, but her spirit was open to the LORD because I had sent my *Heart and Soul Surrender* cassette home with her son, and she had played it for three days before my arrival. This helped to prepare the ground and began to loose her mind from satanic deception. The strongholds were great in her life because her mother had given her to the devil and cursed her as a small child, repeatedly abused her, attempted to kill her, and told her that she was hated and unwanted.

The abuse shattered her personality into fragments, creating an increasing life and death struggle that made it nearly impossible to function normally. There were a number of triggers put in place to control her, and cause extreme fear and anxiety, also serving to make her helpless and dependent on the parent's whims. The mother had selected and given her to her husband as his slave. As soon as they were married he quit working, though he was healthy and strong and fully capable of providing. He made Linda support the family. Linda's family had tried to have her committed because she soon became unable to work. She was living in a home across the street from, and owned by, her mother. Her husband was currently living elsewhere, deep in pornography. He sometimes forced the children to watch porn when they visited, while he lay in bed with strange women. He would come over frequently to bully Linda, with the full blessing of her mother.

I spent over seven hours casting out demons. One was sitting on her chest choking her. I told her to make it go. She began to sob and ask, "What will I do? They've been with me so long I won't know how to act." Finally, she told it she didn't want it anymore and I commanded it to leave in Jesus' Name. We both watched it go out the window. I led her and her children to the LORD. She renounced any involvement with the occult and repented for her sin. I broke the curses spoken against her and at her request filled a garbage bag full of objects of worship to demon gods: talismans from the psychic network, jewelry, statues, posters, a dream catcher, hand-carved voodoo idols, anything she or her children were using as a point of contact with demons. I broke the power of each object off her and the children. We anointed all doorways, windows, pillows, beds and people with oil and drew the bloodline of Jesus at all entrances. Before I left I taught her how to stand against the imminent attack of Satan in Jesus' Name, and wrote down some instructions. When I left, she begged me to take the garbage bag to a dumpster, because if we had set it out on the curb, she said she would not be strong enough to resist bringing it back in.

She called the next day praising God for her glorious new found freedom. She rejoiced that she had used Jesus' Name and made the demons stay away. Monday I began receiving threats from her relatives for helping her and for throwing away the idols. Linda called Monday evening and told me the bizarre events of the day: The one object she was unwilling to part with was the most critical of all. She related the story of how a satanic priest had come to her home and cursed a large mirror on the wall. The mirror immediately developed a "fault" in the center. Demons came and went through this portal. She had also told me she feared she might be pregnant by her abusive husband, from whom she was separated. The divorce would be final in two weeks. She had swelled up and suddenly gained twenty pounds, but the doctor told her that morning she was not pregnant. Linda came home and stood in front of the mirror laying hands on her belly, pushing hard and shouting, "Come out, in Jesus' Name." Blood gushed out and she saw three demons leave her and go into the mirror. Her husband, who was using her as a chalice, was desperately attempting to regain control of her through sorcery, impregnating her with demons to prevent the divorce.

She asked me what to do. I instructed her to get some oil, anoint the mirror, and break the power of the gateway or portal in Jesus' Name. Then I told her to bind up the door to the demonic realm in the mirror, close it and seal it by binding Jesus' blood to the mirror. I held the phone and heard her carrying out these instructions. Then I advised her to get rid of the mirror. She was able to return to work, but much ground was lost when the owners of the house (her parents) and her husband gained reentry and brought many of the demons back with

51

them. Demons respect authority and ownership. If possible, it is best to minister solely on property that is holy or sanctified. I have resolved to ascertain who owns the property before beginning deliverance sessions in the future.

Word Curses

Your situation may not be as dramatic as Linda's, but word curses are just as damaging, such as: "You'll never amount to anything," "You're lazy and stupid, just like your father," "Grandma had breast cancer, mother had it, so I'll probably have it, too," You're too old, too young, too poor, too fat, too short, too tall," etc. The list of possible curses is as endless as the people who make them. They bring destruction to lives and must be broken in Jesus' Name, cancelled, and sealed by the blood of the Lamb.

Generational Curses

There are many who are being overcome by generational curses. These curses come down from relatives living and dead, who sinned against God or were cursed by others. It manifests in a family history of diseases, mental illness, and in a spirit of bondage to things such as liquor, gambling, lust, divination, cigarettes, etc. It may manifest in a propensity to anger, child or wife abuse or clairvoyance. A spirit of divination that attaches itself to a family bloodline down through the generations has the right to be there if any ancestor practiced witchcraft. This spirit is not a wonderful gift like the Hollywood movies teach, but a terrible curse. The strongholds that are nurtured and expanded through demonic attachments must be broken. In my case, since I'm adopted, it had to be done in both my birth parents, and adoptive parent's, maternal and paternal bloodlines.

The deaf and dumb spirit that Jesus cast out was in the boy because of the father's sin of unbelief. *(Matthew 17:21)* This curse was broken when the father repented. Then Jesus cast the demon out of the boy and commanded it not to return. This deliverance was unique in two ways: It's the only instance in scripture where the demon was disarmed before being cast out, and was forbidden to return. Remember this when dealing with generational curses, and the deaf and dumb spirit.

Most generational curses should be broken back to the third and fourth generation. The references to curses that go back to the third and fourth generation for iniquity and transgression are: *Exodus 20:5; Exodus 34:7; Numbers 14:18; Deuteronomy 5:9*. The curse of illegitimacy that goes back to the tenth generation is referred to in Deuteronomy 23:2.

Repenting for sins of forefathers and for the nation

Strongholds that have people in their grip through bloodlines must be broken. We break them off by faith, using the Name of Jesus and pleading His blood. Do this with each ancestor on both sides, beginning with the appropriate generation, and working your way to the first. Often, God will reveal specific sins as you move through this process. There might be an ancestor on your mother's side who practiced witchcraft. Stop at this generation and break the curse in Jesus' Name. Stand in the gap just as if it was you who sinned. Then forbid the evil spirit to return because the open door to curses has been closed. Seal it with the blood of Jesus. Then proceed carefully, expecting more revelation.

I have seen people rush through this process counting down as fast as they can, and I know they mean well. However, it is much more compassionate and effectual to move slowly, allowing the Holy Spirit to speak. The following scriptures are powerful and effectual for repentance.

Let Thine ear now be attentive, and Thine eyes open, that Thou mayest hear the prayer of Thy servant, which I pray before Thee now, day and night, for the children of Israel Thy servants, and confess the sins of the children of Israel, which we have sinned against Thee: both I and my father's house have sinned. (Nehemiah 1:6)

O LORD, according to all Thy righteousness, I beseech Thee, let Thine anger and Thy fury be turned away from Thy city Jerusalem, Thy holy mountain: because for our sins, and for the iniquities of our fathers, Jerusalem and Thy people are become a reproach to all that are about us. Now therefore, O our God, hear the prayer of Thy servant, and his supplications, and cause Thy face to shine upon Thy sanctuary that is desolate, for the LORD's sake...for we do not present our supplications before Thee for our righteousnesses, but for Thy great mercies. O LORD, hear; O LORD, forgive; O LORD, hearken and do; defer not, for Thine own sake, O my God; for Thy city and Thy people are called by Thy Name. (Daniel 9:16-20)

If any man see his brother sin, a sin which is not unto death, he shall ask, and he shall give him life for them that sin not unto death. (1 John 5:16)

Whosesoever sins ye remit, they are remitted unto them; and whosesoever sins ye retain, they are retained. (John 20:23)

Other scriptures for repentance are: *Leviticus 26:39-42; Nehemiah 9:1-4; Jeremiah 3:24-25; 14:20.*

Getting free

1. Confess sins involving the occult. Confess any abortions.
2. Repent and ask God's forgiveness.
3. Break the power of each stronghold over your mind in Jesus' Name.
4. Plead the blood of Jesus over each instance.
5. Cast out any familiar spirits (generational demons), divination, or witchcraft that may be operating.
6. If you believe you are a victim of word curses known (ones you made against yourself, and ones you know others have made against you) and unknown:
    a. Break all word curses against you in Jesus' Name. Render them null and void.
    b. Break off and renounce all psychic power, soul power and satanic power that has been arrayed against you.
    c. Cancel their assignments.
    d. Declare that the blood of Jesus is against these evil curses, and bind the blood of Jesus to yourself.
7. Forbid these demons to return once the curses are broken.

Chapter Sixteen
Bitter-Root Judgments, Inner Vows, Soul Ties

We have all made them! They compel and destroy our lives, and we are not even aware it is happening. Judgments and vows are so easy to make, yet so destructive. Breaking them off my life has made a radical change for the better, and it will for you, as well. Sometimes it takes a long time to remember the judgments and vows, but pray for the Holy Spirit to help bring them to mind in God's order and timing. When I sit down with someone experiencing difficulties in the areas of soul ties, bitter-root judgments, inner vows or generational curses, I make a flow chart while they relate information about family members in detail. A pattern usually emerges showing the same footprints of demonic operation for generations. Once this pattern is brought to the light of the cross, it is easy to diagnose it from knowing the symptoms. This is exactly what doctors do, but we have Dr. Jesus on the case.

Breaking the stronghold of bitter-root judgments

Bitter-root judgments are structures we erect in the soulish realm, when we have judged another. Through the LAW OF SOWING AND REAPING we will receive it back as self-fulfilling prophecy.[50] For example, if one judges his father for abuse, one will reap by becoming an abuser. If a girl judges her father for neglecting her, she will reap through a husband who neglects her. What goes around, comes around. *For they have sown to the wind, and they shall reap the whirlwind. (Hosea 8:7)*

Be not deceived; God is not mocked: for whatsoever a man SOWETH, that shall he also REAP. (Galatians 6:7)

Bitter-root judgments DEFILE others around them and may poison a whole family. The roots are deep and may reach back several generations. Everyone has heard of feuds between clans, such as the Hatfields and the McCoys. Some ethnic groups are particularly vulnerable to bitter-root judgments because it is part of their culture.

Looking diligently lest any man fail of the grace of God; lest any ROOT OF BITTERNESS springing up trouble you, and thereby many be DEFILED... (Hebrews 12:15)

To get free, the person must confess his sin (and forefather's sin) and renounce it. He must repent of making the judgment, no matter how well deserved it was. God cannot forgive us if we do not choose to forgive our offenders. Forgiveness on the victim's part cuts off Satan's right to accuse.

JUDGE NOT that ye be not judged. For with what judgment ye judge, ye shall be judged... (Matthew 7:1-2)

The JUDGMENT can now be broken and the person loosed from it, freeing him from demonic operations. Demons who are attached to these judgments can now be cast out. An oppressed person's expression is hard. He/she resists effectual prayer, and often, words of knowledge as well. I have found that bitterness is a stronghold that most people deny when confronted with the truth. No one wants to admit that he is bitter. Bitter-root judgments cause anger and hatred, eat people alive and destroy relationships. They are one of the main causes of sickness. Failure to repent of bitterness will cause the person to remain sick in body and soul. Let go of the right to seek revenge, or hold grudges and offenses.

Bitterness manifested in sickness

After ministering the song *"Stripes"* at a concert, I called people forward for healing and prayer. I began to minister to a woman with a long list of illnesses. The Father spoke one word to me: "Bitterness." She had a hard look in her eyes and her face was drawn toward her mouth where she pursed her lips continually. I said, "The LORD showed me that you have bitterness." She drew back in resentment and denial. I told her to return to her seat and God could reveal it to her, and that if she would fully repent, she would be healed. This was clearly *not* what she wanted to hear. After the service she rushed up to me and said, "My mother was bitter, my father was bitter, my children are bitter, my first husband was bitter. Do you think I could possibly be bitter?" I told her that she was DEFILED by bitterness and gave her some materials to help her. She repented and broke the bitter-root judgments. After being bound for many years, she was delivered and healed of all her diseases. The truth sets us free. Hallelujah!

Inner vows

An inner vow is a strong statement of determination, usually made in early life, that is usually forgotten, but profoundly affects life in the present. The vow drives the flesh and becomes a self-fulfilling prophecy that compels a person to fulfill the vow, consciously or unconsciously. The person unwittingly becomes a SERVANT of the vow. Some vows have time clocks that eventually go off like a bomb, such as: "When I grow up I'll never... (fill in the blank)!"

Know ye not that to whom ye yield yourselves SERVANTS to obey, his SERVANTS ye are to whom ye obey; whether of sin unto death, or of obedience unto righteousness? (Romans 6:16)

Examples of some typical vows are: "No one will ever tell me what to do!" "All men do is use women and then leave!" "I'll never trust anyone again!" "I'll never be like my Dad (or mother). I'll never treat my children like that!" The person wonders why he becomes just like his dad or mom, yet can't seem to stop. Boys make vows to never share with a woman, then wonder what is wrong with their marriage. Girls make vows to never trust a man if her dad deserted her or let her down. She will never let her true self be known to her husband, always holding something back. A common vow is, "I'll get even with him (her)." This may cause the person to take out vengeance on *all* women (men). What a person sows he will reap *(Galatians 6:7)*, and inner vows will surely bring a day of reaping. Even good vows need to be broken because no one wants to be controlled by the flesh. Inner vows and bitter-root judgments create strongholds in the soulish realm, structures that must be destroyed if victory is to be maintained. [50]

Thou shalt not forswear thyself, but shalt perform unto the LORD thine oaths...SWEAR NOT AT ALL... (Matthew 5:33-37)

Steps for breaking inner vows and bitter-root judgments

1. Pray and repent for making inner vows and bitter-root judgments.
2. Ask the Holy Spirit to bring hidden vows to the surface to be discovered and broken. This is a process that takes time.
3. Confess the vows and judgments as sin and ask the Father for forgiveness.
4. Break each vow and judgment and loose yourself and others from the power of your judgments and vows.
5. Plead the blood of Jesus over each broken vow and judgment; forgive others who drove you to make the vows and judgments.
6. Breaking off inner vows and bitter-root judgments leaves gaps in your soul. Memorize scriptures and speak them often.

Soul ties

When a soul tie is formed, a spiritual transference occurs. A soul tie is the knitting together of two souls.

...lationships, and with God, but it is destructive in ungodly relationships ...ttachments to parents, movie or sports stars, etc. One can also become ...d leaders. I even ministered to a woman who had formed soul ties to ...rce or separation from a sexual partner causes the soul tie to be ripped ...ttered. Sexual soul ties make ungodly relationships hard to break off ...ll the other sexual partners you and they have had. The soul become ...child or adult is molested, there is a transference of evil spirits from ...homosexual spirit if this applies, a perverse spirit, guilt, shame, ...ungodly soul ties, through soulish and sexual links.

...receive and perpetrate physical and emotional abuse. We have all ...use or sexual partner that abuses them. Frequently, people become ...because the soul is being drawn to others through soul ties. Sexual ...er sexual soul ties and links, as well. Dirty, unclean or perverse ...exual sin in a marriage. Some think that spouses should get back ...mmend: dirty soul ties be broken and the couple get counseling. ...new healthy soul ties can be formed.

...f-contact links; objects given to a victim of satanic ritual abuse ...y witches. A young woman I was ministering to had been given rings, jewelry and other objects through which control was maintained. Because she was given at birth to a coven headed by her grandfather, and ritually abused throughout childhood, she had many such "charged" objects in her possession. When the coven felt her slipping away from their control, they sent in a boyfriend who was used to give her necklaces and rings to keep her in bondage. She accepted Jesus Christ as her Savior but continued to struggle. I met her on a mental ward where she was under suicide watch, having sliced up her wrists in an unusual pattern, as the demon of suicide had directed. Ritual carving of wrists is common. Our ministry session included casting out demons, repentance, prayer. However, when we began to break soul ties she shut down and began shaking in fear, unable to continue. At another session, we broke the soul ties. This was hard for her because it involved forgiving her offenders. The demons that were deliberately placed in her through ritual sexual abuse (incubus and succubus) threatened to kill her (also known as a death trigger) and had choked her on several occasions. She was very afraid. When we went deeper, I discovered that at twenty-seven, her current age, she had been programmed to return to the coven as high priestess, groomed to be the bride of Satan. After much prayer, she was able to tell the demons she did not want them and ordered them to leave. Deliverance is a process, particularly for SRA victims. It takes compassion for the victim, patience, and wisdom. (Get my tape or book on *Bitter-Root Judgments, Inner Vows and Soul Ties*, for a much fuller treatment of this vital subject matter.)

Getting free from soul ties

1. Confess the sin of ungodly soul ties.
2. Repent and ask God's forgiveness for each one. Forgive the others involved in forming ungodly soul ties.
3. Break each soul tie and loose yourself and the other person(s) from it in Jesus' Name.
4. Plead the blood over each broken soul tie, and cleanse the memories.
5. Uproot any longings for these sexual partners and renounce them. Cleanse the memories, by pleading the blood over your mind, will, emotions, imagination and memories.
6. Resist any demons that try to return.
7. Break off guilt and shame in Jesus' Name.
8. Learn to hate the sin that caused the soul tie and do not dwell on it any more.
9. Realize that the struggle you have experienced is a spiritual one. Fighting these longings in the flesh will bring failure.

Chapter Seventeen
The Spirit of Rejection

Cycle of failure

When a spirit of rejection is allowed to enter someone, it is because they have judged another for rejecting *them*. The rejected person draws more rejection to themselves, because this spirit can be sensed unconsciously by others, repelling them without even knowing why. Thus, the cycle for rejection becomes set for life, if not dealt with decisively. Spirits named fear of rejection, self rejection and self hatred enter in, along with guilt and shame. The law of sowing and reaping is put into motion through the sin of judging another. *Be not deceived; God is not mocked; for whatsoever a man soweth, that shall he also reap. (Galatians 6:7)* As this person rejects others and continues to be rejected, a lifestyle of failure, defeat and more rejection emerges.

What happens when you try to help a wounded animal? Intentions may be good, but misinterpreted by the animal, who snaps and bites because of fear of further injury. Thus, the person trying to help receives wounds inflicted on *them*. The only choice is to leave the animal (or rejected one) alone to suffer, in order to protect one's self. Hence the cycle of a spirit of rejection perpetuates itself. (See chapter on *Bitter-Root Judgments*)

Rejection from the womb

After birth, I was given up for adoption. A spirit of rejection and a terrible grieving (spirit of heaviness) entered my spirit. I laid in the hospital for six weeks unable to keep any formula down, and had a death wish brought on by a spirit of rejection. When I was adopted, I cried constantly which caused my adoptive mother to be so irritated that *she* rejected me. She constantly criticized me. Nothing I ever did was good enough. I became near-sighted and retreated into reading books to escape her constant wrath. She retaliated by ridiculing me, calling me a book-worm. I developed severe allergies that restricted my activities and kept me away from others, while I retreated deeper into my little world. I judged both my birth mother and adoptive mother for rejecting me. Therefore, I began to reap rejection from others.

Exclusion

I felt excluded from the group, on the outside looking in, unworthy, unwanted. (I actually had many friends over the years.) I felt humiliated by imagined rejection which I was sure was obvious to all. *...a wounded spirit who can bear. (Proverbs 18:14)*

A wounded spirit, which God reveals in His Word, creates an opening for the spirit of heaviness. I used to walk around crying without knowing why, rejecting people before they could reject me, doing everything alone so no one could spurn me. I became very independent. I began acting professionally, and earning a living as a musician. I loved immersing myself into my characters and won many awards. With this taste of success that I desperately needed, it was natural to turn to a career in show business. It was perfect. I could play other likable, successful people, and get paid to do it. I was so good at it that people often confused me with the characters I portrayed. I could hide in my dressing room or hotel room and never deal with real life.

Anorexia

Yet there was deep trouble brewing. I became anorexic, deeply obsessed and dissatisfied with my appearance, starving myself down to 96 pounds. My mother spent the better part of my childhood criticizing everything about me, especially targeting every detail of my appearance, so it was natural that whenever I looked in the mirror I saw an ugly, fat person looking back at me. She, herself, was overweight, filled with bitterness and self-hatred, and took out her dissatisfaction with the hand life had dealt her, on me. A lying spirit and deception entered me, where they continually utilized my mother's sharp tongue to ridicule me and my appearance. Thus, I made an inner vow: "I will never be fat." Now, I was fighting the vow, and a spirit of fear who told me no one would ever like me if I was fat. (Reality check: I was slim and attractive.) My mother entered me in modeling school where I was told my body was too rounded to be a runway model, and I was given a strict diet to overcome this "flaw." My mother sabotaged this diet by making my favorite fatty foods at every meal, while continuing to criticize me. When I lost some weight, the modeling agency began sending me out on assignments as an incentive to lose more weight. Guilt and shame entered in.

Anorexics seek to perfect themselves because of buried anger, guilt, and self-hatred, becoming filled with hatred toward their own bodies. They become afraid of food, and that fear turns into obsession with food. They may measure out impossibly small portions. Because they, themselves, feel out of control, they seek to establish control by refusing to eat. This is exacerbated by guilt due to inner vows and bitter-root judgments, as they try to atone for their own sins. Because of unrepented anger against another, and feeling helpless to control their own lives, they direct this rage against themselves. They see not eating, or binging and purging, as a way of bringing a sense of control back into their lives. The anorexic and bulimic both reek with self-hatred and self-rejection. The spirit of anorexia looks like a rack of bones. It is hollow cheeked, and mocks its victim. It's eyes burn with contempt, yet its voice is seductive until the person is totally under its control. Then, it is demanding and forceful, or desperate and pleading to keep its victims powerless.

A spirit of bondage usually enters in. The bondage, in this case, is to food. The victims either feel helpless to stop starving or binging and purging, or determined to continue starving, even if it means death. It is ironic that in desperation to control their lives, they are spinning ever further out of control. When the situation is allowed to continue this far, a spirit of death enters the person. These hideous spirits must be cast out. It takes time, even after the demons have been expelled, to see as God sees, but that is the ultimate goal. *Our bodies are wonderfully made. (Psalms 139: 14)*

The fighter

Throughout the show biz years when I traveled with my brother, I became a fighter. I had made an inner vow: "No one will ever tell *me* what to do." I thought that if I began defending myself, no one would be able to hold negative thoughts about me. My brother and I had fights, on stage and off, that were infamous. I never allowed anyone to say anything negative against me without a battle, which sometimes resulted in being beaten up. My brother threw me out of his car in the middle of a freeway, in the middle of the night, in the rain, in the middle of nowhere for eating a cookie he thought was his. Once he beat me with a fist covered with rings for arguing with him. Two-inch welts appeared all over my head. Another time he ripped out a handful of my hair as I tried to lock myself in my car after a public battle. Once, I provoked him on stage, and he grabbed my flute and broke it over his knee. Pieces flew everywhere. The whole audience left and we were fired.

The mask

In show business, I learned how to hide behind an impenetrable mask of success and happiness, always getting applause and being loved by my fans, but it was never enough. I would collect my applause like trophies and go back to an empty hotel room. I traveled from place to place for years at a stretch, only being with people at night when I was on stage. I kept them all at a distance, because I thought if they knew the real me, they would reject me. I did a lot of drugs and drank heavily every day to escape the loneliness of rejection. A spirit of rejection and suicide sat on my shoulder and tormented me day and night, telling me how everyone hated me, how worthless I was, how I should commit suicide and do the world a favor.

Spirit of suicide (via abortion)

One night, while on stage, I was having a hard time keeping my persona together, so I ran to my hotel room embarrassed and hurt. The spirit of suicide ordered me to get out my pills and end my life. I took them all. When I didn't return for the next set, the band members had the hotel break into my room, and an ambulance took me to the hospital, parading me right in front of my fans, to pump my stomach. This added further humiliation. When a doctor tried to talk to me, I spit at him and saw him as an enemy through enraged eyes not my own, and spoke with an ugly voice not my own. I was shocked at myself. After returning to my hotel, I looked in the mirror and saw an evil face super-imposed on my own. I was frightened but didn't know how to get free. It is of note that this suicide attempt was on my due date, had I not had an abortion. A spirit of murder entered me during the abortion, along with further self-loathing. After that, I hated children, never wanting to have any of my own.

The chief demons behind abortion are Molech, god of child sacrifice *(Leviticus 18:21; 20:2-4; 1 Kings 11:7; 2 Kings 23:10)*, Ashtoreth (excavations have uncovered thousands of skulls of infants sacrificed to this goddess), and Lilith, a Sumerian goddess, patron saint of infanticide. Rabbinical sources refer to Lilith as "the terror that flies by night." *(Psalm 91:5)* The IUD, a birth control device that causes spontaneous abortions, can also be responsible for unexplained depression, oppression, and activity of evil spirits in a woman's life.[52]

Born again and set free

These demons held me in their grip until I was born again. Then the Spirit of Life in Christ Jesus entered my spirit. At that point, the evil spirits were forced from my spirit but continued to occupy my soulish realm. As I read the Word of God, I learned about the spirit of adoption, and God's great passionate love flooded me. *Having predestinated us unto the adoption of children by Jesus Christ to Himself...wherein He hath made us accepted in the beloved. (Ephesians 1:5-6)*

Love is the key ingredient in the *process* of deliverance. Sometimes I would weep for hours as I meditated on the suffering Christ took for me on the cross. No one had ever loved me in such a complete and unselfish way. I would bask for hours, and delight in God's love. I became a fervent soul winner. I wanted everyone to know the wonder of God's love. I learned that Jesus was despised and rejected of men, yet He bore my rejection on the cross, and carried my sorrows.

> *Surely He hath borne our griefs, and carried our sorrows; yet we did esteem Him stricken, smitten of God and afflicted. But He was wounded for our transgressions, He was bruised for our iniquities: the chastisement of our peace was upon Him; and with His stripes we are healed. (Isaiah 53:4-5)*

I wept for days over these verses when I found them, realizing that Christ had identified Himself with me even in death, that He had felt what I felt, and was wounded as I had been wounded. He was the stone the builders rejected. *(Matthew 21:41)* Here was a Savior Who was rejected by men and by God as He cried out on the cross, *"My God, My God, why hast Thou forsaken Me?" (Matthew 27:46)* He paid a terrible price so that I could be accepted in the beloved. *(Ephesians 1:6)* Some of the layers of deception began to peel off. Hallelujah!

I found the scripture: *When my father and my mother forsake me, then the LORD will take me up. (Psalm 27:10)* I was still plagued, however, by feelings of unworthiness and sorrow, loneliness and failure. I began to break free through praising and worshiping God whenever the evil spirits would torment me, which would force them to leave, but I still needed deliverance. I was sure no one liked me, and constantly misinterpreted things people said and did as rejection. Finally, a dear pastor friend recognized what was going on, and ministered truth and deliverance to me. The deception of that evil influence was broken off. I forgave those who had rejected me, and repented for judgments I made against others. I even repented for rejecting myself.

Glorious change

My life has radically changed. I'm free to enjoy people without twisting every expression and word into rejection in my mind. I rejoice in the wonderful friends God has brought me. I had no idea how great life really is, because a veil was over my eyes all my life that filtered people and circumstances through the wounds and rejection of the past. My prayer is that if you or someone you know is suffering from the torment of a spirit of rejection, you will have compassion on them, look past the wounded-animal reaction, self-preservation tactics, rejection they manifest toward *you*, and deliver them in Jesus' Name. I can spot this spirit a mile away, and so can you. Let us demonstrate the compassion Jesus showed us, by taking the time to deliver the wounded from this hideous, twisted spirit, from the kingdom of darkness into the kingdom of light.

Definition

"Reject," according to *Webster's*, denotes: refusing to accept, recognize, or make use of; to refuse affection or recognition. Problems with rejection often begin in the womb. Perhaps you were unwanted, or of an unwanted gender. Then you built a wall around yourself to be insulated from the pain. Generally, the personality takes one of three paths: the victim, the persecutor, or the phony. All three types may become perfectionistic, impatient, frustrated, haughty or angry. Because of all the introspection, the person usually becomes self-centered, possessive, controlling and manipulative. These three types may have all the traits described below, or manifest only a few; but these are red flags, showing that the person needs help, deliverance, patience and sometimes, tough love.

The "victim," languishes in self-pity, is often sarcastic, withdrawn, pessimistic, lonely, depressed, helpless, listless, suicidal, insecure, fatalistic. They may withdraw into a fantasy world. Many of the people who use drugs do so to escape rejection. They may be overcome with fear, fretting and anxiety. They may become the jealous wife or husband, or feign sickness for attention and play helpless. It is hard for this person to walk in faith and victory, because they get so much attention by always playing the victim. This personality can easily get involved in abusive relationships, which they stay in, to everyone's dismay. Or they take another tack and become a loner. They like to be completely independent so they never have to trust others. Inside, they are hurting, but they look all right to the world.

The "phony" is the life of the party. They talk too loud, boast, wear too much make-up or jewelry, always have to have the best car or house, but are empty inside. They often come too early and stay too late. They are very needy, and wear their friends out wanting attention. The mask they wear is superficial happiness and indifference, and they often have marriages of convenience, with no real intimacy. They can't allow others to really know them because of the fear of rejection. If someone gets too close, they will cut off the relationship. They often have many acquaintances but no friends. Ironically, sometimes this is the person others envy, until their true vapid state is discovered. The "phony" has trouble ever developing deep intimacy with the LORD because of the thick protective wall he has built around his real self.

The "persecutor" is the person full of bitterness, hatred, resentment, rebellion and stubbornness. He has a lot of anger that can turn inward or outward, sometimes both. If he tries to turn it inward, then he can become depressed, suicidal or physically sick, or it will break out periodically into violence toward others. This can be the brooding, angry young man, capable of heinous acts, or the wife abuser who keeps promising to change. Often, the profile will include a father or mother who ignored him, deserted him, or failed to show love. Therefore, he will do whatever it takes to express his anger and get attention, negative or positive. The "persecutor" has trouble trusting God, because often his own father failed him. The cycle of abuse is hard to break, but nothing is impossible with God. I have heard it said that a person's relationship with his father will be reflected in his relationship with God, and his relationship with his mother will be reflected in his relationship with the church. It often seems to be true.

Deliverance

1. First, the person must clearly state that he or she does not want the evil spirit of rejection any more, and the other spirits that came in on its coat tails, are no longer welcome, either.
2. Second, the evil spirits must be cast out. They must be made to leave.
3. Inner vows and bitter-root judgments must be broken.
4. Forgive others who have rejected you. Be specific. This allows God to forgive *you. (Mark 11:25)*
5. Ask God to forgive you for the sin of rejecting others, judgment of others, rebellion, witchcraft, bitterness, etc.
6. Ask God to forgive your offenders. Put your trust in Him to set things straight, and choose this day whom you will serve.
7. Ask God to deal with the deep wounds in your soul, and bring inner healing. Believe God's Word concerning His acceptance and love for you. This is the hardest part. You've been under the influence of rejection for so long that it's hard to believe God truly loves and forgives *you.* Believe it! He really *loves* you!
8. Learn to see yourself as God sees you. When the battle ensues and this demon tries to return, (believe me, he will) putting thoughts of discouragement and rejection, self-hatred and unforgiveness back on you, begin rejoicing in the LORD, speaking forth what God's Word says about you. Always remember that you can *never* be separated from the love of God. *(Romans 8:39)* Pray and read His Word for only His love can truly set you free.
9. The deep inner hurts and wounds must be faced and dealt with. Allow the Holy Spirit to minister His wisdom, comfort and direction to you. Let Him show you the past as it *really* was, and prepare to repent, then forgive.
10. Let go of the right to avenge yourself!!! You will only make yourself sick and bitter, holding on to the hurts of the past.

For more in-depth information on these subjects get the tape or book, *Bitter-Root Judgments, Inner Vows and Soul Ties*.

Chapter Eighteen
Halloween, Witchcraft, Pagan Holidays and Returning Curses

Halloween in "Christian" preschool

When my sons were in preschool at a church near our home, I decided to take authority over the celebration of Halloween in this supposedly "Christian" setting. I tried to talk to the head of the school, but she was very hostile. I gave her some materials about the demonic origins of the holiday, but heard nothing. Finally, I went to the school to discuss it, and encountered her from opposite ends of the hallway. There was a tremendous clash in the spirit realm, yet anyone watching probably wouldn't have seen much. We squared off, and I asked her if she was going to stop the Halloween program. I proclaimed that Christians should have no fellowship with the unfruitful works of darkness. *(Ephesians 5:11)* As I spoke this scripture, she opened her mouth and a demon came roaring out toward me. I was shocked but said, "Stop, in Jesus' Name!" The head of a Christian preschool was possessed with evil spirits, and influencing the children. We removed our sons from this preschool, immediately. Believe me, the next preschool was very carefully screened before placing our sons in that environment.

Demonic origins

Halloween (Samhain, meaning lord of the dead) is a religious celebration of darkness that witches still observe. The Celts and Druids celebrated a three day fire festival from October 29th to October 31st, culminating in their high holy day of the year. They performed animal and human sacrifices and prayed demonic prayers on this day. Celebrated as a time for divination, the origins of Halloween are thoroughly ensconced in Druidic and Celtic paganism. In ancient times the people wore masks to try to fool demons roaming about, thirsty for human sacrifice on this night of the year. It was thought that the demons would see the mask, think it was another demon, and leave them alone. Well known to the people was the fact that the person wearing the mask would assume the identity of the demon portrayed by the mask. (This is one reason why our children should not wear Halloween costumes.) It was thought, and is still practiced by witches today, that the veil separating the third and forth dimensions was at its thinnest on October 31st. People could pass over and visit dead relatives for one night. The spirits might not be friendly, thus they wore masks and costumes to fool the demons. The people set out blood or flesh treats for the demons, hoping they would accept the offering and not molest them. This is where the term "trick or treat" comes from.

The druidic priests also used the term when they went from house to house demanding that each clan give them a victim for sacrifice, who would be a stand-in for the others for the year. If the household did not cooperate, a hexagram was painted on their front door, curses were placed on them, and often their houses would be burned down, someone would die, or some other evil was worked against them. The priest would tie the hapless victim up and drag him along behind the wagon until all the victims were gathered. A bonfire would be built and the person would be asked if he wanted to be killed immediately, or try his luck bobbing for apples in boiling oil. (This is the origin of the custom of bobbing for apples.) Those who bobbed for apples either died or were severely maimed. Other victims were tortured in a man-shaped wicker basket which was set on fire.[53]

Around the Jack O'Lantern the custom was practiced of leaving out a grotesquely carved turnip, filled with human fat and lit. Haunted houses are places where demons live, and are to be avoided. Why would we subject ourselves or our children to this kind of assault? Familiar spirits can possess a person who is participating in Halloween activities. The term "familiars" comes from the witch's practice of using cats and other animals as their familiars, a chalice for demonic spirits. Celts who could not go to the Druidic festival held harvest festivals and performed some of the same rituals on their own, lighting bonfires (bone fires) on every hill top.

Should we allow our children to follow the example of the enemy of their souls by dressing up as demons, witches, vampires, goblins, fairies? Or should we teach them to be like Christ, and be conformed into *His* image? Many children are indoctrinated into the occult, simply through involvement in Halloween practices. They receive a spirit of fear from dressing in frightening costumes, going to haunted houses and walking up to stranger's houses to ask for treats. They can pick up a wrong spirit by threatening to do evil tricks if they are not satisfied with a treat. Just as people once offered food to evil spirits, our children represent these demons when we offer them treats on Halloween.

> *...for what fellowship hath righteousness with unrighteousness? And what communion hath light with darkness? (2 Corinthians 6:14)*

> *Have NO fellowship with the unfruitful works of darkness. (Ephesians 5:11)*

> *...through death He might destroy him that had the power of death, that is, the devil... (Hebrews 2:14)*

> *Ye cannot drink the cup of the LORD, and the cup of devils: ye cannot be partakers of the LORD's table, and of the table of devils. (1 Corinthians 10:21)*

> *Neither give place to the devil. (Ephesians 4:27)*

Our puritan ancestors hated the ungodly pagan holidays, and came to this country to escape them. When other peoples with ungodly pagan practices emigrated to this country they brought their customs with them. Christians should not involve themselves with the demonic celebration of pagan holidays. If you have done so, even as a child, renounce your involvement with the occult. Repent for participating in this and other pagan holidays. Ask God's forgiveness. It is not a cute children's holiday, but a satanic ritual to corrupt our standards and morals, stirring up fear and fascination with the occult. It is not all right to suspend our moral code, even for one day a year! Abstinence from all things demonic must be a way of life for true Christians. The seriousness of this sin is not to be scoffed at or underestimated.

Babylon and the Queen of Heaven

The wickedness of Babylon has polluted the whole earth, and her pagan holidays (holy days) have thoroughly permeated our culture.

> *...COME OUT OF HER MY PEOPLE, that ye BE NOT PARTAKERS IN THEIR SINS, and that ye RECEIVE NOT OF HER PLAGUES. (Revelation 18:4)*

> *Wherefore COME OUT FROM AMONG THEM, and BE YE SEPARATE, saith the LORD, and touch not the unclean (forbidden) thing... (2 Corinthians 6:17)*

> *...the women knead their dough, to make cakes to the QUEEN OF HEAVEN... (Jeremiah 7:18)*

The QUEEN OF HEAVEN worship began in Babylon with the first queen to set herself up to be worshipped, named Semiramis. In addition to calling herself the moon goddess, she was known by many names down through time due to the confounding of languages at the tower of Babel: Diana, Easter, Ishtar, Isis, Europa, Venus, Ceres, Kali, Aphrodite, Ashtoreth, Queen of heaven (still worshipped by Catholics), etc. Her son and husband, Nimrod (also known as Tammuz), was worshipped as the sun god, Baal. Many names were given him in various cultures: Baccus, Apollo, Adonis, Mars, Zeus, Odin, Thor, Jupiter, Osirus, etc.

When Emperor Constantine melded paganism with Christianity, worship of the queen of heaven and her son became, instead, the worship of Mary and Jesus. The goddess was always pictured as an adult and the god as an infant, since Semiramis was literally Nimrod's mother. Because halos (nimbus) were depicted around the sun and moon gods, symbolizing rays of the sun, halos began to be depicted around Mary and Jesus. They literally scratched names off statues to the goddess and her son, and put Mary and Jesus in their stead. Thus, the people maintained their pagan worship of the god and goddess. Before Easter, there were forty days of weeping for Tammuz, which became known as Lent (with the death of our Savior, Jesus, thrown in to match with the story of Tammuz). Tammuz' tale of woe was that of being torn apart by a wild boar in his prime, which instigated the forty days of weeping set up by Semiramis to mourn her son. One of his names, Baccus, literally means weeping. We eat ham on Easter for revenge against the wild boar. Since the "queen of heaven" was supposedly hatched from an egg, we have Easter eggs as part of the holiday (holy day). Newborn infants were sacrificed to the "queen of heaven," and eggs were painted with their blood to worship the goddess. Following pagan traditions, we still paint Easter eggs today.

> *Then he brought me (Ezekiel) to the door of the gate of the LORD's house which was toward the north; and behold, THERE SAT WOMEN WEEPING FOR TAMMUZ...And he brought me into the inner court of the LORD's house, and behold, at the*

door of the temple of the LORD, between the porch and the altar, were about five and twenty men, with their BACKS TOWARD THE TEMPLE OF THE LORD, and their faces toward the east; and THEY WORSHIPPED THE SUN TOWARD THE EAST. (Ezekiel 8:14-16)

Incidentally, Tammuz' birthday was on the twenty-fifth of December. It was celebrated by cutting down trees, and affixing gold and silver balls (symbolizing his testicles) to the tree. Food offerings to the god were added to the tree for decoration (popcorn, cranberries, candy). Pagans also worshiped the tree they had cut down believing it to have a tree spirit, called deva (or diva).

Thus saith the LORD, LEARN NOT THE WAY OF THE HEATHEN…For the customs of the people are vain: for one cutteth a TREE out of the forest, the work of the hands of the workman, with the axe. They deck it with silver and with gold; they fasten it with nails and with hammers, that it move not. (Jeremiah 10:2-4)

Babylon was the seedbed of all pagan religions. Before this, only one God was worshipped. Witchcraft and the mystery religions were all born in Babylon.

Witchcraft in the public schools

At the end of the school year, my son's fifth grade teacher began teaching witchcraft on a Monday morning. My husband and I took authority over the situation, and went up to the school to confront the teacher, who had the temerity to refer to herself as a Christian. I called a lot of parents and the President of the Board of Education. By Wednesday evening the book was removed from the classroom. The teacher's only reaction was to whine that now everyone would think badly of her. My advice: Go straight to the top---it saves time. The President of the Board of Education had the book banned within twenty-four hours. This is a principle that works in the spiritual realm as well as the natural realm.

A number of my children's teachers, over the years, tried to teach Transcendental Meditation in the classrooms. My sons all stood up to their teachers and refused to participate. One fourth grade teacher yelled at my son and ordered him to meditate. He stood up and said he wouldn't. They went back and forth until he was dismissed to the library. Ungodly meditation opens a person's mind up to invasion from demonic spirits.

Every year throughout the entire month of October, every subject in the school was bombarded with Halloween projects, books, paper work, science, reading, math, art, and music. My center son told the art teacher he would not draw a witch. The teacher slammed his fist down so hard he cracked the table trying to force my son to participate in the project. All the other students threw their pencils at the teacher until he relented, and gave my son an alternate assignment.

City of witches

You have heard of the "city of angels," Los Angeles, but when I was on the road, I discovered Casa Dega, the city of witches, a very unpleasant experience, indeed. When I first began to see things in the spirit realm, even before I was saved, I thought I had an over-active imagination. While I was working with a band in Orlando, we had an engagement in Daytona Beach and we drove back and forth each night. Some nights I would see a sign for Casa Dega looming at me on the freeway, and other nights we would pass the same spot, but it was not there. I discovered this town was populated solely by witches and warlocks. They began appearing wherever the band was: in the club, at donut shops, etc. I believe they were using me as a chalice (receptacle for demonic spirits), since Betty and her coven in Little Rock had set me up before (story in Chapter Nineteen). I was very uncomfortable when they were around. They asked us to attend their meetings. Our drummer, who became obsessed with them, wanted to go. They exerted such a strong draw on me that I asked my Jewish agent what to do. He warned me to stay away. Every day there was a struggle inside me; part of me was drawn to them, and part of me was repulsed.

On the last night of our engagement the witches and warlocks showed up in the club, and I began to feel as though I was choking, constricted in my body and throat, and I was very afraid. The whole band was in the same van together going home, and the drummer was driving. Suddenly, he screeched off the road. It was a weird, misty night, with fog rising, yet I could see the moon. He drove like a maniac, and the rest of the guys started crying out in fear, hollering for the drummer to turn around and go home. I was in the front captain's chair and could clearly see his face in the eerie light. He no longer resembled our drummer, but he appeared to be possessed with a vicious, evil spirit.

When we arrived at Casa Dega I noticed all the houses were black. There was a fog rising across the lake, and as I looked I saw evil spirits floating toward us from that direction. Several members of the band burst into tears, and two of the guys wrestled with the drummer, forcibly removing him from the driver's seat, while the car careened all over the road. The keyboard player drove us home, but I knew the witches weren't done with me. I lay down to sleep, still trembling, and closed my eyes. Soon I felt an evil presence in my room, and when I looked I saw the devil, with glowing red eyes. He tempted me, saying that if I would worship him, he would make me a star. I don't know how I knew these words to say, but I said, "Get thee from me, Satan, in the Name of Jesus!" He left out the window.

What can Christians do?

Recently, a couple of weeks before Halloween, I got a call from a missionary friend who wanted to do something in her town to combat Halloween. She'd had some encounters with witches in her area who were planning a big celebration in the park. I told her that the very best thing to do would be to hold a prayer meeting and worship the LORD, then engage in fervent prayer and pull down strongholds. I told her to be prayed up, not to take the battle lightly, to wear her armor, to plead the blood over herself, her family and everyone at the prayer meeting. It is time Christians begin to take back the ground the devil has stolen.

If we sit cowering in our houses, we have lost before we have begun. I have been spit on, cursed at, shoved away, threatened, back-stabbed by school authorities, had other mothers back out on me when we went to confront authorities, schools and principals, leaving me standing alone with egg on my face. I've had teachers hiss at me, shun me, laugh at me, had my life threatened, been ridiculed and even threatened because of my stand against Halloween and witchcraft. There is one answer to all this trouble: Keep on resisting the evil influence of the world and the devil's plan to destroy us. The devil is upset whenever a child of God stands up for what is right, but as long as I know I stand on the scripture and the solid rock of righteousness, there is no devil in hell that can stop the truth. If we had an army of worshippers who were willing to fight for what is right, we would not be facing many of the current predicaments our nation is in. I am just one person, but I invite you to join me today. One of us can put a thousand demons to flight, and two of us can rout ten thousand. *(Deuteronomy 32:30)*

The Bible clearly states that we are not to follow or learn the ways of the heathen, yet Christians not only celebrate pagan holidays, they openly do so right in their churches. Doc Marquis, a former witch, raised in an illuminati family that practiced witchcraft, was shocked beyond measure when he attended church the first Halloween after he renounced witchcraft and was saved. Christians were practicing the same rituals on Halloween, right there in church, that his family had carefully taught him in learning to be a witch, such as dressing up in ungodly costumes, bobbing for apples, carving pumpkins with evil faces, having special foods, trick or treating, etc. He resolved to expose these occult practices and holidays for what they really are.

Satanic holy days

Jan. 7	St. Winebald Day	
Jan. 17	satanic revels	
Feb. 2	Candlemas	
Feb. 25	St Walpurgis Day	
Mar. 1	St. Eichataut	
Mar. 21	Spring Equinox	
Apr. 17	Good Friday	
Apr. 18	Easter Eve Day	
Apr. 26	Grand Climax	
Apr. 30	Walpurgismacht	
May 1	Beltane/May Day	
Jun. 21	Feast Day (summer solstice)	
July 27	Grand Climax (summer solar solstice)	
Aug. 1	Lammas Day	
Aug. 3	satanic revels	
Sept. 7	Marriage to the beast Satan	
Sept. 20	Midnight Host	
Sept. 23	Fall Equinox	
Oct. 28-30	Satanist High Holy Day	
Oct. 31	All Hallows Eve	
Nov. 1	Satanist High Holy Day	
Nov. 4	satanic revels	
Dec. 22	Winter Solstice	
Dec. 24	demon revels [54]	

8 nights of human sacrifice and other pagan holy days—witchcraft

1. Dec. 22 **Yule** (winter solstice)
   Jan. 21 Inauguration Day—thirteen days before Imbold
2. Feb. 1 **Imbold** (Groundhog Day)
   Feb. 14 Valentine's Day—13 days after Imbold
3. Mar. 21 **Ostara** (spring equinox)
4. May 1 **Beltaine** (May Day)
5. June 21 **Litha** (summer solstice)
   July 4 Independence Day—13 days after Litha
6. Aug.1 Lugunasda
7. Sept. 21 **Mabold** (autumn equinox)
8. Oct. 31 **Samhain** (Halloween)
9. Dec. 25 **Saturnalia** (Saturn Festival of Romans—birthday of Tammuz (Baal, Nimrod, Bacchus, etc.)

Notice there are four sets of thirteen weeks. Between the main festivals there are six weeks, then seven, then six, and so on. Six is the number of man, seven the number of God, thirteen the number of depravity and rebellion. The message they are sending is that through depravity and rebellion they place man over God.

The nativity of the sun god, Tammuz (Saturn, Baal, etc.) was actually on December 25th. Jeremiah 10 forbids learning the way of the pagans, such as cutting down a tree (evergreen tree was symbol of fertility) and fixing it in your house with gold and silver balls (symbolic of the testicles of Baal), and putting food on the tree (offering to the god), putting candles in the window (welcoming winter god to bless your house, and symbol of male organs), putting a five-pointed star on the tree (symbol of Nimrod, Baal, etc., the star god, and winter horned or stag god), reindeer (symbolic of stag god), mistletoe (fertility plant), wreath (circular, symbol of female sexual organs, cycle of life), holly (fertility plant). Yahshua the Messiah was born on the Feast of Tabernacles when God came to tabernacle with men (around the end of September or early October).

Easter is the festival of the bare-breasted fertility goddess (Ishtar, Ashtoreth, Isis, Diana, etc.): Easter bonnet (the priestesses had bonnets that looked like baby bonnets, and the priests had new white robes); sun rise services (this was held to worship the sun god, held early so they could disperse and look for the egg the goddess would hatch from. If found, this would bring blessings for the new year); dyed Easter eggs (dipped in the blood of slain infants, sacrificed to the fertility goddess, born of the union of priests with virgins on the altar of Ashtoreth the year before); Lent (40 days of weeping for Tammuz, who was killed at 40 years old, slain by a wild boar); eating ham on Easter Sunday (done for revenge against the wild boar); Easter bunny (symbol of fertility).

Valentine's Day was a pagan fertility festival with sexual orgies, drunkenness and human sacrifice. Cupid, son of Venus, another name for the goddess (Semiramis, Ashtoreth, Easter) was noted for being a troublemaker. Sacrifices were brought to the goddess: sweets, flowers, and the symbol of the holiday was a heart.

Groundhog's Day was another festival of the pagans. The groundhog was said to have powers of divination. If he saw his shadow, six more weeks of winter would follow. If not, the next seven weeks would be good. The groundhog symbolized the earth mother (goddess) who slept until spring. The theme was reincarnation in which the earth goddess (groundhog) reawakened.

Beltaine (comes from Baal) or May Day involved a pagan fertility ritual of recreation. Dancing around the maypole with red and white streamers, men dancing clockwise, women dancing counter clockwise was an ancient practice. The May pole represented the male phallic symbol. The ribbons intertwining symbolized the act of procreation.

On St. Patrick's Day, green symbolized the occult in nature. Earth creatures such as Leprechauns with their schalalies, were to be caught, for if one controlled a leprechaun, they could have his gold. His pot of gold represented prosperity. The shamrock was another occult symbol, used to make wishes.[55]

Returning Curses

Witches send curses. If you do not want their curses, then return them to the senders, as you would food with poison in it. Notice that this is not creating or sending curses, you are not cursing them back, you are simply *returning* the curse. If a witch or Satanist does not want the curse back, then they should not have sent it in the first place. Pains in the body, sickness, marital problems, etc. may all be the result of curses. First, forbid retaliation of any wicked spirit against you, your home, property and family. Pray to undam the wall of protection that witches place around themselves, tear down their protection, and cancel the curse's assignment against you.[56] Then return the curse and demons attached to it, to the senders.

In Charismatic witchcraft, the "Christian" prays prayers that are controlling, destructive or vengeful. These are wicked prayers that must be broken. I had a woman who was jealous of me sending wicked prayers, and I began to have problems as a result. When someone prayed for me they pulled the arrows (curses) out of my back and I was immediately relieved from the attack.

Study Questions: Chapter 18

1. What can you do during the Halloween season with other Christians that is not simply a sugar-coated copy of this pagan holy-day?
2. Have you participated in Halloween? Repent!
3. Have you taught your children the truth about this pagan holy-day?
4. What can you do in your community to make a difference?

Chapter Nineteen
The Spirit of Divination and Familiar Spirits
Same demons, same old tricks, new window dressing

People of every age have been desperate for answers. In ancient times they went to mediums and witches, just as they flock to psychics today. There is a psychic in Texas who actually reads rear ends. Can you imagine baring your bottom to a psychic to have your fortune told? People are desperate for the truth or they would not engage in such foolishness.

In this chapter we will deal with the spirit of divination, and in the next chapter there is a much fuller explanation of the word "python" from which the word "divination" is derived. A familiar spirit is one that attaches to families and is passed on generationally; in other words, it becomes a legal part of a generational curse. King Saul consulted with a witch (medium who consulted with the dead) who used DIVINATION and FAMILIAR SPIRITS, and paid for it with his life and the life of his sons *(1 Samuel 31:2-4)* the very next day.

> *Then said Saul unto his servants, Seek me a woman that hath a FAMILIAR SPIRIT, that I may go to her, and inquire of her. And his servants said to him, Behold, there is a woman that hath a FAMILIAR SPIRIT at En-dor. And Saul...went...and he said...DIVINE UNTO ME BY THE FAMILIAR SPIRIT, and bring me him up, whom I shall name unto thee. (1 Samuel 28: 7-8)*

A spirit of divination is often called a familiar spirit because it is familial, that is, it attaches itself to families, and at the death of one member, will move to another. The penalty for being a witch or for consulting with a medium in the Old Testament is death. A witch is a false prophet who uses occult methods to achieve wicked or deceptive ends.

> *Thou shalt not suffer a WITCH to live. (Exodus 22:18)*

> *There shall not be found among you any one that maketh his son or his daughter to pass through the fire, or that useth DIVINATION, or an OBSERVER OF TIMES, or an ENCHANTER, or a WITCH, or a CHARMER, or a CONSULTER WITH FAMILIAR SPIRITS, or a WIZARD, or a NECROMANCER. (Deuteronomy 18:10-11)*

> *A man also or a woman that hath a FAMILIAR SPIRIT, or that is a WIZARD, shall surely be PUT TO DEATH: they shall stone them with stones... (Leviticus 20:27)*

> *Regard not them that have FAMILIAR SPIRITS (soothsayers), neither seek after WIZARDS, to be DEFILED by them... (Leviticus 19:31)*

God hates all sorcery because it causes people to seek answers from satanic sources rather than seeking God and His Word. Satan twists God's truth to deceive people, even God's own people. He twisted truth in the Garden of Eden and he is still doing it today. *(Genesis 3:1-7)* He can enter into those he has deceived and cause them to betray the LORD, as he did the disciple, Judas. *(Luke 22:3)*

The spirit of divination often speaks using an element of truth. That is the hook. What follows is a mixture of lies and half-truths, designed to deceive. I know many people who call themselves Christians, who participate in practices outlined in this chapter, but they are sadly deceived, for light and darkness cannot have fellowship. C.S. Lewis wrote these words of warning: "There are two equal and opposite errors into which our race can fall about the devil. One is to disbelieve in their existence. The other is to believe, and to feel an excessive and unhealthy interest in them."[57]

The new paradigm is revealing, and the agenda is being pushed by numerous groups: feminists, the New World Order (NWO), the United Nations, Outcome Based Education (OBE), New Age and pagan religions, Disney, video and computer games.

Old Paradigm	New Paradigm
1. Truth	Social and pagan myths
2. Facts	Feeling and experience
3. Observation	Imagination
4. Logic	Speculation
5. Science	Politicized pseudo-science
6. Reality	Fantasy
7. Factual history	Storytelling
8. The Bible	Imagination or experience

9. Spirit given insights..Experience or imagination
10. Experiences that affirm the scriptures...................Selected Bible scriptures that affirm the experience
11. God is personal...God is pantheistic, He's in everything, He's not personal
12. Good and evil are incompatible...........................Joining good and evil brings wholeness
13. The Bible reveals reality....................................Feelings and experience define reality
14. Trusting God is key to success............................Trusting one's inner god-self is key to success
15. Knowing God...Knowing divine self
16. Finding God's will..Getting in touch with one's feelings
17. Loving God, then others....................................Loving self, then others
18. Oneness with God and other Christians.................Unity with everything
19. Love sinners, hate sin.......................................Tolerance for anything (except intolerance)
20. Sin is separation from God................................Sin means separation from spiritual forces in nature [58]

The fool hath said in his heart, There is no God. (Psalm 14:1)

When we think we are capable of being our own gods, we are fools. The scriptures speak of God's way as THE ANCIENT PATHS, from which the people have departed. In the above examples it is clear that the "new paths" have departed from God's plan for our lives, and have produced New Age religions, which can only bring destruction to our souls.

...they have caused them to stumble in their ways from THE ANCIENT PATHS...To make their land desolate...I will scatter them as with an east wind before the enemy...in the day of their calamity. (Jeremiah 18:15-17)

A witch named Betty

I only wish I had been born again and known the Word when I encountered the spirit of divination. I was in Little Rock, in an open state of anticipation after some recent experiences with the occult. A waitress in the club where we were playing asked my brother and me to a meeting, where she hinted that supernatural events took place. I went with her out of curiosity but stood in the lobby, unable to enter the room where they gathered around a person lying on a pallet.

An outgoing, grandmotherly woman named Betty approached me and cooed, "As you stood there, I saw you in a past life, in a long flowing robe. You were a singer in the temple but you were killed, and you have come back to fulfill your destiny." I was taken aback, but intrigued. I asked her what was going on in the other room and she stated they were applying the green healing light to a man that was very ill.

Betty agreed to come and hear me sing, and when she did she insisted that she saw auras on my brother and me. Over the next few weeks she taught me astral travel (silver cord) and past life regression through hypnosis. Often, in her home with groups present, she would hypnotize someone and take them first into the past and then into the future. In the future they would invariably see war and destruction. (One of her incomes on the side was selling bomb shelters and C-rations.) She asked me to visit her "church," so one Sunday morning I went and was asked to sing. I assumed it was a Christian church, so I sang "Amazing Grace" which they loved. Then, we all held hands, and they prayed to impart "power" to me. Without my permission or knowledge, I became their chalice (person who is a receptacle for holding demons). In witchcraft, the magic wand is the male symbol and the chalice is the female symbol of power. It didn't occur to me until later, when I started having mental and emotional problems, that there were thirteen of them, a coven of witches.

Betty was fascinated with my brother's musical talent, so she had him over to a friend's house that had a grand piano. She hypnotized him and guided him to visit the room where she claimed all the music for all time was stored. She instructed him to pull down a piece of music and play it. He did so and it sounded like Mozart, but no work I'd ever heard. Sure enough, he said Mozart's name was on the piece. Later, she took a piece of music my brother and I wrote and offered it up to "god" in a ceremony of fire. I believe she wanted to use my brother's musical gift as a channel to possess others through the medium of music.

There was an incredible amount of deception going on with this one woman, and I was a ripe target because of curiosity and openness. Many people who are drawn into these deceptions are never able to escape the bondage. It was a glittering and enticing counterfeit for the true gifts of the Living God. The hunger in my heart was real, for God Himself placed it there, but I had turned my back on Him because of unpleasant childhood experiences. The past lives, auras, hypnosis, astral projection, green healing light soulish prayers, transfer of evil spirits, covens and guided imagery are all part of both eastern pagan religion and New Age religion. Betty may have appeared like a plump, sweet, grandmotherly person who was caring and helpful, but in reality, she was a wicked servant of Satan. She operated through a spirit of divination, using familiar spirits, sorcery, deception, lying spirits, whoredoms, error, a python spirit, etc. Sometimes I had sharp pains in my body. This is usually witchcraft. If it happened today, I would break the spirit of voodoo and curses. I was grotesquely defiled after my association with her. Thank God, the band moved to an engagement in another town, or she would have wrapped me even tighter in the coils of python.

Harry Potter's school of witchcraft for children

The Harry Potter books look like innocent fun, but a close look reveals a lot of provocative information. The lightening bold on his forehead is the universal sign of Satan. *(Luke 10:18)* The book covers are filled with symbols of witchcraft. The author claims not to be a witch but wears a black robe and displays the witches' salute across her chest in photos.[59]

In the books Harry is a sorcerer and a magician, casts spells, does astral projection, performs blood rituals, sends curses to make pain come on someone, sends killing curses to murder someone, practices alchemy, talks to snakes which are wise, flies on broom sticks, drinks blood, uses a magic wand, has a phoenix for a pet (symbol of reincarnation), uses powers to take revenge, plays quittage on a broomstick, cheats, shape shifts, uses powers from within, uses satanic rituals, walks through walls, levitates, disrespects authority, sacrifices a cat, cuts off the hand of a living person, boils a baby alive, does crystal gazing, divination, stealing, astrology, practices necromancy, takes mood altering drugs, and uses magic charms. Harry Potter awakens a lust in the heart of the reader to seek ungodly, supernatural power.[60] These books are definitely not for Christians.

Strictly forbidden practices

1. Soothsaying, fortune-telling, divination.
SOOTHSAYING (manteuomai) means to divine, to practice divination. The first part of the word, mainomai, means to   rave. The second part, mania, means fury displayed by those possessed by the evil spirit while delivering their oracles, according to *Vine's*.

> *And I will cut off the cities of thy land, and throw down all thy strongholds: And I will cut off witchcrafts out of thine hand; and thou shalt have no more SOOTHSAYERS: Thy graven images also will I cut off (idolatry), and thy standing images out of the midst of thee... (Micah 5:12-13)*

> *Therefore Thou hast forsaken Thy people the house of Jacob, because they...are SOOTHSAYERS like the Philistines... (Isaiah 2:6)*

2. Witch, warlock, wizard, charmer, sorcerer, white or black magic, Satanism. Manasseh, a wicked king of Israel, engaged in practices that caused God to bring the Assyrians to carry them away into captivity.

> *And he (Manasseh) caused his children to pass through the fire in the valley of the son of Hinnom: also he OBSERVED TIMES, and used ENCHANTMENTS, and used WITCHCRAFT, and dealt with a FAMILIAR SPIRIT, and with WIZARDS: he wrought much evil in the sight of the LORD, to provoke Him to anger. (2 Chronicles 33:6)*

WITCHCRAFT, in the above scripture, is the Hebrew word kashaph (3784, *Strong's*) meaning to whisper a spell, enchant or practice magic.

> *Thou shalt not suffer a WITCH to live. (Exodus 22:18)*

3. Rebellion, disobedience, defying the LORD.
The word REBELLION (4805, meriy) in the following scripture means bitterness and rebellion. It comes from the word marah (4784), meaning to disobey, to defy the LORD, provoke, to make bitter, make angry, to reject, not to recognize. The word STUBBORN (sarar) is often added to REBELLION in scripture to strengthen the meaning.

> *For REBELLION is as the sin of WITCHCRAFT, and STUBBORNNESS is as iniquity and idolatry. (1 Samuel 15:23)*

> *...a STUBBORN and REBELLIOUS generation...that set not their heart aright... (Psalm 78:8)*

> *Woe to her that is FILTHY and polluted, to the oppressing city! She OBEYED NOT the voice; she RECEIVED NOT CORRECTION; she TRUSTED NOT in the LORD; she DREW NOT NEAR to her God. (Zephaniah 3:1-2)*

FILTHY (4754, mara) in the above scripture comes from the same prime root as the preceding Hebrew words for REBELLION. In other words, "Woe to her that is FILTHY with REBELLION." This scripture refers specifically to Israel, but certainly reflects accurately upon any rebellious person.

    a. Does NOT OBEY the voice of the LORD.
    b. DOES NOT RECEIVE CORRECTION from the LORD.
    c. DOES NOT TRUST in the LORD.
    d. DOES NOT DRAW NEAR to the LORD.
    e. And to link it with further revelation of the root of REBELLION: the person operates in BITTERNESS, DEFIANCE, DISOBEDIENCE and STUBBORNESS.
    f. Additionally, REBELLION signifies that the rebellious person feels REJECTED and UNRECOGNIZED.

It is well known that many people enter the world of the occult seeking power. Often the person feels angry and restricted by the commandments of a holy God. When a person dabbles in the occult, it can stem from ignorance, or it may be generated by defiance against what they have been taught, however the end result is that it fosters rebellion against the one true God, YHWH. The person will be defiled and embittered through this ungodly link, by the filth of whoring after other gods. Eventually, their conscience becomes SEARED BY A HOT IRON, and they no longer can distinguish between right and wrong, so that wrong actually seems right to them.

> *Now the Spirit speaketh expressly, that in the latter times some shall depart from the faith, GIVING HEED TO SEDUCING SPIRITS and doctrines of devils; Speaking lies in hypocrisy; having their conscience SEARED WITH A HOT IRON... (1 Timothy 4:1-2)*

SEARED (2743, kauteriazo) means to render insensitive, to brand. It is where we derive our word cauterize. The truth is, a person does not become bitter without some kind of wounding. Many rebellious people have cauterized wounds that have never healed, but instead have been covered up with so much scar tissue that they are rendered insensitive. They may seek the occult as an escape.

4. Astrologer, stargazer, zodiac, horoscopes, monthly prognosticators (*Strong's* 3045, yada, meaning new moon observers seeking understanding from the stars). The word ASTROLOGER occurs in Daniel eight times (*Strong's* ashshaph, 825-826), also meaning enchanters, conjurers, to practice enchantments, to lisp. According to *Vine's*, the sick underwent actual surgery while incantations were spoken.

> *And in all matters of wisdom and understanding, that the king inquired of them (Daniel), he found them ten times better than all the MAGICIANS and ASTROLOGERS that were in all his realm. (Daniel 1:20)*

ASTROLOGERS (*Strong's* 1895, habar) appears one more time in Isaiah, meaning to be a horoscopist.

> *Stand now with thine ENCHANTMENTS and with the multitude of thy SORCERIES, wherein thou hast labored from thy youth; if so be thou shalt be able to profit, if so be thou mayest prevail. Thou art wearied in the multitude of thy counsels. Let now the ASTROLOGERS, the STARGAZERS, the MONTHLY PROGNOSTICATERS, stand up, and save thee from these things that shall come upon thee. Behold, they shall be as stubble; the fire shall burn them; they shall not deliver themselves from the power of the flame... (Isaiah 47:12-14)*

> *...neither shall ye use ENCHANTMENTS (sorcery), nor OBSERVE TIMES (astrology). (Isaiah 19: 26)*

> *...Learn not the way of the heathen, and be not dismayed at the SIGNS OF HEAVEN; for the heathen are dismayed at them. (Jeremiah 10:2)*

> *Regard not them that have FAMILIAR SPIRITS, neither seek after WIZARDS, to be defiled by them... (Isaiah 19:31)*

> *And the soul that turneth after such as have FAMILIAR SPIRITS, and after WIZARDS, to go a whoring after them, I will even set My face against that soul, and will cut him off from among his people. (Leviticus 20:6)*

5. Enchanter, hypnotist, augurer, diviner, wizard, witch, charmer, necromancer, medium, etc.
    a. DIVINATION (7081, qecem) means fortune telling including its fee, oracles, revealing occult knowledge.
    b. DIVINERS (7087, qacam) indicates someone who determines future by magic scrolls or dice, a soothsayer.

c. CONSULTER WITH FAMILIAR SPIRITS (7592, sha'al, one who prays, demands, begs, consults) acts as a medium or channeler of communication between this world and the spirit world.

d. NECROMANCER (medium) is a professional who calls up the dead and consults with them; said to have soft, secret incantations while working their abominations, they work with familiar spirits to deceive gullible customers. The spirit of a dead person, really a demon is masquerading as a person, is said to possess the medium to communicate messages.

e. MEDIUM, PSYCHIC, MIND READER, are words that have become familiar to us, however they do not appear in the Bible. Webster's defines medium as a person thought to have power to communicate with the spirits of the dead. This was graphically illustrated in the popular movie, "Ghost."

f. A WITCH (3784, kashaph) is a person who practices sorcery, enchantment, casts spells, uses hexes, curses and bewitching (putting someone under a spell), use of potions (mind altering drugs), superstition, and has dealings with the devil.

g. A WIZARD (3049, yiddeoniy, yidde) is a male spiritist, a conjurer, a ghost. This word appears in the Old Testament eleven times.

h. MAGICIAN (2749, chartom) appears sixteen times in the Old Testament and relates to the study and practice of astrology and magic arts such as the magicians in Pharaoh's court used when contending with Moses. Practices thaumaturgy (wonder working), alchemy, legerdemain (slight of hand).

i. SORCERER: There are three main words translated sorcerer:
1) (3097, magos, Greek) meaning oriental scientist, wise man, magician;
2) (3786, kashshaph, Hebrew) meaning one who whispers spells and practices magic, a magician;
3) (5332, pharmakeus, Greek) meaning spell giver, a poisoner or druggist, magician.

j. PEEP and MUTTER: sounds that wizards make. Peeping means to whisper, or chatter. *(Isaiah 8:19)*

k. CHARMER (3907, lachash) meaning one who whispers or mumbles to cast a spell, from Psalm 58:5. Charmer (328, 'at) means to move softly, secretly. *(Isaiah 19:3)*

l. OBSERVER OF TIMES (6049, 'anan) means to cover, to cloud over, deceive, to act covertly and practice magic. In the Deuteronomy 8:14 context it means astrologer, one who foretells events.

m. MAGICIAN (2748, chartom) means a horoscoper who draws magical lines or circles. *(Acts 13:6, 8)*

n. CLAIRVOYANCE, also known as SECOND SIGHT, another word not found in the Bible, means the power to perceive things beyond normal human senses, according to *Webster's*.

o. TELEPATHY is, "Communication by means other than the senses, as by the exercise of mystical powers." *(Webster's)*

p. The SEVENTH SON OF A SEVENTH SON (or daughter) is said to have mystical powers due to their magical order of birth.

q. PROGNOSTICATION means to predict the future, to foreknow. It involves reading bones, tea leaves, reading bumps on the head, entrails of animals, sortilege (predicting future by drawing lots), etc. The ground hog is said to be a prognosticator.

r. FORTUNETELLER (cartomancy) claims to know future events through use of such devices as crystal balls, palm reading (chiromancy, reading the seven planetary mounds that correspond to the seven astrological deities), tarot cards, horoscope, dice, liquids in a vial, shell hearing, cephalomancy (a black magic practice that uses a skull for divination), conjuring (summoning a spirit by incantation), rahabdomancy (divination by means of a wand or stick), occult graphology (analysis of character through handwriting, mixing fortune-telling with it), gender analysis (a plan to obliterate sexist roles to be controlled by the United Nations), divination by suspended ring, the Bible and key method, dreams producing divination called incubation or temple sleep, sediment in a cup with magical writing on it, inspection of entrails of animals (haruspication), divination by spealbone or shoulder blade (scapulimancy), augury, footprints in ashes, behavior or the cries and flight of birds, meetings with ominous animals, the flight of arrows, patterns or paths of water, telepathy through graves, fire walking (supernatural ability to walk on hot coals without pain or damage, done in hypnotic trance), etc.

There shall not be found among you any one that maketh his son or his daughter to pass through the fire (sacrifice them in fire), or that useth DIVINATION, or an OBSERVER OF TIMES, or an ENCHANTER, or a WITCH, or a CHARMER, or a CONSULTER WITH FAMILIAR SPIRITS, or a WIZARD, or a NECROMANCER. For all that do these things are an abomination unto the LORD... (Deuteronomy 18:10-11)

...I will destroy the counsel thereof: and they shall seek to the idols, and to the CHARMERS, and to them that have FA-MILIAR SPIRITS, and to the WIZARDS. And the Egyptians will I give over into the hand of a cruel lord; and a fierce king shall rule over them, saith the LORD. (Isaiah 19:3)

And when they shall say unto you, Seek unto them that have FAMILIAR SPIRITS, and unto WIZARDS THAT PEEP, and that MUTTER: should not a people seek unto their God? for the living to the dead? (Isaiah 8:19)

For these nations, which thou shalt possess, hearkened unto OBSERVERS OF TIMES, and unto DIVINERS... (Deuteronomy 18:14)

And they caused their sons and their daughters to pass through the fire, and used DIVINATION and ENCHANTMENTS, and sold themselves to do evil in the sight of the LORD, to provoke Him to anger. (2 Kings 17:17)

s. ENCHANTMENT or to enchant (5172, nachash) means to divine, augur, to whisper a magic spell, to hiss, one who reads signs and omens by divination. *(Leviticus 19:26; Numbers 23:23; 2 Kings 21:6; 2 Chronicles 33:6)* In Jeremiah the Israelites were instructed not to follow enchanters, diviners, sorcerers, false dreamers, or false prophets. The word ENCHANTERS (6049, 'anan), in this instance, indicates a clouding over, to act covertly, practice magic.

Therefore hearken not ye to your prophets, nor to your DIVINERS (soothsayers), nor to your DREAMERS, nor to your EN-CHANTERS, nor to your SORCERERS... (Jeremiah 27:9)

The ENCHANTMENTS (3909, lat) or magic used by the Egyptian magicians is documented in Exodus 7:22; 8:7; 8:18. Here it means incantation, secrecy, covert.

The word ENCHANTMENT (3858, lahat) used in Exodus 7:11 is extreme. It means ablaze, flaming, en-wrapping. It indicates that Pharaoh's magicians used some fancy show-biz with their first copycat miracle.

...now the magicians of Egypt, they also did in like manner with their ENCHANTMENTS. For they cast down every man his rod, and they became serpents...(Exodus 7:11)

ENCHANTMENTS (2267, cheber) in the following case means a spell, charmer, company, society. It is clearly stated that using enchantment and sorcery will cause women to be widowed and children to be killed.

But these two things shall come to thee in a moment in one day, the loss of children, and widowhood: they shall come upon thee in their perfection for the multitude of thy SORCERIES, and for the great abundance of thine ENCHANTMENTS. (Isaiah 47: 9)

t. HALLOWEEN: All Halloween practices stem from pagan religious practices.

u. WATCHERS: pictures or objects with eyes on them, acting like a camera to spy on people. Watchers is also the name of a group of witches who practice this form of spying. Watchers is also the name of angels who watch us.

6. Drugs (pharmakos, Greek): This is where we derive the word pharmacy.

Now the works of the flesh are manifest...idolatry, WITCHCRAFT...they which do such things shall not inherit the kingdom of God. (Galatians 5:19-21)

WITCHCRAFT comes from the Greek word pharmakeia (*Strong's 5331*) meaning magic, sorcery, poisoner. According to *Vine's* it means a sorcerer who uses drugs, potions, spells, enchantments. The two scriptures below use pharmakeia, translated SORCERER. Various devas attach to each kind of drug derived from plants, and they enter drug users.[61]

But the fearful, and unbelieving, and the abominable, and murderers, and whoremongers, and SORCERERS, and idolaters, and all liars, shall have their part in the lake which burneth with fire and brimstone: which is the second death. (Revelation 21:8)

Blessed are they that do His commandments, that they may have right to the tree of life, and may enter in through the gates into the city. For without are dogs, and SORCERERS, and whoremongers, and murderers, and idolaters, and whosoever loveth and maketh a lie. (Revelation 22:14-16)

According to *Vine's*, SORCERY is the use of drugs, accompanied by incantations and appeals to occult powers through amulets, ostensibly to keep the victim from the attention and power of demons, but in actuality, it is more to impress the victim with the sorcerer's power. The book of Revelation reveals men will not repent of their sorceries, even during the tribulation, and that by drugs (sorcery), all nations will be deceived.

> *...for by thy SORCERIES were all nations deceived. (Revelation 18:23)*

> *Neither repented they of their murders, nor of their SORCERIES... (Revelation 9:21)*

Lest anyone think sorcery is powerless or harmless, the sorcerers (magicians) of Egypt were able to duplicate several of Moses' miracles and plagues: Both Moses' and the magician's staffs turned into snakes, both turned water into blood, both launched a plague of frogs and a plague of lice. *(Exodus 7:11-12, 22; 8:7, 18)*

7. Water witching, divining rods, dowsing (stocks, staff).
   This occult method of finding water has been used by pagans and Christians alike, over many millennia. When a DIVINER walks a property holding out his rods, a demon actually bends the rods toward a water source.

   > *My people ask counsel at their STOCKS, and their STAFF declareth unto them for the spirit of whoredoms hath caused them to err, and they have gone a whoring from under their God. (Hosea 4:12)*

   The word STOCKS (6086, 'ets) means sticks, planks, wood. The word STAFF (4731, maqqel) means divining staff or rod for guiding.

8. Passive mind states (this is simply inviting demons to take over), dreamers, trance channeling.

   > *...Let not your prophets and your DIVINERS, that be in the midst of you, deceive you, neither hearken to your DREAMS which ye cause to be dreamed. For they PROPHESY FALSELY unto you in My Name: I have not sent them, saith the LORD. (Jeremiah 29:8)*

9. False prophecy, false tongues, lying spirit., false dreams.
   There are several examples of lying spirits that used prophets *(1 Kings 22:20-28)*, and of false prophets in scripture. *(Jeremiah 14:14)*

   > *Beware of false prophets, which come to you in sheep's clothing, but inwardly they are ravening wolves. (Matthew 7:15)*

   > *I have heard what the prophets said, that PROPHESY LIES in My Name, saying, I have dreamed, I have dreamed. (Jeremiah 23:25)*

   > *Behold, I Am against them that PROPHESY FALSE DREAMS, saith the LORD, and do tell them, and cause My people to err by their LIES, and by their lightness; yet I sent them not, nor commanded them... (Jeremiah 23:32)*

   One who uses false tongues is another instrument of Satan. These persons pollute prayer meetings and deliverance services, and should be asked to keep silent or leave. Those operating in this kind of witchcraft usher an unholy presence in. Often, Satan sends them either to hamper the work of our LORD, YHWH, or as a chalice to receive demons when they are cast out of others.

   > *LYING LIPS are an abomination to the LORD... (Proverbs 12:22)*

   > *A LYING TONGUE hateth those that are afflicted by it... (Proverbs 26:28)*

10. Martial arts (meaning military or self-defense arts): karate, T'ai Chi, ninja, kung-fu, Tae Kwon Do, Aikido, jujitsu, judo.
    The root of martial arts is Taoism (or the way; there is no good or evil; belief in yin/yang, where good blends with evil, which is a balance for good, and each supports the other), Buddhism, Zen and Shintoism. Taoism denies Jesus Christ as Savior, for it is pantheistic (everything is god). Marital arts got their start and developed in the Shaolin monastery, where the priests used spiritual power (occult energy) to produce miraculous effects (these are not from YHWH, our God), combined with fighting techniques. These arts are filled with eastern occultism, and were developed as an intricate way to worship pagan gods. The various styles of martial arts are unique to each monastery of pagan monks. They often involve extreme measures using mind control techniques, disciplines, mind-sets, use of deadly force and religious beliefs with requirements that are contrary to

Judeo-Christian ethics. For example, Chi is "another spirit," and an important occult part of these religions. Using chi involves drawing on occult powers to empty the mind, not a practice Christians should engage in. Chi can be used for deadly force or for healing. Ki-ai is the shout when blows are struck, used to channel chi (life force or god energy). Martial arts defile the Christian who should be seeking peace with all men and pleasing the LORD, not how to maim and kill others. The anti-Christ spirit often enters people in the martial arts. They lean on the arm of the flesh rather than YHWH.[62] Martial arts involve acknowledging and ritual bowing (the bow before each fight) to a picture. This is Shintoism (ancestor worship), which is an abomination, opening the participant up to a spirit of whoredoms. Ninja is a highly occult practice; Ninja's are reported to be able to walk up or through walls, become invisible, and practice astral projection.[63] Here is what our God, YHWH, has to say about such practices.

Thus sayeth the LORD, LEARN NOT THE WAY OF THE HEATHEN... (Jeremiah 10:2)

And have NO FELLOWSHIP with the unfruitful works of darkness, but rather REPROVE (expose) them. (Ephesians 5:11)

For ye were sometimes DARKNESS, but now are ye light in the LORD: walk as children of LIGHT... (Ephesians 5:8)

For the wrath of God is revealed from heaven against all ungodliness and unrighteousness of men, WHO HOLD THE TRUTH IN UNRIGHTEOUSNESS. (Romans 1:18)

For ye are bought with a price: therefore glorify God in your body, and in your spirit, which are God's. (1 Corinthians 6:20)

11. EXORCISM: a satanic, magic ritual that derives from ancient pagan sources, adopted by the Catholic Church. It may actually cause the person to be *more* demonized.

12. PARAPSYCHOLOGY: the study of occult phenomena and demonic manifestations.

13. POLTERGEISTS: demons (called ghosts) that manifest by making noises and moving objects.

If you have been involved in any of the above occult practices, repent.

More pagan religious paraphernalia, rituals and practices strictly forbidden by our God

1. Talismans (occult object loaded or charged in a magic circle, carrying occult power), amulets, fetishes, unicorn's horn (talisman to provoke lust), animal energy stones, good luck charms, Egyptian ankh, peace sign (known in Satanism as the witches' foot), pentagram, hexagram (introduced to King Solomon through one of his pagan wives), rosaries (root is Hindu prayer beads).
2. Reading vibrations from crystal, crystal gazing, pyramid symbolism.
3. I.U.D. (women use them without realizing they cause abortions with the monthly cycle and may have suicidal symptoms, anger, depression, remorse, demon infestation, etc., without knowing why).
4. Indian jewelry with religious symbols on it, tiki doll, African masks, foreign religious artifacts (many foreign countries allow witch doctors to pronounce incantations over objects made in their factories).
5. Dream catcher or Mandela (a Native American fetish that supposedly catches bad dreams and lets through the good dreams, usually hung above cribs or beds).
6. Occult practices in Boy Scouts and Girl Scouts such as Micasay; talking to the Indian "great spirit."
7. Witchcraft: when one attains a certain level in the craft, two options are given to enhance the practice:
   a. Lycanthrophy: becoming a werewolf; literally changing oneself into a wolf-like creature that kills (this is more common in areas where voodoo priests control the people). A pastor friend asserted that during a Sunday morning service a woman began to manifest as a werewolf. Her ears grew pointed, her jaw dropped down and out, her eyes changed and she began to grow hair. They cast this wicked spirit out of her and she returned to normal.
   b. Vampirism: becoming a vampire; literally sucking blood or life force from victims (this actually goes on in some covens). The ever increasing rash of TV shows, movies and books about vampires have stirred up an unnatural and unhealthy interest in these creatures. The Anne Rice books, beginning with *Interview With the Vampire*, have caused an amazingly large cult to develop, centered in New Orleans. Thousands have flocked there to learn "the way." Day walkers are another type of vampire that is able to prey on victims in daylight, craving the life force of their victims.[64] Drinking blood is very wicked, for life is in

the blood, and the Bible strictly forbids it. The extreme surge of interest in vampires is a sign that we are in the end times. Some of the fallen angels of ancient times were cannibalistic and drank the blood of their victims. Vampires form feeding circles within which they can sometimes contain their lust for blood. Some fall on innocent prey by taking night jobs or cruising the streets for hapless victims after dark. One man found that after a while he could not contain himself, and nearly attacked women on the street. After that, he nearly killed a willing witch in his coven by taking too much blood.[65] Curses to break are: Dracula, Cain (reported to have become a vampire after being rejected by God), Vlad the Impaler, Lestat (vampire in Anne Rice books), Anubis (Egyptian god of the dead), Lilith (pagan goddess; one of the ruling spirits over abortion; known as a vampire). Break the power of blood lust, the spirit pack, astral projection, mind control, shape-shifting, witchcraft, vampire resurrection, the killer instinct, love of the night, the vampire slave, hypnotism. "Keepers" are psychic vampires that drain energy from others and keep it stored. Supposedly, they can live a long time this way.[66]

8. Angel worship, spirit guides, obsession with ghosts or demons.
9. All incantations; such as peeling an apple in front of a mirror at midnight with incantations to find true love.
10. Levitation, astral travel or projection (the travel of the spirit outside the body), holistic healing, psychic healing and surgery, using the green healing light, c'hi (any kind of healing that does not have our God as the focus), materialization, some forms of homeopathy, metal bending (actually a demon doing the bending), automatic writing, regression therapy, third eye, universal consciousness, wheel of life.
11. Kundalini: (chakras of kundalini yoga use a sexual ritual that joins the sacred female force to the male force.
12. Pornography, Sado-masochism, sexual relations with incubus or succubus, perverse sexual acts, homosexuality.
13. Occult books: such as *Harry Potter*, *Goose Bumps*, casting spells; occult music.
14. Occult games: Ouiji boards, Jumanji, Dungeons and Dragons, Pokemon, Magic—the Gathering, Doom, Quake, Resident Evil, satanic music, many computer games and video games.
15. Occultish TV programs.

Religions

Following are some religions that do not accept Jesus Christ (Yahshua Messiah) as the only Savior and our God (YHWH) as the one true God:
1. New Age Religion: The ultimate eclectic religion of self. Claims tolerance, embracing all religions *except* Christianity and Judaism, against whom they are remarkably *intolerant*. One God simply isn't enough for them. Their agenda to infiltrate the United Nations and the public schools has been very successful. It is acceptable to their agenda to teach Hindu meditation techniques, American Indian religious practices, books that promote witchcraft, etc., but just try to read out of the Bible or a Christian book and see how fast you get fired. It happened to me.
2. Wicca (means to twist or bend; root word: wikke meaning bad or wicked): practice witchcraft: white or black magic.
3. Monism (all is one, all things are connected; the god/goddess is all; most Wiccans and New Agers are Monists).
4. Dualism (our god, YHWH, and Satan are equal).
5. Church of Satan (Anton LaVey), Satanism, Luciferianism.
6. Temple of Set; worship of Set (Egyptian god known as the fallen leader of angelic host); founder: Michael Aquino.
7. Polytheism (many gods, everything is sacred and can be worshipped: animals, rocks, trees, etc.).
8. Paganism (trusting in occult wisdom and powers; rituals similar throughout world).
9. Neo-paganism (blends ancient pagan religions; believe spiritual forces link everyone to every other part of nature).
10. Animism (the belief that inanimate objects are alive and have souls); praying to trees and rocks, demonstrated in the movie, "Pocahontas."
11. Pantheism (the belief that all is god, god is in everything in nature).
12. Gnosticism (holiness and salvation through mystical knowledge, not through Jesus Christ).
13. Naturalism (all religious truth derives from nature and natural causes; there is no supernatural cause for events).
14. Sun worship (the sun god reigned supreme as all powerful source of life and wisdom; required human sacrifice: Baal, Molech, Baccus, Zeus, Osirus, etc.).
15. Tibetan religion; their new age followers employ "tulpa," the ability to materialize actual breathing beings.[67]

16. Chinese "c'hi," the Hindu "prana," and the Hawaiian "mana" form the 'energy' or 'force' behind Chinese acupuncture, Hindu yoga, psychic healings.[68]

17. Great spirit (American Indian god).

18. Rosicrucianism (Fraternity of the Rose Cross; founded by Christian Rosenkreutz, 14th century German nobleman, after studying occultism in the Middle East. They claimed occult powers, secrets lost to science and medicine, and claimed they never felt hunger.) [69]

19. Jungian psychology, Marxism, communism, socialism, shamanism, Satanism, fetishism.

20. Hypnotism, trance channeling through auto-hypnosis, blood pacts, pacts with Satan, séances, mind control.

21. ESP (extrasensory perception), EST, Eckankar, Gurdjieff, yoga, TM (transcendental meditation, the repetition of a certain word is really calling upon the name of a demon to possess you).

22. Nazism (the fanatical religion created by Himmler was a blend of paganism, occultism, Norse and Arthurian legends). The Nazi symbol known as the twin sowelus or SS Runes,[70] was the ancient Norse sun wheel (possibly an ancient Hindu idol). Nazism borrowed from several cultures. Their true stated purpose is to break free of what they call the oppression of Christianity.[71]

23. Jehovah's Witness, Unitarianism, Christian Science, Theosophical Society, Swedenborgism, Silva Mind Control, Zoroastrianism, Anthroposophy, The Way International, Worldwide Church of God (Armstrong), Church Universal and Triumphant, Hari Krishna, Rastafarianism, Roman Catholicism, Scientology, Unification Church (Moonies), Unity, People's Temple, Tara Center, Children of God, Elizabeth Clare Prophet, Spiritualism, I Am Movement, Bahai, human potential movement or humanism, globalism.

24. Buddhism, Hinduism, ancestor worship, reincarnation, yin yang.

25. Islam (worship Allah, not the same as Christian God); a Moslem is a believer in Islam (connected to use of hashish).

26. Mormonism (comes from the pagan god, Mormo; god of ghouls and of the dead) or Latter Day Saints (LDS); center in Salt Lake City, Utah; RLDS or renamed Community of Christ; center in Independence, Missouri. Mormons are taught that the *Book of Mormon* has a familiar spirit (demon)---they do not understand this teaching. Moroni, an Indian demon, is the title of one of the sections in the book.[72]

27. Goddess worship: Great Mother, Ashtoreth, Diana, Semiramis, Isis, Easter, Ishtar, Kali worship, Gaea (earth worship), Sophia worship, feminism, etc.

28. Python worship—snake worship (part of this form of pagan worship is hypnotism, prophecy, human sacrifice).

29. Voodoo, hoodoo, Santeria (a mixture of voodoo and Catholicism), Camdoble, Palo Mayombe, Ju Ju, gris-gris (to bewitch), curse of the Loa (ruling spirit), root workers and witchdoctors, conjure men, Haitian—African—Black Southern voodoo, gove (souls of dead in clay pots), obeah, conjuration, spirit of death, zombie, graveyard dust demons, lust potions, fire walking, spirit of the tree, lefba, ghede, baka, banda, assator, asson, acon, cambe, kombe, chauffer, mambo, mange, saints used as synonym for Loa, verser, wanga, maori, morongo, Agwe, Azacca, Bline Gawd, psychic prayers, false baptism of fire, Petro, Rada, Obatala, etc. The wicked spirits to be broken are all the above, and Samede, Ghede, Abaddon, rhythm, trances evoked through their worship, jerking spirits, candle burning, rosary prayers, false tongues, false prophecy, false dancing in the "spirit," false burning in the stomach called Holy Ghost, Creole curses, curse of roots, use of fetishes, idolatry.[73]

30. Environmentalism, saving the environment, Green Peace: While a reasonable effort to protect the environment is all right, the true nature of this movement at the highest levels is earth goddess worship, which the United Nations has declared a global religion *preferable* to Christianity.

31. Freemasonry: Shriners, Knights Templar, Klu Klux Klan (an organization begun by a Freemason), Mafia (an organization begun by a Freemason), Eastern Star, Daughters of Nile, The Shrine, White Shrine, De Molays, Job's Daughters, Rainbow Girls, Illuminati. Freemasonry is a satanic pagan religion.

32. Cabala (Kabbalah, Kabala, Qabbalah) is a form of Jewish mysticism, dating back to approximately 1200 A.D. Germs of mystical thought can be traced to the first and second centuries A.D., beginning with the contemplation of the throne of God, Merkabah mysticism, characterized by ecstatic visions, focusing only on the Creator aspect of God. Later, came the rise of Hasidim mysticism, 12th and 13th century Germany, steeped in occult sciences with a leaning toward pantheism. The Spanish Cabalists claimed revelations of the prophet Elijah, and the *Sefirot*, or inner life of God. The *Sefirot* are the Mystical Tree or Upper Man symbols, meant to describe a process of divine life, overflowing into the entire creation. Zoharic writings further extended the

mystical contemplation of the Torah, divine commandments, soul, and inner life of the divinity. Later, Cabalists had even more bizarre beliefs concerning the creation, theorizing extensively about the separation of God from His Shekhina, and man's role in restoring their union. Other movements followed: The Lurianic Cabala in the 17th and 18th centuries, the Sabbatian movement, and 18th century Hasidism.[74]

Kabbala (or Cabala) is an ancient, esoteric, satanic cult that grew out of a mystical interpretation of the Hebrew Scriptures, and is a secret group that handed down their doctrines orally to preserve secrecy. (Occult implies hidden.) Their doctrine states that God's attributes are actual beings that emanate from Him. Cabala is a mixture of pantheism and Judeo-Christian doctrine: Their God is impersonal and uncaring. Cabala decodes scripture with notarikon, a system of using the first letter of words in a sentence to form new words. They also use themurah, similar to a cryptogram, where one letter is substituted for another, making codes. Cabalists attach great significance to words that appear by chance. Gematria is used to twist this code into a number system by using it as a way to interpret scriptures. Cabalists see the Word of God as a riddle to be deciphered, rather than truth to be obeyed.

There are other false religions too numerous to name that spring up constantly. The people of the apostle Paul's day engaged in the same foolish practices outlined above that the people of today participate in. They even used some of the same names and rituals. God warned us in His Word what would happen to those who practice any form of pagan idolatry.

Result of the foolishness of pagan religions *(Romans 1:18-32)*

1. They become futile in their thoughts.
2. Their foolish hearts are darkened.
3. Professing to be wise they become fools.
4. They become vain (conceited) in their imaginations.
5. They hold (back) the truth in unrighteousness.
6. They fail to glorify God, though they know Him.
7. They change the truth into a lie.
8. They are unthankful toward God.
9. They worship the creature and creation, rather than the Creator.
10. They have pleasure in unrighteousness.
11. They dishonor their own bodies.
12. God gives them up to vile affections (passions).
13. They may become lesbians and homosexuals.
14. God gives them over to a "reprobate" mind. Reprobate (*Vine's*, adokimos), meaning a mind which God cannot approve, but instead, rejects; the effect of refusing to have God in their knowledge is that the moral sense is perverted, and their minds are beclouded with their own speculations.
15. Then they become filled with all unrighteousness, fornication, wickedness, covetousness, maliciousness; filled with envy, murder, debate (strife), deceit, malignity (*Vine's*, kakoetheia—meaning bad manner or character, evil disposition that puts the worst light on everything, malice, malevolence), whisperers (*Vine's*, psithuristes—occurs in an evil sense), backbiters, haters of God, despiteful (insolent), proud, boasters, inventors of evil things, disobedient to parents, without understanding, covenant-breakers, without natural affection, implacable (*Vine's*, aspondos—indicates one who will not enter into a covenant), unmerciful.

God's antidote for purposely rejecting Him *(Romans 1:18-32; 2:1-9)*

1. They are without excuse. God has shown them the truth.
2. Their error is multiplied back to them.
3. God gives them up to dishonor their own bodies.
4. They will suffer judgment.
5. The wrath of God is revealed against all ungodliness and unrighteousness.
6. Hard hearts receive wrath.
7. There will be tribulation and anguish on every soul that does evil.

For rebellion is as the sin of witchcraft, and stubbornness is as iniquity and idolatry. Because thou hast rejected the Word of the LORD, He hath also rejected thee… (1 Samuel 15:23)

Familiar spirits pass from one generation to another. Christians may be harassed by these spirits that believe they have family rights through bloodlines. Magic in any form, white or black, even if done in a seemingly innocent game, is an abomination to YHWH, our God. Much secular music has ungodly themes that create an open door for satanic attack on the listener. Smash these occult objects to bits and destroy them. If possible, burn them. The value, no matter how high, is not worth the price of your soul. Demons are attracted to "charged" objects, therefore it is important to go through your home and eliminate everything that has an occultic origin.

Many of them also which used curious (magical) arts brought their books together, and burned them before all men: and they counted the price of them, and found it fifty thousand pieces of silver. (Acts 19:18-19)

If you have engaged in any of the activities listed above, or other occult activities, you have opened the door to demonic aggression that ultimately produces strongholds in your life. The devil will take any ground you allow. Deliverance is about closing these doors to the occult. Speak the following steps out loud.

Steps to take for deliverance

1. Realize that all the above practices, listed in this chapter, are sin.
2. Repent!
3. Ask for the strength and power to break away from bondage.
4. Renounce your involvement in each occult and psychic practice you have participated in.
5. Renounce psychic powers.
6. Bind the strongmen of witchcraft and divination, and cast them out.
7. Cast out a spirit of divination, witchcraft, python, voodoo, etc.
8. Cut the link with the spirit of divination (and any other spirits in operation, such as lying spirits and deception) created between soul and spirit.
9. Renounce and break off each sin and subsequent stronghold in Jesus' Name. Chop them off at the roots. Plead the blood of Jesus over each broken root.
10. Renounce any mediums, channelers or gurus, and so-called sacred books, false prophecies or readings received by mediums, psychic connections. Cancel their assignments against you.
11. Renounce use of any so called "light" or "force" in the universe.
12. Destroy all talismans and occult jewelry, art or objects (by fire if possible).
13. Ask God to forgive you and wash you in the blood of Yahshua Messiah (Jesus Christ).
14. Break any ungodly soul-ties you may have to cults or false religious organizations or objects.
15. Accept Yahshua Messiah (Jesus Christ) as your Savior and LORD.
16. Forgive the people who led you in these practices and pray for their salvation.
17. Ask YHWH, our God, to fill you with His Holy Spirit. *(Ephesians 5:18)*
18. Fill your mind with scriptures by reading and studying the Word of God. *(Colossians 3:16)*
19. Witness to others involved in these practices; they, too, can be delivered.
20. Declare aloud that you wish to send or receive *no* messages from the spirit world except from the Holy Spirit.
21. Return any curses or spells and demons sent by Satanists or witches to the sender. Command the Satanists and witches' protective wall be destroyed. Curses may include marital problems, sickness, pain, confusion, driving and compelling lusts, fatigue, etc. Cut all silver cords and lay lines.

Additional steps for white witches and Satanists

White witch (strongmen)
Sophia, Gaea, Diana, Hecate, Aradia (others goddesses)
Pythoness, divination
Hermes
Horned god: Herne, Cernunnos, Pan
Renounce familiars, fetches and demon helpers by name.
Renounce the spirits they have channeled.

Satanists, black witches (strongmen)
Satan, Lucifer, Belial, Leviathan (others)
Lillith, Molech, Kali (human sacrifice)
Incubus or succubus spirits (sexual demons)
Legion, Hermes,
Deaf and dumb spirit
Python spirit, divination

What to renounce

1. Renounce Wicca and goddess worship
2. Renounce high priest as false prophet
3. Renounce the *Book of Shadows* as false scripture
4. Ask forgiveness for trying to converse with the dead
5. Break all soul ties formed through sexual encounters
6. Ask forgiveness for taking illegal drugs
   (seal with The Blood)
7. Ask forgiveness for any blood shed (seal w/ blood)
8. If there are attacks during sleep: pray for protection;
   ask the LORD to send His angels to guard you.
9. Plead the blood of Jesus over your soulish realm.

What to renounce

1. Renounce Satanism
2. Renounce high priest as false prophet
3. Renounce *Satanic Bible*; any other sacred books, as false scrip.
4. Ask forgiveness for making pacts with the devil
5. Same; Ask forgiveness for any of these rites done with demons
6. Ask forgiveness for taking illegal drugs (seal with the blood)
7. Ask forgiveness for any blood shed (seal with blood of Jesus Christ)
8. If there are attacks during sleep: pray for protection...
9. Break all triggers[75]

Getting free from Masonry, Mormonism, and other cults that require oath or covenants

1. Pray over your home. Plead the blood of Jesus (Yahshua Messiah) over your home, yourself and your family.
2. Realize that Masonry (and cultish oaths) is sin.
3. Take authority over lying and deceitful spirits. Cast them out.
4. Turn the issue over to God.
5. Ask forgiveness for seeking occult powers and knowledge and denying the unique deity of Jesus the Christ.
6. Rebuke any lying or deceitful spirits.
7. Ask Yahshua Messiah (Jesus Christ) to give you power to break away from the bondage of the craft.
8. Break any ungodly soul-ties in Jesus' Name.
9. Chop off the cable tow between you and the Lodge or cult with the sword of the Spirit.
10. Seal this with the blood of the Lamb, Jesus the Messiah.
11. Renounce the strongmen of Masonry and other cults; command them to leave your family forever.
12. Renounce and cast out a perverse spirit, a lying spirit, a spirit of error, a seducing spirit, a spirit of whoredoms, spirit of divination, spirit of confusion, spirit of deception, spirit of haughtiness, familiar spirits, anti-Christ spirit, bondage, spirit of fear.
13. Ask God to forgive you for involvement in the Lodge or cult.
14. Seek God, and strengthen yourself through prayer, and meditation on God's Word.
15. Witness to other Masons, Mormons and cultists, and lead them to Jesus.[76]

Masonry (strongmen)

1. Tubal Cain
2. Jah Bal On
3. Hiram Abiff
4. Dagon
5. Molech and Lillith (demanded infant sacrifice)
6. Baal
7. Set
8. Pythoness (spirit of divination)
9. Baphomet (goat in five-pointed star, secret god of Knights Templar) [77]

Mormonism (strongmen)

1. Mormo (god of ghouls and the dead)
2. Moroni (demon of Indian subcontinent)
3. Spirit of priestcraft
4. Spirit of Bishoprick

Masonry: What to renounce

1. Renounce the Lodge and auxiliary bodies as false religion
2. Shriners: renounce temple oaths on the Quran to Allah
3. Renounce false head-ship of the Grand Lodge
4. Renounce Melchizedek priesthood
5. Renounce false Masonic communion
6. Renounce Worshipful Master; declare Jesus as only master
7. Cut all ties and cable-tows (seal with the blood)
8. Repent for denying Jesus as Messiah in Masonic initiations
9. Break covenants, and seal all with the blood (these will be over your family, too)
10. Renounce all blood oaths, covenants and communions
11. Break the curses you've spoken (seal with the blood)
12. Send letter of demit for release from Lodge
13. Destroy Masonic trinkets, rings, jewelry, books, pins, preferably by fire

Mormonism: What to renounce

1. Renounce LDS or RLDS Church as false religion
2. Renounce patriarchal blessing as sin of mediumship
3. Renounce Melchizedek and Aaronic priesthood as the sin of priestcraft
4. Renounce Joseph Smith as false prophet
5. Renounce Book of Mormon and other LDS books as false doctrine and repent for serving other masters
6. Renounce baptismal covenants and any priesthood blessings
7. (Temple Mormons) Renounce temple oaths, temple marriage as sin [78]

Jehovah's Witness (strongman)
1. Ra-Hoor-Khuit (Horus)—Egyptian god of war

Jehovah's Witness: What to renounce
1. Renounce Arian Jehovah-God (false mask of the Jehovah's Witness God)
2. Renounce *New World Translation* as false scripture
3. Renounce Governing Body of Watchtower as false prophet
4. Renounce Watchtower Bible and Tract Society as false religion
5. Renounce baptism into cult
6. Ask forgiveness for denying deity of Jesus Christ and His resurrection
7. Ask forgiveness for denying the Holy Spirit [80]

Christian Science (strongman)
1. Hermes (Greek god of mind and founder of Hermetics)

Christian Science: What to renounce
1. Renounce as false religion
2. Renounce Mary Baker Eddy as false prophet
3. Renounce Science and Health and Key to Scriptures as false
4. Forgiveness for denying unique deity of Jesus and Holy Spirit
5. Repent for sin of seeking occult healing
6. Repent for denying reality of God's creation
7. Repent for seeking psychic powers [79]

Deliverance on yourself?

Yes, indeed! Rebuke or cast out devils as you would if you were ministering to someone else. Most of the time when we are being oppressed, there is no one around who can help. Trust God to help you, even if you don't feel like it. If you are deeply angry, intensely frustrated, depressed, have a lot of evil thoughts, or a lot of fights with others, this is a sign that you are being attacked through areas where you are vulnerable, and you may need deliverance.

When thou passest through the waters, I will be with thee; and through the rivers, they shall not overflow thee: when thou walkest through the fire, thou shalt not be burned; neither shall the flame kindle upon thee. (Isaiah 43:2)

1. Repent before God. Spend time in prayer seeking His face.
2. Fight using the fruit of the Spirit, commanding the devil to leave in Jesus' Name.
3. Put your armor back on.
4. Resist the devil.
5. Clear demons out of your house by ordering them to go in Jesus' Name, and anointing your house with oil.
6. Plead the blood over you, your loved ones and your home.
7. Be strong in the LORD and the power of His might! Don't give up!
8. Find scriptures to stand on and speak them out loud daily. Bind them to yourself, your situation and your loved ones.

Stand fast therefore in the liberty wherewith Christ hath made us free, and be not entangled again with the yoke of bondage. (Galatians 5:1)

Strongholds

If there are strongholds in your life, pride or lusts of the flesh that keep hanging on, this is an indication that Satan is energizing and exploiting your weaknesses so you will doubt your deliverance and subsequent liberation from these weaknesses. The STRONGHOLD is a fleshly pattern reinforced by a demon, which may remain even though the STRONGMAN has been cast out. Fleshly patterns wear a groove in your soulish realm like the permanent pattern on a record. Deliverance is a process. It may take time to tear down what has taken years to establish. Demons are attracted to sinful acts and will fight to maintain their position by throwing a constant stream of thoughts and temptations at the person. Additionally, some of the same problems that Satan caused from within, he can cause from outside the person. One who truly desires deliverance must develop an ever deeper intimacy with the Father, and the Holy Spirit will strengthen and guide the person into the final release of the sin. Remember to trust in God's promises, not in feelings or moods.

...let us lay aside every weight and the sin which doth so easily beset us... (Hebrews 12:1)

Chapter Twenty
The Spirit of Python

Divination: imitation of prophecy; the art of pretending to foretell future events.

The word DIVINATION comes from the Greek word puthon (or pneuma Puthonos), from which we derive the word PYTHON. In the middle column of the Bible, Cambridge University Press, the spirit of divination is referred to as a spirit of python. The intertwining connection of ancient serpent myths seems to spring from the serpent in Eden. The healing arts, to this day, have an ensign called the caduceus; two intertwined snakes on a pole in sexual congress, with wings on the tips. This is the symbol of Hermes, Greek messenger and god of medicine. This spirit mesmerizes or hypnotizes its victims. Python controls minds and lives through suggested sins of the flesh, such as greed, envy, bondages, confusion, lusts, sins, familiar spirits, etc.

The spirit of python's origins are in the Greek cult of Apollo that had a serpent guarding its temple, which was, according to legend, slain by Apollo. According to Greek myth, Pythian was a monstrous serpent (or dragon) dwelling in Pytho at the foot of Mount Parnassus. *(Webster's Dictionary)* Pythian was born out of the same mud of Deucalion's Deluge [81] known as the great flood. The serpent guarded the Delphi oracle, which was the most celebrated citadel of prophecy in the ancient pagan world of the Mediterranean. Delphos of Delphi means womb and was considered the womb of the world. The oracle was situated in a cave. Pythia gave prophecies after inhaling volcanic fumes from the center of the earth guarded by Python. Pytho was also an ancient name for Delphi. According to legend, Python was a child of Gaea (Mother Earth), who traditionally had an oracle at Delphi before Apollo came. Legend holds that Python lived at the center of the earth and held it together. He guarded and controlled the shrine of the oracle Gaia at Delphi, before Apollo came. In the myth, Python was originally female; in later versions of the legend Python was male.[82] According to legend, the serpent was killed because it would not let Apollo establish his own oracle, being accustomed to giving oracles itself.

Pitho (or Pitys) came from Peth or Pet, meaning **to beguile**. The name came from the famous serpent **Python**. The original Pan (Adam), meaning he who turned aside, loved a nymph called **Pitho**, the name of **a beguiling woman** (symbolic of Eve), who, having been beguiled, induced her husband to follow her.[83] Fornication and adultery, both physical and spiritual, are part of python's arsenal. In Greek myth, Dionysus, god of fertility and wine, was originally a serpent, born to Persephone, daughter of Zeus. When murdered, he was reborn in human form. A snake cult sprang up around him. In Greek culture, the daemons (demons) could appear as a serpent or a man. They were assigned by Zeus to every important person or god to give advice.[84]

The cult of Apollo was a snake-worshipping cult, depicted in an amazingly accurate fashion in the movie *Conan the Barbarian*. When Apollo (the sun god) killed Pythian, the name Python was transferred to Apollo himself. Later, the word was applied to diviners or soothsayers, regarded as inspired by Apollo. The woman that the Apostle Paul encountered was possessed by the same demon that was worshipped in the cult of Apollo: a spirit of divination.[85] Any oracles coming from a person possessed with a spirit of divination were considered to be the oracles of Apollo, or words from a deity to be taken very seriously.[86] Utterances from trance speaking or channeling (done by a medium) at high levels, such as the damsel that pursued Paul, are called ORACLES (SOOTHSAYERS), believed to be the result of inspiration from a deity. [87]

The Apostle Paul encountered the spirit of python in Macedonia where a damsel followed him about possessed by a SPIRIT OF DIVINATION, that caused him much trouble. He cast the spirit out, which caused him more trouble.

> *And it came to pass, AS WE WENT TO PRAYER, a certain damsel possessed with a SPIRIT OF DIVINATION met us, which brought her masters much gain by SOOTHSAYING: the same followed Paul and us, and cried, saying, These men are the servants of the most high God, which show unto us the way of salvation. And this did she many days. But Paul, being GRIEVED, turned and said to the spirit, I command thee in the Name of Jesus Christ to come out of her. And he came out the same hour. (Acts 16:16-18)*

I saw a spirit of python standing over the pulpit area of a church. It was about twelve feet tall, hideous, with scales, and it had one snake-like eye in the center of its forehead. I prayed that its power be broken from that church.

Hypnosis is a form of divination

Hypnosis is a form of charming, beguiling or enchantment that takes possession of the soulish realm, and subsequently, the body. During hypnosis the mind is more suggestible, resulting in passivity. Passivity is one of the most dangerous and vulnerable states to allow oneself be in, opening a person up to demonic attack. Hypnosis is ungodly and should be avoided at all costs. We are not to tempt the LORD by engaging in this form of divination.

The hypnotist's power depends upon the level of commitment he has made to the dark side. When I was in the world, I worked as a back-up band several times for two well-known Las Vegas hypnotists, whose acts centered around calling people up from the audience and hypnotizing them. Under hypnosis, the people would behave in a shocking manner, and perform feats of strength impossible under normal circumstances. Both hypnotists would leave some of their victims with triggers before they woke them, then pronounce the trigger later in the show, causing the victim to remove a garment or some other pre-programmed behavior. Often, I witnessed a ninety-pound woman, selected from the audience for each show, suspended across the back of two chairs only by her neck and ankles. As she was ordered to stiffen her body, according to command, the two-hundred pound hypnotist would climb up and stand on the tiny woman for several seconds. One of the hypnotists was slicker, more dangerous and powerful than the other. I am certain many left these shows profoundly slimed and infested by demons.

The damsel who was harassing Paul was a PYTHONESS, a priestess or prophetess of Apollo. A Pythoness needed occult stimulation to attain altered states of consciousness, through which Python entered her and spoke her "oracles." She was charmed (HYPNOTIZED) by a large serpent kept at the oracular temple and acquired skills from being hypnotized. She would have been a channeler of the spirit of DIVINATION, who used a form of hypnosis to open a door to demonic infestation. Often, a Pythoness would sit over a snake pit and prophesy, practicing mind control techniques and using a hypnotic eye or a jewel for this purpose.

Preparing to pray

Notice that the damsel who followed Paul met them just as they were PREPARING TO PRAY. This is often the case. Just as the anointing begins to flow, or someone is getting ready to pray or lead people into repentance, this spirit will use a susceptible vessel to interrupt with a loud *"word"* or a distraction. (Some people seem to always have a *word* no matter where they go. This is a subject not often addressed in the church.) Leaders have learned that confronting the python spirit will bring them persecution or backlash, so they ignore this form of harassment, pretending this *word* is from the Holy Spirit, when they sense deep inside their own spirits it is not. A prophet I know was shocked at a men's meeting when a *word* came forth timed to coincide with the end of a message on repentance: "Everyone must bow their knees to me!" The men all over the hall began to bow, but the prophet discerned it was an evil spirit that had spoken this command. He rebuked this spirit and exhorted the men to stand to their feet. The devil loves to come into meetings and masquerade as the Holy Spirit.

The word GRIEVED (diaponeo) in Acts 16:16, denotes having to work with great toil, being seriously troubled. The damsel was speaking the truth, but with the wrong motivation: greed. The wicked spirit of divination, being promoted through her and her masters, was determined to discredit and foil Paul's efforts, and turn the holy (kodesh, set-apart) ministry of Paul into a money making scheme. When Paul cast the spirit out of the damsel, they threw him in jail.

The constrictor

The spirit of python is a powerful constricting spirit that squeezes the life out of its victims, just like the python snake does. It dangles divine prophecy in front of a person to entice them, while swinging a tail around from behind to knock them down.

The modern day python serpent still has vestiges of hind limbs, visible externally as a pair of claws adjacent to the anal cleft. Their prey is killed by suffocation, as the python takes advantage of the victim's struggles by tightening its coils each time their captive exhales.[88] Notice how the python uses its prey's fear against it. As the victim struggles for breath, it is suffocated. Sometimes a person under attack from a python spirit will manifest choking and coughing, grabbing the throat, helplessly. A python spirit will jump from one person to another, trying to bring confusion. It will try to disrupt meetings, pretending to seek ministry. If allowed to continue, it will either break up the meeting, or demand attention to occupy most of the prayer time of those ministering.

Some manifestations of the python spirit are lack and debt, weariness, fatigue, confusion, frustration, pressure, heaviness, oppression, depression, fear, coughing and choking. The fruits of this spirit are division, factions, poverty, discouragement, frustration. Because python is a spirit of divination, it teams up with the Jezebel spirit, whoredoms, controlling and manipulative spirits, and beguiling and seducing spirits. Jealousy, strife and competitive spirits also work with python.[89] If allowed to continue, it will squeeze the life out of its victims. It causes church and marital splits, businesses to fail, and finances to dry up.

The big squeeze

Python works to squeeze people into a state of poverty, lack and debt. If someone is giving to a ministry or church, python will squeeze them until they have no more finances to give. A couple of years ago I was having a garage sale to help raise funds for a ministry trip. From the first day, no one was coming and no money was being made. I sought the LORD and felt impressed to rebuke and break the spirit of python off my sale. After this, people came and I sold everything of value, making more than enough. This demon works to constrict the flow of finances to churches, homes and businesses. Nothing will seem to go right, business deals will not go through, ministry trips will have to be canceled, funding for church programs will dry up. Python works to break down God's plan.

Chains broken

At a women's convention where I was ministering, an evangelist, who ran a soup kitchen for the poor, came up for prayer. She had been plagued by depression, thoughts of despair, defeat, lack of funds, lack of freedom in her ministry. I discerned chains of bondage wrapped all around her, choking off the life of Christ in her. This is the spirit of python. I picked up my flute and began to play, walking round and round her, while the anointing broke the yokes. The chains began to snap one by one. Her whole body jerked and twitched. Finally, the deliverance was complete. She began to dance and rejoice in the LORD. I received a letter from her two weeks later, declaring God's greatness and her complete victory over python, detailing the freedom and power she now walked in, in her own ministry. A similar thing occurred in the life of David and King Saul. When an evil spirit plagued Saul, David played his harp and the spirit left because of the anointing. *(1 Samuel 16:23)*

Chains around cities

Python holds whole cities in its grip. It fights to remain in control. Have you ever noticed that some cities are desperately poverty stricken, while others seem to burst with success and industry. There are a number of great men and women of God who have suffered burn-out from sheer exhaustion, and died of physical ailments that could have been avoided with proper rest and nutrition. Python seeks to wear out the ministers of God through continuous work without rest, until they collapse.

Breaking python's grip

1. You may be allowing the python spirit access to you through your own words. Watch what you say. Break any curses you or others have made against you. Examples: "You'll never amount to anything." "There's never enough money to pay the bills." "I'll never get out of debt!"
2. Repent for any sins in your life. These will become open doors for demonic activity in your life. Pray for the Holy Spirit to give you wisdom in this area.
3. Cast out the spirit of python. Break this spirit off your finances, church, job, city and family in Jesus' Name.
4. Stand in vigilance against any seduction, deception, poverty, lack and debt. *(3 John 2)*
5. Watch in the financial realm, and guard against the enemy sending in his servants who have division and strife, or who want to constantly take up all your time, but persist in the sins they seek counseling for. Tell them, "When you have followed through with what I told you to do the *first* time, then call me."
6. Don't succumb to guilt. When you're tired, *rest*. After all, *who can you help if you're sick or dead?*
7. Break off and resist any discouragement.
8. Cast out any other spirits in operation, such as, heaviness, fatigue, confusion, depression, frustration, tightness in the throat, chest or belly.
9. Bind the blood of Yahshua Messiah (Jesus Christ) to yourself and your finances.
10. Resist the devil!
11. Resist the temptation to languish in self-pity. Stand up and fight the good fight of faith!
12. Bind scriptures to yourself such as Philippians 4:19; Proverbs 10:22; Matthew 7:11.

Chapter Twenty-One
Basilisk, Leviathan, Dragons

Basilisk

Basilisk means king, or little king of serpents. It comes from the Latin root basil meaning king. This chapter will address the increasing power and authority of the spirit called Basilisk. As the wickedness of our nation grows, Basilisk increases in authority. The serpent theme of the previous chapter will be expanded in this chapter. Pre-Canaanite Phoenicians worshipped a serpent god known as Basilisk, with rituals of a phallic and sexual nature. The proliferation of snake cults was probably a result of the Biblical and historical significance of the serpent in the Garden of Eden, when humans began following the advice of Satan in serpent form. This spirit has been depicted with or without wings, and with or without a crown. Sometimes it had an extra eye in its tail to strike adversaries.[90] The basilisk was said to kill with a glance or with venom.[91]

Legend and myth tie most pagan peoples to snake gods. They willfully worshipped the creature rather than the Creator. Legend and myth dictated that to look at Basilisk was to die. This is carried through the gorgons of Greek mythology, Medusa with snakes for hair, Apollo killing the oracle of Delphi by killing the ruling serpent, the Sumerians and Akkadian's guardian serpent of the "World Tree," which again smacks strongly of the Garden of Eden account. The serpent Hedammu loved Ishtar (Semiramis, Easter, Ashtoreth, etc.). The Sumerians had an arch-serpent that dwelt in subterranean waters, also known as chaos. (Chaos was one of the names of Cush, founder and husband of Semiramis, queen of Babylon.) The cosmic serpent, or chaos, is a twisted symbol of everything evil which must be defeated. The historian, Pliny the Elder, wrote, "It (basilisk) kills not only by its touch but also with its breath scorches up grass and burns rocks." [92] The cockatrice mentioned in Isaiah 11:8; 14:29; Jeremiah 8:17 is believed to be another name for basilisk.

In the Semitic and Indo-European writings the basilisk is called a dragon, a name that Satan himself bears in Revelation. These dragons were serpent-like in appearance. The Persians had a great sky serpent who was creator of the planets and the sky, and mid-eastern peoples deified him as lord of waters. The Hurrians, who dwelt in Turkey, Iraq and Syria brought the serpent god Indra to Egypt. The Egyptian serpent god was also known as Set. The pharaoh's crown of Egypt sported a serpent, Uraeus, who, according to myth had crawled up the tree of life. A serpent is also connected to the god Horus; Pharaoh was thought to be Horus, incarnate. The sun god Ra, who ruled by day, was known by a different name in every culture (Baal, Bacchus, Osiris, and originally as Nimrod, son and husband of Semiramis), and was connected to Uraeus, who also ruled by day.

The spirit of basilisk operates in broad daylight as well as by night. Scriptures revealed this spirit as *"the destruction that wasteth at noonday." (Psalm 91:6)* Basilisk is a legendary, mythical and historical creature that brings destruction, death, plagues, diseases, natural disasters and terrorism. *(Psalm 91:13; Proverbs 23:32; Isaiah 14:29; 11:8; 59:5; Jeremiah 8:17; Luke 10:19)* Several prophets have seen basilisk in visions. It was wearing full armor and had an army ready to do battle.[93]

> *Thou shalt tread upon the lion and the adder... (Psalm 91:13)*

> *Behold, I give unto you power to TREAD on serpents and scorpions, and over all the power of the enemy: and nothing shall by any means hurt you. (Luke 10:19)*

TREAD in the Hebrew (*Strong's* 1869, darak) means to string a bow by treading on it in bending, thresh. The Greek word TREAD (*Strong's* 3961, pateo) means to trample down underfoot, with its root word (*Strong's* 3817, paio) meaning to hit as if by a single blow. We fight this spirit corporately, never individually, by treading on its head, striking a single blow, by threshing it in the winepress of the wrath of YHWH, our God, using scripture to crush its head. Basilisk is believed to be most active from the 17th of Tammuz to the 9th of Av on the Jewish calendar, and most particularly active between noon and three PM.[94] The FIERY FLYING SERPENT is a saraph (seraph), another manifestation of basilisk. *(Isaiah 30:6; Numbers 21:6)*

> *...for out of the serpent's root shall come forth a cockatrice, and his fruit shall be a FIERY FLYING SERPENT. (Isaiah 14:29)*

I saw the basilisk spirit leading a gigantic force of demons, entering America over New Smyrna Beach, late last June. It was an enormous dragon. Behind basilisk was a huge black colossus. I stood on the beach as a witness to the invasion force, and knew something terrible was about to happen to America. In July, shark attacks began all over Florida, because the hedge of protection had been lifted from our shores. There were over twenty attacks at New Smyrna Beach, alone.[95] CNN called it the Year of the Shark. I believe this spirit was one of the principalities behind the September 11th attack against America, but its destructive plans are just beginning. Designs against America include, but are not limited to, political upheaval, weakening national security, military conflict, separating us from Israel, destruction of food supplies.

Leviathan: king of the proud

Leviathan (*Strong's* 3882, Livyathan) means a wreathed animal, a serpent, crocodile or large sea monster. Leviathan …*is a king over all the children of pride. (Job 41:34)* This creature is a sea serpent that goes on land as well, a creature of chaos, a dragon which threatens order and creation, and finally, leviathan is a demon. Leviathan personifies evil which YHWH will conquer and slay.

> *Thou brakest the heads of LEVIATHAN in pieces, and gavest him to be meat to the people inhabiting the wilderness. (Psalm 74:14)*

> *In that day the LORD with His sore and great and strong sword shall punish LEVIATHAN the PIERCING serpent, even LEVIATHAN that CROOKED SERPENT; and he shall slay the DRAGON that is in the sea. (Isaiah 27:1)*

The word PIERCING in the above scripture means fleeing, a fugitive. In Canaanite mythology there was a "fleeing serpent" called Lotan, which had seven heads. IT WAS KILLED BY BAAL.

This spirit promotes presumption, spiritual pride, and false humility, stops deliverance, refuses to leave without a battle. *Upon earth there is not his like, who is made without fear. (Job 41:33)* Leviathan breathes fire out of his mouth, just like the dragons of folklore.

> *OUT OF HIS MOUTH GO BURNING LAMPS, and sparks of fire leap out. Out of his NOSTRILS GOETH SMOKE, as out of a seething pot or cauldron. His BREATH KINDLETH COALS, and a flame goeth out of his mouth. (Job 41:19-21)*

Just like the dragons of old, he has scales like a coat of armor.

> *His SCALES are his PRIDE, shut up together as with a close seal. One is so near to another, that no air can come between them. They are joined one to another, they stick together, that they cannot be sundered. (Job 41;15-17)*

He makes the deep boil like a pot with the heat he creates and swiftness with which he moves. *(Job 41:31)* In the Greek language dragon (*Strong's* 1404, drakon) was a fabulous kind of serpent. Dragon in the Old Testament (*Strong's* 8577, tanniyn) was a marine or land monster, sea serpent, serpent. *Webster's* defines leviathan as a sea monster mentioned in the Old Testament. Dragons and dinosaurs walked with man during the time of Job, and he would have been very familiar with leviathan. (Remember that basilisk was a legendary serpent or dragon with lethal breath and glance.) Man and dinosaur certainly walked together as proven by the Paluxy river tracks, which revealed man's footprint next to dinosaur footprints.[96]

Dragons

The chief dragon is Satan, himself. *(Revelation 12:9)* The dragon is also called a serpent in the same sentence. Definitions for dragons, basilisk and leviathan are very similar. *Vine's* denotes dragons as mythical monsters, large serpents, so called because of their keen power of sight, from a root word, derk, meaning to see. Genesis 1:21 and Job 7:12 both translate "tanniyn" as whales, however the word means sea serpent, or marine or land monster. Thus, we see that God Himself created the dragons. Leviathan and dragons are mentioned together in Psalm 74:13-14. Basilisk, the adder and dragon are noted together in Psalm 91:13. Apparently dragons wailed *(Micah 1:8)*, swallowed people up *(Jeremiah 51:34)*, snuffed loudly when they sucked in air *(Jeremiah 14:6)*, lived in dens *(Jeremiah 9:11)*, inhabited dry places *(Isaiah 35:7)*, and were poisonous *(Deuteronomy 32:33)*. They are all to be trampled under out feet. As we tread on serpents, scorpions, dragons and ALL the power of the enemy, we hearken to the scripture in Genesis 3:15 in which the woman was to bruise his (Satan's) heel through her seed, the Savior.

Deception is one of the main tools of leviathan and the dragon, Satan. Leviathan and python are serpentine demons that work together. The similarities between these creatures are undeniable. When python works with leviathan they are harder to cast out. Eliminate the lesser demons that support them and it will be easier. Leviathan digs its tail into a person like python and chokes the life out of its victim. It brings pain in the body, stops spiritual growth because of pride, and causes learning disabilities.[97]

The pride of leviathan smacks of Satan, himself. Leviathan, basilisk and dragons were all real creatures, and all are the names of demons. They will one day be utterly crushed. Satan will be cast into a lake of fire *(Revelation 20:10)*. The book of Job began with Satan going before the LORD and asking to destroy Job. The book ends with the LORD referring to leviathan as a mighty and proud creature whom the LORD made and can also destroy.

He that made him can make His sword to approach unto him. (Job 40:19)

Chapter Twenty-Two
The Spirit of Suicide and the Spirit of Death

Jesus has already won the battle. We must claim the victory! I was speaking at a Women's Aglow when I looked up and saw two women come in together. One wearing dark glasses sat muttering angrily; the other had clearly dragged her there against her will. At the end of the meeting they stood last in line for prayer. When I reached the angry woman she muttered at me in a strange voice, "There's nothing you can do. I'm going to do it!" I said, "Do what? Suicide?" She roared with an unearthly scream and leaped. While she was in mid-air I commanded, "Come out, in Jesus' Name!" She immediately fell backwards and was out cold, delivered of a spirit of suicide. The important thing was not to just get her delivered, but to fill the clean house with God's Word. I told her sister to arrange for someone to stay with her and read her the Word of God around the clock until it was firmly planted in her spirit, filling up the empty space left by the demon.

Another woman at my church had gone forward to receive a ministry gift during an altar call, but was gloriously delivered when I recognized a spirit of depression and suicide riding on her back. I began to minister to her and she began to shake all over and weep. She confessed that she was planning to leave church and kill herself that very day.

People under the influence of the evil spirit of suicide or death have deep feelings of worthlessness, unloveliness, loneliness, uselessness. Suicide and death are murderous spirits that turn inward. They gain access to an individual through fear, self-hatred and depression. Self-hatred is a form of spiritual suicide, and with low self-image operating, one opens oneself up to sickness and disease.[98]

A spirit of death or suicide, and a lying spirit can gain access to a person when they dabble in the occult. That is because there is a death penalty attached to involvement with witchcraft.[99] *(Malachi 3:5; Jeremiah 17:5; Leviticus 20:2-6, 27; 1 Chronicles 10:13)* If you have been involved in any occult activities, repent. (See the chapter, *The Spirit of Python*, for deliverance.) Praise God! We have the victory through the authority (power) God has given us! *(Luke 10:19)*

Deep wounds and hurts must be dealt with or you will never be free. They become points of entry for demons, that will stubbornly stay until the offense, hurt, bitterness or unforgiveness is dealt with. Ask the Holy Spirit to reveal these hurts to you. Ask YHWH to forgive you. Learn to forgive yourself and learn to love yourself. Self-hatred and self-rejection are against God, Who says you are blessed and loved.

Satanic rock band

I used to know the leader of a famous satanic rock band when my brother and I were on the road together. He was a nice Jewish boy from New York. I asked him at various times how he came to write the terrible lyrics that caused teens to commit suicide, why he had a laser light show that destroyed the retinas of their eyes, and used decibel levels that destroyed their eardrums. He told me his band was in Canada touring when a man came along who told them if they would write satanic rock, he would make them stars.

I asked how the song lyrics were composed. He described how the band would assemble in a room and the lyrics would come by automatic writing (a demon literally moves the pen and writes the words). He also told me when their master tape was completed, they took it to a coven and had witches pray over it, so demons would go home with each album purchased and torment the kids to whom they belong. He felt no apparent remorse for the suicides committed because of his albums, and took no responsibility.

This seemed out of character to me, because the person I knew seemed considerate and caring. He was like two different people. I would sit on stage behind the band, high on the amps, watching the crowd become possessed with satanic frenzy, and wonder who was really entertaining out there. He was not tall, but when on stage, he seemed transformed and elevated. I know now that a demonic spirit would enter him and was using him on stage as a catalyst to possess, gain access, enter into and spiritually destroy the audience members.

I want to caution parents about the music to which their children are listening. Many young people and adults receive demonic spirits through music, and during the concerts. (More detail is available in my book, *Jezebel vs. Elijah*, in the chapter entitled *Exposing Pokemon and Other Games*. Music opens the spirit up and renders the mind in a passive state. Then it is easy for the demons to enter. These evil influences must be removed from the home. Take authority over the demons, get rid of demonic posters, tapes, CDs, and books about demonic subjects which can cause an unnatural curiosity to enter a young heart. Closely monitor TV and radio listening. If your child protests what you are doing, then you are probably doing the right thing. Stand up to them lovingly, but firmly. Use your God-given authority. It is up to you to protect your children from bad influences.

Be not deceived: evil communications corrupt good manners. (1 Corinthians 15:33)

The Mound Indians and sumo wrestlers

It is an amazing fact that the land of the USA was cursed by various groups of Native Americans referred to collectively as the Mound Indians, who lived here long ago and left behind large mounds from the Great Lakes to the Gulf of Mexico. There were burial mounds from two to seventy feet high built beginning around one-thousand A.D. They also built platforms of earth on which as many as fifty structures were built. Pyramid temple structures were built from 700 A.D. in the southeast and lasted until the early historic period. The Great Serpent Mound, found in Ohio, is 1,330 feet long. It involves seven serpentine convolutions with the tail section in three coils. An oval embankment, 125 feet long and 60 feet wide, protrudes from the open mouth of this mound.[100] Clearly, serpent worship was part of the religious beliefs of these tribes.

According to Henry Gruver, a man of God who walks cities throughout the world praying and breaking curses at the direction of the LORD, the young people of these tribes rebelled against authority, liked heavy drum beats in their music, danced wildly, engaged in body piercing, putting multiple rings in their ears, nose, eyelids, chest and genitals. They tattooed themselves all over and wore little or no clothing. (Does any of this sound like the young people of today?) They rushed fiercely when attacking their enemies and murdered all strangers they came in contact with. White men were strongly warned to stay away from these rogue Indians when they first started venturing into the Ohio valley wilderness. Mound Indians were known for cursing the land.

Henry Gruver was recently led by God to walk every area in the USA where the Mound Indians had dwelled. The LORD showed him that their curses had profoundly affected and influenced the people to receive a mindset of rebellion and cause our youth to emulate their practices. Think of it: these Indians, through Satan's evil influence, are responsible for rock and roll's evil influence, the bizarre behavior of our youth today, and have left the land cursed under Satan's authority, until the Holy Spirit found someone to begin breaking the satanic curses, ridding our land of this evil spirit of rebellion, demon worship.

Henry Gruver tells another story of prayer walking in Japan. He went up to a mountain where sumo wrestlers abuse young boys and then throw them down to their deaths. On the path where the bodies fell nothing grew, no vegetation. There was a curse on the land. Henry prayed, remitting the sins committed in that place, and vegetation began to grow there again.

Rebellion

Rebellion enters a child from allowing evil influences, and the lyrics, music and lifestyle of rock stars to work on them.

And have no fellowship with the unfruitful works of darkness… (Ephesians 5:11)

If you, yourself, were rebellious and have not repented, your children will follow in your footsteps. Repent and ask God for His forgiveness before you proceed with your children. You have, in effect, cursed them through your own actions. The sins of the fathers are visited on the children.

Hag attack

I was leading worship one morning at a women's meeting. Afterward, the woman in charge decided to let her trainees practice prophesying on those who were there. One of these women turned and gave me a spooky, wild-eyed look. (The Holy Spirit told me to leave, but I felt a strong pressure holding me down.) She began prophesying evil word curses against me. I was so oppressed by her prophecy that I began to feel physically ill. The other three "prophetesses" jumped on the bandwagon and began giving me more evil "words." Finally, the woman in charge stopped them, but corrected only the last one. I left, feeling beat up, weak, sick, and definitely under attack. By late afternoon, I was crying my eyes out and having thoughts of depression and suicide.

A friend called long distance for prayer, but when he found out the state I was in, he asked me what the women looked like. I described them and he pronounced it a "hag attack." In his church there was a beauty queen with a handsome, wealthy husband. Several women in the church were jealous of her, and they gathered around her "prophesying" death on her husband. The elders in the church had to rebuke them and break the power of the curses spoken. When this kind of attack occurs, it stems from a spirit of envy, jealousy, hatred, hurts, or some other evil influence.

If you find yourself under this kind of attack, don't sit quietly. (Personally, I will *not* sit still for another assault of this kind.) Right then and there, specifically break the words spoken in Jesus' Name, render them null and void and cancel their assignment against you. Bind (and if the circumstance permits, cast out) the evil spirit operating *through* the person, but show love to the person. Exposing the devil's schemes may not always be the popular move, but it must be done.

Take this thought

Picture a hideously ugly imp sitting on your shoulder whispering in your ear. The words are heard in your mind as if they are your own thoughts. Often they are unlovely thoughts about others or yourself, angry thoughts, thoughts of defeat and failure, or self-pity. You have a choice! The demon won't tell you that you have a choice; it's something you must learn by renewing your mind to the Word of God. "Take this thought, take this thought: I am a loser; they really do treat me badly; I deserve to fail; after all, I failed before; no one really cares about how I feel; how dare they say that to me? Who do they think they are? I guess I'm just not good enough, smart enough, rich enough, fast enough, tall enough, educated enough, experienced enough…"

The thoughts from the enemy come *before* the manifestation. If the demon can get you to take his thought, then he can establish a stronghold in your mind. First, he wants you to receive the thought; then believe it. Once you believe it, it will begin to bring forth fruit, manifesting through anger, rejection, sickness, offences. You will actually begin to fail at a task you were previously able to perform. Sometimes we get mad at God when we are taking and acting on these thoughts. We blame God for our failures. God has proclaimed a lot of wonderful things about us in His Word, yet we choose to believe the evil report of the enemy, even when it's fraught with lies. Remember, God didn't permit these things to happen, you did. Resolve right now to change your life!

Make a list of every bad thing you believe about yourself, and that others have asserted about you, your life, finances, children, jobs, etc. Look at it! Every one of these evil reports on this list came from the enemy. He may have begun the attack against you in the womb, so that it looks like you did it to yourself. Rest assured, he is relentlessly pursuing you to bring defeat to your doorstep.

When I was pregnant with my third son, I took a tour of the hospital facilities where he would be born. They showed me the new room where I would deliver and a special room where women with high blood pressure delivered. When they spoke the word eclampsia something rushed at my face and fear tried to attach itself to me. For the next two months this spirit would rush at me several times a day, repeating eclampsia over and over in my ear, trying to get me to receive this physical problem into my body. At first, I would say, "No, I won't take this thought, in Jesus' Name!" Then I began to simply and firmly say, "No, in Jesus' Name!" Soon it stopped. I had a normal delivery with no complications. However, I want to emphasize that the demon was persistent, trying to wear me down with his determination. I knew that I was already victorious, but I had to stand in the authority Jesus gave me.

…because greater is He that is in you, than he that is in the world. (1 John 4:4)

The Battle is the LORD's

We arrive already victorious! Evil thoughts are like a house made of cards: One breath from the Holy Spirit and they all fall down. Stand on a scripture and speak it every time an evil thought comes. This defeats the enemy.

A woman called me long distance in a desperate state. Her very demonized son was about to be committed to an asylum. I prayed for him and broke the demons' power, loosing him from them. She called back a few days later to say that he was so much improved, they had decided not to commit him.

John G. Lake once received a request from a man at one of his meetings to pray for a relative who had been committed to an insane asylum in England. As John entered into prayer his spirit was translated to England. He entered the asylum and cast the demon out of the woman, then his spirit returned to his body. A few days later, her relatives contacted him and said she had left the asylum in her right mind and was completely free. I believe we will see more and more miracles of this kind as the day fast approaches for the return of our Messiah. If we make ourselves available to Him, He can use us to do great exploits, and set the captives free.

Chapter Twenty-Three
The Spirit of Fear

How fear gets in

Fear is a chief prince that has destroyed many. Because of fear we allow ourselves to become subject to bondage. Fear can be very real, extending to phobias, addictions, fear of authority, worry, nervousness, paranoia, schizophrenia, stress, confusion. A root of fear may cause an inferiority complex or bedwetting. It may cause a person to be unable to speak in public or forget what they were supposed to say. I had a recurring nightmare for many years in which I would walk out on a stage and forget all my lines. I took authority over the wicked spirit that caused this nightmare and cast it out. The dreams stopped immediately. A person with this spirit will not feel safe and secure, and may transfer this fear to their children. Demons will congregate around a fearful person and begin manifesting in their house, or appear by the bed at night. Mare is an evil spirit that attacks people in their dreams, producing nightmares.

The spirit of fear gained access to mankind through guilt from sin. Fear entered the human heart in the Garden of Eden.

> *...I heard Thy voice in the garden, and I was AFRAID. (Genesis 3:10)*

The conscience knows it is guilty and subconsciously knows punishment is coming. Unrepented sin brings a spirit of fear. Fear of death enters in and the roller coaster ride begins. If left unchecked, it can end up in insanity, obsessive-compulsive behavior or mental illness. One woman I ministered to was completely immobilized, unable to leave her house where she kept it dark because of fear. Fear can enter a child who is terrorized or neglected. Fear brings terrible bondage: phobias, worry, fretting, dread, nightmares, torment, terror, sickness, fear of death, timidity, anxiety, nervousness, stuttering, stress and heart attacks, fear of disease, fear of loss of control (which can invite in a controlling spirit). Fear is lack of faith in our God, and His ability to save us from destruction. The opposite of fear is faith.

Fear causes a myriad of diseases. Among them are asthma, allergies, angina, ulcerative colitis, acne, heart problems, etc.[101] If we deal with the root of fear and cast it out, people will be healed. *(Luke 21:26)*

Living with witches

When I was in college I moved into a big house with two girls I didn't know, as an emergency place to live. They turned out be drug-dealing witches who positively hated me. They gave me some drugged food and fixed me up with a demon-possessed man, who took me to vampire movies at the drive-in. I started to see vampires everywhere and kept screaming until he took me home and raped me, spreading my blood everywhere. Then he stole my car and left. The witches came in and opened the window, luring me to jump. A psychic friend, who was 6'4", 250 pounds, intervened by racing two blocks down the street and carrying me out. The witches did not mess with him. A spirit of fear entered me that night, and the witches began cursing me, causing all kinds of havoc in my life. The next day my friend found my car by psychic power, stormed in and recovered it for me. He moved me into his house and took care of me while I recovered from drug addiction. During that time the witches and their friends were busted and blamed me, necessitating round-the-clock protection.

Attacked by grizzly demon

When I had my own house a few months later, a demon-possessed man, roaring loudly like an enormous grizzly bear, attacked my house trying to get in, and beat on the walls hard enough to shake the whole house and crack the plaster. I was so afraid that sweat poured off me in great puddles, my mouth went dry and I trembled so hard that I could not dial the phone. A pizza in the oven began to burn and smoke, yet I stood by the door shaking, with a knife and hammer in my hands. When I finally was successful in dialing the police, the phone went dead in my hand. It was then that I realized I had left the lights on, and that he was standing two feet away, right outside my window, looking in. After turning the lights out, the attack continued for about another hour. Incredibly, none of the neighbors heard it. After the attack was over, I ran to my landlady's house, but she didn't believe me, refusing to let me use her phone, until I showed her my cut phone line and cracked plaster. I was doing summer stock theater at the time with Ken Harper, then husband of actress Tess Harper. He gave me a 45 caliber gun. The next time I was attacked, I called the police right away and their comment was, "Why did you call us? You have a cannon sitting right there, but it will probably break your arm if you use it!"

Satan sends more troops

Next, my boyfriend inexplicably flipped out and attacked me outside the club where I was singing, striking me across the left side of the face. I ran and locked myself in my car, then drove to the police station, but they would not come out. I drove home but he blocked my car and beat on the window all night, trying to get in. Satan was working me over with fear, and I could not trust anyone. I got drunk one night and drove off a cliff at Silver Dollar City in my Volkswagen Beetle. There was only one small place that was not smashed flat and I was in it. It was a miracle that I was still alive, and it took a long time to pry me out. The emergency room man in Branson, who sewed my nose back together, made lewd passes at me; the policeman who took me home threatened me, trying to get information. Fear begets fear and draws demonic attacks to you, as more and more demons circled for the kill.

Shot in Kansas City

When I came back to Kansas City, I was shot in the head by a stranger at the Colony Steak House, where my brother and I were playing with our band. The man escaped and was never caught. In the emergency room they dug out the bullet, x-rayed the wound, washed it with salt water and released me. Now, I had a whopping headache and a lot more fear. My brother's friend, who was a nurse, took me to her house, where she and a man tried to hold me down and rape me. My brother arrived in the nick of time and took me home. The next night at the club I sat paralyzed with dread in a corner, watching everyone suspiciously, but my brother told me that if I didn't get back on stage that night, I never would.

The next club we played suddenly hired exotic dancers to perform before, during and after our show. The new, rude clientele started throwing beer cans and bottles at us as we performed. When we wanted to leave, the club owner said we would never live to tell the story, and we were forced to fulfill the contract. Ironically, he was found dead in the trunk of his car a few months later. Several clubs we played burned to the ground. Fortunately, an informant told us in order to salvage our equipment. Another club owner we worked for pulled out his gun at midnight every night for no apparent reason, and started shooting. One night I saw him turn the gun on me. I fell down to avoid being shot and sprained my ankle. I worked in a Las Vegas review for a while, during which time a club owner decided he owned me, informing me I could not leave his club to work elsewhere. I had to get my lawyer, who was Irish mafia, to bring his friends to protect me from the Italian mafia, while I made my escape and hopped a plane. Over the years people tried to break into my hotel room on several occasions. I've been chased down dark streets several times and had guns held on me. I have a list of seventy-five disasters that happened to me during the next few years: plane crashes, towering infernos, etc.

Jesus, my deliverer

Satan sends circumstances to try to destroy all of us. Many terrible things happened to me, but I am still here because SOMEONE WAS PRAYING FOR ME all those years, standing in the gap, never giving up on what must have looked like a hopeless case, until I accepted Jesus Christ as my LORD and Savior. The man who prayed for me came to my wedding, and when he went through the reception line he shook my hand so hard, it felt as if it would break. He asked, "Are you home to stay?" When I responded in the affirmative, he whistled and blew loudly, shaking his head. Two weeks later, he went home to be with Jesus. I thank God for this dedicated man. Prayer really does work.

It should be clear after all this to anyone that the devil had a plan for my life, but God had a much better plan, and sent His intercessor to stand in the gap for me.

Fears

1. Fears, phobias: *...every man's heart shall melt: And they shall be afraid... (Isaiah 13:7-8)*
2. Torment, horror: *Fearfulness and trembling are come upon me, and horror hath overwhelmed me. (Psalm 55:5)*
3. Heart attacks, terror: *My heart is sore pained within me: and the terrors of death are fallen upon me. (Psalm 55:4)*
   Men's hearts are failing them for fear. (Luke 21:26)
4. Fear of death: *...deliver them who through fear of death were all their lifetime subject to bondage. (Hebrews 2:14-15)*
5. Nightmares, terrors, dread: *Thou shalt not be afraid for the terror by night... (Psalm 91:5)*
6. Distrust, doubt: *Why are ye fearful, O ye of little faith? (Matthew 8:26)*
   But the fearful, and unbelieving...have their part in the lake which burneth with fire and brimstone... (Revelation 21:8)
7. Fear of man: *The fear of man bringeth a snare... (Proverbs 29:25)*

God's protection

God has given us His Word that He will cover us with His feathers, and hide us in His secret place. *(Psalm 91:1)* He has given us boldness to stand and take back what the enemy has stolen. He has given us:

Power (authority) to tread on serpents and scorpions, and over all the power of the enemy: and nothing shall by any means hurt you. (Luke 10:19)

…but whoso putteth his trust in the LORD shall be safe., (Proverbs 29:25)

Let not your heart be troubled… (John 14:1, 27)

Men's hearts may fail them for fear, but our God is a strong tower, and we can run into it and be safe. *(Proverbs 18:10)* This is contingent upon learning to dwell in His secret place. This requires speaking our faith and trusting in God's ability to deliver us in times of trouble.

He that DWELLETH in the secret place of the Most High shall ABIDE under the shadow of the Almighty. I will SAY of the LORD, He is my refuge and my fortress: my God, in Him will I TRUST. (Psalm 91:1-2)

Deliverance

1. Rebuke a spirit of fear and cast it out. Break the stronghold of fear off yourself and others.
2. Resist the temptation to entertain thoughts that are anxious, fearful, fretting, etc.
3. Bind faith to yourself. Choose not to fear.
4. Bind a spirit of power and love and a sound mind to yourself. *(2 Timothy 1:7)*
5. Bind a spirit of adoption to yourself. *(Romans 8:15)*
6. Learn scriptures that build trust and confidence in YHWH, our God. When my children were small, they began to be attacked by nightmares. I helped them memorize Psalm 91, Luke 10:19, and Isaiah 54:17. When they were afraid, they would speak out these scriptures and command the devil to go in Jesus' Name. Now they are empowered to handle these situations themselves, and they do so boldly.
7. Bind peace and God's safety to yourself.
8. Ask God to send His angels to surround and protect you, and to go before you into every place you go to prepare the way. *(Exodus 23:20)*

Twenty-Four
The Spirits of Anxiety and Confusion

Anxiety

Anxiety comes in through fear. It is defined in *Webster's* as intense dread, apprehension, nagging worry or uncertainty. Anxiety manifests in phobias and paranoia. Anxiety is crippling and can hold a victim helpless in a darkened house for long periods of time, or prevent a person from even experiencing simple things like going up in an elevator, driving a car, or climbing a ladder. A person may live his whole life, never experiencing the joy of the LORD because of dread, fretting over imagined things that haven't even happened. That is why God tells us to take authority over VAIN IMAGINATIONS that are really STRONGHOLDS in the mind, and bring EVERY THOUGHT CAPTIVE to Christ.

> *...pulling down STRONGHOLDS; Casting down IMAGINATIONS, and every HIGH thing that exalteth itself AGAINST the knowledge of God, and bringing into CAPTIVITY EVERY THOUGHT to the obedience of Christ. (2 Corinthians 10:4-5)*

The word HIGH thing really means "proud" thing. Any evil thought that exalts itself above or against YHWH is wicked and prideful. Begin to train your mind to defeat the evil thoughts Satan wants to plant there. Being in bondage to wicked thoughts is a terrible way to live.

Carefulness

Our loving Father instructs us to:

> *Be CAREFUL for nothing: but in everything by prayer and supplication with thanksgiving let your requests be made known unto God. (Philippians 4:6)*

CAREFUL (*Vine's*, merimnao) means to be anxious, to draw in different directions, distract. When we are drawn in different directions, then we are not on God's straight and narrow path. We are running here and there, inviting in a spirit of confusion. If only we could get a clear picture of God's peace and order, and realize that God can handle our problems! He's older and wiser than us, bigger and stronger than us, and best of all, He knows the future and we do not.

Worry

Can you add one day to your life by worrying? No! In fact, you will cut your life short by being anxious. The LORD desires us to live in His place of safety, His secret place.

> *I will both lay me down in peace, and sleep: for Thou, LORD only makest me dwell in SAFETY. (Psalm 4:8)*

SAFETY (*Strong's* 983, betach) stands for a place of refuge, to be and feel safe, assurance, hope, boldness, confidence, security, care (less). In other words, I couldn't care less, because I know and trust God has me in the PALM OF HIS HAND.

> *Behold, I have graven thee upon the PALMS OF MY HANDS; thy walls are continually before me. (Isaiah 49:16)*

Look carefully at this next scripture.

> *The Name of the LORD is a strong tower: the righteous runneth into it, and is SAFE. (Proverbs 18:10)*

SAFE, in this scripture (*Strong's* 7682, sagab), means inaccessible, defend, exalt, be excellent, set up, be exceedingly strong. God is declaring that He will defend you, be strong for you, make you inaccessible to the enemy if you will totally trust Him!

Confusion

Anxiety brings confusion. A spirit of confusion brings insanity. Insane asylums are full of confused people. The more yielded a person is to demonic influence, the more demons will be present. *(Mark 5:2-5)* A confused person cannot receive truth, their faith wavers and they refuse to listen to solid, godly advice. They will run forward again and again to be "saved." Conversation with a person who has this spirit is disjointed and nonsensical. Thinking is muddled and it seems like the lights are on but no one is home. Sexual sin may be a root problem. The confused person struggles but doesn't seem to improve. God intended us to have sound minds *(2 Timothy 1:7)* and gave us POWER to overcome the enemy.

Behold, I give unto you POWER to tread on serpents and scorpions, and over all the power of the enemy: and NOTHING SHALL by ANY means HURT YOU. (Luke 10:19)

If God has given us this POWER, then why are so many people fearful, anxious and confused? I believe it is because the LORD told us to STAND *(Ephesians 6:14),* and instead we have done the opposite: STAND DOWN. (See section on *Military Readiness*)

Confusion (*Vine's*, akatastasia) represents instability, state of disorder, disturbance, tumult. Taking apart this word is *very* revealing. "Kata" connotes "down," and "stasis" indicates "a standing." Put them together and they mean STAND DOWN! When is the best time for an enemy to attack? When you are not ready, of course. God wants you to STAND in military readiness at all times. *(Ephesians 6:13-14)* The enemy of your soul wants you to STAND DOWN, let down your guard, your alertness. He doesn't want you to recognize his wiles. He wants to lull you into a stupor with the spirit of slumber and ultimately CONFUSE you, until you are a useless casualty. That's what he likes: useless, helpless, hopeless Christians.

As I minister all over the country, I have observed an increase in confusion among Christians. I usually lay hands on the back of their heads and loose them from the confuser's attack, then pray for restoration of their thinking patterns. Sometimes it is a simple adjustment; other times it is a longer process. The devil has gained access to the thought patterns and set up a stronghold in the victim's mind, which must be brought into the obedience of Christ. *(2 Corinthians 10:4-5)* Transformation of the mind through the Word, replacing old, wicked thought patterns with the pure written scripture involves reading the Word, memorizing the Word and meditating on the Word.

And be not conformed to this world: but be ye transformed by the renewing of your mind... (Romans 12:2)

God's plan

God has a better plan for you! He has given you the weapons and Words to defeat the enemy. The way to fight CONFUSION is through the fruit of the Spirit, peace.

For God is NOT the author of CONFUSION, but of PEACE... (1 Corinthians 14:33)

ENVYING and STRIFE can bring CONFUSION. Loose yourself from these evil spirits and thought patterns, for they are sin. Make them leave you and your home.

For where ENVYING and STRIFE is, there is CONFUSION (disorder) and every evil work. (James 3:16)

Just recently my eldest son came into the living room after he had been put to bed. He reported that he looked out his window to see the moon, and instead saw a demon in the form of a hideous bat, with red glowing eyes, clinging to his window. It wanted to enter his room but he said, "In the Name of Jesus Christ, leave and don't come back!" It fled in terror. He lay down and slept peacefully. Teaching children how to defeat the enemy is vital to all families, for the devil has an aggressive plan to destroy them. (See steps for deliverance in the *Spirit of Fear* section.) Bind scriptures to yourself that are God's solutions to the devil's attacks against your mind, and repent for allowing the enemy of your soul to pervert your thought life. If you are being attacked in your dreams with anxiety, fear, worry, etc., then take the following steps:

1. Take authority over your dreams by rebuking the devil off them.
2. Command him to release your dreams.
3. Plead the blood of Jesus over your dreams.
4. Put on your armor, especially the helmet of salvation.
5. Ask God to protect your dreams and send His angels to guard you as you sleep.
6. Bind scriptures to yourself that apply to protection while sleeping. The following are good ones, but search for others, too.

I will both lay me down in PEACE, and sleep: for Thou, LORD, only makest me dwell in safety. (Psalm 4:8)

...thou shalt lie down, and thy sleep shall be sweet. (Proverbs 3:24)

Chapter Twenty-Five
The Religious Spirit

Legalism and stopping the gift of prophecy

The religious spirit works with a spirit of legalism (Pharisee spirit), a controlling spirit, a spirit of bondage and a spirit of haughtiness to keep the Holy Spirit out. Yahshua (Jesus) came against this spirit several times. A church with a religious spirit spends a lot of time accusing the members of sin, and teaching, sometimes in veiled ways, that God is not a God of integrity, and He will not always do what He says he will do. Legalism oppresses women, who are told to be silent and submit to husbands who demand submission, but refuse to follow God's wise council to love their wives as Christ loves the church, and gave Himself for her. These women are seldom allowed to move in the things of the LORD. Often, but not always, there will be dress codes, spoken and unspoken, and frequent contention and strife. This may be concealed from the congregation for a time, but will filter down to them anyway, in their homes and church activities. The religious spirit quenches true agape love.

If someone in the congregation moves in the gift of prophecy they will be hushed, removed. New restrictive rules will be instituted. The religious leadership fears exposure. One prophet was denounced from the pulpit when he tried to prophesy a word the pastor didn't want him to say, and subsequently driven from the church. Another tactic of a controlling or religious spirit is to hush, subjugate and constrict the prophetic voice. Prophetic words must go through discouraging, difficult channels, allowing others to decide if it is "acceptable" to speak. The Bible instructs us to let two or three prophesy, and the others judge, not stifle the prophetic word before it's even spoken. *(1 Corinthians 14:29, 31, 39)* A few public corrections by godly leadership would stop any false prophesying. Then the true prophetic voice could be lovingly nurtured. In 1996 a church in Houston had their pulpit literally split in two by the power of God on Sunday morning. With this sign from the LORD, the leadership yielded up control of the church and congregation to the direction of the Holy Spirit, and they've been in revival ever since.

Quenches healing

A large church's worship leader asked me to come and minister, and the LORD gave me specific directions how to set the captives free and heal the sick. I did not know it but the church didn't allow women to minister. A strong religious spirit had brought everyone under bondage. No one had been healed in a long time. One of the pastors who taught the night classes had instructed the people that God really didn't heal much, and they shouldn't get their hopes up. The senior pastor was new because the first pastor had run off with his secretary, after preaching heavy legalistic bondage on the men and women concerning marriage. What a mess!

Smashing strongholds

The first thing I did in the two Sunday morning services was use my sword to break strongholds, and sing *"Armor of God."* Then I ministered *"Stripes"* for healing. Immediately, after the song was over, I called out words of knowledge, then asked everyone who was healed to stand. Almost thirty people stood in each service. Several people told me afterward that a huge angel stood behind me and drew his sword when I drew mine, ministering with me. A number of women hugged me and thanked me for setting them free from legalistic bondage. The anointing breaks the yoke.

Persecution for the Word's sake

On the following Wednesday, a letter arrived from the night school pastor, denouncing what I had done. He contended that if I was going to *bludgeon* people with Isaiah 53 (I spoke the scripture once), the least I could do was *balance* it by teaching on suffering and death. He was serious! After all, that is what he was doing. No one had faith for healing in his church, and He wanted it that way: helpless, hopeless people under his control. (Members of the congregation who needed healing would sneak off to a little church a few miles away that taught faith in God's healing power, and often received miracles.) He further stated he was sending copies of his letter to all the other pastors he knew, to stop the ministry, which was everyone.

I thought God had betrayed and deserted me. I wailed and cried for three days and would not leave my bed, believing that my ministry was over. Finally, on Friday evening, the LORD spoke to me and said, "Are you done?" I sheepishly said I was. Then, he told me to clean up and go to a church where His servant was the pastor. He was one who had been forced out of the church for trying to speak a prophetic word. When I arrived, the pastor immediately called me up to minister to the sick. Many were healed, delivered and lay slain in the Spirit for hours. Among other things, God taught me the lesson that persecution comes for the Word's sake, and I learned to rejoice *through* the fiery trials.

Stops the true work of the Holy Spirit

The religious spirit is pervasive in the church. Through pride, it seeks to control the true works of the Holy Spirit, and restrict or prevent His operation. Leadership who are threatened, fearful, who acquiesce to the wishes of others, afraid to take a stand, will never see the Holy Spirit move, because they keep a tight fist on everything, and the Holy Spirit is grieved. He will not come where He is not welcome. Only in congregations where controlling and religious spirits are vigilantly kept out, will He come. To be released from the terrible bondage of a religious spirit, humble yourself. Ask forgiveness of others you may have oppressed, and set them free from your judgments. Tell the religious spirit it is no longer welcome and cast it out in Jesus Name. Repent and ask God's forgiveness for allowing the religious spirit to operate. Pray for the Holy Spirit to open your eyes to every area where the religious spirit is operating. Resist the temptation to take back control when things do not go exactly as you planned.

Chapter Twenty-Six
The Controlling Spirit

When people subject themselves to someone with a controlling spirit, they place themselves under enslavement to a demon. The controller is a manipulator and must use witchcraft to achieve his ends. Some religious leaders seek to control "their" flocks by demanding a performance level that puts the people in deep bondage. These leaders are being blinded by fear of the loss of control of finances, or fear of not enough finances (which is unbelief), or fear that there won't be enough workers. Some are motivated by such pride that they think the sheep cannot follow or hear from God on their own. The nature of Satan is that he looks for both weaknesses and strengths that already exist in individuals to exploit. It is especially easy if there are generational familiars at work.

Fear in leadership

Some leaders fear that the people will get into sin unless they are constantly condemning them and putting them under bondage. The message of grace is never preached, because it is considered dangerous. They behave as if the people are their personal property, not adequately encouraging the gifts, quenching the moving of the Holy Spirit through the people. They fear exposure, behaving as if the book of Galatians is not in their Bibles. I've heard it said that grace is the divine influence on the heart that empowers people to do God's work. If these leaders truly understood grace, they would set the people free. The controlling pastor or leader is not trusting God to meet his needs, so he resorts to manipulation and witchcraft to control the people. I know of one church that had the people recite out loud their creed every Sunday. Included in this litany is a vow to give and tithe, and be loyal to *that* church. The sheep don't realize they are being compelled, controlled and manipulated by these ungodly vows. In some situations, a leader orders the flock not to go to meetings at certain places. Some leaders hound their congregations for tithes, and manipulate the people to give beyond their means.

An example I witnessed of manipulation happened on a beautiful summer evening. A sweet family had just purchased a beautiful van. When the pastor saw it in the parking lot he remarked loudly that he'd had a dream in which God had given him a van exactly like it, and how much he needed a new van. The family felt guilty for having a new van, and under pressure, gave the pastor their new van. He bragged continually about the new van *God* gave him but everyone knew he had gotten it with his own manipulations.

One large church asked a tremendous teacher to come who taught on grace. He spoke eloquently on freedom to love and serve the living God. The leadership panicked and verbalized privately, "How will we control the people and keep them from living in sin without keeping them under the law?" When the teacher would not change his message, they threw him out. They believed their job was to keep people holy by putting guilt and bondage on them.

The controller may operate with religious fanaticism. Rigid or finicky demands on housekeeping are common. Harsh treatment of the children is often observed. The tyrannical church leader is extreme in his rejection of other leaders or churches. Those who follow him must exhibit his same views or be fired. He will usually be hard to work with, demanding and unreasonable on certain issues. The controller will have a high turnover in personnel on the job and in the church. The controller may manipulate by using body language, yelling, cursing, pouting, threatening physically or emotionally, or through blackmail. These are all forms of witchcraft. The controller may even pray controlling prayers, which are witchcraft prayers.

Often, the person with a controlling spirit is motivated by fear. If he lets go, he fears chaos, and suffers from lack of trust in God to perform His Word. Therefore, the controller suffers from doubt and unbelief in religious and personal matters. The pastor with a controlling spirit is afraid the people won't give enough, or afraid they might run off to another church and stay.

The attack

When I was new in the LORD, my pastor, who had a controlling spirit, wanted me to use my musical gift to promote his church. When I was asked by a visiting minister to sing at his church in a different city, I was thrilled and instantly sensed that God wanted to use me there. In the parking lot, as I walked to my car, I overheard my pastor telling his wife that he was not going to let me go because he was afraid I would never come back. I was shocked, but managed to get in my car and start home. I thought at the time I had to submit to the unreasonable demands of the pastor and do whatever he wanted. Demons of jealousy, witchcraft and controlling spirits fiercely attacked me when I got to the bridge over the Missouri river. I nearly wrecked before I could command them to go in Jesus' Name. My pastor had unleashed wicked spirits to keep me under his control.

I learned, from this incident, to take authority over controlling spirits the second they begin to manifest. When I finally did minister in the other city, three people were dramatically healed while I sang. One had been dying of an incurable disease. Shortly thereafter, my husband and I left the church we were attending to lead worship elsewhere, after discovering our pastor was in adultery again, after being disciplined for this a couple of years earlier. Later, it was discovered he was a pedophile, too. He lost his church about a year later, and passed away recently, bitter and blaming God for his own failures.

Financial control

A friend came to me and confessed that two different pastors attempted to force him to give them money through control, fear, manipulation and witchcraft. He was turned off to "religion" and wondered if this was right. If God's people would understand that using control and manipulation to gain finances is witchcraft, I believe they would quit and begin trusting in YHWH Jireh, our God Who is more than enough, to supply our needs.

When a person controls others it is witchcraft. God specifically states in His Word that if a person wishes to be great in His kingdom he must be willing to serve others, not lord it over them. ...*whosoever will be chief among you, let him be your servant. (Matthew 20:25)*

Husbands who control their wives and vice versa, through extreme demands, manipulation and forced subservience, are sinning against God. Husbands or wives with controlling spirits often demand to have an accounting of every penny spent and oppress their families under extreme strictness and rigidity. A spouse cannot leave the house without being grilled about her/his every move. A spirit of jealousy, division and strife will accompany the controlling spirit. The controller may exhibit anger if the spouse is gone too long. Fear may enter into the oppressed spouse, or motivate the controller to operate in jealousy. Anger and pouting may be used in an attempt to dominate and control others.

The proper exercise of authority blesses those under it. People are turned off to God when they are put in bondage and forced to obey, not out of love, but out of fear or duty. All submission is to be voluntary. **Love is a greater motivator than fear of punishment**. God longs for us to voluntarily follow Him, not out of duty, but out of love. Each person is free in Christ to obey. This is part of our privilege. (Wives, there is a difference between godly submission to your husband and submitting to a demon.) Controllers aren't willing to serve, but desire others to serve them.

Humility is the key to great leadership. One who yells and demands that others submit is not leading according to biblical standards. Following someone who manifests this behavior is, in reality, following a demon that is using the person. People under this kind of leadership may be stressed, sick (physically or emotionally), fearful and deeply wounded. The likelihood that they will take up offenses and be bitter is very high. Conversely, people under godly leadership will be blessed and honored to follow, not to mention willing.

Paradigm for leadership

The doctrine of the Nicolaitanes is an abomination to the LORD. They lorded it over the flock and exalted themselves, forcing the people to serve them. *(Revelation 2:6,15)* A correct paradigm for true godly leadership of any kind, whether it is in the church, home or workplace, is not a standard pyramid with the leader at the top demanding to be served, abusing his position and authority, with the congregation, or family at the bottom. God's model reveals that the pyramid should be reversed, with the point down: God's people at the wide top, and the leadership at the bottom serving the people, is His righteous design. Husbands who always demand their wives serve them will not have a truly happy home, until they learn to get into the trenches and serve their families. It is not enough to work and come home and sit, demanding to be waited on. This devalues and dishonors the wife. This will cause deep resentment in the wife. Whether it shows or not, she will know deep down that she is not honored or valued. Likewise, the wife should not expect a true demonstration of loving leadership if she constantly complains, refuses to allow the husband to take his rightful place of authority in the home, and usurps authority that has been delegated elsewhere.

Our love for God will fill us with a desire to live holier than ten thousand rules. Telling people of the love of God is a far better way to win souls than using fear and control to get them to accept Him. Salvation is more likely to be genuine when it is received through a heart of love. If a person comes to God through fear, what is to keep them serving Him when the lure of sin is strong. The person is more likely to fall away, unable to deal with the shame and guilt, because they see God as a cruel task master. A person like this will run *from* God, instead of *to* the arms of a loving God, Who is filled with mercy and love.

Repentance

A person with a controlling spirit can, and sometimes does, repent. One pastor at a large church repented publicly after attending a revival. He was deeply convicted of controlling and manipulating the flock, and of his own fear of revival. He secretly thought the people would go wild and he would lose control. Instead, the whole church went into several months of revival, with much weeping, repenting, worship and renewal.

Steps for repentance from a controlling spirit

1. If you have used control, which is really witchcraft, to manipulate others, regardless of whether the motivation for your actions is from fear or ignorance, repent!
2. Ask for God's forgiveness and mercy.
3. Cast out the controlling spirit and resist the temptation to take it up again.
4. Cast out a spirit of fear, deception, witchcraft, murder (if there has been any anger or violence), and any other spirit that is operating and manifesting.
5. Ask the Holy Spirit to reveal areas where you are operating in this spirit. Pray for strength, guidance and wisdom to stop.
6. Learn to hate this sin and the behaviors that go with it.
7. Some controlling behaviors include, but are not limited to: whining, complaining, anger, violence, suspiciousness, playing sick, demanding, shouting, cursing, lying, pouting, slamming things, murmuring, threatening, stubbornness, loud talking, manipulation, micro-managing, inability to delegate, selfishness, self-centeredness, inability to see from others point-of-view, etc.
8. Resist the devil and his schemes to destroy you. Resist the temptation, no matter how things seem, to allow yourself to control or be controlled.
9. Sometimes it seems easier to allow abuse to continue. God is not pleased if you allow a demonic stronghold in your life.

Chapter Twenty-Seven
The Jezebel Spirit

A person with a Jezebel spirit has a combination of wicked spirits working together to form a Jezebel spirit: a controlling spirit, antichrist spirit, a spirit of seduction, lying spirits, a spirit of whoredoms, deception, manipulation, witchcraft, divination, lethargy, a spirit of murder, slumber, error, haughtiness, familiar spirits, doubt and unbelief. This spirit is so powerful that in its presence one feels weak, lethargic, helpless, sometimes unable to move limbs. It is a very strong antichrist spirit and seeks to silence (Jezebel killed) the true prophets. Someone with this spirit will never admit he or she is wrong but will manifest a controlling spirit gone off the deep end out of control. A Jezebel will call herself a prophet, and try to align herself with prophets. She prophesies by a familiar spirit. Jezebel will claim to intercede but never does. Jezebel usurps authority. She may display intense anger and throw fits in order to manipulate and control. They will flatter their victims first to win them over, then turn against them. When trying to minister to a person with a Jezebel spirit, the person may sit steaming in silence, refusing to listen or plotting revenge. Or they may take a different tack, and wear you out, sucking the life out of you as you attempt to minister to them. In the end, they walk away in a huff and the minister is totally drained. He/she may lash out in a vicious counter-attack that is devastating. Those who follow Jezebel will be condemned with her.[102]

Difference between controlling spirit and Jezebel spirit

The difference between the controlling spirit and the Jezebel spirit is not to be taken lightly. There are many people running around accusing others of having a Jezebel spirit when the accused person really has a controlling spirit. Falsely accusing people we feel threatened by, is inappropriate. One must be careful not to start slinging names around. Just because someone has a forceful personality does not mean she/he has a Jezebel spirit, however both the controlling and the Jezebel spirit operate through witchcraft.

A person with a controlling spirit *can* be brought to repentance, but Jezebel never repented; people with Jezebel spirits *rarely* repent. Jezebel manifests a much deeper apostasy than someone who has a controlling spirit. She promotes deviation from the truth of the gospel. She uses and destroys the saints and prophets in order to accomplish her agenda: to turn the people's hearts away from the true God. She is vengeful and wanton in her pursuit of power and lusts of the flesh. She is a master deceiver.

Jezebel seeks worship

Jezebel seeks to be worshipped, using sorcery and manipulation. Jezebel questions the manhood or ability of others, making them feel small. Jezebel is the cause of many divorces. A married person with this spirit will drive his or her spouse to sink into alcohol, TV, adultery, material success, bury themselves in their work, social clubs, the children, excessive golf or other sports, sleep, or the newspaper to escape the wrath of their tongue. Jezebel uses anger or silence to control. Jezebel tries to control pastors and churches. Some pastors have this spirit, and through it they seek to control their congregations.

Jezebel dominates

Jezebel walks in dominance, surrounded by bitter envyings and a constant atmosphere of confusion. Rebellion will play a key role with Jezebel, sowing seeds of turmoil and unrest. Jezebel's find themselves unable to delegate authority. They give orders, then won't allow them to be carried out without humiliating the other person involved. They try to control, arrange, and dominate everyone around them. They keep others in a state of turmoil. Jezebel sometimes seeks to defile through pornography, lulling her victims into gradual, ever harder exposure. Jezebel targets women who are embittered against men, and she won't live with anyone she can't dominate.[103] From her heart she yields to no one, even though for public appearances she will appear to do so, in order to rule through another.

Jezebel promotes pornography

Jezebel is the source of obsessive sensuality, unbridled witchcraft, and hatred for authority. Much of our government is now almost completely controlled by this spirit. I believe President Clinton was ruled during his presidency by Jezebel. A man who is prisoner to Jezebel may manifest bondage to pornography, or be unable to control his sexual desires, filled with guilt and shame. The porn the American people have been exposed to in the media through the President's affairs, has defiled the people, and is evidence that Jezebel has practically taken over the media. This happened because the people have been lulled into submission by this spirit. First, we saw announcements by Gennifer Flowers, then Paula Jones and others followed concerning the President's sexual affairs. These people were used by Jezebel, to widen the gap of what can be acceptably discussed in a public forum.

Jezebel covers truth with distraction

Then came Monica Lewinsky and her graphic testimony. What can we say when the evening news and the newspaper are so blithely explicit that children have to be banned to their rooms in order not to be exposed to this influence. The Lewinsky investigation was dragged out over time to acclimate the public into accepting this kind of information as a regular course with the evening meal. It has brought a spirit of slumber into American households that distracts us from what is really going on behind the scenes in our government, as we gradually turn over our sovereign rights to the U.N., along with our military and our weapons, our military secrets to aggressive foreign nations, and our trading and manufacturing rights to foreign powers. Yet all the people were fed in the news was coverage of the President's affairs. Women continued to come forward with new, even more devastating accusations, but the nation's senses were dulled.

In order to take the heat off herself when she is under attack, Jezebel counter-attacks. A prime example is that every time President Clinton came under attack for his wrong doing, he and his wife would launch a vicious counter-attack against his accusers. We discovered under this assault, that some of the people who were exposing his affairs had engaged in affairs of their own. This was designed to distract us from our beleaguered president. When these tactics slightly delayed, but failed to stop the impeachment proceedings, then on the very day the vote for impeachment was to have gone forth, President Clinton ordered our troops into Albania.

Jezebel promotes hatred and dissatisfaction

Jezebel engenders dissatisfaction between spouses. This spirit is fiercely independent and intensely ambitious for control. Remember when the President was trying to get elected, and his wife had to tone herself down, wearing drab colors and not speaking as much. We were never told she even *had* a middle name, which was her maiden name before marriage. After the election, mission accomplished, *then* came the announcement that the American people were getting *two* for the price of one. The First Lady removed her mask of submissive behavior, and began to wear bright colors, emphatically and forcefully taking control of some investigations. We were immediately informed that she was to be referred to by her *middle* name (a declaration of independence and dominance), insisting that it be announced whenever she was addressed. (Jezebel seeks recognition.) She tried to force a system of health care on the public that would have been Socialism, pure and simple (Socialism seeks to manage all aspects of peoples lives for them, eliminating independence and creating greater dependence on big government). Many of the First Lady's friends, proponents of women's rights and lesbians, were given positions of influence.

Jezebel's agenda—murder

The President, overcome with lust and womanizing because of being a prisoner of Jezebel, seemed helpless to stop his actions. Meanwhile, an astonishingly dominant lesbian was made Attorney General, and others were given positions of influence. They pushed Jezebel's agenda of unlimited abortion; Clinton vetoed the Partial Birth Abortion Bill that the country and congress worked hard to put through. The Attorney General approved ATF and FEMA's attack against the Branch Davidian's and she never apologized for the slaughter of men, women and children in the Waco tragedy. The following day the entire Branch Davidian's compound was bulldozed to the ground, all evidence destroyed, a highly irregular procedure. The Oklahoma City bombing was another cover-up of the Waco tragedy, in which innocent people died. All ATF records were stored there, and the building was bulldozed to destroy evidence. In another unfortunate incident, Ron Brown, National Security Advisor, was killed in a very suspicious plane crash the day after he told Clinton if he was indicted for his crimes, he would take Clinton down with him. No apologies came forth for these, or any other tragedies perpetrated on the American people.

Jezebel brings destruction of family—promotes women's rights and homosexual agenda

As the Jezebel spirit gained influence over our government, it pushed women's rights; feminism. Sexual liberation is mostly a disguise for another form of bondage. While it is being promoted in the media, other forms of bondage in the economic, political and social arenas are being put in place, without the spotlight on them, and increased exponentially. Jezebel is the controlling influence directing the lesser demons of homosexuality and lesbianism. One of the President's first acts as leader of the free world, was to pass legislation promoting gay/lesbian rights in the military and work place. One high ranking military official stated, at a recent briefing, gays had weakened the military in significant ways, and that putting women in combat, despite what Hollywood would have us believe, endangers the men who will want to protect them in combat situations; additionally, the women simply aren't strong enough to carry the equipment or another man out of a situation if necessary.

Meanwhile, the First Lady spent a lot of time promoting a "children's rights" agenda. This looks good on the outside, but it is really a movement to take away "parental" rights. In California, a mother sought to keep custody of her son from her abusive divorced husband, who lived with his gay lover. He, however, retained custody. Fearing for the child, she went into hiding with him, but was caught and thrown in prison. The boy was raised by his father and boyfriend. He was exposed to such abuse and filth that in a desperate act he committed suicide. Jezebel seeks to destroy the family.

Twisted goals through wicked people

It is noteworthy that although the President's actions toward the young intern, Monica Lewinsky, and other women, was obviously chauvinist, manipulative, ungodly, abusive and unacceptable to the stated agenda of women's rights proponents, not one voice was raised in this camp to denounce the President, as it was in the appointment of Supreme Court Justice, Clarence Thomas, (does anyone recall the hoopla?) who allegedly harassed another young woman, Anita Hill, in his employ. It is important to note that this man *did* get approved for the Supreme Court, and now has a strong influence on our justice system. Remember the outcry from women's groups against him?

The White Water intrigue was another interesting twist from the First Lady. Indictments, accusations, and convictions are the tip of the iceberg. All the amazing amount of money that magically appeared in the Clinton's accounts, used for campaigns, has never been explained. The MacDougals suffered greatly, but perhaps Vince Foster suffered the most: He was found dead under mysterious circumstances, supposedly a suicide, while Hillary and an assistant raided his office for sensitive information. Why wasn't anything done about that? Susan MacDougal ended up in jail for refusing to talk. When the Clinton's left office, Susan was pardoned (surprise, surprise), along with Clinton's brother, and several other questionable pardons.

Jezebel creates puppets

Jezebel used our President for her own purposes. He was her puppet. The First Lady fiercely defended the President, and even stated that she was *proud* of him after the Lewinsky affair was finally admitted to. This was the Jezebel spirit speaking directly to truly listening ears. Rather than ever expressing her hurt or concern over her husband's actions, she expressed her anger with those who exposed him. This spirit causes its victims shame and guilt. Anyone recall the public repentance of the President? With tears and hanging of the head, "I have sinned."

Jezebel seeks to kill the prophets

Jezebel's true enemy is the prophet of God. She hates the prophets and seeks to kill them. She murdered hundreds of them in Israel. A true prophet will lead the people to repentance and humility. Jezebel hates repentance, humility and prayer. She seeks to stir the people up against the true prophets, in order to kill and hush the prophetic, because a true prophet will expose Jezebel for who she is. This is why Jezebel always seeks to control pastors and the goings on in the church, persecute the prophets, and denounce their words. If Jezebel controls a pastor, he will run all the true prophets off for fear of exposure. She causes fear and discouragement in God's prophets just as she did in Elijah *(1 Kings 19:4)*, and John the Baptist. Just to demonstrate how powerful this spirit is: Even after his great victory on Mount Carmel, Elijah suffered an attack of fear, heaviness and depression and prayed that he might die after Jezebel threatened him. While John the Baptist languished in prison he began to doubt that Jesus was the Messiah. He sent his followers to question Jesus. *(Luke 7:19)* Jezebel works through doubt and unbelief. Jezebel's ultimate hatred is against God Himself.

The spirit of Elijah

The spirit of Elijah was placed on John the Baptist, who was again confronted by this Jezebel spirit, manifesting through Herodias. She had him killed because he exposed her sin, just as Elijah exposed Jezebel's sin. John became discouraged and fearful and sent his disciples to inquire of Jesus if He was truly the Messiah, even though he had witnessed to others that He was, and had seen the Holy Spirit descending on Him. Jesus proclaimed in Matthew 17 that Elijah will return before the great and terrible day of the LORD. There will be another terrible conflict between Elijah and Jezebel, whom I believe now has dominion over our nation. Jezebel seeks to establish false religions and help them gain strength and credibility. This can be readily seen through the proliferation of witchcraft and New Age religions in our nation.

Jezebel is after the children

A friend of mine who was recently returning from a flight to California, was seated next to a boy and girl, seven and nine years old. All they wanted to talk about were witches and vampires. She tried several times to change the subject, but they chattered incessantly about their idols from TV. She finally had to tell them to stop, and began to share Jesus with them. I told her that with all the TV shows like "Sabrina, Teenage Witch," and "Buffy, the Vampire Slayer," shows full of graphic demonstrations of witchcraft, how can we expect our children not to be heavily influenced and obsessed with this information. We have come a long way since "Bewitched!" If parents will not monitor their children's viewing time, the children will be overcome with unnatural curiosity and obsession with the occult.

Video and computer games have become a training ground for violence and the occult. "Doom" and "Quake" have been linked to the Kentucky and Colorado slayings at schools. Obsession with *Pokemon* has caused violent assaults against teachers, and stabbings between students. One boy, who assaulted his teacher when she took his *Pokemon* cards, stated, "She was trying to take my "power!" The *Pokemon* game repeats over and over in its song, "Gotta catch 'em, gotta catch 'em *all!*" The *Harry Potter* craze is not surprising, since the books are steeped with the occult, even using real magic spells. Jezebel wants to "catch them all," too! (For a much fuller treatment of this subject matter, read *Jezebel vs. Elijah*, by Dr. Bree M. Keyton.)

Warring against Jezebel

Francis Frangipane tells of warring against the spirit of Jezebel through prayer with his church. Right away several gays and lesbians were delivered. Pastors and wives began calling to confess sexual sins, *and persecution began*, mostly from people *who had been friends*. One night the spirit of Jezebel manifested at the foot of his bed and threatened to kill him and his church if he didn't stop praying against it. One week later, a man called and threatened with the exact words the demon had spoken. Jezebel had found a willing vessel. Francis prayed for a snowstorm that very Saturday night, and got ten inches by morning. Few people came to church. The ones who did, prayed fervently. No one was harmed and later this man was saved.[104]

Mercy through our Messiah

Though I have referred to this spirit as a she, it can use *anyone*. If you have been under bondage to a Jezebel spirit, use the steps outlined below.

1. Pray fervently.
2. Seek help from a minister who does not operate with a controlling spirit.
3. Bind up the Jezebel spirit, and all its seductions and operations through you.
4. Plead the blood of Yahshua (Jesus) over yourself.
5. Put on the whole armor of YHWH (God). *(Ephesians 6:11-17)*
6. Renounce all association with Jezebel in Yahshua's (Jesus') Name, and repent for tolerating Jezebel.
7. Cast out this demon and break its influence off your life. You will almost certainly need help with this.
8. Repent of the love for ungodly power and for allowing this demon to operate through you.
9. If you find that you have a Jezebel spirit after reading this chapter, there is always mercy in allowing yourself to be conformed to the image of Christ, our Messiah.
10. Submit to authority, and allow them to help you and show you a better way.
11. This battle must be fought in the spirit, not through the flesh: the flesh *must* loose.
12. You must break free to fulfill God's plan for your life, by doing the opposite of what this spirit dictates. Remember that strongholds in your mind are holding you hostage to ungodly thought patterns. Loose yourself from them.
13. The ultimate answer is humility, and must be sought carefully with tears. Humility is our defense! Much repentance is needed.
14. Bind humility to yourself. Listen to the two songs on the *"Heart & Soul Surrender"* CD, *"I Surrender Myself"* and *"Heart & Soul."* These two songs bring a strong anointing for repentance, total surrender of the heart, a

key to deliverance from a Jezebel spirit, and the spirit of humility. Also listen to the dramatic work, *"Nails,"* on the same album, for deliverance.

15. Cast out a controlling spirit, a spirit of seduction, a spirit of whoredoms, an anti-Christ spirit, doubt and unbelief, deception, manipulation, a lying spirit, witchcraft, divination, lethargy, a spirit of murder, slumber, error, haughtiness, and familiar spirits.
16. Renounce and sever all connections, soul ties and cabal-tows to the demonic realm.
17. Smash every stronghold and trigger that might draw you back into manipulation and power-play (witchcraft), characteristic of Jezebel.
18. Ask God's forgiveness, and plead the blood over yourself.
19. Pray for strength and wisdom. Ask the LORD to soften your heart.
20. Let the Holy Spirit search your heart in a time of fasting and prayer. Ask Him to show you areas where you have been a manipulator. Then repent.
21. Bind appropriate scriptures to yourself concerning humility, peace, and love. Fill yourself up with the Word.

Bitter-root judgments open door to Jezebel

Bitter-root judgments can compel a person to fulfill in their own lives the very thing they judged in others. When judgments are made against offenders, they compel a person, through the law of sowing and reaping, to reap these same judgments back in their own lives. A woman who judges others for being abusive, harsh and unloving, will become the same way through reaping what she has sown, welcoming Jezebel as an avenging angel for the injustices she feels she has suffered. She controls because of fear. She must give up manipulative behavior, and learn to trust God and take every thought captive to the obedience of Christ, our Messiah. *(2 Corinthians 10:4-5)* (For a much fuller treatment of this important subject, see the chapter on *"Bitter-Root Judgments, Inner Vows and Soul Ties."*) To be set free from bitter-root judgments that have opened a door to Jezebel in your life:

1. Seek help from a minister who does not operate with a controlling spirit.
2. Repent wholeheartedly for allowing Jezebel to operate through you.
3. Renounce all involvement with Jezebel.
4. Cast out the Jezebel spirit, and all other spirits operating with her.
5. Submit to a time of correction; learn to trust again.
6. Ask God's forgiveness, and plead the blood over yourself.
7. Pray for strength and wisdom. Ask the LORD to soften your heart.
8. Break every bitter-root judgment you have made, especially against parents, relatives and spouse.
9. Bind humility to yourself, and learn to operate in the fruit of the Spirit.
10. Let the Holy Spirit search your heart in a time of fasting and prayer. Ask Him to show you areas where you have been a manipulator.
11. Repent and renounce witchcraft and manipulation.
12. Follow all other steps for deliverance in the previous chapter.

(For an in-depth study of the Jezebel spirit, get my book, *Jezebel vs. Elijah.* It contains over 150 characteristics of Jezebel.)

Chapter Twenty-Eight
The Ahab Spirit

Where there's a Jezebel there's an Ahab

Where there is a Jezebel there must be an Ahab. In the case where the pastor of a church has a Jezebel spirit, the whole church is defiled by serving as the Ahab. Ahab enables Jezebel to function. Jezebel floods her victim with weakness and helplessness, walking on them until they can't hold up their heads without shame. They become weak and ineffectual individuals. They will be fearful and resentful, dominated by the controlling person who is possessed by Jezebel. Ahab will manifast many of Jezebel's characteristics, for, in many ways, he is a weak reflection of her. In reality, she fulfills his desire for power and lusts of flesh.

Home out of order

An Ahab controlled husband may take his resentment out on other females in the workplace, behaving in a critical and abusive manner. His home is out of order, and he feels helpless to stop it. A man under Jezebel's control must:

1. Repent for allowing an Ahab spirit to operate.
2. Break it's power off him and his home.
3. Take back the head-ship of his home in a firm but loving manner.
4. Remember: Authority is not about domination, but loving leadership.[105]

Ahab considers things of God trivial

Ahab considers the things of God trivial, abdicating his place of authority to Jezebel. Ahab married Jezebel because it was politically strategic and she was seductive. She enhanced her beauty by painting her eyes. She was a high priestess of Ashtoreth, and probably into perverse sex. Through her manipulations and charms, she maneuvered into the power position, usurping Ahab's authority. Jezebel had 850 prophets who served her and her gods, Baal and Ashtoreth. She was the Baal prostitute who led all Israel into sin.

Ahab lusts for material possessions

Ahab lusts for material things. He should have killed Benhadad, instead making a lucrative deal with him. He lusted for Naboth's vineyard, whining to Jezebel. She killed Naboth to satisfy Ahab's competitive lust, while he behaved like a baby, relentlessly seeking for bigger and better things. Because Ahab entered a battle after choosing his sycophant prophet's words over the true prophet, he lost his life. The child on his way to becoming an Ahab will be attacked by Satan with rejection from his father. He will carry many wounds, be bitter, and fearful of relationships.

Ahab abdicates

Ahab is a miserable person. He is really waiting for someone to put him out of his misery and tell him what to do. Ahab will not fulfill the role of leadership in his home, refusing to set a good example for the children, dumping responsibilities on the wife that he should handle. An Ahab becomes a passive quitter, ever weaker as he goes. The wife tries to take up the slack becoming progressively stronger. The more he abdicates, the more she will take up the slack, until she is in complete control. Even though Ahab has abdicated authority, *he* will be the one held accountable by God. Disorder in the home brings the curse of God. This can result in broken homes and children becoming homosexuals.[106]

Repentance from an Ahab spirit

1. Repent of sympathy for Jezebel.
2. Repent of yielding to an Ahab spirit, and allowing it to operate through you. If Ahab is a whole church, the congregation must repent.
3. Ask God's forgiveness for failure to take your proper place in God's plan.
4. Bind up the Ahab spirit's power to operate over yourself and your home. Break this evil influence over your mind.
5. Repent of bitter-root judgments and inner vows made in your youth against aggressive, Jezebelian mothers and fathers.
6. Separate yourself from Jezebel's influence.

7. Hate the garment even spotted by the fleshly sin of following Jezebel.
8. Repent for succumbing to spiritual and perhaps physical adultery.

Deliverance from an Ahab spirit

1. Put on the whole armor of God, that you may be able to withstand the fiery darts of the wicked one.
2. Renounce this evil spirit.
3. Cast out the Ahab and Jezebel spirit.
4. Be strong in the LORD and the power of "His" might. Stand and resist!
5. Break every stronghold off your family, home and church. There will be complex structures (strongholds to break) and this will require time, persistence and faithfulness.
6. Cast out a spirit of fear. Resist the devil, and the temptation to yield or waver under the attacks of Jezebel.
7. Bind a spirit of power and love and a sound mind to yourself.
8. Get proper authority in place and don't yield to the easy way out.
9. Fast and pray for wisdom on how to handle Jezebel.
10. Take back the headship of your home in a firm but loving manner.
11. Remember: Loving leadership is not about domination.
12. Realize that you didn't get in this situation overnight, and you won't get out of it overnight. Be patient!
13. Stand fast, strengthening and encouraging yourself in the Word.
14. If you are attacked with weakness, bind scriptures to yourself for strength such as:

But they that wait upon the LORD shall renew their strength; they shall mount up with wings as eagles; they shall run, and not be weary; and they shall walk and not faint. (Isaiah 40:31)

Remember, if you sincerely desire to break the power of Jezebel and Ahab off your life, God will send His angels to protect you. Bind Luke 10:19 to yourself at all times.

15. Plead the blood over yourself, your household and church, daily. Play Christian music in your home.
16. Expect the LORD (YHWH) to move in your behalf. Rejoice! *(James 1:5)*
17. Put on your armor and don't take it off!
18. Use your faith to stand! *(Ephesians 6:13-14)*

(For more in-depth coverage of the Ahab spirit, read the section on the spirit of Ahab in my book, *Jezebel vs. Elijah.*)

Study Questions: Chapter 24

1. How does anxiety come in?
2. What are some steps you can take to avoid allowing anxiety to dominate your life?
3. What does "be careful for nothing" mean in Philippians 4:6?
4. How can you apply this to your life?
5. What is confusion? Why does the devil use this tactic?
6. If you are being attacked in your dreams with fear:
    a. Take authority over dreams by pleading the blood of Jesus over them.
    b. Ask the Father to send warring angels to protect you as you sleep.
    c. Repent if there is any area of sin in your life.
    d. Wear the whole armor to bed—particularly the helmet of salvation.
    e. Rebuke any demons assigned to you and return them to the sender.
    f. Forbid demons from attacking your dreams and bind scriptures to yourself such as Psalm 4:8 and Proverbs 3:24.
    g. Trust the LORD with all your heart.

Chapter Twenty-Nine
The Spirit of Unbelief

Thomas missed a great blessing by refusing to believe. Jesus admonished him:

>...*be not faithless (UNBELIEVING), but believing. (John 20:27)*

Jesus didn't stop there. He pronounced a blessing on those willing to take the extra step, and believe without seeing. *(John 20:29)* When we only cling to what we see with our eyes, rather than to what God says, we miss God, and we are operating in unbelief. The disciples could not cast out a deaf and dumb spirit because of their unbelief. Jesus said:

>*O faithless (UNBELIEVING) generation, how long shall I be with you? How long shall I suffer (put up with) you? (Mark 9:19)*

The disciples couldn't calm the storm because of their unbelief. Jesus asked them:

>*Why are ye so fearful? How is it that ye have no faith? (Mark 4:40)*

We cannot please God with unbelief. Bluntly stated, the unbelieving will be burned in the lake of fire. *(Revelation 21:8)* Will you choose to trust God or your doctors? Will you choose to trust God's system of finance, or will you trust social security, savings and the stock market? All these things can be wiped out in a moment, but the Word lasts forever.

Poverty and lack

I got a call from someone recently who was languishing in deep unbelief. She called in desperation with no money, no food, no car, no job, no childcare so she could get a job. I began to minister to her, but everything I suggested was met with excuses. I spoke words of encouragement, words of faith. My faith in God's ability to handle the situation was met with her stubborn unbelief. She refused to hear what the LORD was speaking through me. One overriding issue was her bitterness against all rich people. Finally, I stated that we were getting nowhere because she argued over every point. I told her she needed deliverance, and that if she wanted to be free, to come to my concert in two days and God would set her free. She walked a long distance to get there, but at the end of the concert I called her up, and she was delivered of a spirit of bitterness, unbelief, etc. She repented of hating rich people and forgave them all. Her back was healed when she forgave. She called two days later to exalt the Name of the LORD and to thank me for ministering deliverance to her. Her whole life was changed, and she said that she felt free and lighter than she had in years.

Raised in a cult of unbelief

Conversely, at that same concert, there was a young woman who was raised a Jehovah's Witness. She told me right up front she hated religion. I told her I did, too. Being unsaved, she had no understanding that Christianity is not about religion, but relationship. She refused to pray for salvation with the others during altar call, stubbornly standing with her arms crossed. At the end, when I ministered the song, *"Nails,"* for deliverance, she ran out, unable to stay in the presence of the power of God. She came back two days later to the coffee house and claimed she was attacked by demons all the way home, and had terrible nightmares. She needed to be born again to receive the authority to resist the devil. She asked many questions of the shop owner, but unfortunately was told that she could use the Name of Jesus to make the demons flee. This was dangerous advice to give. The seven sons of Sceva tried to use the Name of Jesus, and they were severely beaten because they had no authority, not being born again, to use this Name.

>*And the evil spirit answered and said, Jesus I know, and Paul I know but who are ye? And the man in whom the evil spirit was leaped on them and overcame them, and prevailed against them, so that they fled out of that house naked and wounded. (Acts 19:15-16)*

Who's got the power?

Unwittingly, the producers of the movie, *The Exorcist*, revealed that the priests who were attempting to cast the demon out of the girl, were not born again, because they had no authority (power) to make the demon leave. Authority can be likened to a policeman holding up his hand in traffic. Even the largest trucks stop for him because he is backed by the full weight of the law. The devil has no power (authority) over the children of God, unless they *give* it to him. As a born again believer we have authority (power) over *all* the power (authority) of the enemy because Jesus gave it to us.

> *Behold, I give unto you POWER to tread on serpents and scorpions, and over ALL the POWER of the enemy... (Luke 10:19)*

Definition

Unbelief is the stubborn refusal to hear what God has said. Unbelief is caused by hardness of the heart. Again and again Jesus demonstrated faith and the power of believing, yet the disciples failed to soften their hearts. Unbelief proceeds from:

1. An evil heart. *(Hebrews 3:12)*
2. Slowness of heart. *(Luke 24:25)*
3. Hardness of heart. *(Mark 16:14; Acts 19:9)*
4. Refusal to receive truth. *(John 8:45-46)*
5. Not being Christ's sheep. *(John 10:26)*
6. Devil blinding the mind. *(2 Corinthians 4:4)*
7. Devil stealing the Word out of the heart. *(Luke 8:12)*
8. Seeking honor from men. *(John 5:44)*

A person in unbelief is: rejecting Jesus Christ *(John 16:9)*, rejecting God's Word *(Psalm 106:24)*, rejecting the gospel *(John 12:38; Isaiah 53:1)* rejecting evidence of miracles *(John 12:37)*, questioning the power of God *(2 Kings 7:2; Psalm 78:19-20)*, and staggering at the promise of God. *(Romans 4:20)*

Straight Hair

A woman came forward for prayer at an evangelist's meeting. She was very frustrated because every time she got a permanent in her hair it would immediately go straight. He got a word of knowledge that the demon's name was "straight hair," sent to harass her and he rebuked it. Shortly thereafter she got a perm and her hair remained curly. Remember, demons have been assigned to *you*. What really frustrates you? Rest assured, you will be troubled repeatedly in this area until you learn to resist the devil *(James 4:7)*, by using the Name of Jesus before which every knee must bow *(Philippians 2:10)*. Learn to recognize demonic harassment.

Impediment to miracles

Unbelief is a fierce impediment to miracles.

> *And He could there do no mighty work, save that He laid His hands on a few sick folk, and healed them. And He marveled because of their unbelief... (Mark 6:5-6)*

When I minister the song *"Stripes"* at my concerts, I can strongly sense the faith level rising at the end of the song; when faith arises many get healed. Some places I've ministered have a dark cloud of unbelief hanging obtusely over the area, burdening lives with fear and other strongholds. It takes much longer to build the faith level up to the point where they can receive healing. It's hard to convince an unfaithful servant that he should be faithful.

Never argue with a demon

According to the New Testament, Jesus talked to a demon and asked its name. As soon as He knew, He cast it out. Most of the time He simply told them to be quiet, and cast them out. There may have been other times He got information from them, but it is simply not recorded. Demons may lie, curse, and threaten through a person. Stand your ground in Jesus' Name, and they must leave. Never argue with a demon. They are all liars, so any information obtained through a demon could be false, or a filibuster to keep from being cast out. On the other hand, sometimes they will give you clues from the mouth of the individual you are ministering to that gives them away. The person will sometimes frame it as an "I" message. "I'm not afraid of you." "I can stay because she looked at porn." "I don't have to leave because she wants me to stay."

Power of God

A secular rock station in Kansas City started playing one of our songs frequently on the air. Unsaved people started to respond to it. One day they played it between AC/DC and Judas Priest. The loud speaker was on in the kitchen area of a restaurant. The power of God hit them, and all twelve of the kitchen staff got saved.

Gangs and teenagers saved

At an outdoor event where I was singing, several gang members walked by. I called out to them that today was the day of salvation. They turned and looked at me, their faces frozen. I said to repeat these words after me, and led them in a sinner's prayer. They responded and were saved. At another concert, I barely got to the third song when the power of God hit the kids in the coffee house, and they ran forward crying and begging to be saved. Some screamed, "Get these demons off me!" while others were confessing their sins as fast as they could.

It is the anointing that breaks off yokes of bondage, and without it we might as well all stay home. Jesus came to set captives free, and we are carriers of His anointing. Let's walk in it, and trust the LORD to use us mightily.

Praying for the lost

When I was in the world someone stood in the gap for me or I would not be here. I drove off a cliff, got shot in the head, was shot at other times, and threatened with guns occasionally, was in a towering inferno, plane crash, hurricane, chemical tanker crash, numerous car wrecks, threatened by the mafia, beat up repeatedly and stranded outside in ice storms. I've been robbed, held hostage, had third degree burns on my face, been raped, attacked by demons, stranded in the desert, and a long list of other disasters, seventy-five all together.

I know I looked like a hopeless case. In spite of all these disasters, I still hadn't turned to Christ until one night, in a fit of depression, I got out all my pills to commit suicide. Just as I lifted them to my mouth the phone rang. It was my partner and keyboard player, Steve, who is now my husband. He insisted that I turn on the *700 Club*. When I did, Pat Robertson said, "Put down those pills!" I was shocked and flushed all the pills. Shortly thereafter, I gave up show business, got saved, and Steve and I got married. Then we began to serve the LORD with all our hearts.

At our wedding, the man who prayed for me all those years and held back the forces of darkness from taking my life, came to our wedding. He asked if I was home to stay. When I said yes, he sighed loudly in relief, and went home to be with the LORD two weeks later. Please commit to pray for someone, today. There is always hope. You can hold back the devil with your intercession for as long as it takes, until the person comes to Jesus.

A stronghold

Unbelief is a stronghold that holds many church-goers in its wicked grasp. People who are faithless, persecute those who are faithful servants. *(Romans 15:31)* However, we are admonished to stand against wickedness and rejoice when we are persecuted for righteousness sake. *(Matthew 5:10-12)* Those who have unbelief shall die in their sins *(John 8:24)*, shall not enter into rest *(Hebrews 3:19)*, shall be condemned and destroyed *(Mark 16:16; 2 Thessalonians 2:12; Jude 5)*, shall be cast into the lake of fire *(Revelation 21:8)*, and shall receive their just due:

The lord of that servant will come in a day when he looketh not for him, and at an hour when he is not aware, and will cut him in sunder, and will appoint him his portion with the unbelievers. (Luke 12:46)

Belief

On the other hand, belief means to be *fully persuaded*. Are you fully persuaded that God is Who He said He is, and will do what He said He will do? Then faith is the natural result! Belief signifies reliance on the veracity of the Word. Faith honors YHWH, our God. Is He trustworthy? Belief means putting faith and trust in Him.

Prayer to be set free

Oh, God, hear my cry today. I have been an UNFAITHFUL servant. I repent of entertaining a wicked spirit of UNBELIEF. I loose myself from the power of unbelief, and I break off any spirit of fear, doubt, or lying spirits that I've listened to, instead of Your glorious truth. I cast them out of my life, my home, my marriage, my job. I command them to go in the Name of Jesus Christ (Yahshua Messiah).

I earnestly desire to be a FAITHFUL and profitable servant. I know that without faith I cannot please You. *(Hebrews 11:6)* LORD, I believe. Help Thou my unbelief. Forgive me for my unbelief and strengthen my resolve to take a stand to believe the unshakeable Word above all circumstances, to accept Your truth no matter what things look like to my natural eye. You are faithful God, Who has promised. Let me be full of faith and walk in the divine promises I find in Your Word. Jesus, one of Your Names is FAITHFUL. *(Revelation 1:5; 3:14; 19:11)* Write Your Name on the tables of my heart, that one day I may stand before You unashamed. Now, by faith, I choose to take up my cross, and walk as a faithful witness as You did, never letting unbelief defeat me in battle, but realizing that I'm not going *toward* a victorious battle. I'm coming *from* the victorious battle You've already won for me, as I stand in faith and BELIEVE. Amen.

Chapter Thirty
The Spirit of Doubt

Small faith

A doubter is someone whose faith is small. They are easily perplexed (*Vine's*, aporeo), at a loss, uncertain, they manifest weakness of faith, such as the way the disciples behaved when Jesus was not found in the tomb. *(Luke 24:4)* A doubtful person is anxious, he worries and frets, wavering between hope and fear. *(Luke 12:29)* Sometimes doubt becomes despair. Doubt creeps in through a failure of expectations and gains a stronghold that grows in the believer's heart, chipping steadily away at faith.

Disappointment brings doubt

I know many wonderful pastors who start out full of excitement and faith, but over the years, disappointments and moving in presumption instead of faith, wears them down until they end up preaching a watered down "maybe gospel." Maybe God will and maybe He won't. If this is you, repent quickly and allow God to heal your wounded heart. You really are not covering yourself or helping others by telling stories of how Aunt Disbelief and Sister Mistrust and Brother Skepticism never got anything from God for which they prayed.

Wavering and double-mindedness

WAVERING is another word for DOUBT. WAVERING (*Strong's 1252*, diakrino), in the following scripture, means to hesitate, stagger, doubt, withdraw. WITHDRAW, suggests that someone is pulling back from the battle because of serious doubt festering in their heart about YHWH Nissi, our conqueror. The nagging thought presents itself that He may not have the ability or desire to work in your behalf to defeat the enemy: in other words, the rotten fruit of doubt, coupled with the devil's lies have taken precedence in your heart. The result is that you STAND DOWN.

> *But let him ask in faith, nothing WAVERING. For he that WAVERETH is like a wave of the sea driven with the wind and tossed. For let not that man think that he shall receive anything of the LORD. A DOUBLE-MINDED man is unstable in all his ways. (James 1:6-8)*

The word DOUBLE-MINDED (*Vine's*, dipsuchos) actually means two-souled. This is almost indicative of a split personality: one that has faith and one that is in doubt. Doubt begins to form through the failure of one's expectations being met. Expectation and hope need to be firmly grounded in our God's desires *for* us, not in unreasonable demands we place on Him to perform *our* will. He is not holding us in suspense or *"making us to doubt"* (*John 10:24*), but performing His will as He sees fit. Abraham waited decades before the LORD's promise for a son was manifested.

God asks for our trust. This is not easily given. After all, Brother Falsehood and Sister Slander betrayed us, and so many others have let us down. We prayed for someone's healing and they died. We prayed for relief from some kind of thorn in the side and it remained. Though it seems we have prayed and prayed, our spouse shows no sign of changing or repenting, and our own lives are in shambles; we have trouble believing God's Word is true because we've allowed the "facts" to outweigh the wonderful "truth" contained in God's Word. Yet, I declare to you this day that HE IS FAITHFUL WHO PROMISED. *(Hebrews 10:23)* The worlds were framed by the Word of the living God. You, too, are framing your world by the words you speak. What are you speaking?

Understanding the insidious spirit of doubt

One of the meanings of doubt is "suspense due to lack of light." (*Vine's*) When we fill our hearts with the light of Jesus Christ and the Word, we dispel the darkness of doubt and enter into the kingdom of light where all things are possible to him who believes. *(Mark 9:23)* Doubt brings fear and fear brings torment. No one wants to live in torment, never getting satisfactory answers to prayer. STAND and believe today! Glorify God with your Words of faith. Set aside your cares and roll them all over onto Jesus. Today is the day that will change your life for the glory of God. Use your faith to believe, not to doubt! Only believe! (See the prayer in previous chapter on *Unbelief*. Substitute the word "doubt" for "unbelief" as you pray.)

Chapter Thirty-One
The Spirit of Korah (Rebellion and Pride)

Korah is alive and well

Before an outdoor concert in the summer, I had prayed and fasted for three days. When I arrived, the LORD spoke one word to me: Korah. *(Numbers 16:1-50)* There was a spirit of Korah present amongst the people. The spirit of Korah manifests as REBELLION and pride, a lethal combination that works together. Korah gathered the people together against the LORD. He coveted Moses' position, although he already had a position of service before the LORD. He was deceived and blinded by pride into thinking he could take away Moses' authority. Korah had no reverence for the LORD or the LORD's decisions. He simply wanted a promotion, which he would have taken by force, but for the humility of Moses. When Moses heard Korah's words, he threw himself down in humility, saving countless lives, both in that rebellion and in the one that followed. In Hebrew the word rebellion *(Strong's* 7081, marah) signifies AN OPPOSITION MOTIVATED BY PRIDE. It primarily means to disobey, and signifies a rebellious attitude AGAINST God *(Deuteronomy 9:7)*, defying the command of God. Rebellion means to be bitter, make angry, provoke and REJECT. *(Vine's) Woe to her that is filthy (REBELLIOUS) and polluted, to the oppressing city! She obeyed not the voice; she received not correction; she trusted not in the LORD; she drew not near to her God. (Zephaniah 3:1-2) For REBELLION is as the sin of WITCHCRAFT, and stubbornness is as iniquity and idolatry. (1 Samuel 15:23)*

Korah stood against God and lost

In the first rebellion the Bible says Korah was gathered AGAINST the LORD. *(Numbers 16:11)* In the second rebellion it says they were gathered AGAINST Moses and Aaron. *(Numbers 16:42)* It is extreme presumption to go AGAINST the LORD and the man of God. PRIDE blinds the mind in such a way that people get puffed up in their own self-importance. When this happens, they get the idea they are better than others, particularly God's choice of a leader. *If any man THINK HIMSELF TO BE SOMETHING, when he is nothing, he deceiveth himself. (Galatians 6:3)*

If you, or someone you know, has spoken against God or God's choice for a leader, repent immediately. This is serious sin against the LORD. It is incredible to me that Korah never saw what was coming. How could he have totally missed what God was doing through Moses, or not seen what was going to happen to him, and his family? Pride blinded his mind. The person in pride is consumed with self-love. (Pride can also be self-hatred.) He puffs himself up above others and believes his problems are too big for God. He has no meekness (teachability) or humility (the antidote). Moses was one of the meekest men who ever lived *(Numbers 12:3)* and God responded to Moses when he threw himself on God's mercy, rather than standing in pride like Korah.

Pride

A prideful person cannot accept correction or criticism, always turning the tables on the other person, spending his time in self-defense, never saying, "I'm sorry." Pride is arrogance, placing himself above all others. God resists the proud, but gives grace to the humble. The prideful person has trouble submitting to God and glories in self-hatred, which he thinks is humility, demanding to atone for his own sins, rather than repenting and accepting Christ's forgiveness and atonement.

Leaders in sin

If a leader is found to be in sin or a blatant error, this matter is to be dealt with in the following manner. The Word is very specific. *Against an elder receive not an accusation (do not listen to criticism), (unless presented by) but before two or three witnesses. (1 Timothy 5:19)* Go to this person, and if he can be won back to God's way, good. If not, take others and try to reason with and bring this brother to repentance. If not, *then* go before the congregation publicly. If we are spiritual the Word encourages us: *Brethren, if a man be overtaken in a fault, ye which are spiritual, restore such a one in the spirit of meekness… (Galatians 5:1)*

Abimelech's rebellion and pride

Abimelech was a man deep in rebellion and pride. I believe the cause can be traced to rejection by his seventy brothers. Abimelech was not a legitimate son of Gideon, but was born of a concubine from Shechem. *(Judges 8:31)* In order to take control he had to slay all seventy of his brothers. He usurped the rightful authority over Israel and set himself up as king. God dealt with all the people who sided with unjust Abimelech by allowing an evil spirit to bring enmity between them. Then all of Shechem was slain by Abimelech and his army. He encamped against

Thebiz. During this attack, a woman cast a millstone down on his head causing a mortal wound. Because of his pride, and not wanting it said that a woman killed him, he had his soldiers thrust him through with a sword. The end of rebellion and pride is judgment and death. *(Judges 9:1-57; 2 Samuel 11:21)* Rebellion manifests in many ways: resentment, bitterness, unforgiveness, anger, hardness of heart, violence, holding grudges, murder, uncontrollable temper, backstabbing, refusal to be under authority.

Scriptures for a child in rebellion

If a child is in rebellion, then the parents must go to war in their prayer closet. Bind these scriptures to your child, spouse, and yourself. Some excellent scriptures follow, with personal prayers for you to pray.

But if our gospel be hid, it is hid to them that are lost: In whom the god of this world hath blinded the minds of them which believe not, lest the light of the glorious gospel of Christ, Who is the image of God, should shine unto them.(2 Corinthians 4:4) (I pray that Your light would shine through me, not be hidden. Shine Your light into my child's heart. Use me to be an example of Your unfailing love.)

And that we may be delivered from unreasonable and wicked men: for all men have not faith. But the LORD is faithful, Who shall stablish you, and keep you from evil. (2 Thessalonians 3:2-3) (Protect and deliver my child from evil, and work everything for Your glory in his life. Draw him, by Your Holy Spirit, back into Your protected sheepfold.)

That He may incline our hearts unto Him, to walk in all His ways, and to keep His commandments, and His statutes, and His judgments, which He commanded our fathers. And let these my words wherewith I have made supplication before the LORD, be nigh unto the LORD our God day and night, that He maintain the cause of His servant, and the cause of His people Israel at all times, as the matter shall require... (1 Kings 8:58-59) (Maintain my cause, and move day and night in my behalf to bring my child back to You, to serve You and love You. Cause him to walk in Your way and hear Your voice.)

Sirs, what must I do to be saved? And they said, Believe on the LORD Jesus Christ, and thou shalt be saved, and thy house. (Acts 16:30-31) (Bind this scripture to your child; write it on the tables of his heart.)

For thus saith the LORD God; Behold, I even I, will both search My sheep, and seek them out. I will seek that which was lost, and bring again that which was driven away, and will strengthen that which was sick... (Ezekiel 34:11, 16) (Thank you, that You search daily for my child, and You will bring him back through Your unfailing love.)

And I will give them a heart to know Me, that I Am the LORD: and they shall be My people, and I will be their God: for they shall return unto Me with their whole heart. (Jeremiah 24:7) (Give my child a heart to know You and to seek after You with his whole heart.)

Hast not Thou made a hedge about him and about his house, and about all that he hath on every side? (Job 1:10) (I pray up a hedge around my child to protect him from all the fiery darts of the enemy, until he comes back into God's perfect will.)

So shall My Word be that goeth forth out of My mouth: it shall not return unto me void, but it shall accomplish that which I please, and it shall prosper in the thing whereto I sent it. (Isaiah 55:11) (Praise the Holy Name of God, for You have heard my prayers, and as I speak Your Word over my situation, You will prosper Your Word in my child's life.)

No weapon that is formed against thee shall prosper; and every tongue that shall rise against thee in judgment thou shalt condemn. This is the heritage of the servants of the LORD, and their righteousness is of Me, saith the LORD. (Isaiah 54:17) (I loose myself and my children from the weapon of deception the enemy has used against us, in Jesus' Name. I bind truth and wisdom to my child in Jesus' Name. Satan, you cannot have my child. Take your hands off him for he is my heritage, and IT IS WRITTEN that he will serve the LORD, according to Acts 16:31)

Blessed is the man that feareth the LORD, that delighteth greatly in His commandments. His seed shall be mighty upon earth: the generation of the upright shall be blessed (Psalm 112) (Father, Your Word says that my seed shall be mighty on the earth, and that he shall be blessed. I claim this scripture for my child. I call him a mighty man, and I call those things that be not as though they were. *(Romans 4:17)* This is what You do with Your children, LORD, and it is what I will do with mine.)

Lo, children are an heritage of the LORD: and the fruit of the womb is his reward. As arrows are in the hand of a mighty man; so are children of the youth. Happy is the man that hath his quiver full of them: they shall not be ashamed... (Psalm 127:3-5) (My children are my reward. Help me to *always* see them as You see them. By faith, I claim that my children are mighty arrows, that they bring me happiness. Thank You for my children, Father.)

And all thy children shall be taught of the LORD; and great shall be the peace of thy children. (Isaiah 54:13) (I rebuke a spirit of strife off my household. I command it to leave in Jesus' Name. My children belong to the LORD and He teaches them the way. Thank You that my children live in peace and my household is bathed in peace.)

...for I will hasten My Word to perform it. (Jeremiah 1:12) (Thank You, Father, that You have heard my prayers and supplications and You will swiftly come to my assistance. Rescue my child and our family in our deep distress.)

The perversion of the gifts

Before birth, and from infancy, Satan seeks to defeat us in the areas where God has called and gifted us. As soon as we recognize the attack against the gifts of God, we must break it off, by repenting of sin and closing the door to the deceiver. Many people who have gifts from the Holy Spirit are lured into the occult. The counterfeit gifts will function until the person receives deliverance and repents, breaking its power. A woman I know who was a witch using clairvoyance, tarot card reading, etc., now serves the LORD and has recently begun to be used to bless others with her God-given gift of prophecy. I used my musical talent to serve the enemy until Jesus saved me. Then, my heavenly Father allowed me to use His gifts for His glory.

Heartfelt repentance

1. If you are or ever were in rebellion, repent. Ask God's forgiveness. Holy Spirit will come showing areas that need correction.
2. Loose yourself from and cast out a spirit of Korah, rebellion and pride.
3. Give YHWH, our God, and His will, first place in your life. Don't resist those who are in godly authority over you.
4. Give yourself time to flow with God's plan. Don't try to step right out into ministry. You may be operating in witchcraft.
5. Break these things off your children. Your rebellion and sin will be visited on them until it is broken off and you have repented.

Chapter Thirty-Two
Antichrist Spirit, Lying Spirit, Deception, Error, Seducing Spirit

Deception

In foreign countries the deception is often so strong that people are totally possessed. A missionary to India I met told of a man who loved his little boy and played with him all the time in the park. One day the missionary saw the man in the park with something that was drawing a crowd. When he came closer he saw that it was the little boy's head on a stick, which the man was waving wildly about. When asked why he had killed his son, he answered that his "god" had told him to do it so that his "luck" would change. The word luck derives from the word Lucifer. Many religions base their beliefs on luck and will literally do anything to change it. What a cruel liar the devil is.

Lying

Deception is one of the ways the devil entices us to sin in the area of lying. He drops a thought into our mind that it would be all right to lie because if we tell the truth, then we will have more problems: we might hurt someone's feelings, what will it hurt to lie to them. Lying can be simply keeping silent when we should speak. The possibilities are endless, for Satan, himself, is the father of lies.

> *Ye are of your father the devil, and the lusts of your father ye will do. He...abode NOT IN THE TRUTH, because there is NO TRUTH in him. When he speaketh a LIE, he speaketh of his own: for he is a LIAR, and the father of it. (John 8:44)*

> *...and ALL LIARS, shall have their part in the lake which burneth with fire and brimstone... (Revelation 21:8)*

Our conscience brings conviction. If we will listen, and follow the voice of the Holy Spirit, Who will lead us into all truth, we can avoid many pitfalls in the area of lying. For a lying spirit to freely work, the victim must suppress his conscience and justify his actions in his own heart.

> *Every way of a man is RIGHT IN HIS OWN EYES: but the LORD pondereth the hearts. (Proverbs 16:2)*

Lies include bondage to religious traditions *(Galatians 5:1)*, false accusers *(2 Timothy 3:3)*, gossip (vain babblings) *(1 Timothy 6:20)*, false tale bearers *(Proverbs 26:22)*, slander *(1 Timothy 3:11)*, false teachers and false prophets *(2 Peter 2:1-2; 2 Chronicles 18:22)*, perjury (lying, misleading, or incomplete testimony under oath) *(1 Timothy 1:10)*, luck (based on superstition) *(Acts 17:22)* leading people into such foolishness and sin as gambling, believing old wives tales, sorcery *(1 Timothy 4:7; Romans 8:28)*, flattery (one of the ways the antichrist will come in):

> *...he shall come in peaceably, and obtain the kingdom by FLATTERIES. (Daniel 11:21)*

Finally, strong delusion is a powerful, lying tool of the enemy. The following scripture should be translated THE LIE, not "a" lie.

> *Because they received not the love of the truth, that they might be saved, and for this cause God shall send them STRONG DELUSION, that they should believe A LIE: That they all might be damned who believed not the truth... (2 Thessalonians 2:11-12)*

Antichrist spirit and error

The antichrist spirit has been working its evil from the beginning. It is the spirit that fought to keep the seed of Adam from being pure. It is the spirit that sought to kill Abel and raged in Cain. It is the spirit that stirred up Cush (founder of Babylon), and his son Nimrod to build a tower to defy God. The antichrist spirit brings jealousy, hatred, competition, murder, wars, apostasy. It seeks to discredit the true Messiah and constantly introduces false Christ's. The early Christians had to deal with this spirit and so do we. Eventually, this spirit will gain world dominance. It is gaining power daily, as many other spirits that have influence come under its inevitable rule during the tribulation. The antichrist spirit worked through the Jews of Jesus' day to discredit and kill Him, and it works to destroy the true prophets and servants of YHWH, our God, today. The antichrist spirit knows we are free moral agents. God allows us to lie and believe a lie if that is the direction we wish to go. King Ahab wanted to hear a lie from his prophets, and YHWH, our God, allowed it. *(2 Chronicles 18:20-22)* However, believing this lie cost Ahab his life. The spirit of error renders its victims unteachable, *(2 Timothy 4:3-4)*, unsubmissive and unable to receive warnings *(Proverbs 29:1; 10:17)*, contentious *(James 3:14-16)*, full of false doctrines *(1 John 4:1-6; 2 Timothy 4:3-4)*, and defensive. *(2 Peter 2:1)*

> *…he that is not of God HEARETH NOT us. Hereby know we the SPIRIT OF TRUTH, and the SPIRIT OF ERROR. (1 John 4:6)*

If the principality of error is allowed to operate through a person, sooner or later the antichrist spirit will enter as well. This spirit comes in because of the sin of idolatry. The antichrist spirit brings blasphemous accusation toward the veracity of God's Word such as: the virgin birth; that Jesus is the Son of God, and only He can save your soul. *(1 John 4:3)* This spirit draws people to the occult and pagan religions, humanism (worship of man and belief that man can save himself), salvation by works, and influences people to put material possessions above the one true God.

> *For many DECEIVERS are entered into the world, who confess not that Jesus Christ is come in the flesh. This is a DECEIVER and an ANTICHRIST. (2 John 7)*

The antichrist spirit wants to replace our worship of Christ with self-worship, worship of material things, worship of pagan gods or Satan himself. This is idolatry and opens one up to this wicked spirit. Several new translations of the Bible distort and deceive concerning the basic tenants of the Christian faith, thus they become tools of the antichrist spirit and the spirit of error. Following are certain important scriptures that the NIV Bible translates into heresies and denials that: Jesus is the Messiah and has come in the flesh; the virgin birth; mention of the blood of Jesus that atones for our sins: *(Luke 2:33; Acts 4:27; 1 John 5:7; Colossians 1:14; 1 Timothy 3:16)* There are numerous examples. The spirit of error is countered and overcome by the Spirit of Truth.

The antichrist spirit is that which opposes and attempts to substitute itself and its lies for the TRUTH. The antichrist spirit is against the LORD and His Messiah. He will exalt himself above God, Jesus' teachings, and against Christians. *(2 Thessalonians 2:3-4; Revelations 13:7)* This spirit's main weapon is deception. It uses our senses to deceive us. Our senses are gullible, especially if they are not exercised in the Word of Truth, the Bible. Hollywood and the media know this, and have begun perfecting technology that is capable of causing us to believe what we see, rather than the truth. (The perfect movie to open your eyes to the deception possible through the media is *Wag the Dog*.) The evil antichrist spirit will deceive us through our own senses and stir up lawlessness, profanity, ungodliness, murder, lies, defiling our bodies through sexual sin, and contrariness to sound doctrine. *(1 Timothy 1:9-10)*

Seducing spirits

The antichrist spirit uses seducing spirits to draw its victims off the true path that leads to Christ. There is a powerful pulling and drawing through fascination with strong personalities, "charged" objects and occult rituals. *(Proverbs 12:26)* A SEARED CONSCIENCE is easily deceived and seduced, eagerly choosing to believe the devil's lies over the truth, especially when false signs, wonders and false prophets abound. False new-age religions are seducing and enticing the world to follow and even recruiting Christians at alarming rates. Every year my sons were in public school one of their teachers tried to get the students to perform Transcendental Meditation techniques in class. New age religion has permeated our society on every level and is so commonplace now that most people have accepted it. One of the most popular movies of our time is *Ghost*, which is loaded with witchcraft, mediums, necromancy, deception, murder, lying, and a strong romantic theme to SEDUCE the watcher into viewing the occult events as acceptable. Romantics everywhere hail this film.

> *For false Christs and false prophets shall rise, and shall show signs and wonders, to SEDUCE, if it were possible, even the elect. (Mark 13:22)*

> *Now the Spirit speaketh expressly, that in the latter times some shall depart from the faith, giving heed to SEDUCING SPIRITS, and DOCTRINES OF DEVILS; Speaking lies in hypocrisy; having their CONSCIENCE SEARED WITH A HOT IRON… (1 Timothy 4:1-2)*

> *But evil men and SEDUCERS shall wax worse and worse, DECEIVING, and being DECEIVED. (2 Timothy 3:13)*

Shakespeare wrote, "Oh, what a tangled web we weave, when first we practice to deceive." Have you ever noticed that one little lie creates a huge structure around it, because it requires constant maintenance and cover-up. Thus, more deceptions and lies are born. Soon, it requires an entire web of deception to protect one little lie. A lie acts like a thorn in the heart to wound the conscience. If lies and deception continue, then soon the person has a SEARED CONSCIENCE. This produces a hardened heart.

Blessed are they that do His commandments, that they may have right to the tree of life, and may enter in through the gates into the city. For without are dogs, and sorcerers, and whoremongers, and murderers, and idolaters, and WHOSOEVER LOVETH AND MAKETH A LIE. (Revelation 22:14-15)

Truth vs. lies

Only the truth will set us free. It will explode the myths and lies built up around us. Exercise yourself to godliness *(1 Timothy 4:7)* and do not do things that are contrary to sound doctrine. *(1Timothy 1:10)* True prophecy never contradicts the written Word of God. If you receive a prophecy that does, break the power of the words spoken, cancel their assignment, and speak truth in love to the person being used by a lying spirit. A prophet we know attended a man's meeting in which another man stood up and gave a prophecy that demanded everyone in the room get on their knees and give oblation to a spirit. This word was disguised so that without thinking, most of the men present did so, until our friend went forward and exposed the demonic spirit that was demanding worship. In a room full of godly men, only he and one other man recognized this evil prophecy and had the sense to stop it, directing the others to repent. Satan is full of deadly, vicious lies to destroy ourselves and others. He whispers these lies in our ears, and we sin when we choose to take them and believe them. If we meditate on the things of God, it leaves no room for lies to enter our minds. Each part of the following scripture counteracts one of Satan's deceptions.

…whatsoever things are TRUE, whatsoever things are HONEST, whatsoever things are JUST, whatsoever things are PURE, whatsoever things are LOVELY, whatsoever things are of GOOD REPORT; if there be any virtue, and if there be any praise, think on these things. (Philippians 4:8)

God's truth	Satan's lies
1. Truth	Lies and religious bondage
2. Honesty	Flattery and deception
3. Justice	Perjury and false accusation
4. Purity	Wickedness of the flesh
5. Loveliness	Gossip
6. Good report	Slander and tale-bearing
7. Virtue	False teachers and prophets
8. Praise	Accusations and complaining
9. Think on good things	Strong delusion and superstition

Howbeit when He, the SPIRIT OF TRUTH, is come, He will guide you into ALL TRUTH…He shall glorify Me… (John 16:13-14)

The SPIRIT OF TRUTH will glorify the Truth, Jesus. If we are in Christ, we reflect the truth and live in truth. Because the Greater One lives in us *(1 John 4:4)* we are overcomers. Deliverance can sometimes come through a timely word of knowledge, a word of wisdom, through discerning of spirits, or through a gift of prophecy. If a word comes forth from the LORD, take it seriously. It may reveal something that will help set you free.

Deliverance

1. Repent for lying and believing lies about yourself, spouse, neighbor, friend, boss, pastor.
2. Repent for idolizing worldly goods and allowing the spirits of error and antichrist to influence you.
3. Break the power of the lies spoken by speaking them out, breaking them, casting down vain imaginations about our bodies, our abilities, our fears, others, etc., and render them null and void in Jesus' Name.
4. Ask God to cleanse your mind of all unrighteousness and plead the blood over yourself.
5. Ask others to forgive you if you have lied to them or spread gossip about them, and make restitution if appropriate.
6. Bind the Spirit of Truth to yourself. It will set you free. *(John 8:32)*
7. Ask the Holy Spirit to bring circumstances to your mind that need correction.
8. Follow through.

Chapter Thirty-Three
The Spirit of Heaviness

When a person is overcome with grief or a sense of failure, real or imagined, a spirit of heaviness will attack, energize and amplify the situation through feelings of helplessness and unworthiness. The spirit of heaviness will drag the victim down through self-pity, depression, fatigue, a deeply wounded spirit, failures, loneliness, rejection, grief, thoughts of suicide, despondency, defeat, hopelessness, melancholy, depression, despair, feelings of worthlessness, inordinate grieving, and it will invite the spirit of death to enter. Heaviness can gain access through generational curses and through unresolved hurts if not resolved in a reasonable period of time; tragedy can create an entry way, too, bringing loneliness, guilt, anguish, torment and regret. Heaviness sits on a person and inflicts woeful, despairing thoughts. Demons bearing the name of each emotion will attach themselves. Heaviness is easy to spot. The body, voice and facial expressions will reflect the state of the soul.

Healing for the brokenhearted and hopelessness

Jesus came to heal the broken-hearted and to preach deliverance to the captives, to set at liberty them that are bruised, downtrodden, crushed, and discouraged by life. *(Luke 4:18)* Jesus Himself was nearly overcome by a spirit of heaviness in the Garden of Gethsemane, so that He had to be strengthened by an angel. *(Mark 26:37)* Nehemiah was so full of heaviness that he couldn't hide it from the king. This could have cost him his life, for no one was allowed to display these emotions before the king. *(Nehemiah 2:2)* *...by sorrow of the heart the spirit is broken. (Nehemiah 15:13)*

The spirit of heaviness brings hopelessness to its victims *(2 Corinthians 8:9)*, self-pity *(Psalm 69:20)*, offense toward others who are more successful and offense toward God. This draws one to blame God for failures, which brings despondency and feelings of helplessness against Him. The victim will stop praying, behaving wisely or seeking help. Heaviness will settle like a wet blanket as they continue to blame God for their problems. Usually, upon investigation, presumption will be found in their actions that brought on their situation in the first place. God, on the other hand, has wonderful plans for us and longs to show us His love.

> *For I know the thoughts that I think toward you, saith the LORD, THOUGHTS OF PEACE, and not of evil, to give you an expected end. Then shall ye call upon Me, and ye shall go and pray unto Me, and I will hearken unto you. And ye shall seek Me, and find Me, when ye shall search for me with all your heart. And I will be found of you saith the LORD... (Jeremiah 29:11-14)*

New garments

The spirit of heaviness used to attack me, both before I was saved and afterward, dragging me into melancholy and depression. One of the triggers the enemy used was deep regret over past sins before I accepted Jesus as my Messiah. Also, he constantly badgered me with the things I was struggling with as a new Christian. The disappointment over each failure I experienced in my Christian walk was used as a wedge to bring guilt, shame and regret. One day, while I was spiraling downward toward depression, the Father directed me to turn on Godly praise and worship music and begin to dance before Him. The oppression and heaviness fled through power praise. New wine cannot be put in old wine skins, but many people try to put a glorious slender garment of praise on a body heavy with grief, self-pity or depression. The body and mind must be renewed with God's joy. YHWH, our God, has the antidote for the spirit of HEAVINESS. It is the OIL OF JOY and the GARMENT OF PRAISE.

> *...to comfort all that mourn; To appoint unto them that mourn in Zion, to give unto them beauty for ashes, the OIL OF JOY for mourning, the GARMENT OF PRAISE for the spirit of HEAVINESS; that they might be called trees of righteousness, the planting of the LORD, that He might be glorified. (Isaiah 61:2-3)*

What YHWH, our God, says about you is the Truth. What the devil says is the lie. It's time to stop listening to evil thoughts that are really the devil's thoughts, made to sound like your own, and realize *Whose* you are.

Getting free

1. Resist the devil and his evil thoughts. Command the spirit of heaviness to leave. If ministering to another, they must tell the spirit it is *not* welcome and that it must leave. Then you can cast it out.
2. Put on the garment of praise to defeat this demon. Listen to uplifting worship, upbeat praise and dance before the LORD. (No mournful songs now, designed to elicit strong repentance. There is a time and place for this.)

3. Apply God's oil of joy to yourself; do this spiritually and literally; apply fragrant anointing oil to your forehead and rebuke the spirit of heaviness along with any "symptoms" that evil spirits are striving to strengthen.
4. There really is some truth to aroma therapy. *(Song of Solomon 1:2)* Take a relaxing bath with fragrant oils and gently massage your neck, back and legs.
5. Make new friends, volunteer, break free from the boredom of the same patterns and habits.
6. Get out of the house and walk outside, taking deep breaths.
7. Resist depressing thoughts. Renew your mind by reading what God's Word says about you, and bind His Word to yourself.
8. Bind peace to your mind, emotions, spirit and body. Make the choice to rejoice!
9. If there is insomnia, bind this scripture to yourself: ***Thou wilt keep him in perfect peace, whose mind is stayed on Thee...*** **(Isaiah 26:3)**

Chapter Thirty-Four
The Spirit of Slumber, the Spirit of Delilah, Whoredoms, Gluttony, Guilt

Babylon has invaded the true church, introducing the spirit of Delilah, whoredoms and the spirit of Jezebel. The sleeping church must awaken and divest itself of the trappings of worldly seductions, purposes, agendas, and the filth and slime of wickedness. Babylon will only grow stronger unless the bride of Christ arises to defeat the relentless march of darkness into our lives. A pastor in Florida was in surgery for complications after a triple bypass. His spirit left his body, and the doctors wanted to disconnect him from life support, but the family and church continued to pray for a miracle. The first thing he saw when his spirit left his body was the spirit of Jezebel, the spirit of Delilah and the spirit of whoredoms. They were beautiful, seductive spirits that mocked and ridiculed him, informing him that they had been assigned to him all his life, to destroy the true work of God that he was called to do, and to pull him off the path in order to build his own kingdom. Immediately, an angel appeared and took him into the presence of the LORD where he was rebuked for not carrying out God's plans. After eighteen days his spirit entered back into his body, and he is now setting his course to do the Father's will. We are in a battle, not only for men's souls, but to fulfill the unadulterated calling on our lives. Demonic forces are arrayed against us to defeat these holy purposes.

The goddess on American soil

The single most important symbol of America was placed by a secret, mystical, religious cult on our soil. In the 1880s, when the Statue of Liberty was being sculpted for America, clergymen were worried about having a pagan goddess on American soil. The Masonic lodge kept their involvement low profile, as they did when building the Washington monument, a phallic obelisk symbolizing the worship of Baal. The sculptor, Auguste Bertholdi, was seeking a commission to construct a statue of Isis to overlook the Suez Canal. It was to be a robed woman holding a torch. Bertholdi was a member of a Masonic lodge in Paris. His fellow Masons helped build the Statue of Liberty. Richard Hunt built the pedestal, a ziggurat emulating the tower of Babel. The words on the statue are, "Give me your tired, your poor, your huddled masses..." This is a take on the words of Jesus, *Come unto Me, all ye that labor and are heavy laden, and I will give you rest. (Matthew 11:28)*

There was a Roman goddess named Feronia, worshipped by freed slaves as "The Emancipator." She was the goddess of liberty, linked to Nimrod (Baal). The Roman goddess Cybele is represented with a turreted crown, or crown of towers like a ziggurat, as is the Ephesian goddess, Diana. Ashtoreth (another word for Semiramis, the goddess Queen of Babylon) means Tower Woman. These towers under or on the heads of the goddesses was to represent the tower of Babel. Thus, we have the Queen of Babylon, the goddess Ashtoreth (Isis, Semiramis, Diana, Cybele) in New York harbor.

Some Bible scholars believe New York City may be Mystery Babylon, the mother of harlots. The woman named mystery Babylon is linked to global financial order, merchandise, commodities, international economics. *(Revelation 17:5)* [107]

The spirit of Delilah

The spirit of Delilah is on a mission from Satan: to seduce the people called of God into a state of slumber, so that Jezebel and whoredoms can take over. Delilah works with these two spirits to deceive and rob people of their destinies by confusing them concerning their callings and purposes, and introducing lusts of the flesh. These diversionary tactics are very effectual. Delilah is the same spirit that cut off Samson's power. She seeks to take authority away from the church, and stops the work of God by destroying ministries through seduction.

Slumber

The flesh and blood person, Delilah, seduced and deceived Samson, lulled him to sleep on her lap and shaved his head, sapping his God-given strength as a result of his disobedience and sin. Then he was attacked by the enemy. When a man's conscience is lulled into sleep, the spirit of slumber enters in. Conversely, if a Christian stays awake in the spirit, watches and listens to the warning of the watchman on the wall, the sin of slumber cannot enter in. If we sleep through the attack, other evil spirits are invited to join in the defilement. A spirit of slumber causes sleepiness when one desires to study the Bible and to worship. The spirit of slumber currently has a stronghold in the body of Christ that has lulled the sleeping church into a yawning abyss of fellowship with the world, causing her to close a blind eye to God's teachings, allowing legalized abortion and ungodly, wicked men to hold prominent public office, persecuting the true prophets who are sounding the alarm, and ultimately bringing God's judgment upon themselves; the Laodicean church they have become. It used to be a requirement for holding government office that a candidate be of good reputation and be a standing member of a church.

...God hath given them the SPIRIT OF SLUMBER, eyes that they should not see, and ears that they should not hear... (Romans 11:8)

A spirit of slumber works with a spirit of Delilah, Jezebel and whoredoms. The Clinton administration brought all this to the general public on a seductive platter. The whole nation was affected. The spirit of slumber causes a person to loose his moral compass, rendering him without a sense of right and wrong. When a minister friend of mine discovered the rampant addiction to internet pornography among pastors, he began an outreach to that group, specifically. Several other ministers and intercessors have informed me that over half of the pastors in America are not even born again. Seminary schools no longer require their graduating ministers to be saved. Is it any wonder that they do whatever the government orders them to do, refusing to speak out on issues such as abortion, homosexuality and pornography? The newspaper recently carried a headline that a teacher was suspended from his job for bringing Bibles to school. I, myself, was fired from a public school teaching job for reading from a Christian book to students. This is the antithesis of the original purpose for instituting public education. When I studied for my certification to teach, a class on the history of education revealed that public schools were actually instituted in the USA for the purpose of teaching students how to read the Bible. There is no law concerning the separation of church and state as we have been told. When Christians awake and become vigilant, they can forcefully advance the kingdom of our God, but until then, the deception of the kingdom of darkness is an ever-encroaching storm cloud, that is gathering ominously over our once Christian nation.

...the kingdom of heaven suffereth violence, and the VIOLENT take it by FORCE. (Matthew 11:12)

VIOLENT (*Strong's* 973, biastes) means a forceful or violent man. The word FORCE (*Vine's*, harpazo) indicates those who are possessed of eagerness and zeal, who are not SLUMBERING or yielding to the opposition of religious foes, who press their way into the kingdom. Never before in America has one man so captured a city for the LORD as John Alexander Dowie, whose ministry turned Chicago upside down at the turn of the century. He proved that in spite of persecution by the post office, newspapers, repeated arrests by police, slander, and hatred from religious groups, he stood victorious. His enemies ended up dead, in prison or silent. The police became his friends, and the political officials and Mayer were voted in by Dowie's people. Divine healing and salvation were preached on every street corner in the city.[108] It is not too late to take back America. Awaken to your destiny!

Whoredoms

When an individual or nation allows the spirit of slumber to enter in and control them, an insidious spirit called whoredoms tries to worm its way in, also. The spirit of Whoredoms is an exceptionally powerful spirit. It draws the individual away from the true and living God, and replaces the holy purposes of our heavenly Father with plans and activities that are off course. Sometimes these plans look good, but they are error. Our foolish hearts become darkened through this deviation from the true course. The spirit of whoredom's purpose is to pervert the true mission of the church and silence the prophetic voice. If this spirit cannot silence the true prophetic voice, then it will pollute or pervert it. In addition, whoredoms uses up the financial provisions by tempting and dragging the church away from the true call, and diverting them into the wrong direction. Additionally, whoredoms is a generational spirit that is passed down through families. A spirit of whoredoms brings darkness to the eyes of the Christian's spirit, and introduces perversion, idolatry, spiritual and physical adultery and fornication, defilement, filthy thoughts, homosexuality, all sexual perversion, lusts, pornography, a lust for the things of the world, rather than the things of God. It will lead Christians to pursue Satanism, witchcraft, new age religions. It will bring preoccupation with appearance and drive a person to social and political climbing, spiritual and physical adultery, love of worldly things. It causes leaders to spend their time and money building their own kingdoms, instead of the kingdom of God. Each spirit that comes in riding on the coattails of another spirit is progressively more evil than the previous one. Each new step is more hideously perverse than the last.

Ye adulterers and adulteresses, know ye not that the friendship of the world is enmity with God? Whosoever therefore will be a FRIEND OF THE WORLD is the ENEMY OF GOD. (1 Timothy 4:4)

The spirit of whoredoms comes in when spirit and conscience slumber; true knowledge of God is rejected and evil seems good.

My people are destroyed for lack of knowledge: because thou hast rejected knowledge, I will also reject thee, that thou shalt be no priest to Me: seeing thou hast forgotten the law of thy God, I will also forget thy children. (Hosea 4:6)

When the knowledge of God is not received and pursued, the people are destroyed and they go whoring after other gods.

...thou committest WHOREDOM, and Israel is defiled. They will not frame their doings to turn unto their God: for the SPIRIT OF WHOREDOMS is in the midst of them, and they have not known the LORD. (Hosea 5:3-4)

Sexual sin is against one's own body.

...but he that committeth fornication SINNETH AGAINST HIS OWN BODY. (1 Corinthians 6:18)

No one in their right mind would do such things; only when the conscience is asleep due to a slumbering spirit. When I was in the world, my band played in a small southern town that had a huge passion play. Most of the town worked in it, in one capacity or another. When my band was between concerts I worked as a temporary secretary for the man who owned and ran the play. All day I took calls from all over the world for commodity trading. I would set up meetings in foreign countries and he would fly in as the middleman, make commissions and put it in his Swiss bank account. Then he would bring the money back into the country as "loans" to the Passion Play, a slick money-laundering scheme. This man often played Jesus in the play. He was a convicted peeping Tom and had slept with many women in the cast. Knowing the truth about him and the play really turned me off to religion. There was a religious spirit operating through the cast, and whoredoms operated through the head of it. As a result of this unpleasant experience, I ran even further away from God.

Gluttony

When a spirit of whoredoms begins to manifest in a person, it opens the door to a spirit of gluttony. Gluttony manifests as anything we do *to excess* that takes our attention and focus away from the true and living God. The word glutton (*Vine's*, gaster) denotes a belly. In Titus 1:12 the Cretians are referred to as slow bellies, meaning idle gluttons. Gluttony leads a person into addictive behavior. Anorexia, bulimia, and other excessive behaviors manifest because gluttony produces guilt and SHAME. The person tries to atone for his own sins. The sin of gluttony is lumped in with rebellion, stubbornness and alcoholism in Deuteronomy 21:20, and the people were commanded to stone such a person to death. Proverbs 23:21 states that the drunkard and the glutton will be in poverty. The word poverty (*Strong's* 3423, yarash) in that scripture means to rob, to expel, impoverish, ruin, consume, destroy, disinherit, dispossess, drive. This is certainly what the spirit of gluttony does: it drives a person into excessive and unhealthy behavior, it consumes them utterly so that there is no time left for God, it robs them of their rich inheritance in the LORD, which includes peace and joy.

Meats for the BELLY, and the BELLY for meats: but GOD SHALL DESTROY both it and them...your body is the temple of the Holy Ghost which is in you...ye are bought with a price... (1 Corinthians 6:13-20)

Whose end is destruction, WHOSE GOD IS THEIR BELLY, and whose glory is in their SHAME. (Philippians 3:19)

GUILT, SHAME, frustration and anger can enter in as well, when the victim finds himself unable to quit the sin. Gluttony, the sin, is energized by the presence of the spirit of gluttony, and can manifest in many ways, such as: sports addictions, eating disorders, addiction to gambling, pornography, smoking, unquenchable lust, obsessions and compulsions, drug and alcohol addiction, etc. Gluttony works hand in hand with a spirit of bondage.

Guilt

Sin has built a broad highway by now, to drive guilt into the soul. The person develops a poor self-image and feels unworthy. He can barely hold his head up. Finally, he stops praying and gives up. **The spirit of guilt brings condemnation, whereas the Holy Spirit brings conviction.** Condemnation will cause the person to avoid getting the help they need because of the shame and fear it brings. Fear is really fear of death because one's spirit knows the wages of sin are death. *(Romans 6:23)* If a person suffers from guilt, then repentance is necessary for whatever sins are opening the door. Then the spirit of guilt must be cast out.

The antidote

The antidote is to trust in God's eternal life, and Jesus Who gives it to us, and to stay in a state of purity by frequently confessing sin and repenting. When people run after other gods, it is because they are trying to fill the emptiness in their souls. Only Jesus can fill this void. There is no other act, possession, or religion that can take His place, or satisfy our souls. He Himself designed us to be worshippers of Him alone. We must turn our hearts to the living God Who created us, repent of our adulteries, and let the Holy Spirit lead us and guide us into all truth. We lean into Jesus to fill us with His love.

Who is this that cometh up from the wilderness, leaning upon her beloved? (Song of Solomon 8:5)

He embraces us with His eternal love.

His left hand is under my head, and His right hand doth embrace me. (Song of Solomon 2:6)

Become a worshipper of Jesus, and He will fill your deepest needs.

I am my beloved's and my beloved is mine... (Song of Solomon 6:3)

Breaking free

1. Are you suffering from shame, guilt or condemnation?
2. Repent of any sins and addictive behaviors such as gluttony, abortion, unforgiveness, sexual sin, gambling, etc., that could be causing you to feel this way. While these are sins, there are spirits that attach themselves to these sins and continue to energize them.
3. Cast out a spirit of gluttony, bondage, guilt, shame, and a spirit of slumber.
4. Because these things have become your god, repent.
5. Are you part of the sleeping church? Has your spirit slumbered and allowed a life of compromise? Have you turned a blind eye to sin? Repent and ask YHWH, our God's, forgiveness.
6. Cast out a spirit of Delilah, whoredoms, Jezebel.
7. Fill your heart with the Word of God and let His presence and power direct your life. There is no other true satisfaction: going down to the gambling boats will not fill your lonely, hurting heart, seeking escape in any other way will not fill your heart. Only Jesus can fill that terrible gnawing emptiness. Run to His open arms today and find peace, at last.

Chapter Thirty-Five
The Perverse Spirit, Dumb and Deaf Spirit, Legion, Slothful Spirit, Lethargy, Defiance

Definition of perverse

Perverse (*Strong's* 1294, diastrepho) means to distort, to twist, misinterpret, corrupt, turn aside and away. Perverse thinking is wrong attitudes that come from wrong thinking, that manifest in wrong actions. A perverse spirit twists the truth and actually sees things in an incorrect and perverted way. Perverse, according to *Webster's*, means deviating from what is right or good, obstinately persisting in an error or fault, wrongly self-willed, disposed to oppose and contradict. The perverse spirit causes a stubborn REFUSAL to hear the truth. Jeremiah wrote of the perverseness of Judah:

> *O LORD, are not Thine eyes upon the truth? Thou hast stricken them, but they have not grieved; Thou hast consumed them, but they have REFUSED to receive correction: they have made their faces harder than a rock; they have REFUSED to return. (Jeremiah 5:3)*

Notice the perverse spirit caused them to not repent, to refuse to receive correction, to harden their hearts, and refuse to return to the LORD. In the spirit realm, UNCLEAN SPIRITS that manifest as spiritual or sexual perversion often have the appearance of FROGS. Disobedience is manifest. Because of the twisting and distorting of truth, people with a perverse spirit will follow and even become false prophets. They have twisted sexual tendencies and can be addicted to porn.

> *And I saw three UNCLEAN SPIRITS like FROGS come out of the mouth of the dragon... (Revelation 16:13)*

Legion

The Gadarene demoniac was a man full of fierce, perverse and unclean spirits. When bound in chains and fetters the demons who controlled him empowered him to do violence, easily breaking the chains, terrorizing the town's folk, who drove him into the wilderness, where he shamelessly wore no clothes and lived in the tombs, a dwelling place for demons. He already had rage, and anger, but now he picked up the even more wicked spirits of perversion, homosexuality, heaviness, anxiety, exhibitionism, self-mutilation, eating disorders, rejection, suicidal tendencies, confusion, insomnia, bondage and others as he helplessly cried and cut himself. The unclean spirits of Legion were fearful when Jesus cast them out and begged to be sent into the pigs, thus, we can conclude one or more of the spirits present was fear. By the time our compassionate Savior arrived, the Gadarene had a legion of demons living within him. Fortunately, Jesus cast out the legion and set the man free. *(Luke 8:26-39; Matthew 8:28-34; Mark 4:1-20)* Cutting oneself seems to be a common event with the demonized and SRA (satanic ritual abuse) victims. An SRA victim I ministered to, frequently sliced up her wrists in an unusual pattern when the demons directed her to do so. The prophets of Baal cut themselves and cried out to elicit their god's attention when Elijah challenged them on Mount Carmel. *(1 Kings 18:28)* A person who manifests legion, is often a victim of sexual or ritual abuse and is in deep torment of soul.

Dumb and deaf spirit

When the disciples could not cast out a DUMB AND DEAF SPIRIT, it was due to a LACK OF FAITH, a PERVERSE spirit and UNBELIEF that prevented them from succeeding. *(Mark 9:25-26)* They had closed their ears and eyes to the truth. Sometimes a child with learning difficulties has a dumb and deaf spirit. After deliverance, normal learning ability returns.

> *And Jesus answering said, O FAITHLESS and PERVERSE generation, how long shall I be with you, and suffer you?...Then came the disciples to Jesus apart, and said, Why could not we cast him out? And Jesus said unto them, Because of your UNBELIEF...(Luke 9:41)*

> *He REBUKED the foul spirit, saying unto him, Thou DUMB AND DEAF SPIRIT, I CHARGE thee, come out of him, and enter no more into him. (Mark 9:25)*

NAILS

Jesus CHARGED (*Strong's* 2004, epitasso) the foul spirit to come out, meaning He commanded it. He REBUKED the dumb and deaf spirit meaning He forbid the foul, impure, unclean spirit to operate. A perverse spirit darkened the disciples' minds so they could not understand Jesus' true purpose, or the direction He was heading, the cross. Jesus warned:

> Let these sayings *SINK DOWN INTO YOUR EARS: for the Son of man shall be delivered into the hands of men. BUT THEY UNDERSTOOD NOT this saying, and it was hid from them... (Luke 9:44)*

The very next action the disciples took was to dispute who was the greatest among them. The PERVERSE spirit had twisted their thinking, giving them wrong attitudes and causing them to miss Jesus' direction for them. The DUMB AND DEAF SPIRIT closed their ears and eyes from receiving the truth. Over and over, miracles were done in their presence, yet the next time a similar situation presented itself, they dropped the ball again. First Jesus fed the five thousand. Then He fed the four thousand yet they did not understand. When the storm arose with Jesus asleep in the boat, He had to be awakened to rebuke the storm. Later, when another storm arose, Jesus walked on water and rebuked the storm, again, yet they did not comprehend that they had the authority to do the same things. Jesus now showed them a little child and spoke:

> Whosoever shall receive this child in My Name receiveth Me...for he that is least among you all, the same shall be great. (Luke 9:48)

Our whole world is filled with perverse thinking. It is so commonplace that even sincere Christians find themselves corrupted. SRA victims almost always have a dumb and deaf spirit present, and it is common in children defiled by sexual or occult abuse. SRA looks a lot like Multiple Personality Disorder.[109] Loose this person from suicide, self-destruction and a dumb and deaf spirit .

Manifestations
A dumb and deaf spirit manifests in the following ways: lunacy, sore vexed, or the wicked spirit casts its victim into fire or water to destroy him, instigates suicide *(Matthew 17:15)*, blindness, deafness and dumbness *(Matthew 12:22)*, tears the victim, convulsions, epilepsy, foaming at the mouth, gnashing of teeth, crying, pining away, falling down, wallowing. The victim often has memory gaps, and becomes agitated when one tries to deal with these issues. It also hides behind a host of learning disabilities, and sometimes shows its ugliness through a stubborn refusal to learn.

Boy's hearing healed
At the end of a service where I was ministering, a boy of about twelve and his father came forward. When He told me the boy was deaf, I leaned down and looked into his eyes, detecting demonic activity. I turned to the father and asked him a few pertinent questions, first ministering to him. He was full of UNBELIEF. I encouraged him, and he confessed and repented of unbelief. Heaviness lifted off the boy and I commanded the DUMB AND DEAF SPIRIT to leave in Jesus' Name, putting my fingers in his ears and saying, "Be healed in Jesus' Name!" I turned his head toward me and said, "Can you hear me?" He started jumping up and down and said, "Yes, Yes, Yes!" just as in the example in Mark 9, the father's unbelief opened the door to the son receiving a dumb and deaf spirit. A blind man I ministered to in another city wanted prayer, but clearly needed to repent of unbelief. When he did so, he received his healing quite easily. Children who are struggling terribly with learning sometimes need deliverance from a dumb and deaf spirit.

The glazed look
A dumb and deaf spirit can operate from the inside or oppress from without, causing both believers and un-believers to be unable to understand or comprehend scripture or spiritual things. Sometimes, when I start to minister to someone with this spirit, they get a glazed look in their eyes. A dumb and deaf spirit is attempting to control the person and prevent them from hearing the gospel or receiving deliverance. Take authority over this evil spirit, bind it and cast it out in Jesus' Name.

Slothfulness
Slothfulness is a spirit that can hold whole families in its grip. It tries to keep a person from stepping out to do God's will. Sloth is an aversion to exertion or work. The word slothful (*Strong's* 6102, atsel) is also translated sluggard. The two animals, the sloth and the slug, are perfect namesakes for this evil spirit's manifestations. The sloth moves so slowly that green fungus and mold grow in its hair, and it has a putrid odor. The slug, a nasty

creature, leaves a trail of slime behind it wherever it slowly moves. It destroys vegetables in the garden that people worked hard to plant and cultivate. The slothful person will always have an excuse to stay home when they should be helping or participating. This spirit may influence a person to be slothful in all activities, such as a man who forces his wife to support the family while he drinks or gambles away the money she earns, or it may manifest in a refusal to participate in activities of a godly nature with excessive addiction to couch-potato activities, like TV sports or fantasy shows.

...As the door turneth upon his hinges, so doth the slothful upon his bed...The sluggard is wiser in his own conceit than seven men that can render a reason. (Proverbs 26:13-16)

A picture of sloth with family feud

When I lived in the Ozarks, I was amazed by some of the denizens there. I rented a trailer house from some hillbillies, who sat on their front porch continually rocking and chewing tobacco. They had a cow for only one reason: to keep their grass short. One afternoon I came home and smelled a strong odor coming from inside their house. I was informed that they were making liquor in the bathtub. This, it turned out, was their chosen profession, along with a still they kept in the woods. All I ever saw them do was sit.

A sheriff from Branson told me a tale about the Hatfields and the Blues, families that had been feuding for generations. Howard Johnson's was building a new Inn, and the Blues, who were notoriously lazy sneaked into town late at night and stole Ho Jo's new, red tin roof. They plowed up the road coming into their property, and rain washed out the road. The clan lived under the roof until several weeks later when the Hatfields stole it during a raid. The Sheriff happened by when they were dragging it to their own property.

The slothful spouse

I've ministered to several women and men whose spouses manifest the spirit of sloth. They are worn out from trying to raise their children without help, financially or emotionally. Some spouses lay around all day, refusing to help with the responsibilities. It puts a strain on marriages, and relationships. This spirit often works closely with a spirit of heaviness, because refusing to act out God's plan for your life ultimately brings discouragement and despair. Getting a lazy, slothful person up and moving in the things of God is no small task, and must be a work of the Holy Spirit, with much prayer. It cannot be affected by nagging, yelling or threatening. The victim of this spirit must accept Jesus as their Savior and Messiah, and be filled with the Holy Spirit to be set free. Otherwise, they will go back to old habits that this spirit will energize and encourage. The wicked, old patterns of behavior are strongholds, which must be broken.

Lethargy

Lethargy is born out of unresolved sin, whether it be generational or not. The spirit of lethargy brings apathy toward righteousness, holiness, the things of God such as Bible reading and prayer. It gains a foothold through guilt and remains to defeat all Godly efforts. This spirit overwhelms a person so that they may become weary, have trouble sleeping, find themselves unable to listen to or act on God's Word. They may want to sleep all the time, and find it difficult to get anything done. Everything seems to be in slow motion. Motivation is gone and there will be resistance to making the necessary changes to pull up out of depression.

Defiance

The defiant spirit is boldly resistant to authority. Because of the line of authority set up in God's Word, this spirit seeks to lead its victim out from under the umbrella of God's protection and make him vulnerable to its leading. Rebellious people are not happy people. They are always picking a battle somewhere. They always seem to have a chip on their shoulders. The misery this person goes through in lost relationships is covered up by stubbornness, and barely disguised anger. They challenge all comers and are hard to be around because one can never relax, knowing that every word and gesture will be challenged. Some victims of this spirit cannot keep a job because they always resist authority and constantly justify their actions. They have trouble saying they're sorry and repenting for sin. A defiant person cannot be confronted with the truth. They will only argue. Prayer and intercession must be offered, and the evil spirit's influence must be broken before they will listen and begin to receive ministry and deliverance. It often takes time and patience, and is like pealing an onion; many tears, one layer at a time.

Chapter Thirty-Six
The Spirit of Exhibitionism

Draws spotlight to self, rather than God

A person with the spirit of exhibitionism is often someone who was very wounded in childhood. They look for the attention and approval of others to satisfy feelings of rejection and unresolved hurts. Many famous performers are victims of this spirit. They are desperate for the love of others, but often in private push them away with their behavior, because they are actually filled with self-doubt, self-loathing, and low self-image.

A person with a spirit of exhibitionism will always have to be in the spotlight. They are sometimes led to give false prophecies for the purpose of drawing attention to themselves. They may lead others in a wrong direction, or attempt to correct others with soulish prophecies. In these cases, an antichrist spirit, a controlling spirit, or a Jezebel spirit may be in operation, as well. These can be spotted by discerning believers, because they simply come from a soulish perspective, rather than by the Holy Spirit, and cause others to take their eyes off God. A rule of thumb is whether they glorify themselves, or the LORD.

Sometimes a person with this spirit speaks loudly. They don't listen, but interrupt and attempt to control conversations. They will be competitive and denigrate others to promote themselves.

Sometimes the spirit of exhibitionism will deceive others to curry favor or bring destruction. King Ahab fell victim to the wiles of the spirit of exhibitionism, which was working with a lying spirit to bring about his destruction. He paid with his life. Zedekiah was a useful tool of this wicked spirit who desperately wanted the king's approval.

> *And Zedekiah…made him horns of iron: and he said, Thus saith the LORD, With these shalt thou push the Syrians, until thou have consumed them. (1 Kings 22:11)*

Defiling and enticing

A person with this spirit often likes to dance (sometimes lewdly) in front of others. If someone with this spirit dances in front of a congregation of believers, they will all be defiled. Leaders need to minister to these people firmly, but in love, and remove them from "performing" in front of meetings. During the worship in a church I was visiting, a woman got up and began to dance in front of the whole congregation. There were others dancing, but she began to be more and more suggestive and sensuous. Exhibitionism operated through her to entice and defile the whole congregation. At another meeting where I was to speak, a woman got up during praise and worship and began to dance furiously back and forth, until she was in a sweaty frenzy. Then she proceeded to take over the meeting by prophesying loudly and ordering others about. There *is* godly dancing, but it will not arouse sexuality, rather it will lead others in a holy and pure way to the throne room of almighty God.

Similitudes---a godly gift

There is a godly demonstration of the gifts of the Spirit and sometimes God's people will act out what He shows them, to demonstrate a prophetic word, or make a point. The difference is in which spirit is motivating these actions. Ezekiel acted out a prophetic Word from the LORD by lying on his left side 390 days and his right side forty days. *(Ezekiel 4:4-6)* Jeremiah wore a yoke on his neck to demonstrate God had given Judah to Nebuchadnezzar, the king of Babylon, to rule. Hananiah, a false prophet, took off the yoke and broke it, demonstrating for the king of Judah that Babylon's rule would be broken within two years. Because of this false prophecy, Jeremiah prophesied Hananiah's death within the year, and he died. *(Jeremiah 28)*

Repentance

1. Ask God's forgiveness and the spotlight of the Holy Spirit to shine in your heart to reveal to you the truth of your actions.
2. Repent for allowing the spirit of exhibitionism to operate through you, and for others you may have defiled or led astray.
3. Cast out the spirit of exhibitionism, rejection, seduction, whoredoms, lying spirit., etc.

4. Resist the temptation to show off or brag in word or deed.
5. Bind humility, meekness and self-control to yourself and submit to a godly pastor.
6. Pastors should never meet alone with women for counseling, but have someone else present.
7. The presence of this spirit indicates an emptiness in the soul. Learn to fill your heart with God's Word and seek His presence.
8. Allow the Holy Spirit to fill your heart. The love, attention and favor you seek is from God, not the attention and approval of man.

Chapter Thirty-Seven
The Spirit of Haughtiness, Blindness, the Critical Spirit, Strife

A piece of the puzzle

As I go from place to place and church to church to minister, it amazes me how much revelation and godly activities each denomination and body of believers has to offer, and how each one has a part to play in God's plan. Yet, I often hear how such and such a group are in error, from each of the opposing parties. This self-righteous criticism is born out of a spirit of haughtiness. A number of the Hebrew words translated as both haughty and proud in the Old Testament, come from the primary root, ga'ah (*Strong's* 1342). Another word, ruwm (*Strong's* 7311), is translated both as haughty and proud. The New Testament word for both haughty and proud is huperephanos. This leads me to believe that both haughtiness and pride, though translated differently, are essentially the same word.These words mean high, lofty, presumptuously, arrogant, swelling, proud, haughty.

Haughtiness brings dislike and distrust

Haughtiness influences each individual or group to believe they are the only ones with the truth, or at least the whole truth. Knowledge puffs up, so they start shunning everyone not just like themselves. While I do not believe we should embrace cults, or blatant error, love shown between the members of the body of Christ, rather than the strife, backstabbing, tale bearing, and mistrust that is currently taking place, is the way to join together and win the world for Jesus. When unbelievers see churches fighting, it is a real turn off. Religious excess is another manifestation of the spirit of haughtiness. We have no reason for pride to separate us from our brothers in Christ, whether it is because we have high holiness standards, or because we think we are following the law to the letter, or we believe we are better because we are practicing extreme freedom *from* the law.

Haughtiness lifts itself above God

Many haughty people reject God. The rise of humanism (man exalting himself above God, claiming to be self-sufficient, even calling himself God), Gnosticism, communism, Darwinism and evolution (we evolved from primordial soup; there is no God), and other "isms," has given rise to the mindset that we don't need God. He is seen as a myth for the weak-minded to cling to. Man, in his desperate rebellion against the one true God, has sought to replace Him with other gods. Faith in ones own ability, or riches is no hedge of protection. The god of self emerges in the new religion. They strut about saying, "I am god."

Every way of a man is right in his own eyes... (Proverbs 21:2)

These deluded souls hoard what they have instead of being what they were eternally purposed to be, and in the end will meet their destruction. The rich man went to hell but tried to get the beggar, Lazarus, whom he failed to help in his earthly life, to give him water. Lazarus had a wonderful reward, but the rich, haughty man continued to burn in thirst. *(Luke 16:20-25)*

Judging another brings blindness and a critical spirit

When we judge another, we condemn ourselves, and we open ourselves up to a CRITICAL SPIRIT. As we accuse ourselves and others, we make ourselves targets for an enemy attack on our health and relationships.

...whosoever is angry with his brother without a cause shall be in danger of the judgment: and whosoever shall say to his brother, Raca (worthless), shall be in danger of the council: but whosoever JUDGEST another, thou CONDEMNEST thyself; for thou that judgest doest the same things. (Romans 2:1)

The spirit of haughtiness opens a door to spiritual BLINDNESS. We cannot see how wretched we really are.

Because thou sayest, I am rich, and increased with goods and have need of nothing; and knowest not that thou art wretched, and miserable, and poor, and BLIND, and naked... (Revelation 3:17)

The more self-righteous we become, the more BLIND and CONDEMNING we become.

PRIDE goeth before destruction, and a HAUGHTY SPIRIT before a fall. (Proverbs 6:16-17; Isaiah 2:11)

Repentance

Absolutely everyone has pride. If you want to get right with God, begin by repenting of pride. The pride of life creeps in subtly and most of us do not even know we have it. Yet it is the very goodness of God that leads us to repentance. *(Romans 2:4)* He forgives us if we will REPENT OF THINKING TOO HIGHLY OF OURSELVES. True repentance brings humility *(1 Peter 5:5-6)*, as we humble ourselves under the hand of almighty God.

> *Better it is to be of a HUMBLE spirit with the lowly, than to divide the spoil with the PROUD. (Proverbs 16:19)*

No one has anything God didn't give them, therefore, there is nothing to be proud of. He can just as easily take it away. I tell my children when they forget to rejoice, "Today was a gift from God." Let us rejoice in what God has given us, without pride.

The accuser

Always remember that Satan is the accuser of the brethren. It is self-righteousness that causes us to judge another. When we allow ourselves to listen to, or participate in the accusation of others, it is sin, and Satan is surely using us. There are several preachers with national ministries who specialize in criticizing other ministries. They attack and destroy with a casualness that is an abomination to God. We must guard our hearts from joining in by listening or participating in their wickedness, lest judgment come on us as well, and we begin to pick up a spirit of haughtiness from them.

> *For by thy words thou shalt be justified, and by thy words thou shalt be condemned. (Matthew 12:37)*

We are to pray for those we disagree with, and love the brethren, as well as our enemies. Whenever I participate in the sin of being critical of another's ministry, God chastises me by taking away the anointing from me, This is really mercy, though it doesn't feel that way, because if I was allowed to continue ministering in a wrong spirit, I could do more harm than good. When I repent, and ask forgiveness, the anointing is restored.

> *JUDGE NOT, and ye shall not be judged; CONDEMN NOT, and ye shall not be condemned: forgive, and ye shall be forgiven. (Luke 6:37)*

Our hearts are revealed as desperately wicked, full of accusing and condemning thoughts, words and actions toward others.

> *The heart is deceitful above all things, and desperately wicked: who can know it? (Jeremiah 17:9)*

To be set free, these things must be repented of, and washed in the blood of Christ. Jesus did not come into the world to CONDEMN the world, and neither did we.

> *For God sent not His Son into the world to CONDEMN the world... (John 3:17)*

When we submit to the Holy Spirit's transformation of the inner man we begin on a journey that kills the flesh.

> *And be not conformed to this world: but be ye transformed by the renewing of your mind, that ye may prove what is that good, and acceptable, and perfect, will of God (Romans 12:2)*

The spirit of strife

Because we are discussing PRIDE in this chapter, it is necessary to demonstrate through the Word that STRIFE and CONTENTIONS are generated from pride. PRIDE blinds us to our own weaknesses and causes STRIFE where there would be none. The heart is further deceived *(Obadiah 1:3)* through bitterness, unforgiveness, and judgment is perverted through envy and grudge holding. Keeping an offense is a surefire, long term way to provoke STRIFE.

> *Only by PRIDE cometh CONTENTION... (Proverbs 13:10)*
> *...a PROUD heart stirreth up STRIFE... (Proverbs 28:25)*

> *For where ENVYING and STRIFE is there is confusion and every evil work. (James 3:16)*

129

The Greek word for STRIFE used in James (*Strong's* 2052, eritheia) means factions, contention, intrigue, to stimulate to anger, provoke, rivalry, ambition, jealousy, division. Hatred, anger and wrath stir up strife *(Proverbs 10:12; 15:18; 29:22),* and STRIFE generates ENVY. *(1 Timothy 6:4; James 3:16)* If a person is raised in a family full of STRIFE, it is very difficult to break free. Thus, STRIFE is carried on to the next generation. STRIFE becomes a form of abuse in a home. Soon rebellion manifests in the children. A CONTENTIOUS person engenders STRIFE. *(Proverbs 26:21)* The scribes and Pharisees, a haughty and critical, religious sect, full of strife, brought a woman caught in adultery, but after their hearts were smitten with the truth of their own sin, they left. Jesus invited any man who was without sin to cast the first stone, but *all* were convicted in their hearts. Jesus' question to the woman was:

Woman, where are thine accusers? Hath no man CONDEMNED thee: She said, No man, LORD. Neither do I condemn thee: go, and sin no more. (John 8:10-11)

Every CONDEMNATION we participate in, whether in word or deed, will someday bring us terrible shame. If we are to be conformed into the image of Christ, then we must yield ourselves to correction. A key to breaking strife is to humble oneself, decide without regret that having the last word is not as important as having peace, and give up the right to defend oneself. When you do this, the Father can then step in and defend you. Put a watch over your mouth. The very disciples (sons of thunder) who wanted to call fire down from heaven to kill those who would not receive Jesus were on their way to being beautifully transformed at the last supper. This was evidenced by their reaction when Jesus said that one of them would betray Him.

…they began to be sorrowful, and to say unto Him one by one, Is it I? (Mark 14:19)

It took the beginning of humility working in their hearts to allow their souls to be searched for sin. Yet Luke reveals that immediately they began to have STRIFE about who was the greatest among them. Bragging and arguing are manifestations of haughtiness which engender strife.

And there was also a STRIFE among them, which of them should be accounted the greatest. (Luke 22:24)

This spirit of haughtiness and strife, present in their hearts, is one of the reasons, when the betrayal came shortly thereafter, that a spirit of fear was able to seize the disciples, and they ran away. Jesus corrected them, but He had already shown Peter the danger he was in.

Simon, Simon, behold, Satan hath desired to have you, that he may SIFT you as wheat: But I have prayed for thee, that thy faith fail not: and when thou art CONVERTED, strengthen thy brethren. (Luke 22:31-32)

A look at the word SIFT and the word CONVERTED is revealing. SIFT (*Strong's* 4617, siniazo) means to riddle as through a sieve. It also means to pull out (steal), cast down (kill), and trample underfoot (destroy). The sin of haughtiness, pride, and strife opened Peter up to Satan's attack. Jesus' use of the world CONVERTED (*Strong's* 1994, epistrepho) actually indicated real concern on Jesus' part for Peter. Though he was a born leader, he had not yet learned to LEAD BY SERVING IN HUMILITY. Jesus' demonstration of washing the feet, and modeling true humility was timed to show them and us there is a much better way.

CONVERTED in the scripture above means to turn about, to come again. Use of this word indicates that Peter had temporarily turned away from Jesus, and needed converting (TURNING) AGAIN. We all need to turn again when we sin and grieve the Father. Peter's need for CONVERSION was further demonstrated when he drew his sword and struck off the right ear of the high priest's servant, Malchus. Jesus turned and echoed similar words He had spoken to Peter at an earlier time:

Put up thy sword into the sheath: the cup (of suffering) which My Father hath given Me, shall I not drink it? (John 18:11)

Because of the hardness of Peter's heart, Satan was still using him, trying to prevent Jesus from His destiny of suffering for the sins of the world. *(Matthew 16:23)* Peter continued to backslide, cursing, even denying Christ because of the condition of his heart. He returned to his former profession of fishing. It was in his back-slidden state that Jesus sought him out, just as He seeks us out to restore us. Because of Peter's three denials, Jesus had him speak corrective, redemptive words three times before His ascension into heaven.

Simon, son of Jonah, lovest thou Me more than these? He sayeth unto Him, Yes, LORD; Thou knowest that I love Thee. (John 21:15-17)

Jesus asked him two more times in order to restore Peter to right standing in front of the disciples and the whole spiritual realm. Otherwise, he would have been consumed by guilt and shame.

John---son of thunder, or apostle of love?

The extent we yield our lives to the Holy Spirit's correction, is the extent to which we become conformed into Christ's image, and our actions will reflect His character and likeness. John and his brother James were named the "sons of thunder" *(Mark 3:17)* for good reason.

And when His disciples James and John saw this, they said, LORD, wilt Thou that we command fire to come down from heaven, and consume them, even as Elijah did? But He turned, and rebuked them, and said, Ye know not what manner of spirit ye are of. (Luke 9:54-55)

Thunder (*Strong's* 1027, bronte) means to roar. *Vine's* alludes to their fiery disposition (sons of tumult), and it may have led to James' execution. John wanted to call fire down from heaven, and he sent his mother to ask for **PREFERENTIAL** treatment in heaven. John, known as the one whom Jesus loved, laid his head on the Master's breast at the last supper and allowed Jesus to bring out the best in him and cause his zeal to be turned for the good. He is the only disciple who didn't die a martyr's death, though he was boiled in oil and survived attempted poisoning. Yet, with God, it isn't so much how we begin, as the PROCESS OF TRANSFORMATION, and ultimately how we finish the race. At the end of John's life he is known as the apostle of love, and he was entrusted with Jesus' glorious Revelation on the Isle of Patmos.

Spiritual blindness

A haughty person must have a seared conscience in order to justify his actions and words against others. This blindness manifests to his own folly. We should correct our own errors and leave the correction of others to the LORD. The haughty person is contentious, boastful, scornful, high-minded, self-righteous, unteachable, arrogant, **WRATHFUL**, prideful, and obstinate.

And why beholdest thou the mote (splinter) that is in thy brother's eye, but perceivest not the beam (log) that is in thine own eye? (Luke 6:41)

PROUD and HAUGHTY scorner is his name, who dealeth in PROUD WRATH. (Proverbs 21:24)

…a PROUD heart stirreth up STRIFE… (Proverbs 28:25)

An angry man stirreth up STRIFE, and a furious man aboundeth in transgression. A man's PRIDE shall bring him low: but honor shall uphold the humble in spirit. (Proverbs 29:22-23)

Humility brings God's honor. He will uphold those that humble themselves.

…God resisteth the PROUD, and giveth grace to the HUMBLE. (1 Peter 5:5)

Get set free

If you don't think you have pride, think again. It may actually be pride that is blinding you from seeing it in yourself. When we first point a finger at ourselves and repent, then YHWH, our God, doesn't have to humble us and discipline us so strongly.

1. Repent for allowing the wicked spirit of haughtiness to use and operate through you.
2. Cast out haughtiness, pride, contention, hardened heart, seared conscience, strife, rebellion, and any other evil spirit in operation.
3. Pray for your eyes to be opened, and see yourself as God sees you.
4. Ask forgiveness of others you treated with haughtiness.
5. Bind a spirit of humility to yourself, and ask God to begin speaking to you. Allow the Holy Spirit to do a work in your heart, to cleanse you of all unrighteousness. Purpose in your heart to love others with agape love, no matter who they are.
6. Realize you have nothing God didn't give you and begin giving to those less fortunate, but tell no one.
7. Fast to break off deception from your heart, and fill yourself with scriptures such as 1 Corinthians 13.
8. Walk in the Spirit and you will not fulfill the lust of the flesh and pride of life.

Chapter Thirty-Eight
The Spirit of Envy, Jealousy, Hate, Unforgiveness

Envy and jealousy

Envy is a pervasive spirit and causes bitterness and jealousy. (Refer to the connection between envy and strife discussed in the previous chapter.) Wars are caused by envy. Envy and jealousy are both translated from the same two words in *Strong's* (7065, 7068; qana, qinah). Qana has a strongly competitive sense, and means zealous, in a bad sense, to become intensely red, to provoke to anger. Further, it means the act of advancing one's rights to the exclusion of the rights of others. In no passage is our God described as envious, but as jealous (zealous) of advancing His right to be the only God we worship.

> *If ye have bitter ENVYING and STRIFE in your hearts, glory not, and lie not against the truth. (James 3:14)*

> *...From whence come WARS and FIGHTINGS among you? Come they not hence, even of your lusts that war in your members?...The spirit that dwelleth in us lusteth to ENVY? (James 4:1-5)*

> *For JEALOUSY is the rage of a man...neither will he rest content, though thou givest many gifts. (Proverbs 6:34-35)*

One man wants what another man has, thus he becomes envious. According to *Vine's* (phthonos), ENVY is the feeling of displeasure produced by witnessing or hearing of the advantage or prosperity of others. There are pastors who will not let others into their pulpit because of envy. They are afraid the people will run off and follow someone else. The difference between envy and jealousy is that ENVY desires to deprive another of what he has. An example of envy gone mad is the woman who killed a cheerleader thinking her daughter would take her place. She was willing to deprive a fellow human being of life to satisfy her envy.

JEALOUSY desires to have the same or the same sort of thing for oneself. The result of JEALOUSY is that it is never satisfied. (See *Proverbs* above.) An example of ENVY: When a woman envies another woman of her husband and sets out to steal the husband through seduction. JEALOUSY can be demonstrated by keeping up with the Jones's: In our neighborhood, one neighbor saw another with a new riding lawn mower, and found they could not bear to go on without one, though they had a perfectly good push mower in the garage. Then the neighbor on the other side discovered that they, too, could not live without a new riding mower. Within a matter of one month, five neighbors all had riding mowers. A family I know bought a new maroon van with racing stripes. Within two weeks their next door neighbor had purchased an identical van. This caused the first family to be angry with the neighbor, because they wanted to be the only ones with a new van of that color. When I played in nightclubs, another singer heard our band one night, and was so overcome with jealousy that she tried to destroy me, and my band. First, she bought clothes similar to mine and started to do her hair like mine. Next, she tried to hire my brother for her own band. When that failed, she offered our musicians more than we paid, stealing several of our sidemen. She learned my songs and began trying to book herself in the same clubs where we had appeared. I have always believed that God created each of us to be unique, and placed a specific call on each of our lives that no one else can fulfill. If we believe God loves each of us as we are, then we are free to walk in that uniqueness, without fear.

JEALOUSY causes resentment, anger, cruelty, rage, competitiveness, revenge, greediness, exalting oneself above others, vengeance and a lack of rest in God. No matter what God gives a jealous man, or what he gets from others, he will never be content. Lucifer was jealous of God and wanted to be like God. That brought in iniquity and war, resulting in him being cast down from heaven. PRIDE had entered in because of his physical beauty.

> *Thou wast perfect in thy ways from the day that thou wast created, till iniquity was found in thee...Thine heart was LIFTED UP (PRIDE) because of thy beauty, thou hast corrupted thy wisdom by reason of thy brightness: I will cast thee to the ground...(Ezekiel 28:13-19)*

> *...Thy pomp is brought down to the grave...How art thou fallen from heaven, O Lucifer...For thou hast said in thine heart, I will ascend into heaven, I will exalt my throne above the stars of God...I will be like the most High... (Isaiah 14:9-20)*

If one of the most beautiful beings ever created can fail so miserably, so can we. He tempts us with JEALOUSY and ENVY because he hates us, since he can never be redeemed, but we can. He thinks this is unfair, so he accuses us day and night. He demands that we receive the same justice he got, but we receive God's mercy when we ask for it and repent of our sins. It could be said that he is JEALOUS of us.

Hatred and unforgiveness

Envy and jealousy require a lot of energy to maintain. They will eat you alive and never bring satisfaction. Repentance and forgiveness toward those who elicited the envy, or whom you feel owe you something is the believer's only option. If you allow bitterness to arise in your heart, you must ask God to forgive you. (See section on *Bitterness* for steps to take.) Unforgiveness causes a vengeful spirit to arise in your heart. God says vengeance is His alone *(Romans 12:19)*, therefore forgiveness is the only option available to the believer. Unrepented jealousy brings hatred, and hatred brings destruction. If a man does not forgive, God will not forgive him.

> *And his lord was wroth, and delivered him to the tormentors, till he should pay all that was due unto him. So likewise shall my heavenly Father do also unto you, if ye from your hearts FORGIVE not every one his brother their trespasses. (Matthew 18:34-35)*

> *Whosoever HATETH his brother is a murderer: and we know that no murderer hath eternal life abiding in him. (1 John 3:15)*

Hatred is the same as murder in God's eyes and must be repented of. If one continues to hate another person he will not have eternal life.

> *We know that we have passed from death unto life, BECAUSE WE LOVE THE BRETHREN. He that loveth not his brother abideth in death. (1 John 3:14)*

A pastor friend once told me when he realized God had made him unique, and no one else could take away or do precisely what God had called him to do, he repented of ENVY and JEALOUSY. He said it was very liberating. Shortly after this, he began, without fear, to let the flock get up and take turns preaching short sermons or sharing a word from the LORD. The people began to develop their gifts and grow in the things of God as they were challenged to let God bring forth their gifts in the body.

Getting free

The love of YHWH, our God, shed abroad in our hearts by the Holy Ghost is the only antidote.

1. Repent of operating in the sin of jealousy, envy, unforgiveness and hate.
2. Repent of ungodly actions you've committed.
3. Ask God's forgiveness.
4. Cast out a spirit of jealousy, envy, unforgiveness and hatred.
5. Break these strongholds off your life.
6. Bind the love of God to yourself.
7. Look up all the scriptures on love and bind them to yourself.
8. Vigorously resist the temptation to operate in envy, jealousy, unforgiveness and bitterness.
9. Rejoice in the success of others. Pray for those whom you are tempted to be envious of, that they would prosper and be in health, even as their soul prospers. *(3 John 2)*
10. Study 1 Corinthians 13 in the Amplified Bible. Ask the Holy Spirit to lead and guide you in love. The Word of God planted deep in your heart will change your life.

> *...love never is ENVIOUS nor boils over with JEALOUSY; is not boastful or vainglorious, does not display itself HAUGHTILY. It is not conceited—arrogant and inflated with PRIDE...(1 Corinthians 13:4-5 Amp.)*

Chapter Thirty-Nine
The Spirit of Infirmity

Infirmity—mental and physical weakness

Infirmity (*Strong's* 769, astheneia) means feebleness of body or mind, malady, moral frailty, disease, sickness, weakness. This word for infirmity can indicate *both* mental and physical sickness. The spirit of infirmity is often the result of a generational curse, a bitter-root judgment, or an inner vow. It may find entrance through self-pity, excessive stress, strife, or self-hatred. The following women in the New Testament were both demonized and sick. Often this is the case. If you cast out the demon, the person will recover. Sometimes deep wounds open a legal door for a spirit of infirmity to enter.

> *And certain women, which had been healed of evil spirits and infirmities, Mary called Magdalene, out of whom went seven devils... (Luke 8:2)*

This next scripture is very revealing when we look at it carefully. Notice that Jesus was TEMPTED as we are in the area of INFIRMITY, yet without sin.

> *For we have not a high priest which cannot be touched with the feeling of our INFIRMITIES: but was in all points TEMPTED like as we are, yet without sin. (Hebrews 4:15)*

TEMPTED (*Strong's* 3985, peirazo) in the above scripture means to test, to try, scrutinize, entice, to discipline, examine, to prove. Sickness can be TEMPTATION. It takes strength to say no when the temptation comes to "take" a cold or disease. Likewise, mental and emotional weakness must be resisted in Jesus' Name, just as Jesus overcame with the power of His Word. *(John 16:33)* We can speak the Word and overcome sickness and the temptation to be weak. We can help others also, who suffer from mental or physical infirmity.

Infirmity—weak conscience

Infirmity (*Strong's* 771, asthenema) means a scruple of conscience. This kind of infirmity is more in the line of weakness of morality. *We then that are strong ought to bear the infirmities of the weak, and not to please ourselves. (Romans 15:1)* This can mean giving emotional support to others, and building them up in the things of God, so they can learn to stand strong in the LORD. God wants us to be patient and forbear others, comforting them and teaching them the way, in love.

> *Now the God of patience and consolation (comfort) grant you to be likeminded one toward another according to Christ Jesus... (Romans 15:5)*

Infirmity—mental illness

Infirmity (*Strong's* 3554, nosos) means sickness, disease. According to *Vine's* it is used metaphorically to mean mental ailment.

> *And in that same hour He cured many of their INFIRMITIES (sicknesses) and plagues (diseases), and of evil spirits; and unto many that were blind He gave sight. (Luke 7:21)*

Jesus healed all who came to Him, whether it was sickness or disease, mental, physical, or spiritual, an evil spirit, a generational curse, or birth defect; whether it was because of sin or not. Isaac was blind in his old age but the Word doesn't say he sinned. *(Genesis 27:1)* Jesus healed the people because that is what He was sent to do, and because of the love and compassion He had for the people.

> *...He hath sent Me to heal the broken-hearted, to preach deliverance to the captives, and recovering of sight to the blind, to set at liberty them that are bruised... (Luke 4:18)*

Impatience

Impatience is a manifestation of the spirit of INFIRMITY. An impatient person will not wait for things to work out. They become upset and easily frustrated, opening themselves up to the spirit of anger. This weakness of the flesh must be dealt with, because anger brings strife, and where strife is, there is every evil work. If infirmity has an open invitation to manifest, continual anger and bitterness can cause infirmity, as the unrepented sin eats away at the body and mind.

I speak after the manner of men because of the INFIRMITY of your flesh: for as ye have yielded your members servants to uncleanness and to iniquity unto iniquity; even so now yield your members servants to righteousness unto holiness. (Romans 6:19)

Infirmity causes anger and mental anguish

I was having a garage sale with a friend at her house. Just as we got set up, an elderly man with a spirit of infirmity backed out across the street. He just kept coming until he destroyed most of my baby furniture, hit the house, shifted into forward and headed toward the other side of our sale. I shouted, "Jesus, Jesus help!" Miraculously, he barely missed my van and hit a tree next to our clothing racks. He began gunning the motor angrily. A neighbor called the police, and I began pounding on his window since the door was locked. I called out to him until he rolled down his window a bit, saying, "What do you want? I've got to drive..." I reached across him turned off the engine, and pulled out the keys. He was more upset then, and fuming. He was a small, frail man, his back bent and face shriveled in bitter lines. I sensed he was a very bitter, angry man, filled with self-hatred. He was also suffering from Alzheimer's. His motor started again just as the police arrived, and he started to back out. The policeman pounded on the window and he stopped and got out, yelling and threatening the cop, making fisticuffs to hit him. He even took a swing. The policeman took the keys out and turned his back to talk to me; suddenly the car started again. This time he began backing out and nearly succeeded before the cop could get the third set of keys. Later, another set was discovered in his pocket.

The man's children told me he insisted on being independent and living alone, and would howl when they locked his car up in the garage to keep him from driving. He would call locksmiths to open the garage, and make new keys. After this incident, however, they took away his car and sold it. He died shortly thereafter.

The root of the spirit of infirmity is self-hatred. The spirit of infirmity manifests in various diseases. It also comes from bitterness of soul, and can be demonstrated through self-pity, anger, rage, resentment.

Walking in forgiveness

Forgiveness in every area of our lives is imperative, in order to walk in divine health. Otherwise, Satan can gain an advantage and attack you with sickness.

...for if I forgave any thing, to whom I forgave it, for your sakes forgave I it in the person of Christ; Lest Satan should GET AN ADVANTAGE of us: for we are not ignorant of his devices. (2 Corinthians 2:10-11)

When we yield ourselves to be the servants of sin, then we become malleable in the enemy's hand.

Know ye not, that to whom ye yield yourselves servants to obey, his servants ye are to whom ye obey; whether of sin unto death, or of obedience unto righteousness: (Romans 6:16)

Satan uses weaknesses already present

Often, back troubles are the result of a spirit of infirmity.

...there was a woman which had a SPIRIT OF INFIRMITY eighteen years, and was bowed together, and could in no wise lift up herself. And when Jesus saw her, He called her to Him, and said unto her, Woman, thou art LOOSED from thine IN-FIRMITY. (Luke 13:11)

Jesus LOOSED her and He will loose YOU. Notice what He says after this:

And ought not this woman, being a daughter of Abraham, whom Satan hath bound, lo, these eighteen years, be LOOSED from this bond on the Sabbath day? (Luke 13:16)

The SPIRIT OF INFIRMITY usually uses weaknesses *already present* in its victims to bind them and afflict them with sickness. The infirmity is further energized by demons that know how to exploit a weakness, mental or physical. This spirit enters through our own death wishes and self-hatred, and pushes it to the limit. Jesus took stripes to deliver us from our infirmities, just as He died to deliver us from sin and death. *(Isaiah 53:5)*

The thief

A man with an infirmity for 38 years was made whole when Jesus told him to rise and walk. *(John 5:5)* Long illnesses, frailty, lameness, arthritis, weakness; none of these are a problem to Jesus. He wants to set you free. It is the enemy who wants to keep you weak and sick, and who puts sickness on us.

> *The thief cometh not, but for to steal, and to kill and destroy: I Am come that they might have life, and that they might have it more abundantly. (John 10:10)*

If you are not walking in abundant life, the thief is robbing you and you don't have to take it anymore. Fight the good fight of faith. Jesus set those free who were oppressed by the devil.

> *...God anointed Jesus of Nazareth with the Holy Ghost and with power: Who went about doing good, and healing ALL that were oppressed of the devil... (Acts 10:38)*

This is such good news! He healed them ALL—all who were oppressed of the devil. Since Jesus would not do anything that was against God's will, then we know that it is God's perfect will to heal all who need healing. Sometimes Jesus cast the devil out of people to heal them, and sometimes He simply healed them.

Breaking the stronghold of infirmity

1. Repent of any unhealthy habits or of sins such as unforgiveness, bitterness, anger, impatience, immorality, strife and stress that may have contributed to your illness. Ask YHWH, our God's, forgiveness.
2. Set yourself in agreement with the Word that your body is the temple of the Holy Ghost, and you must take care of it by eating healthy, living healthy, and thinking healthy.
3. Tell the spirit of infirmity you don't want it anymore, it is not welcome, and you won't listen to its lies anymore.
4. Cast out a spirit of infirmity if that is the reason for the illness.
5. Use your faith to stand and believe the Word of God, more than how things look or feel. Appearances and feelings can change, but God's wonderful Word does not.

> *Every good gift and every perfect gift is from above, and cometh down from the Father of lights, with Whom is no variableness, neither shadow of turning. (James 1:17)*

> *For I Am the LORD, I change not... (Malachi 3:6)*

6. Bind these scriptures to yourself.

> *Who His own self bare our sins in His own body on the tree, that we, being dead to sins, should live unto righteousness: by Whose stripes ye were healed. (1 Peter 2:24)*

> *...Himself took our INFIRMITIES, and bare our SICKNESSES. (Matthew 8:17)*

7. Loose yourself from the sickness, disease or oppression that is afflicting you.

> *Trust in the LORD with all your heart; and lean not unto thine own understanding. In all thy ways acknowledge Him, and He shall direct thy paths. (Proverbs 3:5)*

8. When the devil comes back again to attack you with fear, resist it. When he taunts you, telling you you're a fool to believe God's promises, stand on the Word: "It is written, 1 Peter 2:24 says that by His stripes I am healed." Force Satan's knee to bend under the power (authority) of the Word spoken out of your mouth. He will be persistent. You must be *more* persistent. Resist the devil and he will flee. *(James 4:7)*
9. After you pray to receive your healing and speak the Word over your body, receive your healing by faith. Believe you are healed right now!
10. Deliverance is a process! It may happen all at once or over time. Fasting and praying for wisdom is a wise step during this season of standing for your healing. *(Ephesians 6:13-14)*

(See the *Stripes* section of this book for much more information on healing, and the spirit of infirmity.)

Chapter Forty
The Spirit of Mammon and Greed, the Devouring Spirit, the Buffeting Spirit

The spirit of mammon and greed

The spirit of mammon affects both rich and poor. Many serve this wicked spirit, consciously or unconsciously. It causes one to fear the loss of wealth, or greedily pursue wealth, never finding peace or satisfaction.

The Bible says YHWH Jireh is my provider and He will never leave me or forsake me. It further states that blessings will overtake me if I keep the LORD's commandments.

The love of money is the root of all evil. *(1 Timothy 6:10)* Greed is rooted in the lust of the flesh. If we are centered in the Father's will for our lives, provision will be available from Him. Confusion manifests in not understanding who your provider is. Are you your own provider? Is your job your provider? Is your mate your provider? If you believe this, then YHWH, is not your provider, and you will always be running after money, but you will never have enough.

Mammon is a wicked spirit that deceives us into taking our eyes off our true provider. *(Matthew 6:24)* Mammon wants to be served, but it is IMPOSSIBLE to serve both God and mammon. Mammon was a deity that ancient peoples worshipped as their god of finance. People believe there is power in money. This is a lie of the devil. The real power is in YHWH, our God.[110] People are deceived into believing power comes from wealth and power is the real goal. This is one of the reasons people get involved in witchcraft, and bow their knees to the god of mammon. We are not the servant of money—money is our servant.[111] The Holy Spirit should lead our lives, not the desperate pursuit of money.

The love of money (*Strong's* 5365, phil-argria) means fondness of silver. The root word, argos, means shining; the ever present passion to know intimately that which shines. What shines for you? A big house, fancy car, lots of money, success, approval of man, power? God instructs us to cleanse our hands and purify our hearts. If we allow the god of mammon and greed to grip our hearts we are walking in spiritual adultery. Without clean hearts we will fall wounded or killed in the battle for our souls.[112] Some prosperity teaching demands God to be our servant to get us money. Just the opposite is true. God is our Master, and money is our servant to expand the kingdom.[113]

The demon of greed

The demon of greed looks like a human, wears a business suit (according to Howard Pittman), and traffics in human souls. I see greed personified like the pirates of Wall Street. It sets snares to entrap unsuspecting victims. The eyes are cat-like, glittering with delight as greed makes conquest after conquest. Its followers worship at it feet in this age, without pity or remorse, as greed foments insatiable avarice by promising wealth and power. This demon is one of the princes of this age.[114] If we allow mammon and greed to grip our hearts, we are walking in spiritual adultery. Without clean hearts we will fall wounded or killed in the battle for our souls.

In our economy, are well lined pockets more important than godliness and righteousness? The voters of this nation thought so, overwhelmingly. Because the people elected Clinton, not once but twice, we signaled our holy God that His laws meant nothing to us. Worshiping at the feet of mammon was more important than having godly leaders who would steer the ship of state toward morality.

The god of greed motivates the abortionists. Take away the profit and abortion will stop. Notice that all the people who want abortion are now living. The supercilious diatribe of feminists, who constantly promote so-called women's rights, is hollow rhetoric when one considers that their platform is built on the tenuous foundation of greed. The second the opportunity was made available in 1973, doctors became licensed killers for profit. They no longer even have to take the Hippocratic Oath to preserve life, because of the changing moral climate in this country. What is the difference between a knife in the hand of a mercenary and a knife in the hand of an abortionist? It is legal to sell the body parts of freshly aborted babies right there in the clinic, to the highest bidder. President Clinton vetoed a bill to stop partial birth abortion, one of the most gruesome procedures in the slaughtering arsenal of abortionists. This was a bill congress passed and the majority of American people wanted.

Breaking mammon and greed's power

1. Repent of allowing the spirit of mammon and greed to rule in your life.
2. Ask God's forgiveness for serving mammon.
3. Turn from greed and fear of loss and give your heart to the true and living God.
4. Tell the Father that you are making a paradigm shift. It all belongs to Him. You will serve Him and money will serve you, to be used to further the kingdom.
5. Trust the LORD to be your provider.

The devouring spirit

The devouring spirit manifests, along with the spirit of destruction or darkness. It is released in a person's life through disobedience and manifests in poverty, lack and debt. A person may suffer illness that lingers without a cause or deep discouragement, depression, hopelessness. The person suffering from this spirit's attack will be in debt. They won't know where their money has gone for there is never enough. Tithing is a key to getting out of debt, for the LORD will rebuke the devourer. *(Malachi 3:8-12)*

The buffeting spirit

The buffeting spirit works covertly against ministries to undercut and rob them of the abundant life and those who give to them, their jobs, and any income. It plagues ministers who really want to do the Father's work but seem to be unable to move forward. Needs go chronically unmet. *(2 Corinthians 12:7)* This spirit's assignment must be cancelled, and any curses returned to the senders seven-fold.

The blocking spirit

The blocking spirit prevents breakthrough in every area. It places a cloaking device around a person or minister that renders them invisible. They will not be noticed, even when they are right under someone's nose. They will be passed over and ignored. Connections will be difficult. Even a very talented individual can have this spirit assigned to them and languish anonymously for life, unless this spirit's assignment is broken.

Study Questions: Chapter 29
1. What evidence do we have in the Bible that God's Word is truth?
2. Name three times when the disciples displayed hardness of heart (unbelief) and failed to act on Jesus' instructions.
3. Name three times when the disciples did respond correctly to Jesus' instructions.
4. Think about two specific times when you failed to respond quickly and correctly to God's Word (His instructions).
   a. What were the consequences?
   b. What could you have done differently?
   c. What did you learn from this situation?
5. Are you a winner or a loser? Give scriptures to back this belief.
6. Are you a carrier of God's anointing? Back this with scripture.
7. What really upsets you? Give this some thought. Do you fly off the handle in anger? Do you get fearful over finances, children, job, etc?
8. After careful consideration: list two things that you can do differently to cooperate with the Holy Spirit, defeat unbelief, and change your life.
9. Repent of unbelief. Study the chapter's definitions of unbelief.

Study Questions: Chapter 32
1. What is a little white lie? What can the consequences be?
2. Can you remember an unfortunate incident in your life when you lied, and what the ramifications were?
3. Is deceiving someone to protect yourself ever a good idea?
4. How does our God feel about deception?
5. What is flattery?
6. What is exaggeration? Whom does it serve?
7. What should you do if someone in your family or your boss asks you to lie?
8. If you struggle in these areas, will you ask the Holy Spirit to help you daily, even hourly?

Chapter Forty-One
Two Ways to Live

Two kinds of people
1. Faithful, just, loyal, wise, productive, righteous, trusting the LORD, successful in God's eyes.
2. Unfaithful, unjust, disloyal, foolish, unproductive, wicked, fearful, missing the mark in God's eyes.

The kingdom of heaven is like the parable of the faithful and unfaithful servants. *(Matthew 25:14-30)* The LORD gives us gifts and talents and waits to see how we will use them. Every man receives a gift, no matter how great or small. What he does with it is up to him. If he takes it and uses it for God's glory, God will give him more. If he hides it, believing God is stingy with the gift, then God disciplines him. If he uses his God given talent for wickedness he will be punished.

> *...Thou wicked and slothful servant...cast the unprofitable servant into outer darkness: there shall be weeping and gnashing of teeth. (Matthew 25:30)*

The defeated life
The defeated person wakes up one morning and realizes he has never lived. He has been afraid to step out and take chances, knowing that disappointment may lurk around the corner. The old expression "Nothing ventured, nothing gained" never fazes him because he will never dream big dreams. He sticks to well-worn patterns that don't challenge him, and in turn, he is angry deep down with God. He feels he got the short end of the stick when God was passing out gifts, because he doesn't believe he really has anything important to offer, and even if he did, he'd bury it under a bushel. He is the man who took the LORD's talent and hid it instead of investing it in the kingdom, because he was fearful of losing it. After all, he might lose it on the way to the bank, and then where would he be? This man doesn't comprehend the love of God.

Will you live in victory or defeat?
You are in a battle for your life. Wake up! You are a winner! Greater is He that's in you than he that's in the world. *(1 John 4:4)* Get your life back on track by confessing your sins to God. Don't be ashamed to get help. When geese are flying in formation, they let the old, the sick and the very young fly in the rear where the air resistance is much less. They constantly switch the ones flying in front where it is the hardest to fly. If we would recognize the great pressure on our leaders and relieve them from time to time, we would not have sick and dying churches or burned-out leaders. Christians are to be overcomers, who take the land for Jesus Christ. The trumpet is sounding. Stand and fight the good fight!

Model of true servants of YHWH, our God
1. Humility and obedience
2. Serving Him in submission
3. Serving others
4. Profitable servant
5. Using gifts and talents wisely.
6. Allow Holy Spirit to lead through seasons of repentance and lay bare the soul.
7. Walks in love.
8. Time spent with The Father in prayer and meditation on the Word.

Taking possession of the land
If you are a born-again believer, you belong to God. He tells you to take the land just as he told the Israelites they were the owners of Canaan, but they had to fight to take it, and fight to keep possession. You must drive the demons out of your soulish realm and body. Vigilance is a necessary part of the Christian walk. In areas where you had trouble in the past, the enemy will attempt to regain access. He sometimes works this through discouragement and rejection. Temptations will come but we don't have to take them. The kingdom of heaven is forcefully advancing and forceful men lay hold of it. *(Matthew 11:12)* Our members are at war within us. The war, ultimately, is over our eternal salvation. If we walk in the Spirit, we will not fulfill the lusts of the flesh.

> *For the flesh lusteth against the Spirit, and Spirit against the flesh: and these are contrary the one to the other: so that ye cannot do the things that ye would. (Galatians 5:17)*

Chapter Forty-Two
Walk in the Spirit

Much has been made of warring in the Spirit, and that is very important, but walking in the Spirit, daily, enables us to avoid some of the battles and to overcome the enemy before he can get a foothold in our thought lives. Following is a discussion of how to war using the fruit of the Spirit. This is the key: Don't engage in warfare for someone else if you are operating in fear, doubt or unbelief, if you are anxious, angry at someone, depressed, or if you are *currently* suffering from the same problem. Living life in the Spirit causes fewer battles, much larger victories and smaller wars, making life less difficult.

WALK IN THE SPIRIT, and ye shall not fulfill the lust of the flesh. (Galatians 5:16)

But the fruit of the Spirit is love, joy, peace, long-suffering, gentleness, goodness, faith, meekness, temperance: against such THERE IS NO LAW. And they that are Christ's have crucified the flesh with the affections and lusts. If we live in the Spirit, let us also WALK IN THE SPIRIT. (Galatians 5:22-25)

Love

To war using YHWH's fruit of the Spirit means that if someone attacks you with anger or hatred, you do the opposite: show them love and operate in the fruit of the Spirit, LOVE. Agape love (*Strong's* 26, agape) means affection, benevolence, a love feast, a feast of charity. It is the God kind of love. The *Bible* promises that by their fruits we will know them *(Matthew 7:20)* Let's make sure that we are walking the love walk in all our dealings with others. We are commanded to abide in love and love our neighbor *(John 15:10)* even as we love ourselves. You cannot truly move in faith unless you operate in love because faith works by love. *(Galatians 5:6)* God will not forget your work and labor of love. *(Hebrews 6:10)* There is a great reward coming for those who choose to defeat temptation by exercising the love walk. When we are perfected in mature love we can cast out fear, anger, strife, and other temptations of the flesh. Finally, as believers our ultimate goal is to be with the LORD forever, thus we must be conformed into the image of our Messiah and pass from death to eternal life by loving the brethren.

Blessed is the man that endureth temptation: for when he is tried, he shall receive the crown of life, which the LORD hath promised to them that LOVE Him. (James 1:12)

...but perfect LOVE casteth out fear... (1 John 4:18)

We know that we have passed from death unto life, because we LOVE the brethren. (1 John 3:14)

Joy

Joy (*Strong's* 5479, chara) means cheerfulness, calm delight, gladness, exceedingly joyful, overflow with joy. If someone is operating against you with depression or heaviness, sad stories, bad news, or pouting, respond with the fruit of the Spirit, JOY. The JOY of the LORD is our STRENGTH *(Nehemiah 8:10)* against attacks of the enemy, and joy cannot be manufactured. Some of the most joyful people I know have been through great adversity, endured fiery trials, and come out the other side with joy wrought in the furnace of affliction. You cannot take their joy away from them. When they enter a room they carry it with them and affect others around them with their glorious fruit.

My brethren, count it all JOY when ye fall into divers temptations; Knowing this, that the trying of your faith worketh patience. (James 1:2-3)

Peace

If the enemy sends someone against you with anxiety, fear, fretting, frustration, or who is continually upset, bringing confusion, stress, or strife: war using the fruit of the Spirit, PEACE. Peace (*Strong's* 1515, eirene) means quietness, rest, set at one again, harmonious relationships between God, men and nations. God wants us to live in harmony with others. A soft answer turns away wrath. *(Proverbs 15:1)* Walking in PEACE can test our faith to the limit if we live in a home filled with strife and confusion. Peace, when someone is screaming accusations in your face, is the toughest fruit of all to walk in. It requires humility in abundance, and must not insist on always winning or having its own way. To experience peace requires giving up the right to self defense, and then truly and finally trusting God to defend you. To walk in God's shoes of PEACE necessitates setting aside our own agenda and walking in God's plan. Otherwise, there will be no PEACE in your soul. You will operate in constant turmoil and will have trouble sleeping. Speak PEACE to your spirit.

Thou wilt keep him in perfect PEACE, whose mind is stayed on Thee... (Isaiah 26:3)

Longsuffering

If the enemy sends someone against you who is irritating and difficult, despondent, angry, or provokes you: war against this attack using the fruit of the Spirit, LONG-SUFFERING. Long-suffering (*Strong's* 3115, makrothumeo) means forbearance and patience. It is the quality of self-restraint in the face of provocation, which does not hastily retaliate or promptly punish. (*Vine's*) It is the opposite of anger, and it manifests in mercy. It does not surrender to circumstances or succumb under trial. It brings hope, since patience is hard to develop. God gives us lots of opportunities to work on it. We will go around the mountain again and again until we develop this fruit.

I had a neighbor who constantly operated his CB. It caused interference on my TV, telephone, radio, and musical equipment. I could not talk on the phone, hear my TV or do recording for weeks on end. For several days in a row, every time I tried to record my new tape he would come on with the most obnoxious sounds and talk, to attract other CB operators to talk to him. Then, being a drug-dealing homosexual, he would try to lure others to come to his house. He would often start up his broadcast during church service that we held in our home, and interfere with the PA. Finally, I flew into a rage and stomped down the hall, yelling that I could not accomplish anything for God because of this man. The LORD rebuked me, immediately. I repented and began to pray for the neighbor. God loves him. Additionally, I did warfare, coming against the demons that operated through him. Without being asked, another neighbor went over and talked to him, asking him not to broadcast during church service hours. Within a couple of days he began constructing a huge tower and soon was broadcasting high enough above the power lines that it no longer affected my electronics. Long-suffering sometimes means waiting on God to handle the situation, while loving your enemy, and seeing him through God's eyes.

Gentleness

If the enemy sends someone to attack you with error, defiance, stubbornness, rudeness, inconsideration: war using the fruit of the Spirit, GENTLENESS. Gentleness (*Strong's* 5544, chrestotes) means kindness, goodness of heart, excellence in character or demeanor. Our kindness toward our enemies, or those who are unkind toward us, frees God to deal with them, and brings the conviction of the Holy Spirit into their lives.

Dearly beloved, avenge not yourselves, but rather give place unto wrath: for it is written, Vengeance is Mine; I will repay, saith the LORD. Therefore if thine enemy hunger, feed him: if he thirst, give him drink: for in so doing thou shalt heap coals of fire on his head. Be not overcome of evil, but overcome evil with good. (Romans 12:19-21)

Goodness

GOODNESS (*Strong's* 19, agathosune) means virtue, moral quality, desire after goodness, a kindly activity on the behalf of someone. It includes the sterner qualities by which doing good to others is not necessarily by gentle means. An example is when Jesus drove out the money-changers and cleansed the temple. *(Matthew 21:12-13)* In other words, sometimes doing good may seem harsh, as in purging with zeal, but it must always be done in love.

Purge me with hyssop and I shall be clean: wash me, and I shall be whiter than snow. (Psalm 51:7)

Hyssop has no thorns, and ends in a cluster of heads having a pleasant aromatic odor. It was used in ritual purification sprinkling. In its dried state, it may have been used to scrub and cleanse, and its leaves eaten with bread. A sponge was put on a branch of hyssop and offered to Jesus on the cross.[115]

When I was about ten, I skidded with my bike in gravel and fell, tearing up my knees and legs. When I came home bloody my mom put me in the tub, and began scrubbing out the deep dirt and gravel with a strong brush. I screamed and fought, while my brother tried to drag her away from me, hollering over and over, "You're killing her!" Mom had to lock him out of the bathroom in order to continue. I know the pain she inflicted while scrubbing the wounds upset my mom (she referred to it for years), but because she loved me and knew that if she did not do it I would be scarred for life, she took the hits, the screams and accusations for my sake. That is what Jesus did for us on a much greater scale when He suffered on the cross. He did it because only He was virtuous, holy and filled with goodness enough to take the terrible abuse for us, to clean us up, remove the deep dirt of sin, and take away the scars of life, leaving us scrubbed, fresh and beautiful.

Faith

Healing works by faith. Faith works by love. *(Galatians 5:6)* All the fruit of the Spirit work together in harmony, not in isolation. When someone is operating in doubt and unbelief, if they behave untrustworthily, faithlessly, as an unbeliever, distrustful, as one not worthy of confidence, lying: Respond by fighting the good fight of faith using the fruit of the Spirit, FAITH, standing on God's truths no matter what the circumstances appear to be. Faith *(Strong's 4102, pistis)* means truth itself, assurance, belief, fidelity, reliance upon Christ for salvation, moral conviction of religious truth, persuasion, trusting, relying. Appearances are deceiving. True faith does not operate through emotions or feelings, which can change minute to minute, but follows God's truth which is unchangeable. True, Godly faith is not based on the facts, the circumstances or people, but finally, stands alone. The truth resides in us when we are born again and we must operate with our loins girt about with truth, having the shield of faith. Make it a big shield by exercising your faith to believe for the impossible. *(Hebrews 11:6; 1 Timothy 6:12)*

Meekness (Humility)

MEEKNESS *(Strong's 4236, praotes)* means humility *(Vine's, prautes or praotes)* and consists of one's behavior toward fellow men, an inwrought grace of the soul; it covers the temper of spirit in which we accept God's dealings with us as good and therefore without disputing or resisting. It is closely linked with the word tapeinophrosune, meaning humility. They that oppose themselves are to be corrected in meekness. *(2 Timothy 2:25)* Toward all men *(Titus 3:2)*, and especially in dealing with the ignorant and erring, we are to show meekness. *(1 Corinthians 4:21)* We are even to follow after meekness. *(1 Timothy 6:11)* Meekness before God means we do not fight against Him, but learn to flow with His plan. It means that even when evil men do insult and injure us, we respond with humility and meekness. We endeavor to keep the unity of the Spirit in the bond of peace. *(Ephesians 4:2-3)*

Meekness, as manifested by Jesus, is a fruit of great power. Jesus was not a wimp, nor was He helpless. Indeed, meekness describes a condition of mind and heart. It is precisely because Jesus manifested meekness that He walked in great power, rather than pride and haughtiness. He had the infinite resources of the universe at His fingertips, yet He would say to someone He healed, "Tell no one." He only commanded the storm to be still when the disciple's lives were in danger, not just to make an impression. Though Samaria wouldn't receive Him, and He certainly could have called down fire from heaven, He cautioned His disciples that this was a wrong spirit. *(Luke 9:54-56)*

Temperance (self-control)

TEMPERANCE *(Vine's, enkrateia)* means self-control. It comes from kratos, indicating strength of will. Because God gave us a free will, we have the right to choose sin, but the child of God must exercise the strength of character to resist sin. Our will must be under the control of the Holy Spirit in order to manifest this fruit in our lives. We fight against temptation and the devil's wiles and deception with the fruit of the Spirit, temperance. When we fill ourselves with God's knowledge through reading and studying the Word, we can then gain temperance (self-control).

...add to your faith virtue; and to virtue knowledge; And to knowledge TEMPERANCE... (2 Peter 1:5-6)

An excellent spirit

Daniel had such an EXCELLENT spirit that even the heathens and pagans recognized it. Nebuchadnezzar was the first king to rely on him for interpretations of dreams, and he made Daniel ruler and chief over Babylon. Nebuchadnezzar's son, Belshazzar, also made Daniel third ruler over all the kingdom.

Forasmuch as an EXCELLENT spirit, and knowledge, and understanding...were found in the same Daniel... (Daniel 5:12)

EXCELLENT *(Strong's 3492, yattiyr)* means preeminent, very exceedingly excellent. Even when King Belshazzar was slain after Daniel's interpretation of the writing on the wall, astonishingly, the next king, Darius, made him first president over all the kingdom. Daniel continued even into the third year of King Cyrus. *(Daniel 10:1)*

Daniel had an excellent spirit because he sought the LORD, not in an ideal vacuum, but right in the midst of a pagan nation, filled with astrologers, magicians, and "wise men" all around him. He kept himself pure from their worldly values, beliefs, and foods. When he refused to defile himself, the Bible says God gave him knowledge and skill in all learning and wisdom and understanding, and of visions and dreams. *(Daniel 1:17)* He refused to stop worshiping his God even when it endangered his life, and endured the lion's den victoriously, seeing his enemies slain with the same treatment they intended for him. *(Daniel 6:14-24)* Daniel was a man who refused to compromise his principles. He fasted and prayed, humbling himself with sackcloth and ashes. *(Daniel 9:3)* He sought the LORD fervently on troubling issues. Most of all, Daniel trusted totally in the LORD and His ability to deliver him. May we all seek to manifest an excellent spirit.

A faithful spirit

A FAITHFUL spirit is to be highly prized in the kingdom. *(Proverbs 11:13)* FAITHFUL is one of the attributes of God.

> *Let us hold fast the profession of our FAITH without wavering; (for He is FAITHFUL that promised...) (Hebrews 10:23)*

When we walk as FAITHFUL servants, our heavenly Father will protect us.

> *The LORD preserveth the FAITHFUL... (Psalm31:23)*

The LORD will lift up the FAITHFUL.

> *...well done thou GOOD and FAITHFUL servant: thou hast been FAITHFUL over a few things, I will make thee ruler over many things: enter thou into the joy of the LORD. (Matthew 25:21)*

The LORD will establish the FAITHFUL and keep them from evil.

> *But the LORD is FAITHFUL, Who shall stablish you, and keep you from evil. (2 Thessalonians 3:3)*

Yes, we are to be faithful unto death so that we may receive a crown of life. *(Revelation 2:10)* Jesus is called a FAITHFUL High Priest. *(Hebrews 2:17)* In Revelation His Name is revealed as Faithful and True. *(Revelation 19:11)* As we allow ourselves to be conformed into His image, we, too, will be known as FAITHFUL and true.

A right spirit

We must long for a RIGHT spirit. It is not something that happens by accident. As we cry out for God to cleanse us and prepare us for His service, there is a process: the potter's wheel where we are molded; the anvil where we are heated in the furnace of affliction and then shaped according to the Master's plan; the polishing process; the cleansing and washing process. A right spirit has to be renewed by staying in the Word, which exerts a molding, shaping, polishing and cleansing action on us.

> *...that ye may be perfect and entire, wanting nothing. (James 1:4)*

> *If a man therefore purge himself from these, he shall be a vessel unto honor, sanctified, and meet for the Master's use, and prepared unto every good work. (2 Timothy 2:21)*

> *Create in me a clean heart, O God; and renew A RIGHT SPIRIT within me. (Psalm 51:10)*

This must ever be our heart's cry, and then we will have A RIGHT SPIRIT. The grain and the grape must be crushed to provide the bread and the wine. Jesus exhorted us to partake of this because it represented His body and blood. When we allow ourselves to be ground by the millstone and crushed by the wine press, we lose our old identity and become increasingly more like Christ.

Daily repentance

Daily repentance is one of the most powerful weapons we have at our fingertips to keep our lives clean, to keep the flow of communication open between the throne room of God and our spirit, and to make sure our prayers are not hindered. The accuser of the brethren brings up our sins and faults unceasingly.

> *...for the accuser of our brethren is cast down, which accused them before our God day and night. (Revelation 12:10)*

Satan is enraged because when he sinned, he didn't get forgiveness, nor did any of the angels who followed him. That is one of the reasons he hates us so much, and why he has appointed himself our prosecutor. He received justice, and he is demanding that we receive justice, too. Yet, when we sin, we have Jesus, Who took upon Himself the sins of the world, and He is the attorney for our defense, our advocate.

> *...sin not. And if any man sin, we have an ADVOCATE with the Father, Jesus Christ the righteous: And He is the propitiation for our sins: and not for ours only, but also the sins of the whole world. (1 John 2:1-2)*

Praise Yahshua Messiah (Jesus Christ) that we have been given a clean record, so that the devil has nothing to accuse us of. We keep our lives clean through fervent, daily repentance. Then, when Satan accuses us, the Bible says God remembers no more. Our sin is forgotten. *As far as the east is from the west, so far hath He removed our transgressions from us. (Psalm 103:12)*

Renewal imperative

For a person to remain free, he must RENEW his mind daily. *...though our outward man perish, yet the inward man is RENEWED day by day. (2 Corinthians 4:16) To be strengthened with might by His Spirit in the inner man. (Ephesians 3:16)* Renewing the mind brings strength. We all need strength to stand against the wiles of the enemy. The devil can be particularly persistent against someone who has just been delivered, because their bodies and minds are familiar with the taste of sin, like the grooves on a record. It requires total reprogramming of the mind not to play the same old tune. Smash the old record through deliverance and prepare to fill your mind with God's Word and presence. Recognize the need for change and seek God daily by praying and reading the Word. The living Word will transform us into Christ's image.

> *And be not conformed to this world: but be ye transformed by the RENEWING of your mind that ye may PROVE what is that good, and acceptable, and perfect will of God. (Romans 12:2)*

The word PROVE, in that scripture, means to DEMONSTRATE. We must demonstrate our continuing transformation by becoming renewed in the spirit of our minds. *(Ephesians 4:23)* The spirit of your mind means even your attitude, and what and how you think. It is God's will for us to be sanctified. *(1 Thessalonians 4:3)* Keeping your mind and heart fixed on Jesus is imperative in order to walk holy before our God. We cannot do this in our own strength. It will no longer be us, but Christ living in us. He is our only hope for remaining free. We must allow ourselves to be CRUCIFIED WITH CHRIST.

> *I am CRUCIFIED WITH CHRIST; nevertheless I live; yet not I, but Christ liveth in me: and the life which I now live in the flesh I live by the faith of the Son of God Who loved me, and gave Himself for me. (Galatians 2:20)*

The next scripture is my prayer for you as you continue walking in your deliverance.

> *I beseech you therefore, brethren, by the mercies of God, that ye present your bodies a living sacrifice, holy, acceptable unto God, which is your reasonable service...For this cause I bow my knees unto the Father of our LORD Jesus Christ, of Whom the whole family in heaven and earth is named, That He would grant you, according to the riches of His glory, to be strengthened with might by His Spirit in the inner-man; That Christ may dwell in your hearts by faith; that ye, being rooted and grounded in love, May be able to comprehend with all saints what is the breadth, and length, and depth, and height; And to know the love of Christ, which passeth knowledge, that ye might be filled with all the fullness of God. (Ephesians 3:14-19)*

Armor of God

from the *Heart & Soul Surrender* CD   Quadrilogy Publishing 1997
Lyrics by Bree Keyton

I come clothed in the armor of God *(Ephesians 6:14-17)*
You come to me with your sword;
Poverty, sickness, fear and doubt, *(John 10:10)*
But I come in the Name, I come in the Name,
I come in the Name of the LORD. *(1 Samuel 17:45)*

God will give you into my hand, *(1 Samuel 17:47)*
This day, the giant falls; *(1 Samuel 17:49)*
And all the people will know the truth,
Through Christ we conquer, through Christ we conquer,
through Christ we conquer all! *(Romans 8:37)*

(Chorus)
Greater is He that's in me; greater is He that's in me;
Greater is He that's in me,
Than he that's in the world. *(1 John 4:4)*
Angels will bear me up in their hands, *(Psalm 91:10)*
With wings unfurled.

You come to me with lies and deceit, *(John 8:44; Revelation 12:9; 20:3)*
Murder, rebellion and strife; *(James 3:16; John 10:10; Galatians 5:20)*
But the sword of the Spirit is in my hand, *(Ephesians 6:17)*
And Jesus is LORD, and Jesus is LORD,
And Jesus is LORD of my life. *(1 Corinthians 1:2)*

Forty-Three
A Close Look at Our Armor

Stand therefore, having your LOINS GIRT about WITH TRUTH, and having on the BREASTPLATE OF RIGHT-EOUSNESS; And your FEET SHOD with the preparation of the GOSPEL OF PEACE; Above all, taking the SHIELD OF FAITH, wherewith ye shall be able to quench all the fiery darts of the wicked. And take the HELMET OF SALVATION, and the SWORD OF THE SPIRIT, which is the word of God. (Ephesians 6:14)

Put on the armor

In Ephesians 6:10-11, God commands us: *...be strong in the LORD, and in the power of His might. PUT ON the WHOLE ARMOR OF GOD...* Colossians 3:12 exhorts us to PUT ON a heart of mercy, kindness, humbleness of mind, meekness, long-suffering, forgiving and forbearing one another. PUT ON (*Strong's* 1746, enduo) means to sink into a garment, to invest with clothing, array, endue. We are to fully invest ourselves, holding nothing back, sinking utterly into the image of our Messiah. To accomplish this impossible task, we immerse ourselves in Him, not the things of this world. The Roman soldier had the insignia of Rome burned into his palm, an act of total commitment, no turning back. He was a soldier until his death. He only thought of serving the empire. Our ensign should be plain to see for all the demons and holy angels. Our loyalty is to the one true God. WHOLE ARMOR (*Strong's* 3833, panoplia) means ALL the full armor. Our English word, panoply, derives from the Greek word, panoplia. Pan (means all), plus hoplon (meaning weapon), according to *Webster's*, is the complete array of warrior's armor and weapons, a protective covering, an impressive display. Our God wants us fully protected, no pieces missing. We are fully armed soldiers marching to war. Paul states we are wrestling in close personal conflict against Satan's army, which is organized by rank. God further commands us to STAND THEREFORE. Stand is a military term meaning to be in readiness. (See Chapter Three) Are you ready?

And having spoiled principalities and powers, He (the Messiah) made a show of them openly, triumphing over them in it. (Colossians 2:15)

Behold, I give you [that's you and me] power to tread on serpents and scorpions, and over all the power of the enemy: and nothing shall by any means hurt you.

He has already won the battle for us. When we resist *(James 4:7; 1 Peter 5:8-9)* we overcome. *(Revelation 12:11)*

Put off darkness and put on light

Colossians 3:8-9 exhorts us to PUT OFF the works of darkness: anger, wrath, malice, blasphemy, filthy communication. PUT OFF (*Strong's* 659, apotithemi) means put away, cast out. We must be ruthless with sin, because it exposes us to the attacks of Satan. Works of darkness are the devil's schemes and cunning devices to ensnare us. He needs darkness to operate. We must cast off darkness (evil works). Notice that God's armor is light, and it dispels darkness. Who is the light? Yahshua the Messiah, Jesus the Christ! We are to clothe ourselves with Him, for each part of our armor is intimately related to the person and character of Christ. We must increase in our desire to be conformed into His image. *(Ephesians 5:8-14)*

...let us put off the works of darkness, and let us put on the armor of light... (Romans 13:12)

The roaring lion

The Bible compares Satan to a roaring lion. *(1 Peter 5:8)* The devil roars all the time. We must get it in our heads that we do not wrestle against flesh and blood. *(Ephesians 1:21)* Our weapons are not the arm of the flesh but the sword of the Spirit, and they are mighty through God to the pulling down of strongholds. *(2 Corinthians 10:4-5)* We are to be sober and vigilant *(1 Peter 5:8)*, and confident in our God's armor. 1 John 4:4 tells us the One living in believers, the Lion of the tribe of Judah, is greater than the one who is god of this world, the lion who roars only to frighten and deceive.

Call to arms

In a world of spiritually challenged Christians, where weariness abounds, and the flesh is ceaselessly warring with the spirit, our God still declares that we must fight. When you are weary, then you are the most vulnerable. This is decidedly not the time to lay down your armor and take a nap. Satan doesn't give up. Ephesians 6 is a call to arms. The battle is the circumstances of life. The protection is God's armor and His blood. The victory is in Yahshua the Messiah.

...stand your ground in the evil day...having fought to the end, to remain victors on the field. (Ephesians 6:13, Weymouth Bible)

When we learn to fight wearing God's armor using the fruit of the Spirit, we blind and defeat the enemy with the sheer brightness of our shining armor. God's love must abound in us, for this is the true key that points to our victory through the cross.

Roman soldiers had seven pieces of armor. In the following study of each piece of armor the reader will notice that one piece is missing—the leg guards, known as greaves. Greaves are not needed in the Christian's armor because we are kneeling (in prayer) when we go to war.

For the warring believer, the backside is not covered because we are to ADVANCE, not RETREAT. A danger with over-zealous but unwise warriors, is that they often advance too far, beyond where the Father is actually commanding the troops. This exposes the backside to attack. This soldier may get hit with friendly fire, or be vulnerable to deep enemy incursions from behind.

Victory is in our faith

God's Word reveals that whatsoever is born of God overcomes the world *(1 John 5:4)*, and the victory that overcomes the world is our faith. *(Isaiah 54:17)* When David ran toward Goliath, his faith was not in the five stones he had, but in YHWH, his God. He refused Saul's armor because he had much better armor. Our faith is not in the armor, but in the God Who told us to put it on. Once on, we must never, ever take it off.

How do we take off our armor? By walking in darkness, cares of this world, lusts of the flesh, lust of the eyes, pride of life, *(1 John 2:16; Mark 4:19)*, and making choices based on selfish motives rather than God's will for us. How can we expect to recognize Satan's deceptions, and learn to walk in God's protection (armor of light), if we won't walk in the light of God's commandments, the fruit of the Spirit, prayer and study of the Word.

Chapter Forty-Four
Having Your Loins Girt About With Truth

The Roman GIRDLE (BELT) was six to eight inches wide, made of leather or metal, worn around the lower trunk. It suspended the other armor securely and tightly against the body, while it supported the sword, and carried money and valuables; just as all the parts of God's Word are suspended by the TRUTH. The BELT was worn in the center of the body, as the TRUTH is at the center of the gospel. The belt of truth secures our breastplate of righteousness firmly against us. Girt (*Strong's* 4024, perizonnumi) means to gird all around, to fasten on one's belt. So, also, should we fasten truth securely all about us. There are no dark secrets or lies for demons to attach themselves to. The light of truth expands our authority to new levels and gives no place to the enemy, who loves to defeat us with our own guilt.

The BELT OF TRUTH is mentioned first in YHWH's list of armor because everything hangs on it. Truth is the key, and our greatest challenge. Jesus said:

> *I Am the way, the TRUTH, and the life. (John 14:6)*

We must have TRUTH in us to bring forth TRUTH.

> *Behold, Thou desire TRUTH in the inward parts... (Psalm 51:6)*

> *He that believeth on Me, as the scripture hath said, out of his BELLY shall flow RIVERS OF LIVING WATER. (John 7:38)*

The RIVER OF LIFE and TRUTH, is brought forth purely by the Holy Spirit. When the belt of truth is removed or askew from the pollution of lies, the river has a stench that kills life.

TRUTH isn't relative, or a personal opinion or interpretation, as they teach in public school. It's absolute! The devil bends the TRUTH to be his servant. He twisted scripture in the Garden of Eden, at the temptation of Christ, and he twists it now. The following scripture is eye-opening.

> *Open ye the gates, that the righteous nation which keepeth the TRUTH may enter in. (Isaiah 26:2)*

What do you think God would say to a nation where politicians purposely misquote and bend scripture for political speeches; a nation that classifies secular humanism as a religion, bans prayer and Bible reading in schools, and the Ten Commandments from courtrooms? God's TRUTH should be the standard in the land, for His Word endures to all generations. Our generation will be judged with the same plumb line He judges all the others. *(Amos 7:8)* As the leaders *we* elect lead, so will we be judged.

> *He shall judge the world with righteousness, and His people with the TRUTH. (Psalm 96:13)*

> *His TRUTH shall be thy shield and BUCKLER. (Psalm 91:4)*

BUCKLER (*Young's Concordance*, socherah) means "target." Contemplate TRUTH as a target. TRUTH, the desired goal, means fidelity to the original standard, God's Word. It's something we shoot for to determine the accuracy of our aim. But is also the target of Satan. Twisting of TRUTH and perverting of scripture is commonplace. When you hear this happening (as the serpent's lie in Eden, "Ye shall not surely die"), it brings bondage. LOINS (*Vine's*, osfoos) means the hips and procreative power. Girding our loins with TRUTH brings life; freedom from the curse of sin and death; freedom to know the TRUTH and let it set us free. *(John 8:32)* The Word is life! *(Proverbs 4:20-22)*

Satan hits below the BELT with accusations, fear, doubt, poverty, sickness, and a host of other lies. Accusation, tale-bearing, judging, carrying offences, and gossip weaken the belt. They are based on hearsay and half-truths, and based in judging which we are commanded not to do. In sports, decency dictates that hitting below the BELT is illegal, yet Satan does not feel bound by the rules of decency. We fight with the Word of TRUTH. The Holy Spirit is the Spirit of TRUTH, and He will guide you into all TRUTH. *(John 16:13)* When a weight lifter is preparing for a lift, he puts a strong leather BELT around his abdominal muscles to protect him from injury. The LORD Jesus and Holy Spirit are our BELT OF TRUTH. We need the strength of this foundational garment, God's girdle, in these last days more than ever, for a great deception is coming.

Now the Spirit speaketh expressly that in the latter times some shall depart from the faith, giving heed to seducing spirits and doctrines of devils. (2 Corinthians 4:4)

Howbeit, when He, the Spirit of TRUTH IS COME, He will guide you into all TRUTH. (John 16:13)

Chapter Forty-Five
The Breastplate of Righteousness

With fully revealed truth in place, we are ready for the breastplate of righteousness. The BREASTPLATE OF RIGHTEOUSNESS had to be very strong and always in place, held by the BELT OF TRUTH. The BREASTPLATE (*Strong's* 2382, thorax) covered much of the upper body. The Roman BREASTPLATE was usually bronze, backed with leather. It protected the heart, lungs, stomach, liver, bowels and other vital organs. These are critical areas, both spiritually and physically. God's BREASTPLATE is so glorious that when we put it on, it protects our hearts. We wear His RIGHTEOUSNESS, because our RIGHTEOUSNESS is as filthy rags. *(Isaiah 64:6; 2 Corinthians 7:1)* Our hearts are desperately wicked, and only the LORD truly knows us. *(Jeremiah 17:9-10)* Therefore, we must put off the old man, and put on the new man, which is created in RIGHTEOUSNESS. *(Ephesians 4:22, 24)* We must put on Christ *(Romans 13:14)*

Part of our obedience to God is protecting our hearts with God's RIGHTEOUSNESS. We can do this by hiding the Word in our hearts *(Psalm 119:11)*, making God the treasure we hide there *(Matthew 6:21)*, and by fixing our desire upon the LORD. *(Psalm 108:1)* The first commandment is to love the LORD with all our hearts. If we do this we will please Him and avoid many pitfalls. By simple acts of love for God, we avoid self-righteousness, a true stumbling block. *(Ezekiel 33:13)*

> *...not having mine own RIGHTEOUSNESS, which is of the law, but that which is through the faith of Christ, the RIGHTEOUSNESS which is of God by faith. (Philippians 3:9)*

> *For He put on RIGHTEOUSNESS AS A BREASTPLATE... (Isaiah 59:17)*

If Satan accuses us every time we approach God, perhaps our armor is not properly in place. Prayer is an indispensable weapon of warfare. Before we pray we must cleanse ourselves, asking God's forgiveness, and binding the blood of Jesus to ourselves. When Satan brings his accusations against you, then remind him you've already washed that sin in Christ's holy blood, and it's gone. Remind the devil you're RIGHTEOUS because of Jesus' RIGHTEOUSNESS, imputed to you. Satan wants to hold us up on this piece of armor with guilt and shame, so we will become ineffectual for God. 1 Thessalonians 5:8 shows us we should be putting on *faith* and *love* as a BREASTPLATE. What good is RIGHTEOUSNESS without love? Love is the key to all the armor. It never fails or condemns as Satan does; and as we do when we become self-righteous. Matthew 19:17 tells us there is none good. No, not one. Except Jesus! We can only fight the devil with our Savior's own BREASTPLATE of RIGHTEOUSNESS shining over our hearts.

Your Holiness and righteousness is what the devil is after. He plots and schemes to steal our BREASTPLATE (positioned over our hearts) through bitterness, hatred, revenge, defeat, wealth, fame, success, failure to have our priorities in order. Therefore, we must be careful to heap coals of fire on our enemies' heads by loving them. We fight using the fruit of the Spirit, (love, joy, peace, long-suffering, gentleness, goodness, faith, meekness and temperance) never avenging ourselves. God wants us to love (love becomes a form of warfare) our enemies and pray for them. This releases Him to act in our behalf. Only then will our armor stay in place, protecting our hearts. If we allow the BREASTPLATE to be dented with wounds and blows from enemies, rusted with bitterness, knocked aside by lack of reliance on Jesus, or trying to earn our own RIGHTEOUSNESS, then we are vulnerable to enemy attack, and we are deceived. Let us put on the BREASTPLATE OF RIGHTEOUSNESS right now, and be conformed to our Messiah's image, will and purpose in our lives.

> *For with the heart man believes unto RIGHTEOUSNESS... (Ephesians 10:10)*

> *For He hath made Him to be sin for us, Who knew no sin; that we might be made the RIGHTEOUSNESS of God in Him. (2 Corinthians 5:21)*

Chapter Forty-Six
Feet Shod with the Preparation of the Gospel of Peace

Unlike the SHOES you are wearing, the SHOES OF PEACE never wear out. Roman soldiers had well-fitted SHOES for protection and maneuverability in action. They were sturdy and fitted with metal cleats for sure foot-edness. These cleats enabled a sure grip with the soldier's feet, so he could dig in and not be moved. We, too, are to dig deep into PEACE, that we will not be moved by the stress and strife of this world. SHOD (*Vine's*, hupodeo) means to under bind or bind on. PREPARATION (*Vine's*, hetoimasia) denotes a readiness, a firm footing on a solid foundation. The believer's walk is to be grounded with firm footing in the gospel. His walk should be a worthy testimony of his resolve. Putting on God's SHOES is preparation for action. God's PEACE makes it possible to walk in His strength on impossible paths, never letting the devil have a foothold, for God Himself under girds us.

> *...guide our FEET in the way of PEACE. (Luke 1:79)*

Putting on the SHOES OF PEACE enables us to crush Satan and his tactics under foot.

> **And the God of PEACE shall bruise Satan under your FEET shortly. (Romans 16:20)**

We can't defeat the enemy if he's ensnared us in his trap. *...fear hath torment... (1 John 4:18)* A wonderful picture of PEACE is shown in Psalm 23: still waters, green pastures, fearing no evil. If you are wrestling with fear, meditate on the 23rd Psalm allowing His PEACE to fill your soul. Then resist the devil. We must first make our PEACE with God, then He brings PEACE to our troubled souls.

> **Thou wilt keep him in perfect PEACE, whose mind is stayed on Thee: because he TRUSTETH in Thee. (Isaiah 26:3)**

Torment comes from Satan having a foothold in your life. If you worry, fret, are fearful, or are anxious, then you have allowed the enemy of your soul access to your life. You have not TRUSTED your God. TRUST (*Strong's* 982, batach) means to be confident and sure. Garrison your heart.

> *Be careful for nothing; but in every thing by prayer and supplication with thanksgiving let your requests be made known unto God. And the PEACE OF God, which passeth all understanding, shall keep your hearts and minds through Christ Jesus. (Philippians 4:6-7)*

There is no PEACE in living in the past or the future; there is only PEACE in the I Am, the now.

> *PEACE I leave with you, My PEACE I give unto you: not as the world giveth, give I unto you. Let not your heart be troubled, neither let it be afraid. (John 14:27)*

> *...in Me (Jesus) ye might find PEACE. In the world ye shall have tribulation: but be of good cheer; I have overcome the world. (John 16:33)*

Jesus gave PEACE to His disciples, and He could not have imparted what He did not possess. He gave us a wonderful gift, Himself, the PRINCE OF PEACE. The very government is on His shoulders. As His government increases, so shall peace. *(Isaiah 9:6-7)* Embrace this gift by filling yourself up with the Word, and when tough problems arise, the Word will arise in you to defeat the circumstances. Then you are well on the way to victorious living. Confusion and strife come when we fail to pursue PEACE. *(1 Corinthians 14:33)* Always be careful to be found of Him in PEACE. *(2 Peter 3:14)*

The SHOES of our warfare are really God's SHOES OF PEACE. This seems a contradiction to our minds, but God's ways are higher than our ways. (Fight using the fruit of the Spirit, PEACE.) Satan is the one who brings chaos and torment; who comes to steal our PEACE. Jesus is the perfect calm in the eye of the storm. He walked through a crowd that was trying to throw Him off a cliff, submitted tamely to physical and emotional abuse, ultimately death, and thereby defeated death. He taught His disciples to turn the other cheek, to bless their enemies, doing good to those who abuse them. His calm brought fear to Pilot's heart. He walked on water in a raging storm in perfect PEACE, and overcame His enemies by shedding His own blood. Remember that vengeance belongs to God alone. *And be not overcome of evil, but overcome evil with good. (Romans 12:19-21)*

Pursue PEACE! *(1 Peter 3:11)* Let it rule and reign in your heart. Wisdom and PEACE go hand in hand. Without the one, you will never have the other. *(Proverbs 3:13-17)* Wise counselors of PEACE will also find joy. *(Proverbs 12:20)* God said angels will bear us up lest we dash our FEET against a stone *(Psalm 91:10)* through a right relationship with Him in all our trials. Isaiah 52:7 reveals that the FEET of him who brings good news (the gospel), and spreads PEACE are beautiful. Be prepared to witness wherever our feet take us. The great evangelist, John Wesley, witnessed to two highwaymen as they robbed money from his saddlebags. Are we tale-bearers, gossipers, whisperers, do we cause strife with our tongues, are our FEET always running to do mischief? We need to wash our FEET in the cleansing water of the Word, and run to meet Jesus, our true PEACE. *Now the LORD of PEACE Himself give you PEACE always (in every way) by all means. (2 Thessalonians 3:16)*

Chapter Forty-Seven
Take up the Shield of Faith, to Quench All Fiery Darts of the Wicked

When there were holes in a soldier's shield from battle, he repaired them before the next battle. His life depended on it, as our lives depend on repairing damage done to our FAITH on a daily basis. The Roman SHIELD was about four feet high and two and one half feet wide. The shield had three layers of wood strips covered with leather, and the edges were bound with rawhide or bronze. It protected the soldier from arrows or spears as he moved it around. The curved shield protected the whole body, so that the soldier could defend all the other armor with it.

Roman soldiers had another tactic that was very effectual. When under a hail of arrows or fiery darts, they would hook their shields together, top and sides, which prevented them from harm as a group. We, as prayer warriors could take a lesson from them. If we link arms in prayer, to stand in the gap, then we, too, could defeat the onslaught of the enemy.

Sometimes the soldiers put oil on their SHIELDS, so the SHIELD would shine and blind their enemies. Often, they soaked the shield in water to quench the fiery darts of the enemy. Fiery darts were arrows dipped in tar and set afire. The thick, black, nasty stench and quality of tar is a perfect metaphor for the missiles of demons. Once temptation is yielded to, soldiers of the cross are slimed with sin. It burns into the flesh, and it is hard to get it off.

The word for SHIELD in Ephesians six (*Vine's*, thureos) means a BIG SHIELD that is large and oblong, and covers the whole body, providing protection for every part of the soldier. Used metaphorically of FAITH, the believer is to take up FAITH in all that affects the whole of his activities, moving the shield strategically to protect all of the armor.

> *...You surround them with Your favor as with a SHEILD. (Psalm 5:12)*

> *...He is a SHIELD to those who take refuge in Him. (Proverbs 30:5)*

The SHIELD OF FAITH protects us from the fiery darts of the wicked one, Satan. FIERY (*Vine's*, puroo) means to be ignited, inflamed with anger, grief, lust, to burn, be on fire, to try or refine. Refining from **without** is manifested as Satan's attack mode, through circumstances, persecutions, trials, tribulations, sickness, poverty. DARTS (*Vine's*, belos) means a missile, spear or arrow. This kind of attack pierces **into** us, therefore this attack comes from temptations, enticements, suggestions to your mind, fear, doubt.

How do we activate the SHIELD? By FAITH in the God Who made it. Without FAITH it is impossible to please God. *(Hebrews 11:6)* When you are in difficult situations, He wants you to hide behind His SHIELD. He is your SHIELD. *I Am thy SHIELD, and thy exceeding great reward. (Genesis 15:1)* Satan wants to start lots of little brush fires, so that you are distracted and unfocused. Then he launches a big attack. Remember, the SHIELD OF FAITH wraps all around you, it is big, and it will help give you the victory. *Thou hast also given me the SHIELD of Thy salvation. (2 Samuel 22:36)* The oil we apply to the SHIELD is the anointing and presence of the Holy Spirit, and His fragrance. The water we soak it in daily is prayer, so our SHIELD will not become brittle and cracked, keeping us pliable, and preventing the enemy from getting in. Part of His ministry to us is to surround us with aid and assistance. Our FAITH in His deliverance puts out ALL the enemy's fiery darts. Above ALL, take up the SHIELD OF FAITH.

Chapter Forty-Eight
The Helmet of Salvation

The Roman helmet protected the soldier's head and bore the insignia of his army. Does your HELMET clearly show what army you belong to? The HELMET OF SALVATION protects us from the attacks of Satan against our MINDS. *(1 Thessalonians 5:8)* (See *Thorns* section of this book) Attacks on the MIND are a huge part of the enemy's arsenal. We must be alert to spiritual attacks of depression, anger, revenge, bitterness, evil thoughts, dwelling on problems, self-pity.

YHWH, our God, wants to impart to us the MIND OF CHRIST! Often we fill our thought lives with junk. We all have our excuses for what we allow ourselves to see and hear, but we need to concentrate, instead, on the "good news." We become enemies of God when our minds are full of evil thoughts and images. *...you, that were sometime alienated and enemies in your mind by wicked works...(Colossians 1:21)* Smith Wigglesworth, one of the world's greatest evangelists, did many miracles and exploits for his God. The only book he ever read was the Bible. He refused to even ride in a car for fifteen minutes without talking about Jesus, and He never allowed even so much as a newspaper to enter his home. He knew the secret to his success was to keep his mind unpolluted with worldly thoughts, and to fill it, instead, with God's Word. Smith had thousands of miracles in his ministry because he knew His God intimately, with no obstacles hindering his ability to hear God's voice. We clog our pipeline to God with enormous amounts of unnecessary information.

We allow our reasoning to get in the way so often that we end up resisting God, instead of the devil. God uses the foolish things of this world to confound the wise. *(1 Corinthians 1:27)* Let us stop worrying about what people think and how foolish we may look, and step out to do great exploits for God, bringing glory to His Name. *(Mark 16:15-20)*

> *For to be carnally minded is death; but to be spiritually minded is life and peace. Because the carnal mind is enmity against God: for it is not subject to the law of God, neither indeed can be. So then they that are in the flesh cannot please God. (Romans 8:6-8)*

Romans 12:2 exhorts us not to be conformed to this world, but to be transformed by the RENEWING OF OUR MINDS. We do this by reading the Word, and through prayer. In the book of Acts people were filled with the Holy Ghost again and again. *(Acts 4:31)* We need a fresh in-filling for boldness in this last great move of God. Those who are boastful or filled with pride will miss God; those who demand that God fit into their finite religious boxes will miss God. While the HELMET OF SALVATION protects our minds, it also opens our minds to the mind of Christ, His Word, and the way of salvation.

SALVATION comes in the person of Jesus Christ. There is no other path by which we may be saved. *(Acts 4:12)* Jesus rescued us from certain death, and gave us eternal life. The complex meaning of the word salvation (sozo) is an all inclusive word, that includes the mind of Christ, which it is our privilege to possess as we are fully yielded to Him, and everything Jesus accomplished on the cross: rescue, safety, preservation, freedom, liberty, peace, righteousness, victory, deliverance, forgiveness, protection, health and prosperity. By it we are pardoned, recreated, healed, restored, made strong and whole, spiritually, physically, mentally, and materially.

Our minds are not His until He fully owns us. Ownership is a question of territory. The more territory we win from the enemy, the more we can yield and allow to be conformed to Christ. We are in the process of becoming fully His. Since we know the main battleground for a Christian is in the mind, having salvation to protect it is vital. A head injury (unresolved hurts and wounds in the soulish realm) can be fatal or cause serious complication. We must fill our MINDS with the Word, which acts as a preservative to protect our MINDS. *(1 Thessalonians 5:8-9)* SALVATION is a free gift, but it is a choice you alone must make. Let us put on the HELMET OF SALVATION right now!

Chapter Forty-Nine
The Sword of the Spirit

The Roman SWORD was a short SWORD, which enabled the soldier to be mighty in combat. It was twenty-four inches long and was sharpened on both edges. It required rigorous training to develop good combat techniques. We, too, must work hard to develop proper techniques to be victorious in battle. Planting a lot of God's Word in our hearts and minds is the first step. Then, when we need it in the heat of battle, we will be ready. The SWORD must be sharpened through prayer and *Bible* study, so that it is a worthy weapon, for quick kills.

The SWORD OF THE SPIRIT is the WORD OF GOD. Hebrews 4:12 tells us the WORD is sharper than any two-edged SWORD; it is quick (alive) and powerful (energetic); and, the WORD, divides even the soul (psyche) from the Spirit (pheuma). When you put the SWORD (WORD) in your mouth, you can discern and defeat the enemy, just as Jesus is going to do at the final battle. *(Revelation 19:15)* He will come back wearing a garment dipped in His own blood. He is the WORD OF GOD (logos), and out of His mouth will go a sharp SWORD (rhema, the spoken Word for a specific circumstance). By the WORD of our testimony and the blood of the Lamb, we can overcome the devil. *(Revelation 12:11)*

> *For the Word of God is quick (living, active, operative, energizing, effective) and powerful, and sharper than any two-edged SWORD, piercing even to the dividing asunder of soul and spirit, and of the joints and marrow, and is a discerner of the thoughts and intents of the heart. (Hebrews 4:12)*

The SWORD OF YHWH is the only piece of armor that is an aggressive weapon. Our liberal and constant use of scripture should be aggressive, too. The expression, "You are what you eat," is a case in point. If you eat a lot of cooked, dead food (religion, dead works, no action to your faith, TV) instead of fresh, live vegetables and fruit (reading the Word and acting on it, spending time in prayer, being doers of the Word), you will reap failure, doubt, sickness, discouragement, fear, and weakness in spiritual matters. If you sow the living WORD into your mind and heart, you will reap abundant life and victory over your circumstances. The WORDS OF GOD are: *...life unto those that find them, and health to all their flesh. (Proverbs 4:22)*

The best defense is a good offense. How would a football team ever win if all they did was defend their own goal? They would never taste victory. Self-defense in spiritual things is important, but can only be called maintaining. The real testimonies and great victories only come through offensive ventures into the devil's territory. Nothing ventured, nothing gained. You need boldness for the days ahead. The body of Christ must become a team and begin carrying the WORD to others, speaking it over their circumstances. Teach others how to have victory, and multiply the blessing.

The SWORD IS THE WORD, and the WORD was first and last, the beginning and the end. This SWORD divides sheep (God's people) from goats (Satan's followers). It cuts away deception, religion, and reveals truth. It will cause people's hearts to smite them, and it will bring clarity, allowing the Holy Spirit to move in and bring conviction and repentance, or deliverance and help. The WORD brings comfort, allowing the Comforter (Holy Spirit) to minister. When the Holy Spirit breathes on the WORD (logos), it brings the quickening of life and understanding to your heart (rhema). During Satan's temptation of Jesus, Satan left when Jesus used the SWORD (WORD) against him. Satan will also leave you, if you are bold and persistently use the WORD. When the SWORD OF THE SPIRIT is used, demons will flee.

The WORD cannot be applied in a harsh, haughty, or presumptuous way to God's people. Attack the devil with the WORD, and love the people. Always fight using the fruit of the Spirit, doing the opposite of what the devil wants you to do. If someone says harsh words about you, say kind words about them. If the devil attacks you through someone with hatred, respond in love. Refrain from beating people up with the *Bible*; it is the Holy Spirit's job to bring conviction.

If your confession is how sick you are, or constantly cataloging problems, then you are really exalting your problems over the WORD OF GOD. This is sin. Is anything too hard for God? Take the SWORD and aggressively smash the strongholds in your life and in other's lives. Find scripture for every problem, and do not allow the situation to exalt itself above God or His Word. *(1 Corinthians 10:4-5)* Hack the problem up with your SWORD until it is small in your mind, and witness for yourself the awesome power of the WORD to overcome your circumstances.

Change defeat into God's stepping stones for personal success with the WORD. *Let the high praises of God be in their mouth, and a two-edged SWORD in their hand. (Psalm 149:6)*

Praying always

Part of taking up the SWORD OF THE SPIRIT is that we pray with the WORD OF GOD coming out of our mouths. When we do this we are wielding His SWORD and making it our sword, invincible in battle.

PRAYING always with all PRAYER and SUPPLICATION in the Spirit, and WATCHING thereunto with all PERSE-VERANCE and supplication for all saints... (Ephesians 6:18)

1. PRAY always.
2. PRAY with all manner of PRAYER and SUPPLICATION.
3. PRAY in the Spirit.
4. WATCH (*Strong's*, agrupneo) means to keep awake in prayer for all other saints. PERSEVERE in watching.

Study Questions: Chapters 43-49
1. What does YHWH, our God, command us to put on in Ephesians 6?
2. In Romans 13:12-14, what are we instructed to put on?
3. What is the purpose of the armor? Why do we need it?
4. How can this armor withstand the attacks of the enemy? *(2 Corinthians 10:4-5)*
5. In what way can 1 John 4:4 affect your life?
6. In what ways do we let our armor slip?
7. What armor did David wear when he fought Goliath?
8. Why do you think God mentioned the belt of truth first?
9. What does Satan do with truth? What are some of his tactics?
10. Why is truth worn in the middle of the body?
11. Why does our heavenly Father say "above all" take the shield of faith?
12. What is the importance of our helmet of salvation?
13. What is different about the sword from the other armor?
14. Why is the sword mentioned last?
15. Put on the armor. Is it always in place?

Chapter Fifty
Garments of Vengeance Cloak of Zeal

The following passage of scripture is a reflection of how our Savior will return. He came the first time meek and mild, but next time there will be judgment and retribution.

> *For He put on righteousness as a breastplate, and a helmet of salvation upon his head; and he put on the GARMENTS OF VENGEANCE FOR CLOTHING, and was clad with ZEAL AS A CLOAK. (Isaiah 59:17)*

On His enemies He will unleash FURY (*Strong's* 2534, chemah) meaning anger, hot displeasure, heat, indignation, poison, rage, wrath. He will LIFT UP A STANDARD (*Strong's* 5127, nuwc), meaning chase, impel, deliver, make to flee, put to flight.

> *According to their deeds, accordingly He will repay, FURY to His adversaries, recompense to His enemies...When the enemy shall come in like a flood, the spirit of the LORD shall LIFT UP A STANDARD against him. And the Redeemer shall come to Zion... (Isaiah 59:18-20)*

We really do not have a clear idea of the power and terror to be unleashed when our Savior returns in VENGEANCE, FURY and ZEAL. His judgments are righteous and true. Because wickedness abounds so extensively in our world, many will say they do not know better, and never had a good example to follow, but in the end there will be no excuse.

> *Wherefore art thou RED in thine apparel, and thy garments like him that treadeth in the winefat?...for I will tread them in Mine anger, and trample them in My FURY; and their blood shall be sprinkled upon My GARMENTS, and I will stain all My raiment. For the day of VENGEANCE is in Mine heart, and the year of My redeemed is come...My FURY, it upheld Me. And I will tread down the people in Mine anger, and make them drunk in My FURY... (Isaiah 63:2-6)*

We, as believers, are to be full of ZEAL for the LORD and willing to war for Him. However, our battle truly begins on our knees, cloaked with zeal, which keeps us from growing lukewarm or cold.[116]

> *...The EFFECTUAL FERVENT prayer of a righteous man availeth much. (James 5:16)*

The word EFFECTUAL (*Strong's* 1754, energeo) means to be active, fervent, be mighty in, show forth self. The word used for FERVENT (*Strong's* 2205, zelos) means ardor, zeal, fiery hot, full of burning zeal, inflamed by the Holy Spirit. These words impart a powerful mandate to us concerning our God's attitude toward prayer and spiritual warfare. It is not something we undertake lightly. It must be with zeal (zelos) and energy (energeo). In effectual fervent prayer, Jesus' own BLOOD-STAINED GARMENT surrounds us, not just in one area, as the various pieces of armor do, but rather it is positioned under our armor.[117] It covers our entire body with His divine protection as we cry out through intercession and spiritual warfare. The blood of the Lamb cries out with us from the GARMENT OF VENGEANCE, all the way to the throne room of God. Having this GARMENT next to the flesh continually cleanses us with Jesus blood-bought redemption as we pray, and His blood intimately connects us to Him for protection and holiness. The CLOAK OF ZEAL covers the body armor.

> *And He (Jesus) was clothed with a VESTURE (GARMENT) dipped in BLOOD... (Revelation 19:13)*

Yahshua Messiah (Jesus Christ) is the Word. He will open His mouth at the great battle of Armageddon and the Word will come forth as a sharp sword. *(Revelation 19:15; Hebrews 4:12)* This Word will defeat His enemies. On His VESTURE will be written His Name, King of Kings, and LORD of LORDS. *(Revelation 19:16)*

The zeal and vengeance our God is calling us to manifest is the antithesis of what the church currently reflects in our present age. The Laodicean church was noted for making an eyesalve that healed eye disorders. Yet, they themselves could not see the truth: The lukewarm, nauseating state of compromise they were in, and that the church languishes in today, full of blind pride, a stench to our ZEALOUS God.[118]

And unto the angel of the church of the Laodiceans write; These things saith the Amen, the faithful and true witness, the beginning of the creation of God; I know thy works, that THOU ART NEITHER COLD NOR HOT: I would thou wert cold or hot. So then because thou art LUKEWARM, and neither cold nor hot, I will SPEW thee out of my mouth. Because thou sayest, I am rich, and increased with goods, and have need of nothing; and knowest not that thou art wretched, and miserable, and poor, and blind, and naked... (Revelation 3:14-17)

Think of the nauseating properties of being LUKEWARM. While God's people are lulled into slumber and deception through pride and self-righteousness, their passivity and self-absorption consume them. No wonder YHWH wants to SPEW them out of His mouth.

The true bride of Messiah will be covered with the GARMENT OF VENGEANCE, filled with white-hot, burning, fervent, fiery passion. Her greatcoat will be ZEAL for the blood-bought lost of this world, and she will wear her armor without fear. She will not shrink from the battle, but will run *toward* the enemy knowing *Whose* she is. The fire of the Holy Spirit will both cleanse and prepare her, and flow through her to bring power-packed healing and conviction to a sin-sick world. She will not cower behind the walls of a compromised church, but she will carry her victorious message into all the world. She will not flinch at the persecution that is sure to come. [119]

Let us pray

I bow my knee before You, my LORD and my God, YHWH. I lift the Name of Yahshua Messiah (Jesus Christ) above every Name spoken, in this world and in that to come. I worship You, and praise You for the wonderful armor You so lovingly provided for me. I put on the LORD, Yahshua Messiah (Jesus Christ), my righteousness, my truth, my peace, my faith, my only salvation. *(Ephesians 6:11-17; 1 Corinthians 10:4-5)* I make my choice to be offensive against the enemy, by continually speaking the Word over my life. I put on the armor of light, to destroy the works of darkness. Truth shall be my shield and buckler. I will stand and defy the enemy with the Word of truth, the blood of the Lamb, and the word of my testimony. *(Revelation 12:11)*

First, I apply the blood-soaked garment of vengeance underneath my armor, as I set myself in agreement with El Elyon, the Most High God, YHWH, King of the Universe, through effectual, fervent prayer. Blood cries out from this GARMENT OF VENGEANCE as I pray according to His perfect will, reaching all the way into the Holy of Holies in heaven. It cleanses and prepares me as I wear Yahshua Messiah's blood on my own flesh. His holy, perfect blood purifies and protects me.

I put on the BELT OF TRUTH. Holy Spirit, I invite You to lead and guide me into all truth today as I put on the belt of truth. *(John 16:13)* Forgive all the lies I have spoken. Bring clarity to my mind, so I may know the truth and the truth will set me free. Holy Spirit, guard me from speaking or believing a lie. Strengthen me, with the belt of truth.

Only You, Jesus, are righteous. I put off the old nature, and put on the BREASTPLATE OF RIGHTEOUSNESS right now, which emanates only from the Messiah and His glory. My fleshly and unrighteous works are wood, hay and stubble, to be burned up in the fire. But the things I do for God, with His direction and a pure heart, will stand the test of Your fire, and only these will last. His breastplate will protect me from blows against my heart. Jesus' perfection is my protection!

Right now, I put on the SHOES OF PEACE. I receive the peace only You can give me: The calm assurance You are Who You said You are, and You will do what You said You would do. I will fill my heart with scriptures to keep my mind at peace, as I keep it stayed on You. *(Isaiah 26:3)* I resist the fleshly human tendency to fret and fear, and choose this day to fight using the fruit of the Spirit, peace.

I take up the SHIELD OF FAITH, and I ask God to give me strength and dexterity to move it around to protect the other armor, as needed. I fight the fiery darts of the wicked one with the fruit of the Spirit, faith! My shield is huge, for God Himself is my shield. With faith I will quench all the enemy's fiery darts. I pour the oil of the Holy Spirit all over my shield to blind the enemy and defeat his tactics.

I put on the HELMET OF SALVATION to protect my mind and thought life from the accuser, the liar, and every evil thought of the wicked one, the devil. This helmet will protect me from the pollutions and deceptions of this world and the cares of this life that weigh me down. I put on the Messiah as my helmet to preserve my thought life from the constant onslaught of Satan. I ask You, LORD, that this helmet would protect my ears from listening to evil, my eyes from dwelling upon evil, and my mouth from speaking evil. I resist evil thoughts and distractions, and command them to flee from me. LORD, cause me to meditate on the fullness of Your salvation and Your protection. Help me to focus on You, and not on the cares of this life. Help me to choose the better part, as Mary did, and stay at Your feet, Jesus. According to 2 Corinthians 10:4-5, I cast down vain imaginations from my mind; I pull down strongholds and every high thing that exalts itself against the knowledge of God. I bring into captivity every single thought to the authority and obedience of the Messiah. Thank You, YHWH, my God, for this helmet.

I put on the cloak of zeal, to remain zealous, white-hot, full of burning, fiery passion for the things of God, willing to war for righteousness, to stand strong with the angels, and to do battle against the enemies of my God.

Finally, with all my defensive weapons in place, I take up the wonderful offensive weapon, the SWORD OF THE SPIRIT, THE WORD OF GOD. I wield it with boldness, advancing steadily into the enemy's camp, to take back what he has stolen from me, and from others. I will defend what is mine with the Word of God, which is more powerful than any two-edged sword. I will proclaim the Word to others to set the captives free. Almighty God, I humble myself under Your mighty hand, so You may teach me and lead me into all truth, so I can correctly apply the truth inherent in the Word. Thank You, God, for Your armor, which I will faithfully wear. I will be part of the great army of YHWH Nissi, my conqueror, forcefully advancing, and taking the enemy by force! Amen.

Bibliography for *Nails*

1. Schnoebelen, *Blood On the Doorposts*, , P. 128
2. Justin Martyr, *Second Apology*, Ch. 6
3. Tertullian, *Apology*, Chap.23, 197 A.D.
4. *The Ante-Nicene Fathers*, Vol. IV, p. 190
5. *The Divine Institutes*, Book V, p.22
6. Origen, *Against Celsus*, Book I, p.46, 230-254 A.D.
7. Theophilus, *Theophilus to Autolycus*, Book II, p.8, 160-180 A.D.
8. Milligan, *The Anatomy of A Scorpion*, Servant Ministries 1989, pp. 47-48
9. Ibid.
10. Ibid.
11. Ibid.
12. Ibid.
13. Ibid.
14. Kraft, *Defeating Dark Angels*, p. 139
15. Ibid, p. 227
16. Schnoebelen, *Blood*, pp.267-8
17. Milligan, *Understanding The Dreams You Dream*, Treasure House 1993, p. 161
18. Ibid. p. 146-146
19. Zugibe, "*Two Questions About Crucifixion,*" Bible Review, April, 1989, pp. 35-42
20. Barbet, "*A Doctor At Calvary,*" p. 174
21. Mordder, "*Die Todesursache bet der Kreuzigung,*" 1947, pp. 50-59
22. Zugibe, Ibid.
23. Tzaferis, "*Crucifixion—The Archeological Evidence,*" BAR, Jan./Feb. 1985, pp. 44-53
24. Zias & Skeles, "*The Crucified Man From Givat ha Mivtar,*" IEJ, 35 1985, pp. 22-27
    Shanks, "*New Analysis of the Crucified Man,*" Nov./Dec. 1985, p. 20-21
25. Primrose, "*A Surgeon Looks At Crucifixion,*" Hibbert Journal, 47, 1949, pp. 382-388
26. Zubige, Ibid. pp. 40-41
27. Storms, "*Jesus, the Suffering Savior: The Obscenity of the Cross,*" pp. 3-4
    (Personal thanks to Dr. Sam Storms: assistance in gathering info. on the crucifixion)
28. Ibid. p. 45
29. Milligan, *Anatomy*, p. 48
30. Garlock, *A Woman's Guide To Spiritual Warfare*, Servant Publications 1991, p. 35
31. Joyner, *The Hordes of Hell Are Marching*, pp. 10, 17
32. Kraft, *Deep Wounds*, p. 256
33. *Book of Enoch*
34. *Book of Jubilees*
35. ftec.net./~bric
36. Sichin, *12th Planet*, p. 327
37. Sichin, *The Stairway to Heaven*, p. 100
38. Lloyd, *The Queen of Heaven*, p. 4
39. Sumrall, *Demons*, Thomas Nelson Publishers 1979, pp. 11-25
40. Ibid. p. 101
41. Annacondia, *Listen To Me Satan*, 1998, p. 70
42. Schnoebelen, *Wicca*, Chick Publications *1990, pp. 109-111;* Schnoebelen, *Blood On the Doorposts, p. 186*
43. Annacondia, *Listen To Me, Satan*, Creation House 1998, p. 46
44. Ibid. p. 82
45. Benny Hinn (video)
46. *Prophetic Insight and Family Focus*, Issue 17, May/June, 1999, p. 10
47. Milligan, *Anatomy*, p. 69
48. Annacondia, Ibid. p. 70
49. Hovind, "*Creation Seminar, Age of the Earth,*" (Video 1)
50. Sanford, *The Transformation of the Inner Man*
51. Greenwald, *Seductions Exposed*
52. Schnoebelen, *Blood*, p. 108-109
53. Marquis, "*Occult Holidays*" (cassette series)
54. *America's Best Kept Secret*, Passport Magazine, 1987
55. Marquess, *Pagan Holidays*, Video
56. demonbuster.com
57. Lewis, *The Screwtape Letters*, p. xiii
58. Kjos, *A Twist of Faith*, New Leaf Press 1997, pp. 62, 80, 83, 136, 139
59. Dollins, *Harry Potter* (video)

60. Schnoebelen, *Straight Talk on Harry Potter*, p. 6
61. Schnoebelen, *Blood*, footnotes
62. Schnoebelen, *Straight Talk on the Martial Arts*, 1992
63. Schnoebelen, *Blood*, p. 334
64. demonbusters.com
65. Schnoebelen, *Blood*
66. demonbuster.com
67. Pittman, *Demons--An Eyewitness Account*, p. 31
68. Sumrall, *Supernatural Principalities and Powers*, Thomas Nelson Publishers 1983, pp. 61-69
69. Schnoebelen, *Masonry, Beyond the Light,* Chick Publications 1991, p. 176; Daraul, p. 162
70. Schnoebelen, *Blood*, p. 143
71. Keyton, *Jezebel vs. Elijah*, Black Forest Press 2001
72. Schnoebelen, *Blood on the Doorposts,* Chick Publications, 1994, p. 290
73. demonbuster.com
74. *Encyclopedia Britannica*, Vol. 4, 1970, pp. 536-639
75. Schnoebelen, *Blood,* pp. 297-300
76. Schnoebelen, *"The Light Behind Masonry,"* (video)
77. Schnoebelen, *Blood*, pp. 293-294
78. Ibid. p. 289-290
79. Ibid. p. 291-292
80. Ibid. p. 290-291
81. *Smith's Bible Dictionary*, Crusade Bible Publishers, p. 77
82. *Encyc. Brit.*, Vol. 18, p. 908
83. Hislop, *The Two Babylons,* A & C Black 1916, p. 311
84. geocities.com/Delphi
85. Vine's, *An Expository Dictionary of Biblical Words*, p. 320
86. Ibid.
87. *Encyc. Brit.*, Vol. 7, p. 506
88. Ibid. Vol. 18, p. 907
89. Merck, *Spoiling Pythons Schemes,* A Great Love, Inc. 1990, pp. 10-11, 22
90. Charbonneau-Lassay, *The Bestiary of Christ*, 1991, p. 423
91. Blumenberg, *Work on Myth*, Cambridge: MIT Press, 1985, p. 116-117
92. *Natural History*, Vol. 1-10, Cambridge: Harvard University Press
93. Jones, Johnson, Davis, *The Lance of Basilisk*, pp. 2-9
94. Ibid. p. 6
95. Keyton, *911 America*, Quadrilogy Pub., 2001
96. Morris, *Vital Articles on Science/Creation*, Institute for Creation Research, May 1976
97. demonbuster.com
98. Wright, *A More Excellent Way,* Pleasant Valley Publications 2000, pp. 274-275
99. Ibid. p. 274
100. *Encyc. Brit.,* Vol. 15 p. 940; Vol. 20 p. 255
101. Wright, *A More Excellent Way*, p. 226
102. Keyton, *Jezebel vs. Elijah*, Black Forest Press, 2001
103. Croft, *The Jezebel Influence*, pp. 1-11
104. Frangipane, *The Jezebel Spirit*, pp. 17-18
105. Ibid. p. 20
106. Bell, *The Ahab Spirit*
107. Lloyd, *Beyond Babylon*, p. 43
108. Liardon, *God's Generals*, Albury Publishing 1996, pp. 30-34
109. Kraft, *Deep Wounds, Deep Healing*, Servant Publications 1993, p. 249
110. Hill and Pitts, *Wealth, Riches and Money*, 2001, Family Foundations Pub., p. 14
111. Ibid., p. 18
112. Keyton, *Vision Behind the Songs*, Quadrilogy Pub., 1997
113. Hill, *Wealth...*, p. 19
114. Keyton, *911 America*, 2001
115. *Smith's Bible Dictionary, Webster's, Vine's*, Hovind, Creation Seminar (Video 3)
116. Schnoebelen, *Blood*, p. 181
117. Ibid. p. 171
118. Keyton, *Jezebel vs. Elijah*, Black Forest Press 2001, p. 189
119. Ibid. p.190

Part Three

The Blood

We are overcomers
through the blood of the Lamb

The Blood

from the *Heart & Soul Surrender* CD   Quadrilogy Publishing, 1997
Lyrics by Bree Keyton

We are overcomers through the shed blood of the Lamb *(Revelation 12:11)*, and it's power to save, protect, redeem and continuously cleanse us. *(Revelation 7:14)* The first Adam had his side opened in a deep sleep and a bride was taken out. *(Revelation 2:21-22)* The last Adam's side was pierced while in the deep sleep of death, and a bride was taken out, created through His blood. *(John 19:34)*

Jesus sweat as great drops of blood at Gethsemane *(Luke 22:44)*, to set us free from rebellion, fear, and stubbornness, that in our moments of weakness, we are made strong. *(2 Corinthians 12:9; 13:4)* He took blows to His face, received stripes, wore the crown of thorns, His hands and feet nailed to the cross, His side pierced, until blood streamed from every part of His body, to make us free from head to foot. *(John 18:22; Matthew 26:67; Mark 15:17-19; John 19:34; John 20:25)*

God spared not His own Son *(Romans 8:32)* that He may freely give us all things. Jesus was punished that we might be forgiven. *(Colossians 1:14)*

He took the cup of suffering *(John 18:11)*, that we might drink from the well of living water. *(John 4:10)*

He was betrayed for thirty pieces of silver *(Matthew 26:15; Zechariah 11:12)*, that we might receive the priceless riches of His free grace. *(1 Peter 3:7)*

He was betrayed by the kiss of a friend *(Mark 14:10; Psalm 49:1)*, that He could be our friend, Who sticks closer than a brother. *(Proverbs 8:24)*

Jesus was sorrowful and very heavy *(Matthew 26:38)*, suffering emotionally to the point of death *(Luke 22:43)*, that we could wear the garment of praise *(Isaiah 61:3)* in all life's circumstances.

There were false witnesses *(Matthew 26:60-61)*, that we might have an advocate, Who ever makes intercession for us. *(Hebrews 7:25)*

He was hated without a cause *(John 15:23-25; Psalm 69:4)*, that we could be loved as sons. *(1 John 3:2)*

He spoke truth that sealed His death *(Mark 14:62)*, that we might speak the truth of eternal life. *(1 John 5:13)*

He was abused and mocked by the chief priests, by Herod's men, and by Pilot's men, that we might all know the need for a Savior. *(Matthew 26:67-68; 27:28; Mark 14:65; Luke 23:10-11)*

He wore scarlet to bear the scarlet sins of the world. *(2 Corinthians 5:19)*

He was blindfolded that we might see *(Mark 14:65; Luke 22:64)*, and bound to set us free. *(John 8:36)*

Guards smote Him on the head with a reed *(Mark 15:19)*, that we might be conformed to the image of Christ. *(Romans 8:29)*

They spit on Him *(Isaiah 50:6)*, heaping on rejection *(Isaiah 50:3)*, that we could be accepted in the beloved. *(Ephesians 1:6)*

They plucked out His beard *(Isaiah 50:6)*, humbling Him, that we might be exalted. *(James 1:9)*

They reviled Him *(Psalm 109:25)* and set Him at naught *(Luke 23:11)*, that we might be seated in heavenly places. *(Ephesians 2:6)*

He was vehemently accused *(Luke 23: 10)*, that we might be justified by grace, through faith. *(Romans 3:24-25)*

He was delivered for envy *(Mark 15:10)*, **that all things may work together for good to them that love God.** *(Romans 8:28)*

He received blows to His face *(Mark 14:65)*, **that our wounded hearts may be healed. They smote Him with their hands** *(John 18:22; 19:3; Matthew 26:67)*, **that we might turn the other cheek.** *(Matthew 5:39)*

He was dumb before His shearers *(Isaiah 53:7; Matthew 26:62-63)*, **that we might have an answer for every accusation.** *(Luke 12:11-12; Matthew 27:37; 1 Peter 3:15)*
He was stripped *(Matthew 27:28)*, **that we might be clothed with humility.** *(1 Peter 5:5)*

The first Adam stripped us naked through rebellion *(Genesis 2:17)*, **shamed when he knew he was naked.** *(Genesis 3:10)* **The last Adam suffered shame in public nakedness** *(Hebrews 13:12-13)*, **and by obedience to the cross, clothed us in robes of righteousness.** *(Isaiah 61:10)*

By the offense of one, judgment came on all; by the righteousness of the other, eternal life came to all who receive it. *(Romans 5:18)*

His visage was so marred, He didn't look human *(Isaiah 52:14)*, **that one day we might behold His matchless beauty.** *(Revelation 1:13-18)*

He was condemned and punished *(Mark 14:64; Matthew 26:66; Isaiah 53:3-5)*, **so that God could be for us and none could stand against us.** *(Romans 8:31)*

He gave His back to the smiters *(Isaiah 50:3; Matthew 26:67)*, **to break off our rebellion.** *(Proverbs 17:11)*

He bore the cross *(John 19:17)*, **that we can roll our cares on Him.** *(1 Peter 5:7)*

He stumbled and fell, that we might receive strength for every trial. *(Hebrews 12:10)*

Another man picked up His cross *(John 12:32)*, **that we might pick up our crosses and follow Christ.** *(Matthew 16:24)*

He was crucified in disgrace outside the city *(Hebrews 13:11-13)*, **where all that passed at the crossroads set eyes on Him, that we may enter into the presence of our heavenly Father without shame, and preach the gospel to all who stand at the crossroads of life.**

He was lifted up on the cross, as the serpent was in the wilderness *(Numbers 21:9)*, **that all who look to Him for healing may also find salvation, and that He could draw all men to Him, bearing our wickedness and bringing healing to our souls and bodies.** *(John 12:32)*

He bore our sins in His own body on the tree *(1 Peter 2:24)*, **that we could be trees of righteousness.** *(Isaiah 61:2)*

He was crucified in weakness *(1 Corinthians 13:4)*, **but we shall live with Him forever by the power of God.** *(2 Corinthians 13:4)*

He became a curse, that we might receive the blessing. *(Galatians 3:13-14)*

He was despised *(Isaiah 53:3)*, **that we might receive honor** *(2 Timothy 2:21)*, **and rejected** *(Isaiah 53:3)* **that we might have acceptance.** *(Ephesians 1:6)*

He was oppressed *(Isaiah 53:7)* **and derided** *(Luke 23:35)*, **that we might be conformed into His image.** *(Romans 8:29)*

He was acquainted with grief *(Isaiah 53:3)*, **that we might rejoice in our salvation.** *(1 Peter 1:8)*

He carried our sorrows, yet we esteemed Him stricken, smitten of God and afflicted. He was wounded for our transgressions, He was bruised for our iniquities, the chastisement of our peace was upon Him, and with His stripes we are healed. *(Isaiah 53:3-5; 1 Peter 2:24)*

Jesus took all of this in order to satisfy the great and wonderful and intense love with which He loved us, that God might clearly demonstrate through the ages to come, the immeasurable, limitless, surpassing riches of His free grace and unmerited favor, in kindness of heart toward us. *(Ephesians 2:4-7)*

They offered Him vinegar mixed with gall *(Matthew 27:34)*, but He refused to take the bitterness, that we might walk in love *(Ephesians 5:2)*, and that He might experience the full extent of suffering for us. *(Mark 9:12)*

They parted and ripped the garments worn closest to His flesh *(Psalm 22:18)*; just as the veil was rent in twain in the Holy of Holies *(Matthew 27:51)* that symbolized His body, to open a way for us to God. *(Hebrews 9:28)* They cast lots for His outer vesture, which was left whole *(John 19:24)*, for it was a valuable and seamless garment, as our new relationship with God through Christ is a valuable and seamless garment.

He forgave them *(Luke 23:34)*, and it was a vital part of the release of the power of the Holy Spirit into the earth, enabling Him to be raised from the dead *(Colossians 1:18; Acts 2:24)*, that we too, through forgiveness, can be raised up to sit together in heavenly places with Him. *(Ephesians 2:6)*

He thirsted and took plain vinegar *(John 19:28-30)*, that we might hunger and thirst after righteousness *(Matthew 5:6)*, drink of Christ, and be filled.

They railed on Him *(Mark 15:29)*, that we may glory in our weakness. *(2 Corinthians 12:9)*

He hung in darkness *(Luke 23:44)*, that we might walk in the light. *(1 John 1:7)*

He was forsaken by God *(Matthew 27:46)*, so that God would never leave or forsake us. *(Hebrews 3:5)*

He took God's wrath *(1 Thessalonians 1:10)*, that we might know God's mercy. *(Ephesians 2:4-7)*

He cried with a loud voice, "It is finished!" *(John 19:30)* The old covenant was fulfilled, and through it we received salvation. *(John 3:16)*

In death, He commended His spirit into His Father's hands *(Luke 23:46)*, that we may die to self *(1 Corinthians 15:31)*, and yield our will, trusting all in the Father's hands.

God's earthquake released such power that death lost its grip on many captives. *(Matthew 27:51)*

No bones were broken *(John 19:36)*, for He gave His body as a bridge between God and man.

Jesus tasted death for every man, that we might have life everlasting. *(1 Timothy 1:16)* Through His death He destroyed him who had the power over death *(Luke 23:46; John 19:30)*, the devil *(Hebrews 2:14)*, and He led captivity captive. *(Ephesians 4:8)* He died our death, that we might share His life.

Spices and myrrh were used for His burial. *(John 19:14)* The vessel that was His body was broken *(1 Corinthians 11:24)*, that the precious ointment, His blood, could pour forth as a sweet fragrance on all flesh, for His love is as ointment poured forth. *(Song of Solomon 1:3)*

Though He was bound in grave clothes *(Matthew 27:59)*, He cast them off and rose from the grave a victorious champion *(1 Corinthians 15:54-57)*, that we too could be unchained, and cast off the grave clothes. *(Hebrews 10:9)*

An angel's voice trumpeted the good news that He is risen *(Matthew 28:6)*, for Jesus Christ conquered hell and death *(Psalm 16:10; Revelation 20:13-14)*, the strongest enemy of all, and He ascended into heaven *(Ephesians 4:8)*, that we too, at the voice of the archangel and the trump of God, shall rise and meet Him in the air, and so shall we ever be with the LORD. *(1 Thessalonians 4:16)*

Nothing shall separate us from the love of God, for as Jesus Christ arose a conqueror, we are made more than conquerors through Him that loved us. *(Romans 8:35-39)*

Chapter Fifty-One
Isaiah 53: A Deeper Understanding

Enhancing our understanding

Because we are partakers of Yahshua Messiah's suffering, Isaiah 53 is an excellent place to begin our study of the suffering of Christ, and the blood He shed for our sins. Isaiah 53 was written to prophetically speak YHWH, our God's plan into existence, to prepare God's people, to supply sufficient detail to be able to recognize the Messiah when He came, and to announce the coming of a Messiah so great He would be the perfect Lamb of God. In Him was embodied the perfection the first Adam in the garden failed to achieve. Jesus fulfilled all of the law given to mankind through Moses; an impossible task, yet He accomplished it.

Hardness of the heart

The terrible suffering foretold by Isaiah should have made it easy to identify God's suffering Savior, yet they all missed it. Incredible as it seems to us today, a careful look at the prevailing attitudes of Jesus' day: hardness of heart, a strong pharisaical spirit, contentiousness by the religious crowd, their refusal to hear Jesus' Words, the spirit of envy that permeated their hearts causing them to plot against Him every time He spoke or performed a miracle. All these were factors that contributed to them missing His coming.

Woe unto you, scribes and Pharisees, hypocrites! For ye pay tithe of mint and anise and cumin, and have omitted the weightier matters of the law, judgment, mercy, and faith: these ought ye to have done, and not to leave the other undone. Ye blind guides, which strain at a gnat, and swallow a camel. Woe unto you, scribes and Pharisees, hypocrites! For ye make clean the outside of the cup and of the platter, but within they are full of extortion and excess. (Matthew 23:23-25)

Verse by verse expository of Isaiah 53

Isaiah 53:1 Who hath believed our report? And to whom is the arm of the LORD revealed?

It is clear the LORD knew only those who would open their hearts to the Him, would recognize His coming.

Isaiah 53:2 For He shall grow up before Him as a tender plant, and as a root out of a dry ground: He hath no form nor comeliness; and when we shall see Him there is no beauty that we should desire Him.

The LORD knew that the spiritual mind set at the time of Jesus' birth would be very dry. Jesus was a refreshing drink of cool water. However, one would have to look closely to know Who He was, because He would look like an ordinary man. Invariably, people look on the outward appearance, but YHWH looks on the heart.

Isaiah 53:3 He is DESPISED and REJECTED of men; a man of SORROWS, and ACQUAINTED with GRIEF: and we hid as it were our faces from Him; He was DESPISED, and we ESTEEMED Him not.

The scribes and Pharisees hid their stony hearts, and refused to recognize the One for Whom they claimed to be waiting.

DESPISED: (*Strong's* 959, bazah) meaning disdain, condemn, scorn, vile person.

REJECTED: (*Strong's* 2310, chadel) meaning he who forbears, frail. REJECTED (*Vine's*) means forsaken.

> He endured rejection so we might have acceptance.

ACQUAINTED: (*Strong's* 3045, yada) meaning to have understanding, to know, with which to feel endued.

> To be a perfect high priest Jesus had to experience our grief so we could trust and know His delivering power by faith.

ESTEEMED: (*Vine's*) meaning reckoned.

> (For the meaning of SORROWS and GRIEF see verse 4)

Isaiah 53:4 Surely He hath BORNE our GRIEFS, and CARRIED our SORROWS: yet we did esteem Him STRICKEN, SMITTEN of God, and AFFLICTED.

BORNE: (*Strong's* 5375, nacah) meaning to carry, accept, suffer, to bear, carry away.

> Carried refers to Jesus' atoning work on the cross.

> Borne means to take upon oneself, to carry as a burden: vicarious suffering.

GRIEF: (*Strong's* 2483, choliy) meaning malady, anxiety, calamity, disease.

> (*Vine's*) meaning sicknesses; both spiritual and physical.

CARRIED: (*Strong's* 5445, cabal) meaning to bear, strong labor.

SORROWS: (*Strong's* 4341, makobah) meaning anguish, afflictions, grief, pain and sorrow.

(*Vine's*) definition is: pains, sickness both spiritual and physical.

God punished Jesus with all sicknesses. Jesus took our GRIEFS and SORROWS. These are both spiritual and physical sicknesses, so that we would not have to bear them.

STRICKEN: (*Strong's* 5060, naga) meaning violently to strike, punish, to beat, bring down, plague.

SMITTEN: (*Strong's* 5221, nacah) meaning to strike, beat, cast forth, kill, murder, punish, stripes, wounded.

(*Vine's*) definition is struck down.

AFFLICTED: (*Strong's* 6031, anab) meaning browbeating, abase self, afflict self, chasten self, defile, force, humble.

Isaiah 53:5 But He was WOUNDED for our TRANSGRESSIONS, He was BRUISED for our INIQUITIES: the CHASTISEMENT of our PEACE was upon Him; and with His STRIPES we are HEALED.

WOUNDED: (*Strong's* 2490, chalal) meaning to wound, to dissolve, to begin by opening a wedge.

(*Vine's*) definition is pierced through.

TRANSGRESSIONS: (*Strong's* 6588, pesha) meaning a revolt (national, moral, or religious), rebellion.

(*Vine's*) definition is wickedness.

By the offense of one (Adam) judgment came on all. *(Romans 5:12-21)*

BRUISED: (*Strong's* 1792, daka) meaning to crumble, beat to pieces, break, crush, destroy, humble, oppress, smite.

INIQUITIES: (*Strong's* 5771, avon) meaning perversity, moral evil, fault, punishment.

(*Vine's*) definition is rebellion.

CHASTISEMENT: (*Strong's* 4148, muwcar) meaning reproof, warning, chastening, correction, discipline, rebuke.

PEACE: (*Strong's* 7965, shalom) meaning safe, well, happy, favor, health, rest, safety, welfare.

STRIPES: (*Strong's* 2250, chaburah) meaning to bruise, hurt, stripe, wound.

(*Vine's*) definition is blows that cut in.

HEALED: (*Strong's* 7495, rapah) meaning to cure, repair, thoroughly make whole, to mend.

Isaiah 53:6 All we like sheep have gone astray; we have turned every one to his own way; and the LORD hath laid on Him the INIQUITY of us all.

INIQUITY: (*Strong's* 5771, avon) meaning perversity, moral evil, fault.

Isaiah 53:7 He was OPPRESSED, and He was AFFLICTED, yet He opened not His mouth: He is brought as a lamb to the slaughter, and as a sheep before her shearers is dumb, so He openeth not His mouth.

OPPRESSED: (*Strong's* 5065, nagas) meaning to harass, tyrannize, distress, a taskmaster, to drive an animal, worker, or debtor.

AFFLICTED: (*Strong's* 6031, anab) meaning browbeating, abase self, afflict self, chasten self, defile, force, humble.

Isaiah 53:8 He was taken from prison and from judgment: and who shall declare His GENERATION? for He was CUT OFF out of the land of the living: for the transgression of my people was He STRICKEN.

GENERATION: (*Strong's* 1755, dowr or dor) meaning posterity, an age or revolution of time.

STRICKEN: (*Strong's* 5061, nega) meaning a blow, infliction, sore, stricken, stripe, stroke, wound.

Daniel 9:26 And after three score and two weeks shall Messiah be CUT OFF, but not for Himself...

CUT OFF: (*Strong's* 1504, gazar) meaning to cut down or cut off, to destroy.

Isaiah 53:9 And He made His grave with the wicked, and with the rich in His death; because He had done no violence, neither was any deceit in His mouth.

He was the sinless Lamb of God. Being laid in the grave of a rich man was an additional prophetic Word that should have tipped the people off that Yahshua (Jesus) was Messiah.

Isaiah 53:10 Yet it pleased the LORD to BRUISE Him; He hath put Him to GRIEF: when thou shalt make His soul an offering for sin, He shall see His seed, He shall prolong His days, and the pleasure of the LORD shall prosper in His hand.

BRUISE: (*Strong's* 1792, daka) meaning to crumble, beat to pieces, break, crush, destroy, humble, oppress, smite.

BRUISE: (*Strong's* 4937, suntribo) meaning to crush, completely, to shatter, broken to shivers.

It (the seed of a woman) shall BRUISE his head, and thou (the serpent) shalt BRUISE His heel. (Genesis 3:15)

BRUISE: (*Strong's* 7779, shuwph) meaning overwhelm, break.

Jesus, Himself, fulfilled the prophecy of Genesis 3, that the God of peace shall BRUISE Satan. *(Romans 16:20)*

GRIEF: (*Strong's* 2470, chalah) meaning rubbed or worn, weak, sick, afflicted, grieve, infirmity, put to pain, wounded.

Isaiah 53:11 He shall see of the TRAVAIL of His soul, and shall be SATISFIED: by His knowledge shall My righteous Servant JUSTIFY many; for He shall bear their INIQUITIES.

TRAVAIL: (*Strong's* 5999, amal) meaning wearing effort, worry of body or mind, grievousness, sorrow, toil, trouble, painful.

SATISFIED: (*Strong's* 7646, saba) meaning to sate, fill to satisfaction, have enough, to be full.

JUSTIFY: (*Strong's* 6663, tsadaq) meaning to be or make right in a moral sense, cleanse, clear self, to be or to turn to righteousness.

INIQUITIES: (*Strong's* 5771, avon) meaning perversity, moral evil, fault.

Isaiah 53:12 Therefore will I divide Him a portion with the great, and He shall divide the spoil with the strong; because He hath poured out His soul unto death: and He was numbered with the TRANSGRESSORS; and He bare the sin of many, and made intercession for the TRANSGRESSORS.

TRANSGRESSORS: (*Strong's* 6586, pasha) meaning to break away from just authority, trespass, apostatize, offend, revel, revolt, transgress.

Yahshua Messiah was despised, disdained, condemned, scorned and treated like a vile person. He bore our rejection, was violently struck, punished, beaten, pierced through, smitten, wounded, abased, chastised, defiled, humiliated and plagued. The sinless Son of God took upon Himself our afflictions and carried, accepted and bore our burdens, griefs, pain and sorrows, through vicarious suffering for our sins. He was murdered for you and me.

He endured strong affliction to intimately know the full extent of sorrow, anguish, malady, anxiety, calamity and every disease known to mankind. He travailed and took all this for our national, moral, and religious rebellion, revolt, wickedness, perversity, moral failure, faults, transgressions and offenses. He was bruised, hurt, beat to pieces, punished, broken, crushed, shattered, overwhelmed and put to pain to set us free.

He bore our destruction, oppression, reproof, discipline and rebuke. He carried the stripes on His back that should be ours. He was harassed, tyrannized, distressed, cut off, driven like an animal and a debtor. He bore our infirmities and sicknesses, spiritual, mental, physical and material.

Yahshua the Messiah, Jesus the Christ of Nazareth, endured this horror to satisfy, fulfill and sate God's wrath, to right us morally, cleanse us, to clear the slate against us, and to wipe out our trespasses, rebellion, revolt and wicked revelings. In turn, He provided us with safety, healing, deliverance, happiness, favor, health, rest, safety and welfare. He repaired the breach between God and man, tore down the wall of separation between us, mended and thoroughly made whole our relationship with our Creator. Only He, being perfect, could oversee His own sacrifice.

The full weight of the horror

After studying the meanings of the above words in Isaiah 53, the full weight of what Jesus took for us becomes horrifically apparent. It is no wonder that Jesus sweat great drops of blood before His arrest at Gethsemane. He alone understood the full import of the words of the prophecy concerning His passion. As the "Word," He fully understood the extreme suffering: the SORROW, GRIEF, AFFLICTION, BRUISING, TRAVAIL, OPPRESSION, REJECTION, DESPISING, and CHASTISEMENT He would have to suffer. He, alone, grasped the depth of TRANSGRESSION and INIQUITY He must bear for the wickedness of mankind.

Sweating blood

Medical science has documented cases of humans sweating blood under extreme duress. We all know sweat pours off under intense emotional pressure. In the sweat of our faces, we have brought forth thorns and thistles, for the ground was cursed. We are delivered from the curse through His redeeming blood. *(Genesis 3:17-19)*

...was as it were great DROPS OF BLOOD. (Luke 22:44)

Guilt and shame

Jesus died for the guilt and the shame of our sins. The Jews were looking for a Messiah who would take back Judah from the Romans by force. Herod and the Jews greatly feared Jesus, because the people loved and followed Him. He was perceived as a threat to their positions given to them by Roman rule. They never grasped Jesus' true purpose because of the hardness of their hearts, fear of losing their positions, and the envy that consumed them.

Redeemed from the curse

Jesus had to be crucified to redeem us from the curse of the law. Redeem (Strong's 1805, exagorazo) means to buy up, ransom, rescue from loss, to purchase. God spared not His own Son *(Romans 8:32)* that we might be saved.

> *Christ has REDEEMED us from the curse of the law, being made a curse for us...that the blessings of Abraham might come on the gentiles. (Galatians 3:12-14)*

Study Questions: Chapter 51

1. What was the state of the pharisees' hearts at the time of Jesus coming?
2. Were they looking for the Messiah?
3. Did Jesus fit their profile for the Messiah? Why or why not?
4. According to Jewish traditions, what are some of the things Jesus did that offended the scribes and Pharisees?
5. What actions did they take to counteract Jesus' ministry?
6. Name three things that affected the political climate and religious community of Jesus' day.
7. Place yourself in the Pharisees shoes. How would you have reacted to Jesus' ministry?
8. Did Jesus condemn them? Give scripture to support your view.
9. What did you learn from a close analysis of Isaiah 53?
10. To whom will the LORD reveal His heart? Give scripture.
11. Name four people who recognized Jesus shortly after His birth. By what means were they able to do this?
12. Should the priests, scribes and people of Jesus' time have been able to recognize Jesus as the Messiah? Give three scriptures.
13. What is the meaning of "esteemed" in Isaiah 53:3? How does this word affect the total meaning of this scripture?
14. Look carefully at the word "sorrows" in verse four. What is the full meaning of this word, and what specific areas of your life does it affect?
15. In verse four of Isaiah 53, study *borne, grief, stricken, smitten* and *afflicted*. How much and how many kinds of suffering did Jesus bear for you?
16. Does this analysis of Isaiah 53 help you more fully appreciate the suffering of our Savior? Does it lead you into a deeper and more profound worship?

Chapter Fifty-Two
The Betrayal

The sorrow and suffering our Savior took for us is most painfully portrayed through the kiss of a friend. When we say we are the friend or servant of God, and we betray Him through disobedience, or failure to show our love for Him by keeping His commandments, it is just as painful to Him. Yet, in His mercy, He continues to love us.

The cup of suffering
He took the CUP of suffering so we might drink from the well of living water. *(John 4:10)*

The CUP which My Father hath given Me, shall I not drink it: (John 18:11)

Betrayed by a kiss
The KISS of Judas is the worst betrayal in history, accomplished through a sign of love and friendship. *(Luke 22:48; Matthew 26:49; Mark 14:45)* Judas was counted as one of the chosen twelve disciples, someone Jesus trusted.

Faithful are the wounds of a friend; but the KISSES of an enemy are deceitful. (Proverbs 27:6)

Acquainted with grief
YHWH, our God, put Yahshua Messiah to GRIEF. *(Isaiah 53:10)* Definitions of GRIEF follow:
(*Strong's* 2483, choliy) malady, anxiety, disease, calamity.
(*Vine's*) meaning sicknesses, both spiritual and physical.
(*Strong's* 2470, chalah) meaning to be weak, sick and afflicted, grievous, put to pain, be wounded, woman in travail.

Sorrow
SORROW: (*Strong's* 4341, makobah) anguish, grief, sickness, both spiritual and physical, affliction, pain. Our griefs and sorrows were carried by our Savior.

He hath borne our GRIEFS and carried our SORROWS. (Isaiah 53:3-4)

SORROW: (*Strong's* 3077, lupe) meaning grief, heaviness, sadness.

He found them sleeping for SORROW. (Luke 22:45)

SORROW: (*Strong's* 4036, perilupos) meaning grieved all around, intensely sad, almost dying of sorrow.

...exceeding SORROWFUL unto death. (Matthew 14:24)

SORROW: (*Strong's* 6089, etseb) meaning grievous, painful toil, labor.

...cursed is the ground for thy (Adam) *sake; in SORROW shalt thou eat of it. (Genesis 3:17)*

SORROW: (*Strong's* 6093, itstabown) meaning toil, labor, pain.

I will greatly multiply thy (Eve) SORROW. (Genesis 3:16)

SORROWFUL: (*Strong's* 3076, lupeo) meaning to distress, cause grief, be in heaviness, to be sorry.

He took with Him Peter and the two sons of Zebedee and began to be SORROWFUL and very HEAVY. (Matthew 26:37)

SORROWFUL: (*Strong's* 4036, perilupos) meaning intensely, exceedingly sad, grieved all around.

Then He said unto them, My soul is exceeding SORROWFUL, even unto death... (Matthew 26:38)

Heavy

Jesus suffered emotionally to the point of death, before any physical suffering began, so that an angel had to come and strengthen Him. *(Luke 22:43)*

HEAVY: *(Strong's 85, ademoneo)* meaning to be in distress of mind; full of heaviness.

I Am

Six hundred men, plus chief priests and others who had come to arrest Jesus fell backward, knocked down by the power of God, through the spoken Name "I Am." This Name represents the eternal, uncreated God, the Holy One of Israel. How easy it would have been for Jesus to simply walk away from the agony yet to come. *(John 18:5)*

False witnesses

There were false witnesses so our loins could be girt about with truth. *(Ephesians 6:14; Psalm 27:12; Matthew 26:60-61)*

Two trials

One trial was Jewish, one was Roman.

Three stages:

Jewish trial
1. Examination before Annas. *(John 18:12-23)*
2. Hearing before Caiaphas and Sanhedrin with false witnesses. *(Matthew 26:57-64)*
3. Trial: Chief priests and elders took counsel and sentenced Jesus to death, bound Him and delivered Him to Pilate.

   (Matthew 27:1-2)

Roman trial
1. Examination of Pilate. *(Luke 23:1-7)*
2. Interrogation of Herod. *(Luke 23:8-11)*
3. Meeting with Pilate before crowd and sentencing. Pilate washes his hands of the matter, but again the chief priests and elders persuaded the multitude to request Barabbas' release and Jesus' death. "His blood be on us, and on our children," they cried. *(Matthew 27:15-31; Luke 23:13-25)*[1]

Two high priests

Annas was Caiaphas' father-in-law. Annas was deposed by the Romans, but he was technically still high priest. Thus, Jesus was brought before both high priests.

"For the absolutely sinless One to be subjected to a trial conducted by sinful men was in itself a deep humiliation. To be tried by such men, under such circumstances made it infinitely worse. Greedy, serpent-like, vindictive Annas; rude, sly, hypocritical Caiaphas; crafty, superstitious, self-seeking Pilate; and immoral, ambitious, superficial Herod Antipas; these were His judges!"[2]

Fear in the Sanhedrin

The Sanhedrin had seventy members: twenty-three constituted a quorum. There were three groups: priests, teachers of the law and elders. The perceived threat of violence against the temple was enough to convict Jesus, but the witnesses lied and said He threatened to destroy it. *(John 2:18-21; Mark 14:59)*

Blasphemy

Blasphemy is dishonoring God by diminishing His glory or claiming rights He alone possesses. Following are the reasons they used to accuse Jesus of blasphemy.
1. Jesus claimed He would be seated at the right hand of God, a position only God's Son could hold.
2. One as apparently helpless as Jesus could not be the Messiah. They were expecting a Messiah who would take over the government and defeat the Romans.
3. Jews believed God alone had the right to enthrone Messiah. Jesus' claims enraged them.

Interrogation

Jesus' response to interrogation was that He clearly claimed to be the Messiah.

...Thou hast said: nevertheless I say unto you, Hereafter shall ye see the Son of man sitting on the right hand of power, and coming in the clouds of heaven. (Matthew 26:64)

...the Son of man came with the clouds of heaven, and came to the Ancient of days... (Daniel 7:13)

The LORD (YHWH) *said unto my LORD* (Adon, master, Jesus), *Sit Thou at My right hand, until I make Thine enemies Thy footstool. (Psalm 110:1)*

Chapter Fifty-Three
The Passion

Jesus was abused twice

1. By the religious crowd. *(Matthew 26:67-68)*
2. By Pilate's soldiers. *(Mark 15:19)*

Blindfolded

This was mockingly done because of a Jewish test that the Messiah would need neither eyes nor ears to identify people.

Scarlet robe

They stripped Him, put on Him a scarlet robe, and mocked His kingship, so that we might be kings and priests. *(Matthew 27:28)*

The scepter

The soldiers of the governor humiliated Jesus and mocked His claim that He was a king by placing a scepter, symbol of authority and power made of a reed, in His hand. *(Mark 15:19)*

Hit on His head with a reed

To maximize His suffering and humiliation, and to prove His weakness and inability to defend Himself, they took the reed they had given Him and struck Him on the head and shoulders, driving the thorns in deeper.

Mocked three times

Before Jesus got to the cross, He was mocked three times and denied three times, so we might be empowered to resist pride, rebellion and hardness of heart through humility.

1. Caiaphas and the chief priests mocked Him. *(Matthew 26:67-68)*
2. Herod's soldiers mocked Him. *(Luke 23:10-11)*
3. Pilate's men mocked Him. *(John 19:1-3)*

Mocked

Jesus was crowned with thorns, adorned with a robe of purple, they mockingly kneeled before Him, hit Him with the reed they had placed in His hand as a scepter, and yelled, "Hail, King of the Jews." *(John 19:1-3)* They spit upon Him and shouted, ***Prophesy unto us, Thou Christ, who is he that smote Thee.*** *(Matthew 26:67-68; Isaiah 50:6; Mark 14:65; Psalm 22:7-8)*

MOCKED: *(Strong's* 1702, empaizo) meaning to jeer at, deride. *(Matthew 27:29, 31, 41; 27:29-30; Mark 15:20, 31;15:19; Luke 18:32; 22:63; 23:11, 36)*

Accused

He was accused of being a criminal, so we might be justified by grace through faith. *(Romans 3:24-25)*
ACCUSED: *(Strong's* 2722, kategoreo) meaning to charge with some offense. *(Luke 23:10)*

Vehemently

Vehemently: *(Strong's* 2159, eutonos) meaning fiercely, mightily.

And the chief priests and scribes stood and VEHEMENTLY accused Him. And Herod with his men of war set Him at naught and mocked Him... (Luke 23:10)

Blows to His face

Jesus took blows to his face so we might have healing for our offenses and wounded hearts; interesting to note this was done by the religious crowd. Of further note are the various intensities and kinds of blows to our Savior's face.

BUFFET: *(Strong's* 2852, kolaphizo) meaning to rap with fist. *(Mark 14:65)*
STRIKE: *(Strong's* 906, ballo) meaning violent or intense; thrust, to throw. *(Mark 14:65)*

SMOTE: (Strong's 4474, rhapizo) meaning to slap, smite. *(Matthew 26:67)*
SMOTE: (*Strong's* 3317, paio) meaning to sting as a scorpion; strike, hit. *(Matthew 26:68)*
SMITEST: (*Strong's* 1194, dero) meaning to thrash, beat, scourge. *(John 18:23)*
STRUCK: (*Strong's* 5180, tupto) meaning to pummel with repeated blows with stick or fist, beat, smite, strike, wound. *(Luke 22:64)*
STRUCK: (*Strong's* 3960, patasso) meaning to knock with a weapon or fatally smite, strike. *(John 18:22)*
SLAPPED CHEEK: denotes feelings, deliberate humiliation.

Creation mocks the Creator
God's own creation, man, mocked His Son: they esteemed Him not. *(Luke 22:63)*

Guards spit
The guards spit and kept on SPITTING, heaping scorn on Him. This action was prophesied in the Old Testament.

> *...I hid not my face from shame and SPITTING... (Isaiah 50:6)*

Plucked His beard
He was humbled so we might be exalted. *(James 1:9)* He led captivity captive. PLUCKING out the beard was prophesied in the Old Testament.

> *I gave My back to the smiters, and My cheeks to those who PLUCKED off the hair... (Isaiah 50:6)*

Reviled
The word reviled comes from the word blaphemeo, meaning to blaspheme, rail on, speak evil of. *(Psalm 109:25)*

Set at naught
He was treated with contempt. *(Luke 23:11)*

Envy
ENVY: (*Strong's* 5355, phthonos) meaning ill-will, spite, jealousy.

> *...Pilate...knew that the chief priests had delivered Him for ENVY. (Mark 15:10)*

Dumb before His shearers
He was dumb before His shearers, so we might have an answer for every accusation raised against us. *(Isaiah 53:7; Matthew 26:63)* He didn't try to justify, or deliver, or defend Himself. He said nothing, though He could have summoned twelve legions of angels *(Matthew 26:53)*, so that when we stand before our accusers, the Holy Spirit will give us the words to speak. *(Matthew 27:37; 1 Peter 3:15; Luke 12:11-12)*

Mocked
While on the cross they mocked Him saying if He was the Son of God, then He should come down off the cross and save Himself. Others He saved, they jeered at Him, yet Himself He could not save. *(Isaiah 50:6; Luke 18:33)*

Visage
Jesus' body and face were so MARRED He didn't even look human. He endured the penalty and was reckoned and regarded as guilty of our sins. This was the ultimate sacrifice. The suffering and physical disfigurement were unparalleled. His body carried every disease known to man.

> *As many were astonished at thee; His VISAGE was so MARRED more than any man, and His form more than the sons of men... (Isaiah 52:14)*

Back
The BACK symbolized rebellion against YHWH and His Torah. Yahshua willingly took this beating to set us free.

I gave My BACK to the smiters... (Isaiah 50:6)

Scourged

The flagellum (Latin word) was a terrible instrument *(Mark 15:15)*, with thick strips of leather platted with bits of metal or bone into a chain, designed to tear away the flesh, leaving it hanging in bleeding shreds. The Flagellum *(Strong's* 5417, phragelloo) is taken from the presumed equivalent of the Latin flagellum, meaning to whip, lash as a public punishment. Under Roman law there was no maximum number of strokes, unlike Jewish law.

...and by His STRIPES we are healed. (Isaiah 53:5; 1 Peter 2:24)

Administering the STRIPES was referred to as "being examined." Thirteen went to the back, thirteen to each shoulder, for a total of thirty-nine. This number was set in order not to break the law, which allowed only forty, in case of a miscount. Many men died from the stripes alone. When the flagellum struck it would wrap around the body as it brutally tore and pulled the flesh away, often exposing bone.

Chapter Fifty-Four
The Passion of the Cross

Bore the cross

Yahshua (Jesus) bore the cross. *(John 19:17)* He bore the weight that so easily besets us. *(Hebrews 12:1)* Now, we can roll the weight of our cares onto Him, for He cares for us. *(1 Peter 5:7)* He carried our sorrows. *(Isaiah 53:4)*

Crucified outside the gate of the city

This was done because of the extreme shame of the cross. *(Hebrews 13:12)*

Hung on a cross

Being lifted up *(John 12:32)* meant crucifixion, which was a Roman form of execution. Romans had to be involved to fulfill this prophecy. The height of the cross was no more than one or two feet off the ground, so that dogs and wild beasts could feed on the corpses. Crucifixion was done in very public places such as a crossroads for maximum exposure and humiliation. The sedecula was a small peg or block fixed midway up the vertical beam to provide a seat, preventing premature collapse, and deliberately prolonging the agony. The scarcity of references to crucifixion in literature and the *Bible* is probably because there was such revulsion, disgust, reproach and degradation associated with this form of punishment. Writers probably didn't want to defile or disgrace their work by referring to it. The cross was considered the worst of human obscenities. (See Chapter Five)

Hung on a tree

He became a curse for us by hanging on a TREE.

> *Cursed is every one that hangeth on a TREE. (Galatians 3:13)*

> *Who His own self bare our sins in His own body on the TREE. (1 Peter 2:24)*

Parting garments, lots cast

The following prophecy, given by King David, is one of the most convincing proofs that Jesus was Messiah.

> *They part My GARMENTS among them, and cast lots upon My VESTURE. (Psalm 22:18)*

The GARMENT (or raiment) referred to in Psalm 22:18 and John 19:23 went from the shoulders to the ankles and was torn in four pieces by the soldiers.

The COAT referred to in John 19:23, is the same VESTURE prophesied in Psalm 22. It was valuable, woven without seam throughout, short-sleeved and to the knees. Soldiers cast lots rather than tear such a fine garment. Because it was a tunic like the high priest wore, if it had been torn, the priesthood it represented would have been nullified.

Naked

He was uncovered, not under grace, but shamefully exposed. Shame came in the garden when Adam and Eve knew they were naked through sin. *(Genesis 3:7)* Our shame comes when our sin isn't covered by the saving knowledge of Jesus, and repentance. He was naked on the cross, that we might be clothed in robes of righteousness. *(Isaiah 61:10)*

Shame worse than pain

Personal humiliation, public nakedness on high ground, degradation, obscenity, reproach, and disgust of the cross were all borne by Jesus, to take away both our guilt and shame. *(Hebrews 13:2, 12-13)* He bore our shame, so we might share His glory. When Adam and Eve knew they were naked, they hid from the LORD. Jesus suffered public nakedness, unable to hide from the wrath against sinful mankind. He was exposed for us, so we might receive the covering of His robe of righteousness.

Crucified with sinners

The sinless Son of God hung in shame between two sinners. One reviled Him, the other defended Him. The first went to everlasting death, while the other was taken to paradise. *(Isaiah 53:12; Matthew 27:38)*

Three crosses, three deaths

On opposite sides of the Messiah hung two thieves. They represented the sides or choices of fallen man. The first thief railed on Messiah, bitter and angry. He demanded a pardon without repentance. The second thief defended the Messiah, calling out to the other thief for the proper fear of God. Even in his hour of death, he asked to be saved. The third man on the cross, our Passover Lamb, hung between opposing forces, sacrificing Himself to take away the sins of the world.

On Passover, there were three main sacrifices of lambs at the temple, rather than the usual two. The high priest always stood and did not sit until the last sacrifice. The first lamb was slain at the third hour, 9 AM (Mark 15:24), the time when they nailed Jesus to the cross. The second sacrifice was at the sixth hour, 12 PM, when darkness covered the land, the time when the first thief spoke bitterly to Jesus. (This darkness could not have been an eclipse, as some have postulated. Passover always occurred at the time of a full moon.) The temple sacrifice of the third lamb, our Passover lamb, was at the ninth hour, 3 PM, at the very moment Jesus died to take away the sins of the world. (2 Corinthians 5:19) After this final sacrifice, the high priest sat down, as our High Priest, Yahshua Messiah, sat down at the right hand of YHWH, our God, for all time.

The first thief represented all who are deceived by the darkness of pride and unrepented sin, and died choosing to reject Messiah. The second thief chose the light, to follow Messiah even when things looked impossible. He represents all who will not fall away or accept deception, even during trials or great offense. Jesus hung between the two—a choice for all mankind—for all time. He was a Savior willing to humble Himself even to the shame of the cross, to show us the way to truth, light and salvation.

Numbered with the transgressors

Isaiah prophesies that Yahshua will be numbered with the TRASNGRESSORS (*Strong's* 6586, pasha) meaning to break away from authority, trespass, rebel, revolt. He was numbered with them for our rebellion. *(Isaiah 53:12)*

And with Him they crucify two thieves, the one on His right hand, and the other on His left. (Mark 15:27-28)

Derided

DERIDED: (*Strong's* 1592, ekmukterizo) meaning to sneer outright at.

...And the rulers also with them DERIDED Him, saying, He saved others; let Him save Himself, if He be Christ... (Luke 23:35)

Gall

GALL: (*Strong's* 5521, chose) meaning a soothing or pain relieving agent, bile, a poison. He refused to be bitter. The vinegar mixed with gall was probably laced with a bitter narcotic to deaden the pain, a common practice. He refused the drink with gall that would have dulled His senses, so that He might know the full extent of suffering for us on the cross.

They gave Him vinegar to drink mingled with GALL. (Matthew 27:34)

...in the GALL of bitterness. (Acts 8:23)

Forgiveness

When Yahshua forgave His murderers it released the power of the Holy Spirit in the earth. This forgiveness enabled Him to be raised from the dead *(Acts 2:24)*, just as Stephen's forgiveness enabled Saul to become Paul *(Acts 7:57-60)*, a great apostle. When Jesus forgave from the cross, He, Himself, could then be the first born raised from the dead *(Colossians 1:18)*, that we, too, could be raised up to sit together with Him in heavenly places. *(Ephesians 2:6)*

Father, forgive them; for they know not what they do. (Luke 23:34)

Thirst quenched with vinegar

Vinegar was soured wine, plain and unmixed. This was given to Jesus when He said, *I thirst! (John 19:28-30)* He took the bitter fruit, that He might bear much good fruit through us.

Railed

His accusers RAILED on Him, with accusations based on false assumptions. God did not deliver His Son from the cross, in order that He could offer salvation to all who would receive it. Because Yahshua did not come down, the accusers walked away satisfied that He was not the Messiah. This is the worst His enemies could say. It is precisely because He did not come down from the cross that we believe on Him. If only our enemies could say we spent our lives helping others and trusting God. Satan was using these men to taunt Jesus into actually coming down. Jesus did something greater than coming down from the cross. He rose from the dead, and they still did not believe Him.

> *And they that passed by railed on Him, wagging their heads and saying, Ah, Thou that destroyest the temple and buildest it in three days, Save Thyself, and come down from the cross. Likewise also the chief priests mocking said among themselves with the scribes, He saved others; Himself He cannot save. Let Christ the King of Israel descend now from the cross, that we may see and believe. And they that were crucified with Him reviled Him. (Mark 15:29-32)*

David prophesied this would occur. *All they that see Me laugh Me to scorn: they shoot out the lip, they shake the head, saying, He trusted on the LORD that He would deliver Him... (Psalm 22:7-8)*

Darkness

The darkness on the earth reflects the darkness of man's sin borne by Christ's soul as He suffered divine wrath *(Romans 5:9)* for sinners. *(Luke 23:44)* The hideousness of sin being borne by the sinless Son of God could only be expressed and symbolized by the darkness over the land and the people. A foolish speculation continues by scientists, that it could have been an eclipse, or some other coincidental weather phenomenon.

> *And it shall come to pass in that day, saith the LORD God, that I will cause the sun to go down at noon, and I will DARKEN the earth in the clear day: And I will turn your feasts into mourning, and all your songs into lamentation; and I will bring up sackcloth upon all loins, and baldness upon every head; and I will make it as the MOURNING OF AN ONLY SON, and the end thereof as a bitter day. (Amos 8:9-10)*

Forsaken

Yahshua's plaintive cry from the cross is really the fulfillment of David's prophetic Psalm concerning the Messiah. This Psalm begins with Jesus' words from the cross, and ends with His words.

> *MY GOD, MY GOD, WHY HAST THOU FORSAKEN ME?...All they that see Me laugh Me to scorn: they shoot out the lip, they shake the head, saying, He trusted on the LORD that He would deliver Him: let Him deliver Him, seeing He delighted in Him...Thou hast brought Me into the dust of death. For dogs have compassed Me: the assembly of the wicked have inclosed Me: they pierced My hands and My feet...They part My garments among them, and cast lots upon My vesture...that HE HATH DONE THIS. (Psalm 22)*

Notice the final words, HE HATH DONE THIS. In Hebrew this is really, *IT IS FINISHED!*, Jesus final words. Some scholars believe He shouted the first and last words of this Psalm, and quietly spoke the rest in between. Using the Name "God," in this instance, instead of His usual "Father" indicates something has transpired. Something is different. The supreme deity and righteous judge is punishing Him. Still, He calls Him "My God," reaching out to Him. The crowds that had once followed Him forsook Him, Judas betrayed Him, the disciples hid, Peter denied Him, and finally God forsook Him.

The punishment for sin is separation from God. This was the worst part of Yahshua's death. We do not have to suffer separation from God because Jesus did this for us. He took God's wrath for us. *(Roman's 5:9)* He laid the foundation for our deliverance from spiritual and physical corruption. He secured the blessing, and took away the curse. He was forsaken so God would never leave or forsake us. *(Hebrews 3:5)* The fulfillment of a millennia of prophecy is that *God's wrath is quenched through His Son's sacrifice* and He is SATISFIED. *He shall see of the travail of His soul, and shall be SATISFIED... (Isaiah 53:11)*

Chapter Fifty-Five
The Finished Work of the Cross

Through Yahshua's (Jesus') death we have reconciliation, redemption, righteousness, sanctification and salvation. Jesus' ministry on earth was *finished*, the old covenant law had been fulfilled. Even in death Jesus was in control of when He gave up His life. He had certain things to accomplish before He could release His spirit from His body. He resumed calling God His Father. It is finished in a victory cry, a triumphant exclamation! The redemption was complete. He commended (*Strong's* 3908, paratithemi) Himself into His Father's hands. COMMEND means to deposit as a trust for protection, commit to the keeping of.

Veil torn
Solomon's temple was 30 cubits high, but Herod had increased it to 40 cubits, according to the historian Josephus. The veil was between 60 and 90 feet high, and several feet thick. Only God Himself could have torn the veil in two, from top to bottom. This act alone should have awakened the religious Jews, but their eyes were blinded to the truth.

The veil represented separation of man from God, through sin. Only the high priest was able to enter beyond this veil once a year. At the moment of Christ's death, this veil was torn in two, revealing that the perfect sacrifice was made and there was now no longer any separation between man and God. The veil symbolized His flesh, torn to open a way to YHWH, our God, through Him. *(Hebrews 9:7, 28; Exodus 30:10; Matthew 27:51)*

Earthquake
The earthquake at Jesus' death cracked the ground, moving aside the lid on the container holding the Ark of the Covenant, buried in a chamber directly below the cross where Jesus hung. Additionally, it caused stones to roll away from certain tombs, saints arose from their graves after Jesus' resurrection, and were seen in Jerusalem. *(Matthew 27:51-52)* Death lost its grip on many captives. The earth itself was shaken to its very foundation, for Jesus was the Chief Cornerstone. *(Ephesians 2:20)* *The earth did quake, and the rocks rent. (Matthew 27:51)*

There was another earthquake when the angel of the LORD descended from heaven and rolled away the stone from the door of the sepulcher, and sat upon it. *(Matthew 28:2)*

Pierced by spear in side
He gave His flesh for the fulfillment of the law. *(1 Peter 4:1)* The curse of the law separated us from God. *(Galatians 3:13)* He gave His flesh to break the curse of the law, so the Spirit could be poured out on all flesh. *(Acts 2:17)* Being PIERCED in the side *(John 19:34)* was the fulfillment of another prophecy that cannot be denied, for usually they just broke the legs without any piercing. *They shall look on Him Who they PIERCED. (Zechariah 12:10)*

Blood on the mercy seat
Jesus was probably speared on the left side under the fifth rib, the location of the spleen. The water separated on top of the heavier blood. Probably three to five units of blood were spilled. When the rocks split in the earthquake, this created an opening on the left side of the cross, where the blood splashed down on the mercy seat of the Ark of the Covenant, buried there 600 years before, in Jeremiah's Grotto, located directly below Golgotha, awaiting the perfect fulfillment of Messiah's blood sacrifice.[3] Archeologist, Ron Wyatt, uncovered the Ark several years ago during a dig, and took scrapings of the blood which was splattered everywhere in the chamber, including on the mercy seat. When tested by two independent laboratories, the blood was found to have unusual properties. It had 23 female chromosomes, and only one male chromosome (normal blood has 23 of each). He believed this was truly the blood of the Son of God.

Innocent blood
Jesus' innocent blood began to be shed at Gethsemane when He sweat blood, and continued until after His death. The infinite power of the blood of Christ has not even begun to be comprehended by finite man. His precious blood:

THE BLOOD

1. Forgives the sins of those who repent, accept His forgiveness, and believe. It brings redemption. *(Ephesians 1:7)*

   For this is My blood of the New Testament, which is shed for many for the remission of sins. (Matthew 26:28)

2. Ransoms all believers from the power of Satan and evil powers.

   …to feed the church of God, which He hath purchased with His own blood. (Acts 20:28)

   …ye know that ye were not redeemed with corruptible things. (1 Peter 1:18-19)

   Thou wast slain, and hast redeemed us to God by Thy blood… (Revelation 5:9)

   And they overcame Him by the blood of the Lamb… (Revelation 12:11)

   Who hath delivered us from the power of darkness, and hath translated us into the kingdom of His dear Son. (Colossians 1:13)

3. Justifies all who believe in Him. His shed blood makes salvation a possibility.

   …Whom God hath sent forth to be a propitiation through faith in His blood, to declare His righteousness for the remission of sins… (Romans 3:24-25)

4. Cleanses believer's consciences so they might serve God without guilt, in full assurance.

   How much more shall the blood of Christ, Who through the eternal Spirit offered Himself without spot to God, purge your conscience from dead works to serve the living God? (Hebrews 9:14)

   Let us draw near with a true heart in full assurance of faith, having our hearts sprinkled (with Christ's blood) *from an evil conscience. (Hebrews 10:22)*

5. Sanctifies God's people.

   Wherefore Jesus also, that He might sanctify the people with His own blood, suffered without the gate. (Hebrews 13:12)

   …the blood of Jesus Christ His Son cleanseth us from all sin. (1 John 1:7-10)

6. Opens the way (access) for believers to come directly before God through Christ in order to receive grace, mercy, help and salvation.

   Wherefore He is able also to save them to the uttermost that come unto God by Him, seeing He ever liveth to make intercession for them. (Hebrews 7:25)

   Having therefore, brethren, boldness to enter into the holiest by the blood of Jesus. (Hebrews 10:19)

   But now in Christ Jesus ye who sometimes were far off are made nigh by the blood of Christ. (Ephesians 2:13)

7. Guarantee of all promises of the NEW eternal COVENANT.

   For how much sorer punishment, suppose ye, shall he be thought worthy. Who hath trodden under foot the Son of God, and hath counted the blood of the covenant, wherewith he was sanctified, an unholy thing, and hath done despite unto the Spirit of grace? (Hebrews 10:29)

   For this is My blood of the NEW TESTAMENT. (Matthew 26:28)

   This cup is the NEW TESTAMENT in My blood which is shed for you. (Luke 22:20)

   And to Jesus the mediator of the NEW COVENANT, and to the blood of sprinkling, that speaketh better things than that of Abel. (Hebrews 12:24)

   In Whom we have redemption through His blood, the forgiveness of sins, according to the riches of His grace…(Ephesians 1:7)

8. The blood saves, reconciles, purifies, there is power in the blood to continually cleanse us from sin. Jesus is our Passover Lamb. *(Exodus 12:7-8; 1 Corinthians 5:7; Hebrews 7:25; 10:22; 1 John 1:7)* We are forbidden to drink any other blood, yet we are to symbolically consume His blood. *(John 6:53-56)*

9. Is central to the New Testament concept of redemption.

> *The cup of blessing which we bless, is it not the communion of the blood of Christ: (1 Corinthians 10:16)*

> *But now in Christ Jesus ye who sometimes were far off are made nigh by the blood of Christ. (Ephesians 2:13)*

> *Elect according to the foreknowledge of God the Father, through sanctification of the Spirit, unto obedience and sprinkling of the blood of Jesus Christ... (1 Peter 1:2)*

> *...These are they which came out of great tribulation, and have washed their robes, and made them white in the blood of the Lamb. (Revelation 7:14; 12:11)*

10. Shed blood removes our sins and reconciles us with God.

> *...by the obedience of One shall many be made righteous. (Romans 5:19)*

> *And being found in fashion as a man, He humbled Himself, and became obedient unto death, even the death of the cross. (Philippians 2:8; Leviticus 16)*

11. He died as a ransom to free us from sins committed under the first covenant.

> *And for this cause He is the mediator of the New Testament, that by means of death, for the redemption of the transgressions that were under the first testament, they which are called might receive the promise of eternal inheritance. (Hebrews 9:15)*

12. He entered the most holy place with His own blood, once for all, and obtained our redemption with His blood.

> *Neither by the blood of goats and calves, but by His own blood He entered in once into the holy place, having obtained eternal redemption for us. (Hebrews 9:12)*

13. We overcome by the blood. *(Revelation 12:11)*
14. We will wash in the blood during the tribulation. *(Revelation 7:14)*
14. His blood was a trespass offering. *(Leviticus 7:2)*
15. His blood was a peace offering. *(Exodus 29:20-21)*
16. His blood was atonement for sins. *(Leviticus 16:14-15, 18-19, 27; 17:11)*
17. His blood took our judgment. *(Ezekiel 16:38; Revelation 16:6)*
18. His blood took our oppression and cruelty. *(Habakkuk 2:12)*
19. His blood took our guilt. *(Leviticus 20:9; 2 Samuel 1:16; Ezekiel 18:13)*
20. Through His blood we have remission of sins, sin offering, atonement. *(Leviticus 4; 8:15; Exodus 29:12; 30:10)*

> *For this is My blood of the New Testament, which is shed for many for the remission of sins. (Matthew 26:28)*

> *Then Jesus said unto them, Verily, verily, I say unto you, Except ye eat the flesh of the Son of man, and drink His blood, ye have no life in you, Whoso eateth My flesh, and drinketh My blood, hath eternal life; and I will raise him up at the last day. (John 6:53)*

> *...to feed the church of God, which He hath purchased with His own blood. (Acts 20:28)*

> *Being justified freely by His grace through the redemption that is in Christ Jesus: Whom God hath set forth to be a propitiation through faith in His blood, to declare His righteousness for the remission of sins that are past, through the forbearance of God... (Romans 3:24)*

> *Much more then, being now justified by His blood, we shall be saved from wrath through Him...by Whom we have now received the atonement. (Romans 5:9-11)*

> *The cup of blessing which we bless, is it not the communion of the blood of Christ? (1 Corinthians 10:16)*

21. His blood makes us perfect (complete), and righteous.

> *...our LORD Jesus, that Great Shepherd of the sheep, through the blood of the everlasting covenant, Make you perfect (complete) in every good work... (Hebrews 13:20-21)*

> *...through faith in His blood, to declare His righteousness for the remission of sins... (Romans 3:25)*

22. New covenant ratified with shed blood. Jesus is the mediator of the new covenant. *(Hebrews 9:15)*

> *But now hath He obtained a more excellent ministry, by how much also He is the mediator of a better covenant, which was established upon better promises. (Hebrews 8:6)*

23. Protected by the blood. Evil passes over us through the applying of the blood of the Lamb of God.

> *...take you a lamb...and kill the passover. And ye shall take a bunch of hyssop, and dip it in the blood that is in the basin, and strike the lintel and the two side posts with the blood... (Exodus 12:21-22)*

Three who bear witness on earth
The Spirit, the water, the blood, and they all agree. *(1 John 5:8)*

No bones broken
His sinless body became a bridge. *(John 19:36; Psalm 34:20)*

The water and the blood
Sacrificed animal parts were washed in the water of the laver in the outer court of the temple. The water that came out of Jesus' side represents the washing of the Word. *(Ephesians 5:26)* The first high priest, Aaron, had his ear, thumb and toe anointed with blood. *(Leviticus 8:23)* Jesus had thorns placed on His head, causing blood to run to His ears, and He had nails driven through His hands and feet from which His blood flowed, that the Old Testament shadow-picture of a high priest could be fulfilled in Him. The blood is life (in the Spirit). *(Leviticus 17:11)* The blood continuously cleanses and justifies. *(Ephesians 1:7)* We have redemption through His blood, forgiveness of sins. Being now justified by His blood, we are saved from the wrath we deserve. *(Romans 5:9)* The blood of Christ purges (cleanses) us from dead works. *(Hebrews 9:14)* We are sanctified through the blood of Jesus once for all. *(Hebrews 10:9)* His blood speaks, it shouts the victory He won for us. *(Genesis 4:10)* His shed blood released us from Satan's power.

> *...that through death He might destroy him that had the power of death, that is, the devil and deliver them who through fear of death were all their lifetime subject to bondage. (Hebrews 2:14-15)*

Sacrificed innocent Lamb of God
He became sin for us. He took our wrath and judgment, so we might live with Him forever. *...while we were yet sinners Christ died for us. (Romans 5:8)*

Sinless blood
Jesus, the last Adam, had blood that was unique, for it was not sin-filled. He was not born of Adam's blood, but was fathered by God Himself, and born of a virgin, *(Matthew 1:22)* yet His body was from the sinful flesh of His mother. No one with the first Adam's blood could have offered himself for our redemption and ransom, because all human blood had sin. We know from scripture that life is in the blood *(Leviticus 17:11)*, and from medical science that blood type is conveyed entirely by the father. The Messiah was safe in His mother's womb because blood cells and bacteria are too big to pass through the placenta to the unborn child.[4]

With no blood passing from mother to child, it became necessary for YHWH to place His seed by the Holy Spirit into a virgin to prevent wicked blood from passing to His son. The father's protoplasmic seed is made of fluid and plasma (water and blood). *(1 John 5:6)* [5] Thus, only Jesus could sanctify us through His own blood and redeem us. Faith in His blood brings us salvation. *(Revelation 5:9)* Because His blood was sinless, it did more than cover sin; it literally did away with it. The last Adam, Yahshua the Messiah, had undefiled sinless blood *(1 Corinthians 15:45)*, enabling Him to become our high priest *(Romans 5:9)*, and we are gloriously born again into a new blood type when we receive Yahshua as our Messiah. While man's blood cleanses his own body of impurities, the Messiah's blood cleanses man from sin.[6] Sin circulates throughout man's body, soul and spirit, but Jesus provides us with a blood cleaning procedure we cannot afford to miss. Once His sinless blood has purified our spirits through becoming born again, the man becomes part of the "body" of Messiah.

Chapter Fifty-Six
Burial and Resurrection of the Messiah

Spices

Myrrh was given to Jesus at His birth and used on Him at His burial. *(John 19:40)* Mary brought an alabaster box and broke it to anoint Jesus for His burial. This event's importance, recorded in all four gospels *(Matthew 26:7; Mark 14:3; Luke 7:37; John 12:3)*, refers to how costly and precious myrrh *(Strong's 3464, muron)*, the death to self, really is to the Father. The high priest was anointed with oil *(Leviticus 8:30)*, just as Yahshua Messiah, our high priest, was anointed with oil before His passion. Jesus had to die to fulfill His destiny, as we must cover ourselves with the precious oil of death to self, and allow ourselves to be broken, to fulfill our destiny in Him.

He led captivity captive

Though we spit on Him, reviled Him and rejected Him, He set us free from the bondage of sin and eternal death.

...When He ascended up on high, He led captivity captive, and gave gifts unto men. (Ephesians 4:8)

Grave clothes

The grave clothes were made of fine linen. *(Matthew 27:59; John 19:40; Mark 15:46)* He was bound in grave clothes *(Matthew 27:59)* and obedient to the death. *(Philippians 2:8)* He threw off the grave clothes at His resurrection so we cannot be held by the law of sin and death.

New sepulcher

He was buried in the grave of a rich man, Joseph of Arimathaea, a member of the Jewish Sanhedrin *(John 19:41)*, fulfilling prophecy.

And He made His grave with the wicked and with the rich in His death; because He had done no VIOLENCE, neither was any DECEIT in His mouth. (Isaiah 53: 9)

Risen

He fulfilled this prophecy even in death, to deliver us from violence and deceit. VIOLENCE *(Strongs 2555, chamac)* means oppressor, unrighteous, unjust gain, cruelty, wrong, damage. DECEIT *(Strongs 4820, mirmah)* means trechery, guile, fraud, false.

The angel said, *He is risen, as He said. (Matthew 28:6; Mark 16:6)* Jesus conquered the strongest enemy of all, death. This is proof He is the Son of God, the first man to ever experience death and conquer it, never to die again.

The Gospels

Matthew: He is the King Who is obeyed (purple).
Mark: He is the man Who identifies with you (white).
Luke: He is the Savior Who took away your sins (scarlet).
John: He is the Son of God Who is worshipped (blue).

These four colors: purple, white (fine linen), scarlet and blue were on the gate that was the entrance into the outer court of the tabernacle of God. These colors were hung all around the tabernacle itself and they were all four in the veil at the entrance of the Holy of Holies. *(Exodus 25:26)* The fence surrounding the outer court and the ark of the covenant were made of shittim wood. This special wood did not decay and represents Jesus flesh which never saw corruption, because He rose from the dead.

Caiaphas

Caiaphas, the high priest, was deposed shortly after Jesus' crucifixion. He killed himself in 35 A.D.

There were four signs that proved Messiah was the true Savior *after* His resurrection

1. The lot for the LORD's goat did not come up in the right hand of the high priest for 40 years. Then the temple was destroyed.
2. The scarlet cord tied to the door of the temple on the day of atonement, stopped turning white after the scapegoat had been cast over the precipice. (In Isaiah it says that though your sins be as scarlet, they shall be white as snow.)
3. The western most light on the temple candelabra would not burn. This light was used to light the other lights.
4. The temple doors would open by themselves as an ominous fulfillment of Zechariah 11:1. This prophecy foretold the destruction of the temple by fire.[7]

What sin did the Jews commit to cause YHWH to no longer accept their sacrifices? What sin caused the above signs and other signs to occur? They rejected the Messiah when He came. For almost 2,000 years Jews have been dispersed before returning to Israel as a nation. As the world looks for the Messiah's second coming, they still look for His first. They will embrace the anti-christ false messiah, instead, who will offer world peace.

Bibliography for *The Blood*

1. Storms, *Jesus, The Suffering Savior*, pp. 2-3
2. Wyatt, *Discovered*, Volume, pp. 95-101 (further reference from Ron Wyatt, archeologist and anesthesiologist, through phone conversation)
3. *Parade Magazine*, Feb. 16, 1992
4. Wooten, *In Search of Israel*, pp. 103-107
5. Wooten, *Who Is Israel?* pp. 63-69
6. Brown, *Are the Rabbis Right?*, (cassette by Messianic Vision)
7. Spurgeon, *The Death and Suffering of Jesus* (general reference guide)

Part Four

STRIPES

The Son of Righteousness arise with healing in His wings

Stripes

from the *Heart & Soul Surrender* CD   Quadrilogy Publishing 1997
Lyrics by Bree Keyton

The Son of Righteousness arise with healing in His wings. *(Malachi 4:2)*

1. Heart disease, lung disease, cholera, rheumatic fever
2. Tuberculosis, strep throat, malaria, leprosy, bubonic plague
3. Digestive disorders, intestinal disorders, fiber cystic breast disease
4. Child bearing difficulties, toxic shock syndrome, hepatitis
5. Measles, chicken pox, bronchitis, emphysema, anthrax
6. Osteoporosis, Parkinson's disease, gall bladder disease, influenza
7. Encephalitis, small pox, dysentery, thrombosis, sickle cell anemia
8. Angina, mumps, hypoglycemia, diabetes
9. Brain and neurological disorders, rabies, rubella
10. Kidney and bladder disease, liver disease, pancreatic disease

---

11. Lupus
12. Bone and joint disease, plague, whooping cough, endometriosis
13. Tumors
14. Glandular disorders, lyme disease, Chron's disease, hypertension, parasites
15. Viruses
16. Cerebral palsy, multiple sclerosis, mental illness, ulcers, Gulf War Illness
17. Alzheimer's
18. Blood disease, depression, malnutrition, pellagra, rickets, scurvy
19. Back pain
20. Bursitis, tetanus, phlebitis, bacterial disease, inflammations

---

21. Genetic and birth defects
22. Cystic fibrosis
23. Migraines, burns
24. Muscle and skin disease
25. Gynecological disorders
26. Gum disease, Hodgkin's disease
27. Lou Gerrig's disease (A.L.S.)
28. Colitis, epidemics
29. Anemia
30. Allergies
31. Fever
32. Headaches
33. S.I.D.S.
34. Arthritis
35. Psoriasis, leukemia, *all* curses
36. Cancer; *all* infections, *all* addictions, *all* injuries

---

37. A.I.D.S., sexually transmitted disease, pneumonia, cirrhosis, bacterial meningitis
38. Muscular dystrophy, blindness and eye disease, poisoning, spider and serpent bites, and scorpion stings.

39. **I Am the LORD, that healeth thee.** *(Exodus 15:36)*
    Jesus took our infirmities and bore our sicknesses. *(Matthew 18:17)*
    He was wounded for our transgressions, He was bruised for our iniquities *(Isaiah 53:5)*,
    And by His stripes we were healed. *(1 Peter 2:24)*

Introduction: Healing Scriptures

Introduction

This work is dedicated to the healing virtue and compassion of our LORD: YHWH Rapha, our Healer. *(Exodus 15:26)* God introduced us to this part of His character and nature because He loves us. This was the first redemptive Name He gave His people after the defeat of Pharaoh's army at the Red Sea. Healing is a part of Jesus' work (atonement) on the cross. Denying that it is God's will for us to be healed is the same as denying we can be saved from our sins through His death on the cross. Both sin and sickness were caused by the fall: both are cleansed by Jesus' shed blood.

Virtue is defined in *Vine's* as the manifestation of His divine power, an essential quality in the exercise of faith, compassion, to be moved in one's inward parts toward individual sufferers; to suffer with another. Jesus has a heart of compassion. He is moved with compassion toward us. God sent His Word and healed us. His intention is always that we walk in divine health, and that healing would be a natural outgrowth of our salvation. Part of the meaning of salvation (sozo) is healing and deliverance. If you have received salvation, then also receive your right to healing. Embrace your healing as you do the truth in Jesus' Words:

> *...by Whose stripes ye were healed. (1 Peter 2:24)*

We must not limit God, but **only believe**. Jesus exhorted people many times, "*Your* faith has made you whole." He performed many unusual healings and miracles. He is the LORD. He changes not. He is the same yesterday, today and forever. He is waiting for you to ask, believe and receive, with effectual fervent prayer. We are not the sick *trying* to get healed, we are *already* healed. It is not that God *can* heal you, He can, but the fact that He *already* has healed you is the greater point. He has finished the work!

If you often have hindering thoughts of your own unworthiness, you are absolutely right. But thank God your own unworthiness is not what qualifies you for healing. It is Jesus' righteousness that enables you to be healed. Healing belongs to you. It is the children's bread, and you are a child of God. You have not, because you ask not.

Faith moves the hand of God. Faith is the substance of things hoped for. In other words, faith is the currency of heaven. Healing is received by faith. Faith comes by hearing. Preaching healing by faith will cause faith to rise in the hearts of the listeners. Testimonies of healing build faith, but ultimately the individual must exercise his own faith. He must see healing as part of his inheritance as a Christian, and as much a part of Jesus' finished work as being born again. When this knowledge and faith coincide, healing will occur.

> *Heal me, O LORD, and I shall be healed; save me, and I shall be saved; for Thou art my praise. (Jeremiah 17:14)*

Both sin and sickness manifested at the fall: Both are cleansed by our Redeemer. Adam and Eve lost salvation, healing, and divine health, when they broke God's command. They received curses and were expelled from the garden. God said that in the day they ate of the tree of the knowledge of good and evil, that very day they would surely die. A day with the LORD is as a thousand years. Death came in a day for them. Yet Jesus redeemed us from the curse of the law of sin and death, and He gave us the law of the spirit of life.

> *For the law of the Spirit of life in Christ Jesus hath made me free from the law of sin and death. (Romans 8:2)*

Recently, I developed laryngitis the day of a concert. I was whispering all day but immediately declared that by His stripes I was healed. I declared in a whisper that when I began to minister I would have a voice to sing and minister. The LORD was right on time. I preached and ministered for three hours that night and many were healed. Glory!

The song "*Stripes*" (above) has a powerful healing anointing on it. In May of 1993, God gave me a vision of Jesus receiving His stripes before He went to the cross. It was a horrific bloody vision. The LORD spoke to me and told me to write a song and He would heal His people. I wrote the song "*Stripes*" and debuted it at a crusade two weeks later. Many were miraculously healed when I ministered the song. Since then, at concerts and through TV and radio airplay, thousands have been healed through the power of God's anointing on this song. I encourage you to acquire the "*Heart & Soul Surrender*" CD (or cassette), and also "*Healing Scriptures*," a 100 minute long cassette with scriptures, exhortation and music, through which many have received faith for healing.

Chapter Fifty-Seven
The Mouth is a Wellspring of Life

If ye abide in Me, and My Words abide in you, ye shall ask what ye will, and it shall be done unto you. Herein is My Father glorified, that ye bear much fruit: so shall ye be My disciples. (John 15:7)

…the MOUTH of the upright shall deliver them…a man shall be satisfied with good by the FRUIT OF HIS MOUTH…the TONGUE of the wise is HEALTH. (Proverbs 12:6, 14, 18)

The MOUTH of a righteous man is a well of LIFE… (Proverbs 10:11)

But the Word is very nigh unto thee, in thy MOUTH, and in thy heart, that thou mayest do it. See, I have set before thee this day LIFE and good, and death and evil. (Deuteronomy 30:14-15)

A wholesome TONGUE is a tree of LIFE: but perverseness therein is a breach in the spirit. (Proverbs 15:4)

A gentle TONGUE with it's healing power is a tree of LIFE, but willful contrariness in it breaks down the spirit. (Proverbs 15:4 Amplified)

The LIPS of the wise shall preserve them. (Proverbs 14:3)

He that keepeth his MOUTH keepeth his LIFE: but he that openeth wide his lips shall have destruction. (Proverbs 13:3)

Understanding is a WELL SPRING OF LIFE unto him that hath it: but the instruction of fools is folly. The heart of the wise teacheth his mouth, and addeth learning to his LIPS. Pleasant WORDS are as a honeycomb, sweet to the soul, and HEALTH to the bones. There is a way that seemeth right unto man: but the end thereof are the ways of death. (Proverbs 16:22-25)

My son, attend to my WORDS: incline thine ear unto my sayings. Let them not depart from thine eyes: keep them in the midst of thine heart. For they are LIFE unto those that find them, and HEALTH to all their flesh. Keep thy heart with all diligence; for out of it are the issues of life. (Proverbs 4:20-23)

Words are health to the flesh

Health to all their flesh means ALL. This scripture covers everything from a sore toe to A.I.D.S.. It is very simple; all means all. When Jesus healed ALL the people, He didn't leave anyone out because they did not fit His profile of a perfect candidate for healing. He healed ALL, rich and poor, short and tall, wise and ignorant, young and old. You are not the exception to Jesus' rule. You are included in this wonderful ALL about which the Bible talks.

Death and life are in the power of the tongue: and they that love it shall eat the fruit thereof. (Proverbs 18:21)

Blessing or cursing?

Have you ever thought of your tongue as a wellspring of life? Do you realize your tongue can deliver you, cause you to walk in health, keep your life? Did you know your tongue has healing power, it can preserve you; your tongue is health to your bones and your flesh? You have life in the power of your tongue through what you say! According to James 3:10-12, out of the same mouth can proceed both blessing and cursing, but God plainly states it should not be so. Think of your tongue as a tree of life *(Proverbs 15:4)*, for that is how God sees it. How does a fruitful tree live?

1. It must have water (Jesus is the living water).
2. It must have fertile soil (be rooted and grounded in the Word).
3. It must have plenty of sunlight (Jesus is the "Son" light of the world).
4. It must be pruned to bear good fruit (God brings His correction, so we may bear good fruit).

Going for the gold

How can this be accomplished? First we bathe ourselves in the living water. Then we fill our hearts and minds with the Word and sweet water will come forth, for out of the abundance of the heart the mouth speaks. We want to be trees planted by the rivers where the most fertile soil is found. The following Psalm speaks of being a tree planted by the rivers of water. It says we are to spread out our roots (which is strengthening ourselves in the LORD and expanding our intimacy and knowledge of God and His Word), so when heat (trials, temptations, and pressures) and drought (sickness and spiritual barrenness) come, we stand strong, with a good root system, which enables us to tap into God's Word, and His will. Let us be trees tapping into the pure river of the waters of life. *(Revelation 22:1)* Then, as Jeremiah 17:8 declares:

…he shall be as a tree planted by the waters, and that spreadeth out her roots by the river, and shall not see when heat cometh, but her leaf shall be green: and shall not be careful in the year of drought, neither shall cease from yielding fruit.

Chapter Fifty-Eight
Abundant Life

It is the spirit that quickeneth; the flesh profiteth nothing; the Words that I speak unto you, they are spirit, and they are LIFE... (John 6:63)

The thief cometh not, but for to steal, kill, and to destroy: I am come that they might have LIFE, and that they might have it more ABUNDANTLY. (John 10:10)

In the way of righteousness is LIFE; and in the pathway thereof there is no death. (Proverbs 12:28)

I shall not die, but LIVE, and declare the works of the LORD. (Psalm 118:17)

...if the Spirit of Him that raised up Jesus from the dead dwell in you, He that raised up Christ from the dead shall also QUICKEN YOUR MORTAL BODIES by His Spirit that dwelleth in you. (Romans 8:11)

The fear of the LORD is a fountain of LIFE, to depart from the snares of death. (Proverbs 14:27)

I will extol Thee, O LORD; for Thou hast lifted me up, and hast not made my foes to rejoice over me. O LORD my God, I cried unto Thee, and Thou hast healed me, O LORD, Thou hast brought up my soul from the grave; Thou hast kept me ALIVE, that I should not go down to the pit. Sing unto the LORD, O ye saints of His, and give thanks at the remembrance of His holiness. For His anger endureth but a moment; in His favor is LIFE: weeping may endure for a night, but joy cometh in the morning. (Psalm 30:1-5)

And I will RESTORE to you the years that the locust hath eaten...and ye shall eat in plenty, and be satisfied, and praise the Name of the LORD your God, that hath dealt wondrously with you: and my people shall never be ashamed. (Joel 2:25-26)

...God, Who QUICKENETH the dead, and calleth those things which be not as though they were. (Romans 4:17)

Declare abundant life

The Word of God is life! Abundant life! We can declare God's healing over our lives. God's favor is life! His healing is His good pleasure, His grace and abundant favor. He wants to restore, to you, the years the devil has stolen. God calls those things that be not as though they were. So should we! God, I'm healed! God, I'm restored! Praise the Name of the LORD. God, You have dealt wondrously with me!

Prayer

Oh, God, I believe I hear Your voice and am counted among Your sons. I pray for Your direction and Your will, so I may perform it daily. As Jesus was the perfect example of Your will, so may I be so conformed into His image, so I reflect that same light in my life, for I am the dwelling place of my Father's Spirit. Hallelujah (praise ye Yah)!

Study Questions: Chapter 57
1. In what way is the mouth a wellspring of life?
2. Name two things you can do immediately to begin to make your mouth a blessing.
3. How many did Jesus heal that came to Him?
4. Has Jesus or His Word changed since He walked the earth?
5. What kind of fruit can the tongue bring forth? What kind of fruit has your tongue brought forth lately?
6. Name four points to making your tongue a tree of life?

Study Questions: Chapter 58
1. What is the pathway of life?
2. What can we expect to receive when we are in God's favor?
3. How does God quicken our mortal bodies?
4. Who came to give us abundant life? How did He accomplish this.
5. What are the promises of Joel 2?

Chapter Fifty-Nine
Wisdom and Understanding

My son, forget not my law; but let thine heart keep my commandments: for length of days, and long life, and peace shall they add to thee. Let not mercy and truth forsake thee: bind them about thy neck; write them upon the table of thine heart: so shalt thou find favor and good UNDERSTANDING in the sight of God and man. Trust in the LORD with all thine heart; and lean not unto thine own UNDERSTANDING. In all thy ways acknowledge Him, and He shall direct thy path. Be not wise in thine own eyes: fear the LORD, and depart from evil. It shall be health to thy navel, and marrow to thy bones. (Proverbs 3:1-8)

Happy is the man that findeth WISDOM, and the man that getteth UNDERSTANDING: for the merchandise of it is better than the merchandise of silver, and gain thereof than fine gold. She is more precious than rubies: and all the things they canst desire are not to be compared unto her. Length of days is in her right hand; and in her left hand riches and honor. Her ways are ways of pleasantness, and all her paths are peace. She is a tree of life to them that lay hold upon her: and happy is every one that retaineth her. (Proverbs 3:13-18)

According as His divine power hath given unto us all things that pertain unto life and godliness, through the KNOWLEDGE of Him that hath called us to glory and virtue: Whereby are given unto us exceedingly great and precious promises: that by these Ye might be partakers of the divine nature, having escaped the corruption that is in the world through lust. (2 Peter 1:3-4)

He that followeth after righteousness and mercy findeth life, righteousness, and honor. (Proverbs 21:21)

Wisdom brings joy

Let us follow God's commandments with joy, be conformed into His image and follow righteousness. He has given us His divine wisdom, and all things that pertain to life and godliness; the mind of Christ, and the wisdom of God. The Word says we have long life, peace, health and length of days. Through our growing knowledge of Him we become partakers of His divine nature. Thank You, YHWH, for the truths You are quickening to us through Your Word. Thank You for long life and health as we grow in Your wisdom.

Study Questions: Chapter 59
1. Name three steps to having God direct your path.
2. If we follow righteousness and mercy, what three things will we find that will bless our lives?
3. Why does Proverbs 21:21 combine righteousness and mercy together?
4. What is righteousness without mercy, or mercy without righteousness?
5. What is wisdom likened to in Proverbs 3?
6. Name six benefits to getting wisdom.
7. How can you relate life and godliness in 2 Peter 1:3-4, to righteousness and mercy in Proverbs 21:21?
8. What are the exceedingly great and precious promises?
9. You are a partaker of the divine nature from the moment you are born again. What scripture can you believe and stand on to walk in this knowledge?

Chapter Sixty
Unity of the Spirit

Endeavoring to keep the UNITY OF THE SPIRIT in the bond of peace. (Ephesians 4:3)

Till we all come into the UNITY OF THE FAITH, and of the knowledge of the Son of God, unto a perfect man, unto the measure of the stature of the fullness of Christ... (Ephesians 4:13)

Behold, how good and how pleasant it is for brethren to DWELL TOGETHER IN UNITY: It is like the precious ointment upon the head, that went down upon the beard, even Aaron's beard: that went down to the skirts of his garments; as the dew of Hermon, and as the dew that descended upon the mountains of Zion: for there the LORD commanded the BLESSING, even life for evermore. (Psalm 133)

Let BROTHERLY LOVE continue. (Hebrews 13:1)

We know that we have passed from death unto LIFE, because we LOVE THE BRETHREN. He that loveth not his brother abideth in death. (1 John 3:14)

Lift up the hands which hang down, and the feeble knees; And make straight paths for your feet, lest that which is lame be turned out of the way; but let it rather be healed. FOLLOW PEACE with all men, and holiness, without which no man shall see the LORD: Looking diligently lest any man fail of the grace of God; lest any ROOT OF BITTERNESS springing up trouble you, and thereby many be defiled... (Hebrews 12:12-15)

Reconciliation and healing

Our LORD desires reconciliation. He wants to heal our relationships. He knows that discord, strife and bitterness can make us sick! Dwelling together in unity is likened to the anointing oil; a fragrant oil, costly and precious. What does God say to do? He says to anoint the sick with oil and they will be healed. The fragrance of the unity of the Spirit, which God is working in us, is vital. Following after peace, and digging up any root of bitterness will bring healing to many of God's people. But it will cost us something. We must lay aside our own pride, our own agendas, our own hurts and wounds. We must be an olive branch, lay ourselves out on the bitter waters and make them sweet. We must be a tree of life.

The level to which we are able to walk in unity of the spirit with our fellow believers, close family and friends, will be reflected in the state of our mental and physical health. How can we pretend to love God when we can't even get along with our family and neighbors? Turmoil in relationships will bring about physiological changes in our bodies and minds that profoundly affect our health. Jesus bore all our sorrows and suffering so you and I could walk in peace and victory. Inability to walk in peace and unity can be traced back to pride, which brings contention, a spirit of haughtiness, bitterness (a refusal to forgive our offenders), and selfishness.

Only by pride cometh CONTENTION...(Proverbs 13:10)

A fools lips enter into CONTENTION... (Proverbs 18:6)

He that is of a proud heart stirreth up STRIFE... (Proverbs 28:25)

It is an honor for a man to cease from STRIFE... (Proverbs 20:3)

Prayer

Father, I fervently desire to please You in all my ways. Let my life be a reflection of Your love to all who cross my path. I admit I have had trouble with others, but I choose this day to serve You, Father. Create in me a clean heart and renew a right spirit within me. As LORD of my life You have great blessings planned for me that I have never walked in because of strife, pride and refusal to love my neighbor or spouse as You intended. I acknowledge I am weak and I need Your help to strengthen me in all my trials, so I may choose to walk in love. Come Holy Spirit and dwell in me. Fill me again with Your presence and power to overcome evil with good. In Jesus' Name I pray. Amen.

Chapter Sixty-One
The Secret Place

He that dwelleth in the SECRET PLACE of the Most high shall abide under the shadow of the Almighty. I will say of the LORD, He is my refuge and my fortress: my God in Him will I trust. (Psalm 91:1)

Thou are my HIDING PLACE; Thou shalt preserve me from trouble; Thou shalt compass me about with songs of deliverance. (Psalm 32:7)

Thou shalt HIDE them in the SECRET of Thy presence from the pride of man: thou shalt keep them SECRETLY in a pavilion from the strife of tongues. (Psalm 31:20)

Thou art my HIDING PLACE and my shield... (Psalm 119:114)

These are mighty scriptures of deliverance and protection. When we are hurting and fearful, we must seek God and hide ourselves under His wings, always remembering He has provided mighty legions of angels for our protection. God says we will tread on the lion and adder and the dragon, and He will deliver us and satisfy us with long life. *(Psalm 91)* The secret place of the Most High is really our hiding place.

Study Questions: Chapter 61
1. Whom do we place our trust in?
2. Name three specific promises God makes to protect us in Psalm 91:1.
3. Give the conditions to provide this protection.
4. What is the definition of trust according to Psalm 91:1? Does God ever lie?
5. What is the "secret place" of the Most High?

Chapter Sixty-Two
Healing for Barrenness

This next section is for the many couples who are barren, to give them hope by looking at what YHWH, our God has already done for His people. Do not despair: God is faithful! Many couples today, are willing to spend tens of thousands of dollars to conceive, but God will hear your prayers and grant you children today, just as He did from the beginning. Only believe! Our wonderful God is the same yesterday, today and forever. *(Hebrews 13:8)* Children are a blessing from the LORD *(Deuteronomy 28:4)* and you can stand on His Word.

Every good and every perfect gift is from above, and cometh down from the Father of lights, with whom is no variableness, neither shadow of turning. (James 1:17)

There shall nothing cast their young, nor be BARREN, in thy land: the number of thy days I will fulfill. (Exodus 23:26)

Thou shalt be blessed above all people: there shall not be male or female BARREN among you, or among your cattle. (Deuteronomy 7:14)

Sarah, Isaac's mother
And God said unto Abraham, As for Sarai thy wife, thou shalt not call her name Sarai, but Sarah shall her name be, And I will bless her, and give thee a son also of her: yea, I will bless her, and she shall be a mother of nations; kings of people shall be of her. Then Abraham fell upon his face, and laughed, and said in his heart, Shall a child be born unto him that is a hundred years old: and shall Sarah, that is ninety years old, bear?
...And the LORD visited Sarah as He had said, and the LORD did unto Sarah as He had spoken. For Sarah CONCEIVED, and bare Abraham a son in his old age, at the set time of which God had spoken to him...And she said, Who would have said unto Abraham, that Sarah should have given children suck: for I have born him a son in his old age. (Genesis 17:15-19; 21:5-7)

So then they which be of faith are blessed with faithful Abraham...Christ hath redeemed us from the curse of the law, being made a curse for us: for it is written, Cursed is every one that hangeth on a tree: That the blessing of Abraham might come on the Gentiles through Jesus Christ; that we might receive the promise of the Spirit through faith. (Galatians 3:9, 13-14)

Rebekah, Jacob's mother
And Isaac was forty years old when he took Rebekah to wife...And Isaac entreated the LORD for his wife, because she was barren: and the LORD was entreated of him, and Rebekah his wife CONCEIVED. And when her days to be delivered were fulfilled, behold there were twins in her womb. And the first came out red all over like an hairy garment; and they called his name Esau. And after that came his brother out, and his hand took hold on Esau's heel; and his name was called Jacob: and Isaac was three score years old when she bare them. (Genesis 25:20-21, 24-26)

Leah and Rachel, Isaac's wives
And Jacob did so...And he went in also unto Rachel, and he loved also Rachel more than Leah...And when the LORD saw that Leah was hated, He opened her womb: but Rachel was BARREN. And Leah conceived, and bare a son, and she called his name Reuben: for she said, Surely the LORD hath looked upon my affliction...(Genesis 29:28, 30-32)

...And when Rachel saw that she bare Jacob no children, Rachel envied her sister; and said unto Jacob, Give me children, or else I die. And God remembered Rachel, and God hearkened to her, and opened her womb. And she CONCEIVED, and bare a son; and said, God hath taken away my reproach: And she called his name Joseph: and said the LORD shall add to me another son. (Genesis 30:1, 22-24)

Manoah and his wife, Samson's mother
And there was a certain man of Zorah, of the family of the Danites, whose name was Manoah; and his wife was BARREN, and bare not. And the angel of the LORD appeared unto the woman, and said unto her, Behold now, thou art barren, and bearest not: but thou shalt CONCEIVE, and bear a son. Now therefore beware, I pray thee, and drink not wine nor strong drink and eat not any unclean thing: For, lo, thou shalt conceive, and bear a son; and no razor shall come on his head: for the child shall be a Nazarite unto God from the womb: and he shall begin to deliver Israel out of the hand of the Philistines...And the woman bare a son, and called his name Samson: and the child grew, and the LORD blessed him. (Judges 13:2-5, 24-25)

Hannah, Samuel's mother
Now there was a certain man...and he had two wives; the name of the one was Hannah, and the name of the other Peninnah: and Peninnah had children, but Hannah had no children...unto Hannah he gave a worthy portion; for he loved Hannah: but the LORD had SHUT UP HER WOMB. And her adversary also provoked her sore, for to make her fret, because the LORD had shut up her womb.

...So Hannah rose up after they had eaten, in Shiloh, and after they had drunk...And she was in bitterness of soul, and prayed unto the LORD, and wept sore. And she vowed a vow, and said, O LORD of hosts, if thou wilt indeed look on the affliction of thine handmaid, and remember me, and not forget thine handmaid, but wilt give unto thine handmaid a man child, then I will give him unto the LORD all the days of his life, and there shall no razor come upon his head...and Elkanah knew Hannah his wife; and the LORD remembered her. Wherefore it came to pass, when the time was come about after Hannah had CONCEIVED, that she bare a son, and called his name Samuel, saying, Because I have asked him of the LORD. (1 Samuel. 1:1-2, 5-6, 9-11, 19-20)

Elisabeth, John the Baptist's mother

There was in the days of Herod, the king of Judea, a certain priest named Zechariah...and his wife...her name was Elisabeth...And they had no child, because that Elisabeth was BARREN, and they both were now well stricken in years. And it came to pass, that while he executed the priest's office...there appeared unto him an angel of the LORD...the angel said unto him fear not, Zechariah: for thy prayer is heard; and thy wife Elisabeth shall bear thee a son, and thou shalt call his name John. And thou shalt have joy and gladness; and many shall rejoice at his birth. For he shall be great in the sight of the LORD, and shall drink neither wine nor strong drink; and he shall be filled with the Holy Ghost, even from his mother's womb.

And after those days his wife Elisabeth CONCEIVED, and hid herself five months, saying, Thus hath the LORD dealt with me in the days wherein He looked on me, to take away my reproach among men. Now Elisabeth's full time came that she should be delivered; and she brought forth a son. And her neighbors and her cousins heard how the LORD had showed great mercy upon her; and they rejoiced with her. (Luke 1:5-15; 24-25; 57-58)

Standing in your faith

Men and women of faith have stood on God's promises all down through the centuries, from Abraham until the present, to receive healing in their bodies to have children. Since God is the same now and forever, you can stand in faith to conceive a child just as Abraham and Sarah, just as Elisabeth and Zechariah, just as Manoah, Hannah, Rachel and Jacob, Rebekah and Isaac. The hand of God is moved by faith. *Now faith is the substance of things hoped for, the evidence of things not seen. (Hebrews 11:1)*

Receiving healing

1. Speak life to your womb and your reproductive organs.
2. Command the malfunctioning part of your body to line up with the Word of God.
3. Memorize scripture and speak it over your body, nothing wavering.
4. Give God all the credit and glory *before* you see the manifestation.
5. Reread the scriptures above carefully noting the many remarkable similarities.
6. Write them down and stand on them for your miracle.
7. Now, lay your hand on your body and ask God to heal you and give you the desire of your heart. If parts are missing, ask for a creative miracle.
8. Ask in faith, nothing wavering *(James 1:6)*, and you shall have whatsoever you say. *(Mark 11:23-25)*
9. Realize it is God's will for you to be healed.
10. Stand in your healing until you see the manifestation of your healing.

Study Questions: Chapter 62

1. Why do you think God changed Sarai and Abram's names?
2. Are names important to God?
3. How did Abraham and Sarah conspire to "help out" God?
4. Name similarities between Sarah, Elisabeth and Samson's mother.
5. Discuss the similarities between instructions to Samson's mother and Hannah's vow to God and instructions.
6. What are similarities between Hannah and Rachel?
7. In what similar circumstances do Isaac and Jacob find themselves?
8. What do you make of the fact that three progenitors through which YHWH made His covenant, Abraham, Isaac and Jacob, all had barren wives?
9. Why did Elisabeth hide herself when she found she was pregnant?
10. How do the customs and social practices of her day vary from those of today?

Chapter Sixty-Three
God's Faithfulness

Greater is He that is in you, than he that is in the world. (1 John 4:4)

Now thanks be unto God, which always causeth us to TRIUMPH IN CHRIST, and maketh manifest the savor of His knowledge by us in every place. For we are unto God a sweet savor of Christ... (2 Corinthians 2:14)

...I will NEVER LEAVE THEE nor forsake thee. (Hebrews 13:5)

...it is God which WORKETH IN YOU both to will and to do of His good pleasure. (Philippians 2:13)

There FAILED NOT ought of any good thing which the LORD had spoken unto the house of Israel; all came to pass. (Joshua 21:45)

Let us hold fast the profession of our faith without wavering; for HE IS FAITHFUL that promised... (Hebrews 10:23)

The LORD is good, a STRONGHOLD in the day of trouble; and He knoweth them that trust in Him...affliction shall not rise up the second time. (Nahum 1:7, 9)

...the JOY of the LORD is your strength. (Nehemiah 8:10)

Triumphing in the LORD

If you believe in Jesus Christ to save your soul, then it follows you must believe in Him to heal your body. In God's economy they go together, hand in glove. Both were paid for on Calvary, both bought with a price, both to be believed equally in the Christian's heart.

Heal me, O LORD, and I shall be healed; save me, and I shall be saved... (Jeremiah 17:14)

If you have faith to be born again, then you do have faith to be healed. To every man is given THE measure of faith. *(Romans 12:3)* We are all given the same measure; some take time to develop it more than others. By reading this book and listening to the tape or CD, "*Heart & Soul Surrender*," you are making an extraordinary step in the right direction. Do not be discouraged. Jesus spoke the truth, and He has already set you free and made you whole. His suffering was not in vain, and must not be lost on a single one of His followers. Be encouraged today to believe and receive your healing. We may fail, but remember, Jesus never fails! Search your heart right now. If you are experiencing discouragement or anger toward God, repent and start filling your heart with faith in His Word. You *can* do all things through Christ Who strengthens you. *(Philippians 4:13)*

Chapter Sixty-Four
Sickness from Unforgiveness or Sin

Some people languish in sickness because of unforgiveness. It is important to make sure your heart is clean. Ask the Holy Spirit to search your heart before you ask for healing.

CAST ALL CARES UPON HIM; for He careth for you. Be sober, be vigilant; because your adversary the devil, as a roaring lion, walketh about, seeking whom he may devour: Whom resist steadfast in the faith, knowing that the same afflictions are accomplished in your brethren that are in the world. (1 Peter 5:7-9)

For verily I say unto you, That whosoever shall say unto this mountain, Be thou removed, and be thou cast into the sea; and shall not doubt in his heart, but shall believe that those things which he sayeth shall come to pass; he shall have whatsoever he sayeth. Therefore I say unto you, What things soever ye desire, when ye pray, believe that ye receive them and ye shall have them. And WHEN YE STAND PRAYING, FORGIVE, IF YE HAVE OUGHT AGAINST ANY: that your Father also which is in heaven may forgive you your trespasses. (Mark 11:23-25)

Calling for the elders to pray

Calling for the elders is a biblical and time-honored way to receive your healing. The elders of the church anoint the sick person with oil, pray over him and he receives his healing. This prayer should be accompanied by repentance of any sins committed. Sin and unforgiveness can cause sickness, but confessing your faults, praying and asking forgiveness can set you free.

Is any among you afflicted? Let him pray. Is any merry? Let him sing psalms. Is any sick among you? Let him call for the elders of the church; and let them pray over him anointing him with oil in the Name of the LORD: And the prayer of faith shall save the sick, and the LORD shall raise him up; and IF HE HAVE COMMITTED SINS, THEY SHALL BE FORGIVEN HIM. CONFESS YOUR FAULTS ONE TO ANOTHER, AND PRAY ONE FOR ANOTHER, that ye may be healed. The effectual fervent prayer of a righteous man availeth much. (James 5:13-16)

Fasting to break bondages

Fasting is another way to break strongholds off your life. God's promise to us is through fasting, repenting and praying with a contrite spirit. He will deliver us, heal us and the glory of the LORD will surround us. Furthermore, the LORD will answer our prayers and be a strong tower for us where we may dwell in safety. Recognize the devil is your enemy and your adversary, not people. Forgive and love the people, but do warfare against the devil and defeat him in Jesus' Name.

Is not this the FAST that I have chosen? To LOOSE THE BANDS OF WICKEDNESS to undo the heavy burdens, and to LET THE OPPRESSED GO FREE, and that ye BREAK EVERY YOKE? Then shall thy light break forth as the morning, and THINE HEALTH SHALL SPRING FORTH SPEEDILY: and thy righteousness shall go before thee; the glory of the LORD shall be thy rereward. Then shalt thou call, and the LORD shall answer; thou shalt cry, and He shall say, Here I Am. (Isaiah 58:6, 8, 9)

Chapter Sixty-Five
Thy Name is as Ointment Poured Forth

Because of the savor of Thy good ointments THY NAME IS AS OINTMENT POURED FORTH... (Song of Solomon 1:3)

And if thou draw out thy soul to the hungry, and satisfy the afflicted soul; then shall thy light rise in obscurity, and thy darkness be as the noonday: And the LORD shall guide thee continually, and satisfy thy soul in drought, and make fat thy bones: and thou shalt be like a watered garden, and like a spring of water, whose waters fail not. (Isaiah 58:10)

For I WILL RESTORE HEALTH UNTO THEE, and I WILL HEAL THEE OF THY WOUNDS, saith the LORD... (Jeremiah 30:17)

He HEALETH THE BROKEN IN HEART, and BINDETH UP THEIR WOUNDS. (Psalm 147:3)

...the LORD WILL TAKE AWAY FROM THEE ALL SICKNESS, and will put none of the evil diseases of Egypt, which thou knowest, upon thee... (Deuteronomy 7:15)

...Bless the LORD, O my soul, and forget not all His benefits: Who forgiveth all thine iniquities; WHO HEALETH ALL THY DISEASES; Who redeemeth thy life from destruction; Who crowneth thee with lovingkindness and tender mercies; Who satisfieth thy mouth with good things so that thy YOUTH IS RENEWED LIKE THE EAGLE'S. (Psalm 103:1-5)

And even to your old age I Am He; and even to hoar hairs will I carry you: I have made, and I will bear; even I will carry, and will deliver you. (Isaiah 46:4)

...know ye not that your body is the temple of the Holy Ghost which is in you, which ye have of God, and ye are not your own? For ye are bought with a price: therefore glorify God in your body, and in your spirit, which are God's. (1 Corinthians 6:19-20)

If thou wilt diligently hearken to the voice of the LORD thy God, and wilt do that which is right in His sight, and wilt give ear to His commandments, and keep all His statutes, I will put none of these diseases upon thee, which I have brought upon the Egyptians: FOR I AM THE LORD THAT HEALETH THEE. (Exodus 15:26)

Hope thou in God: for I shall yet praise Him, Who is the HEALTH OF MY COUNTENANCE, and my God. (Psalm 42:11)

...Peace, peace to him that is far off, and to him that is near, saith the LORD; and I WILL HEAL HIM. (Isaiah 57:19)

And ye shall serve the LORD your God, and He shall bless thy bread, and thy water; and I WILL TAKE SICKNESS AWAY FROM THE MIDST OF THEE. (Exodus 23:25)

HE SENT HIS WORD AND HEALED THEM, and delivered them from their destruction. (Psalm 107:20)

But unto you that fear My Name shall the Sun of righteousness arise with HEALING IN HIS WINGS... (Malachi 4:2)

Surely HE HATH BORNE OUR GRIEFS, and CARRIED OUR SORROWS: yet we did esteem Him stricken, smitten of God, and afflicted. But He was wounded for our transgressions, He was bruised for our iniquities; the chastisement of our peace was upon Him; and WITH HIS STRIPES WE ARE HEALED. (Isaiah 53:3-5)

Yahshua Messiah accepted our diseases, grief and anguish through great agony and labor, both spiritual and physical. He was violently punished, pierced through for our wickedness and rebellion; He was crumbled and shattered, crushed for our perversity and moral evil, so you and I might have peace (health, safety, favor, happiness). (The above scripture is outlined in detail in *The Blood* section of this book.) Let us receive our healing with thankful hearts and faith in what He has already accomplished for us.

Let Us pray

Father, help me get it down deep in my heart that the Name of Jesus is as ointment poured forth on me!!! Like a healing balm of Gilead, that is what Your Name and Your stripes have accomplished for me. YHWH Rapha, my Healer! By Your Name and the power of Your Name, and the stripes You bore, I AM HEALED! Thank You, for pouring Your fragrant presence out on my hurting body, soul and emotions. You are like a fresh drink of water to my desperate thirst, and You are aromatic bread to my hungry heart. There is none like You. I humble myself under Your mighty hand. Fill me with Your Holy Spirit and let me bask in Your presence, for only in Your presence is there fullness of joy. Bring Your peace into my midst like never before. I cry out for visitation of the precious Holy Spirit and for His comforting presence. I yield my body to be a temple and a living sacrifice to You, my Father and my God, YHWH. Cleanse me of all unrighteousness; create in me a clean heart, O God, and renew a right spirit within me. Make me an instrument of praise and a light in the darkness. Bless me and make me a blessing, Father, and make my life significant.

Chapter Sixty-Six
As He Was, So Are We

We are anointed, called and appointed to do the work our Savior did. Gifts have been given to us to do great exploits for His glory. We have been called to do even greater works than Yahshua (Jesus) did. *(John 14:12)*

...the manifestation of the Spirit is GIVEN TO EVERY MAN TO PROFIT withal...To another faith by the same Spirit: to another the GIFTS OF HEALING by the same Spirit; To another the WORKING OF MIRACLES... (1 Corinthians 12:7, 9-10)

...God hath set some in the church, first apostles, secondarily prophets...after that MIRACLES, then GIFTS OF HEALINGS, helps, governments, diversities of tongues. (1 Corinthians 12:28)

...GRANT UNTO THY SERVANTS, that with all boldness they may speak Thy Word, By STRETCHING FORTH THINE HAND TO HEAL; and that signs and wonders may be done by the Name of Thy holy child Jesus. (Acts 4:29-30)

The Spirit of the LORD [is] upon Me, because He has anointed Me [the Anointed One, the Messiah] to preach the good news (the Gospel) to the poor; He has sent Me to announce release to the captives, and RECOVERY OF SIGHT TO THE BLIND; to send forth delivered those who are oppressed—who are downtrodden, bruised, crushed and broken down by calamity; To proclaim the accepted and acceptable year of the LORD—the day when salvation and the free favors of God profusely abound. (Luke 4:18-19 Amplified)

...great multitudes came together to hear, and to be HEALED BY HIM OF THEIR INFIRMITIES. (Luke 5:15)

...the POWER of the LORD was PRESENT TO HEAL THEM. (Luke 5:17)

...great multitudes followed Him; and HE HEALED THEM THERE. (Matthew 19:2)

...the blind and the lame came to Him in the temple; and HE HEALED THEM. (Matthew 21:14)

And He spake to His disciples, that a small ship should wait on Him because of the multitude, lest they should throng Him. For He had HEALED MANY; insomuch that they pressed upon Him for to touch Him, as many as had plagues.(Mark 3:9-10)

Who His own self bare our sins in His own body on the tree, that we, being dead to sins, should live unto righteousness: BY WHOSE STRIPES YE WERE HEALED. (1 Peter 2:24)

HIMSELF TOOK OUR INFIRMITIES, AND BARE OUR SICKNESSES. (Matthew 8:17)

...as He is, so are we in this world. (1 John 4:17)

...Jesus went forth, and saw a great multitude, and was moved with compassion toward them, and HE HEALED THEIR SICK. (Matthew 14:14)

And at even, when the sun did set, they brought unto Him all that were diseased, and them that were possessed with devils. And all the city was gathered together at the door. And He HEALED MANY THAT WERE SICK OF DIVERS DISEASES, and cast out many devils; and suffered not the devils to speak, because they knew Him. (Mark 1:32-34)

...His Name, THROUGH FAITH IN HIS NAME hath MADE THIS MAN STRONG, whom ye see and know: yea, the faith which is by Him hath given Him this perfect soundness in the presence of you all. (Acts 3:16)

Through faith in His Name

As He is, so are we! Think about it! Messiah means the Anointed One. We are anointed. We are to do what He did: Heal the sick, cast out devils. How? Through faith in His Name!!! Let us think about this: If we are like Him, we, too, are anointed. We are joint heirs; reborn sons of God. Jesus was the first born, and we came after Him counted among the sons of God by Christ Himself, the first born of many brethren. In His Name we can heal the sick, the broken-hearted, oppressed, bruised, crushed, marginal, blind, demonized, and those who are held captive by false religion, demons, ignorance and unbelief.

Verily, verily, I say unto you, He that believeth on Me, the works that I do shall he do also; and greater works than these shall he do... (John 14:12)

Chapter Sixty-Seven
Power to Cast Out Devils

Go ye into all the world, and preach the gospel to every creature. He that believeth and is baptized shall be saved; but he that believeth not shall be damned. And THESE SIGNS SHALL FOLLOW THEM THAT BELIEVE; In My Name shall they CAST OUT DEVILS; they shall speak with new tongues. They shall take up serpents; and if they drink any deadly thing, it shall not hurt them; THEY SHALL LAY HANDS ON THE SICK, AND THEY SHALL RECOVER. (Mark 16:15)

Then He called His disciples together, and gave them POWER and AUTHORITY OVER DEVILS, and to cure diseases. And He sent them to preach the kingdom of God, and to heal the sick. (Luke 9:1-2)

When He had called unto Him His twelve disciples, He gave them POWER AGAINST UNCLEAN SPIRITS, TO CAST THEM OUT, and to heal all manner of sickness and all manner of disease. (Matthew 10:1)

…as ye go, preach, saying, The kingdom of heaven is at hand. Heal the sick, cleanse the lepers, raise the dead, CAST OUT DEVILS: freely ye have received, freely give. (Matthew 10:8)

And they went out, and preached that men should repent. And they CAST OUT MANY DEVILS, and anointed with oil many that were sick, and healed them. (Mark 6:12-13)

…UNCLEAN SPIRITS crying with loud voice, CAME OUT OF MANY THAT WERE POSSESSED WITH THEM: and many taken with palsies, and that were lame, were healed. And there was great joy in that city. (Acts 8:7-8)

…God anointed Jesus of Nazareth with the Holy Ghost and with power: Who went about doing good, and HEALING ALL THAT WERE OPPRESSED OF THE DEVIL; for God was with Him. (Acts 10:38)

And behold, there was a woman which had a SPIRIT OF INFIRMITY eighteen years, and was bowed together, and could in no wise lift up herself. And when Jesus saw her, He called her to Him, and said unto her, Woman, THOU ARE LOOSED FROM THINE INFIRMITY. And He laid His hands on her: and immediately she was made straight, and glorified God. (Luke 13:11-13)

As they went out, behold, they brought to Him a DUMB MAN POSSESSED WITH A DEVIL. And when the DEVIL WAS CAST OUT, the dumb spake: and the multitudes marveled, saying, It was never so seen in Israel. (Matthew 9:32-33)

Then was brought unto Him one POSSESSED WITH A DEVIL, BLIND, and DUMB: and HE HEALED HIM, insomuch that the blind and dumb both spake and saw. (Matthew 12:22)

And, behold, a man of the company cried out, saying, Master, I beseech Thee, look upon my son: for he is mine only child. And, lo, A SPIRIT TAKETH HIM, and he suddenly crieth out; and it teareth him that he foameth again, and bruising him hardly departeth from him. And I besought Thy disciples to cast him out; and they could not. And Jesus answering said, O faithless and perverse generation, how long shall I be with you, and suffer you? Bring thy son hither. And as he was yet a going, the devil threw him down, and tare him. And Jesus REBUKED THE UNCLEAN SPIRIT, and healed the child, and delivered him again to his father. (Luke 9:38-42)

And, behold, a woman of Canaan came out to the same coasts, and cried unto Him, saying Have mercy on me, O LORD, Thou Son of David; my daughter is GRIEVOUSLY VEXED WITH A DEVIL. But He answered her not a word. And His disciples came and besought Him, saying, Send her away; for she crieth after us. But He answered and said, I Am not sent but unto the lost sheep of the house of Israel. Then came she and worshipped Him, saying, LORD, help me. But He answered and said, It is not meet to take the children's bread, and to cast it to dogs. And she said, Truth, LORD: yet the dogs eat of the crumbs which fall from their master's table. Then Jesus answered and saith unto her, O woman, great is thy faith: BE IT UNTO THEE AS THOU WILT. And her daughter was made whole from that very hour. (Matthew 15:22-28)

And they came over unto the other side of the sea, into the country of the Gadarenes. And when He was come out of the ship, immediately there met Him out of the tombs a MAN WITH AN UNCLEAN SPIRIT, who had his dwelling among the tombs; and no man could bind him, no, not with chains: Because that he had been often bound with fetters and chains, and the chains had been plucked asunder by him, and the fetters broken in pieces: neither could any man tame him. And always night and day, he was in the mountains, and in the tombs, crying and cutting himself with stones. But when he saw Jesus afar off, he ran and worshipped him, And cried with a loud voice, and said, What have I to do with Thee, Jesus, Thou Son of the most high God? I adjure Thee by God, that Thou torment me not. For He said unto him, Come out of the man, thou unclean spirit. And He asked him,

What is thy name? And he answered, saying, MY NAME IS LEGION: FOR WE ARE MANY. And he besought Him much that He would not send them away out of the country. Now there was there nigh unto the mountains a great herd of swine feeding. And all the devils besought Him, saying, Send us unto the swine, that we may enter into them. And forthwith Jesus gave them leave, And the UNCLEAN SPIRITS WENT OUT, AND ENTERED INTO THE SWINE: and the herd ran violently down a steep place into the sea, (they were about two thousand;) and were choked in the sea. And they that fed the swine fled, and told it in the city, and in the country. And they went out to see what it was that was done. And they come to Jesus and see Him that was possessed with the devil, and had the legion, sitting, and clothed, and in his right mind: and they were afraid. (Mark 5:1-15)

Jesus took authority over demons

It is clear, from these scriptures, that having demons can cause sickness, physical ailments such as deafness and inability to speak, infirmities, mental illness, blindness, and all manner of infirmities. The bowed back was probably arthritis or scoliosis, caused by a demon. Bitterness and unforgiveness are two of the sins that demons piggyback on to enter a person, causing a myriad of diseases. The most common diseases caused by bitterness are arthritis, cancer (such as breast and colon cancer), leukemia, and others. Jesus healed all the people and cast devils out of every one who sought him for deliverance. When He cast out demons, it often resulted in a healing, as well.

Casting out devils is an important part of preaching the gospel. When Jesus rebuked or cast out the demon at work in a person, the person received healing. When Jesus sent out the disciples to minister, He not only told them to preach, but also told them to heal the sick and cast out devils. If true compassion fills a Christian's heart for the sick and oppressed, then he/she will boldly cast out demons just as Jesus demonstrated and told us to do.

Study Questions: Chapter 65
1. What does the phrase mean, "Thy Name is as ointment poured forth?"
2. The Word heals us. Name three scriptures that prove this.
3. If we serve the LORD, He stated three things He will do for us. What are they? *(Exodus 23:25)*
4. 1 Corinthians 6:19-20 shows us our body is the temple of the Holy Ghost. What does this mean?
5. What does "ye are bought with a price" mean? *(1 Corinthians 6:20)*

Study Questions: Chapter 67
1. Mark 16:15-20 lists seven things the disciples were commissioned to do. What are they?
2. Are you a disciple?
3. What did Jesus give His disciples authority over, in Luke 9:1-2?
4. When we preach the kingdom of God, what else are we to do?
5. What did Jesus do for those oppressed of the devil? What should you do for them?
6. What did Jesus and His disciples go through right before they arrived at Gadara?
7. Is there a connection between what happened in Mark 4:35-41 and Mark 5?

Chapter Sixty-Eight
He Healed Them All

...great multitudes followed Him, and HE HEALED THEM ALL... (Matthew 12:15)

Jesus went about all Galilee, teaching in their synagogues, and preaching the gospel of the Kingdom, and HEALING ALL MANNER OF SICKNESS AND ALL MANNER OF DISEASE among the people. And His fame went throughout all Syria: and they brought unto Him ALL SICK PEOPLE that were taken with divers diseases and torments, and those which were possessed with devils, and those that were lunatic, and those that had the palsy; and He healed them. (Matthew 4:23-24)

When the even was come, they brought unto Him many that were possessed with devils; and HE CAST OUT THE SPIRITS WITH HIS WORD, and HEALED ALL THAT WERE SICK... (Matthew 8:16)

...for there went virtue out of Him, and HEALED THEM ALL. (Luke 6:19)

...He received them, and spake unto them of the kingdom of God, and HEALED THEM that had need of healing. (Luke 9:11)

Jesus went about all the cities and villages, teaching in their synagogues, and preaching the gospel of the kingdom, and HEALING EVERY SICKNESS AND EVERY DISEASE among the people. (Matthew 9:35)

...great multitudes followed Him, and HE HEALED THEM ALL... (Matthew 12:15)

...all they that had any sick with divers diseases brought them unto Him; and HE LAID HIS HANDS ON EVERY ONE OF THEM, AND HEALED THEM. (Luke 4:40)

Beloved, I wish above ALL things that thou mayest prosper and be in health, even as thy soul prospereth. (3 John 2)

...If thou canst believe, ALL THINGS ARE POSSIBLE TO HIM THAT BELIEVETH. (Mark 9:23)

And when He had called unto Him His twelve disciples, He gave them power against unclean spirits, to cast them out, and to heal ALL manner of sickness and ALL manner of disease. (Matthew 10:1)

Behold, I give unto you power to tread on serpents and scorpions, and over ALL the power of the enemy: and nothing shall by any means hurt you. (Luke 10:19)

What is ALL?

Webster's defines ALL as the total entity or extent of, the whole number, amount, or quantity of, the utmost possible of, any whatsoever, each and every thing, wholly, entirely. ALL (*Strong's* 3956, pas) means any, every, the whole, all manner of, every, as many as, whatsoever, whosoever. *Vine's* defines ALL as the totality of things referred to, anything whatsoever, the maximum of what is referred to. That just about sums it up! ALL is complete, leaving no room for speculation.

Notice how Jesus healed ALL the people. It is mentioned so many times we really must pause and give glory to God for being no respecter of persons, for doing what He promised, for being full of mercy and grace for us who believe; for loving us so much He sent His only begotten Son to die for us, and suffer for us, so we might ALL have healing in the precious Name of Jesus. Realize right now, today, YOU are included in the magnificent ALL that Jesus healed. He already did it. **It is finished!** Now, ALL you have to do is appropriate Jesus' promises by faith in Him. The time of salvation (Healing is included in sozo—salvation) is now! What are you waiting for? Receive your healing right now in Jesus' Name!

Chapter Sixty-Nine
Miracles in the Old Testament

Healing the leper

Now Naaman, captain of the host of the king of Syria, was a great man with his master, and honorable, because by him the LORD had given deliverance unto Syria: he was also a mighty man in valor, but he was a leper…

…Naaman came with his horses and with his chariot, and stood at the door of the house of Elisha. And Elisha sent a messenger unto him saying, Go and wash in Jordan seven times, and thy flesh shall come again to thee, and thou shalt be clean. But Naaman was WROTH, and went away, and said, Behold, I thought, HE WILL SURELY COME OUT TO ME, and stand, and call on the Name of the LORD his God, and strike his hand over the place, and recover the leper.

Are not Abana and Pharpar, rivers of Damascus, BETTER THAN ALL THE WATERS OF ISRAEL? May I not wash in them, and be clean? So he turned and WENT AWAY IN A RAGE. And his servants came near, and spake unto him, and said, My father, if the prophet had bid thee do some great thing, wouldest thou not have done it? How much rather then, when he saith to thee, Wash, and be clean? Then went he down, and dipped himself seven times in Jordan, according to the saying of the man of God: and his flesh came again like unto the flesh of a little child, and he was clean. (2 Kings 5:1, 9-14)

In Numbers 12:10, Miriam was struck with leprosy because she spoke accusations against Moses. There is resentment, anger, pride and jealousy in her attitude. In the above scriptures, similar attitudes of pride, rage, accusation are displayed by Naaman, indicating that he probably suffered from some unrepented sins such as bitterness, unforgiveness, etc. When he humbled himself and obeyed the prophet he was healed.

Sick unto death

In those days was Hezekiah SICK UNTO DEATH. And the prophet Isaiah the son of Amoz came to him, and said unto him, Thus saith the LORD, Set thine house in order; for thou shalt die, and not live. Then he turned his face to the wall, and prayed unto the LORD, saying, I beseech thee, O LORD, remember now how I have walked before Thee in truth and with a perfect heart, and have done that which is good in Thy sight. And Hezekiah wept sore. And it came to pass, afore Isaiah was gone out into the middle court, that the Word of the LORD came to him saying, Turn again, and tell Hezekiah the captain of My people, Thus saith the LORD, the God of David thy father, I have heard thy prayer, I have seen thy tears: behold, I WILL HEAL THEE: on the third day thou shalt go unto the house of the LORD. And I will add unto thy days fifteen years… (2 Kings 20:1-6)

Raising the dead

And it came to pass after these things, that the son of the woman, the mistress of the house, fell sick: and his sickness was so sore, that there was no breath left in him. And she said unto Elijah, What have I to do with thee, O thou man of God? Art thou come unto me to call my sin to remembrance, and to slay my son? And he said unto her, Give me thy son. And he took him out of her bosom, and carried him up into a loft, where he abode, and laid him upon his own bed. And he cried unto the LORD…And he stretched himself upon the child three times, and cried unto the LORD, and said, O LORD my God, I pray thee, let this child's soul come into him again. And the LORD heard the voice of Elijah: and the soul of the child came into him again, and HE REVIVED. And Elijah took the child, and brought him down out of the chamber into the house, and delivered him unto his mother: and Elijah said, See, THY SON LIVETH. (I Kings 17:17-19, 21-23)

And when Elisha was come into the house, behold, the child was dead, and laid upon his bed. He went in therefore, and shut the door upon them twain, and prayed unto the LORD. And he went up, and lay upon the child and put his mouth upon his mouth, and his eyes upon his eyes, and his hands upon his hands: and he stretched himself upon the child; and the flesh of the child waxed warm. Then he returned, and walked in the house to and fro; and went up, and stretched himself upon him: and the child sneezed seven times, and the CHILD OPENED HIS EYES. And he called Gehazi, and said, Call this Shunammite. So he called her. And when she was come in unto him, he said, Take up thy son. (2 Kings 4:32-36)

Both in the Old and New Testaments, several people were raised from the dead. The great healing evangelist, Smith Wigglesworth, raised several people from the dead. I love the story he told of raising his wife from the dead. When her spirit returned to her body she told Smith she wanted to go back and be with Jesus. He loved her so much he let her go. I know a man in Kansas City who was dead in the lobby of a church I used to attend, for nearly an hour. A group of people gathered around him and raised him up. He had not completed his work for the LORD, and is still alive at this writing. I know an evangelist who has raised over 250 people from the dead in central and South America. I met a woman who lives close to Springfield, Missouri, who raised her infant son from the dead after he had died in his crib. God says to only believe; all things are possible to him who believes.

Chapter Seventy
Miracles in the New Testament

And great multitudes came unto Him, having with them those that were lame, blind, dumb, maimed, and many others, and cast them down at Jesus feet; and He healed them: insomuch that the multitude wondered, when they saw the dumb to speak, the maimed to be whole, the lame to walk, and the blind to see: and they glorified the God of Israel. (Matthew 15:30-31)

...believers were the more added to the LORD, multitudes both of men and women. Insomuch that they brought forth the sick into the streets, and laid them on beds and couches, that at the least the shadow of Peter passing by might overshadow some of them. There came also a multitude out of the cities round about unto Jerusalem, bringing sick folks, and them which were vexed with unclean spirits: and they were healed every one. (Acts 5:14-16)

And God wrought special miracles by the hands of Paul: So that from his body were brought unto the sick handkerchiefs or aprons, and the diseases departed from them, and the evil spirits went out of them.

Serpent bites
And when Paul had gathered a bundle of sticks, and laid them on the fire, there came a viper out of the heat, and fastened on his hand. And when the barbarians saw the venomous beast hang on his hand, they said among themselves, No doubt this man is a murderer, whom though he hath escaped the sea, yet vengeance suffereth not to live. And he shook off the beast into the fire, and felt no harm. (Acts 28:3-5)

Fever and bloody flux—dysentery
And it came to pass, that the father of Publius lay sick of a fever and of a bloody flux: to whom Paul entered in, and prayed, and laid his hands on him, and healed him. And when this was done, others also, which had diseases in the island, came, and were healed... (Acts 28:8-9)

Issue of blood
...a certain woman, which had an issue of blood twelve years, And had suffered many things of many physicians, and had spent all that she had, and was nothing bettered, but rather grew worse, When she had heard of Jesus, came in the press behind, and touched His garment. For she said, If I may touch but His clothes, I shall be whole. And straightway the fountain of her blood was dried up; and she felt in her body that she was healed of that plague. And Jesus, immediately knowing in Himself that virtue had gone out of Him, turned Him about in the press, and said, Who touched My clothes? And His disciples said unto Him, Thou seest the multitude thronging Thee, and sayest Thou, Who touched Me? And He looked round about to see her that had done this thing. But the woman fearing and trembling, knowing what was done in her, came and fell down before Him and told Him all the truth. And He said unto her, Daughter, thy faith hath made thee whole; go in peace, and be whole of thy plague. (Mark 5:25-34)

Lame or crippled
Then Peter said, Silver and gold have I none; but such as I have give I thee: in the Name of Jesus Christ of Nazareth, rise up and walk. And he took him by the right hand, and lifted him up: and immediately his feet and ankle bones received strength. And he leaping up stood and walked, and entered with them into the temple, walking, and leaping, and praising God. (Acts 3:6-8)

When Jesus saw him lie, and know that he had been now a long time in that case, He saith unto him, Wilt thou be made whole? The impotent man answered Him Sir, I have no man, when the water is troubled, to put me into the pool: but while I am coming another steppeth down before me. Jesus saith unto him Rise, take up thy bed, and walk. And immediately the man was made whole, and took up his bed, and walked... (John 5:6-9)

And there sat a certain man at Lystra, impotent in his feet, being a cripple from his mother's womb, who never had walked: The same heard Paul speak: who steadfastly beholding him, and perceiving that he had faith to be healed, Said with a loud voice, Stand upright on thy feet. And he leaped and walked. (Acts 14:8-10)

But He knew their thoughts, and said to the man which had the withered hand, Rise up, and stand forth in the midst. And he arose and stood forth. Then said Jesus unto them, I will ask you one thing; Is it lawful on the Sabbath days to do good, or to do evil? To save life, or to destroy it? And looking round about upon them all, He said unto the man, Stretch forth thy hand. And he did so; and his hand was restored whole as the other. (Luke 6:8-10)

Deafness
And they brought unto Him one that was deaf, and had an impediment in his speech; and they beseech Him to put His hand upon him. And He took him aside from the multitude, and put His fingers into his ears, and He spit, and touched his tongue; And looking up to heaven, He sighed, and saith unto him. Ephphatha, that is, be opened. And straightway his ears were opened, and the string of his tongue was loosed, and he spake plain. (Mark 7:32-35)

Palsy—paralytic or feeble

There came unto Him a centurion, beseeching Him, And saying, LORD, my servant lieth at home sick of the palsy, grievously tormented. And Jesus saith unto him, I will come and heal him. The centurion answered and said, LORD, I am not worthy that Thou shouldest come under my roof: but speak the Word only, and my servant shall be healed. For I am a man under authority, having soldiers under me: and I say to this man, Go, and he goeth; and to another, Come, and he cometh; and to my servant, Do this and he doeth it. When Jesus heard it, He marveled, and said to them that followed, Verily I say unto you, I have not found so great faith, no not in Israel. And Jesus said unto the centurion, Go thy way; and as thou hast believed, so be it done unto thee. And his servant was healed in the selfsame hour. (Matthew 8:5-10, 13)

But that ye may know that the Son of man hath power upon earth to forgive sins, (He said unto the sick of the palsy,) I say unto thee, Arise, and take up thy couch, and go into thine house. And immediately he rose up before them, and took up that where on he lay, and departed to his own house, glorifying God. (Luke 5:24-25)

Dropsy—swelling of lymph and body tissues

And it came to pass, as he went into the house of one of the chief Pharisees to eat bread on the Sabbath day, that they watched Him. And behold there was a certain man before Him which had the dropsy. And Jesus answering spake unto the lawyers and Pharisees, saying, Is it lawful to heal on the Sabbath day? And they held their peace. And He took him, and healed him, and let him go… (Luke 14:1-4)

Leprosy

And as He entered into a certain village, there met Him ten men that were lepers, which stood afar off: And they lifted up their voices and said, Jesus, Master, have mercy on us. And when He saw them, He said unto them, Go show yourselves unto the priests. And it came to pass, that, as they went, they were cleansed. And one of them, when he saw that he was healed, turned back, and with a loud voice glorified God, And fell down on his face at His feet, giving Him thanks; and he was a Samaritan. And Jesus answering said, Were there not ten cleansed? But where are the nine? There are not found that returned to give glory to God, save this stranger. And he said unto him, Arise, go thy way: thy faith hath made thee whole. (Luke 17:12-19)

And there came a leper to Him, beseeching Him, and kneeling down to Him, and saying unto Him, If Thou wilt, Thou canst make me clean. And Jesus moved with compassion, put forth His hand, and touched him, and saith unto him, I will; be thou clean. And as soon as He had spoken, the leprosy departed from him, and he was cleansed. (Mark 1:40-42)

Sick unto death

The nobleman saith unto Him, Sir, come down ere my child die. Jesus saith unto him, Go thy way; thy son liveth. And the man believed the Word that Jesus had spoken unto him, and he went his way. And as he was now going down, his servants met him, and told him, saying, Thy son liveth. (John 4:49-51)

Raising the dead

And there came thither certain Jews from Antioch and Iconium who persuaded the people, and having stoned Paul, drew him out of the city, supposing he had been dead. Howbeit, as the disciples stood round about him, he rose up, and came into the city: and the next day he departed with Barnabas to Derby. (Acts 14:19-20)

Now there was at Joppa a certain disciple named Tabitha, which by interpretation is called Dorcas: this woman was full of good works and almsdeeds which she did. And it came to pass in those days, that she was sick, and died: whom when they had washed, they laid her in an upper chamber. And forasmuch as Lydda was nigh to Joppa, and the disciples had heard that Peter was there, they sent unto him two men, desiring him that he would not delay to come to them. Then Peter arose and went with them. When He was come, they brought him into the upper chamber: and all the widows stood by him weeping, and showing the coats and garments which Dorcas made, while she was with them. But Peter put them all forth, and kneeled down, and prayed; and turning him to the body said, Tabitha, arise. And she opened her eyes: and when she saw Peter, she sat up. And he gave her his hand, and lifted her up, and when he had called the saints and widows, presented her alive. (Acts 9:36-41)

And there sat in a window a certain young man named Eutychus, being fallen into a deep sleep: and as Paul was long preaching, he sunk down with sleep, and fell down from the third loft, and was taken up dead. And Paul went down, and fell on him, and embracing him said, Trouble not yourselves for his life is in him. When he therefore was come up again, and had broken bread, and eaten, and talked a long while, even till break of day, so he departed. And they brought the young man alive, and were not a little comforted. (Acts 20:9-12)

Now when He came nigh to the gate of the city, behold, there was a dead man carried out, the only son of his mother, and she was a widow: and much people of the city was with her. And when the LORD saw her, He had compassion on her, and said unto her, Weep not. And He came and touched the bier: and they that bare him stood still. And He said, Young man, I say unto thee, Arise. And he that was dead sat up, and began to speak, And He delivered him to his mother. (Luke 7:12-15)

…Take ye away the stone. Martha, the sister of him that was dead, saith unto Him, LORD, by this time he stinketh: for he hath been dead four days. Jesus saith unto her, Said I not unto thee, that, if thou wouldst believe, thou shouldest see the glory of

God? Then they took away the stone from the place where the dead was laid. And Jesus lifted up His eyes, and said, Father, I thank Thee that Thou hast heard Me, And I knew that Thou hearest Me always: but because of the people which stand by I said it, that they may believe that Thou hast sent Me. And when He thus had spoken, He cried with a loud voice, Lazarus, come forth. And he that was dead came forth, bound hand and foot with grave clothes: and his face was bound about with a napkin. Jesus saith unto them, Loose him and let him go. (John 11:39-44)

…there cometh one…saying to him, thy daughter is dead; trouble not the Master. But when Jesus heard it, He answered him saying, Fear not: believe only and she shall be made whole. And when He came into the house…He said, Weep not; she is not dead, but sleepeth. And they laughed Him to scorn, knowing that she was dead. And He put them all out, and took her by the hand, and called saying, Maid, arise. And her spirit came again, and she arose straightway…(Luke 8:49-55)

Healing the blind

And when Jesus departed thence, two blind men followed Him, crying, and saying, Thou son of David, have mercy on us. And when He was come into the house, the blind men came to Him: and Jesus saith unto them, Believe ye that I Am able to do this? They said unto Him, Yea, LORD. Then touched He their eyes, saying, According to your faith be it unto you. And their eyes were opened. (Matthew 9:27-30)

And He cometh to Bethsaida; and they bring a blind man unto Him, and besought Him to touch him. And He took the blind man by the hand, and led him out of the town; and when He had spit on his eyes, and put His hands upon him, He asked him if he saw ought. And he looked up, and said, I see men as trees, walking. After that He put His hands again upon his eyes, and made him look up: and he was restored, and saw every man clearly. (Mark 8:22-25)

And they call the blind man, saying unto him, Be of good comfort, rise; He calleth thee. And he, casting away his garment, rose, and came to Jesus. And Jesus answered and said unto him, What wilt thou that I should do unto thee: The blind man said unto Him, LORD, that I might receive my sight. And Jesus said unto him. Go thy way: thy faith hath made thee whole. And immediately he received his sight, and followed Jesus in the way. (Mark 10:49-52)

…there are also many other things which Jesus did, the which, if they should be written every one…even the world itself could not contain the books that should be written… (John 21:25)

The currency of heaven

YHWH, our God, gives us His healing as a free gift. It cannot be bought with silver or gold because the currency of heaven is faith. Your faith makes you whole. This is definitely good news to the majority of the world's population. Only the rich will grieve, for their money will perish with them. As they store up riches, the world is dying and going to hell. In the country of Nepal, the average yearly income is $190.00. Yet, we possess something worth more than all the world's riches: salvation, the gospel and gifts of the Holy Spirit. A healing evangelist was driving through a rural part of Mexico when a very poor woman, who had attended his crusade, flagged him down. Her son had broken his leg and she asked for healing. He was in a hurry and told her to go to a doctor. She said, "I can't afford a doctor. You heal him!" The evangelist laid hands on the boy and his leg snapped back together. What a great and compassionate God we serve.

Ho, every one that thirsteth, come ye to the waters, and HE THAT HATH NO MONEY; come ye, buy and eat; yea, come, buy wine and milk WITHOUT MONEY AND WITHOUT PRICE. (Isaiah 55:1)

Let Us pray

Father, I recognize You are YHWH Rapha, my healer. It was Your desire to heal everyone when Jesus walked the earth and You have not changed. I am the one who must change. I must allow my thinking to line up with the immutable, unchangeable, everlasting truth of Your Word. I repent of my fear, doubt and unbelief, and my stubborn refusal to receive and believe the truth. Fill me now with Your presence, and anoint my ears to hear and my eyes to see. Your Word, O God, is irrefutable proof that You are Who You said You are, and You will do what You said You will do! Heal me LORD, in the Name of Yahshua Messiah (Jesus Christ). I receive my healing by faith, knowing He is faithful Who promised. Thank You, Father. Amen.

Chapter Seventy-One
Is God Glorified by Your Sickness?

Can everyone be healed?

If sickness glorifies God, then we had better stop robbing God of His glory by going to doctors and hospitals, and taking medicine. Yahshua Messiah must have robbed God of a lot of glory by healing ALL who asked Him. To follow this line of thinking, then God's promise that ...*by Whose stripes ye were healed. (1 Peter 2:24)* must be for only an exclusive group God chooses at His whim. If this is the case, then we must question the statement by Jesus that ...*whosoever believeth on Him should not perish, but have everlasting life. (John 3:16)* Being born again and being healed are inextricably entwined through Jesus' completed work at Calvary. Jesus did more than die: He suffered emotionally almost to the point of death, received stripes, was beaten, whipped, a crown of thorns jammed on His head, His hands and feet were nailed rather than tied.

Every aspect of Jesus' suffering had meaning and purpose for us. Isaiah 53 plainly states by His stripes we are healed. His stripes were as much a part of His passion, as His death was for our sins. If everyone cannot be healed, then it follows that everyone cannot be saved. Have we been deceived by God? Or can we count on His infallible Word that says He is no respecter of persons *(Acts 10:34)*, and God is not a man that He should lie? *(Numbers 23:19)* If ALL cannot expect to be healed, then faith does not come by hearing, as the Word states, but rather by special preferential treatment. Remember, God is the same yesterday, today and forever. *(Hebrews 13:8)* If He was ever faithful to His Word, then He is still faithful. If He healed ALL the people then, He will heal ALL the people now.

Healing the man born blind

Let us look at one of the traditional stumbling blocks in scripture that seems to contradict our understanding of God. This scripture, at first glance, seems to go against the personality and character of Jesus.

> *And as Jesus passed by, He saw a man which was blind from his birth. And His disciples asked Him, saying, Master, who did sin, this man, or his parents, that he was born blind? Jesus answered, Neither hath this man sinned, nor his parents: but that the works of God should be made manifest in him. I must work the works of Him that sent Me, while it is day: the night cometh, when no man can work. As long as I Am in the world, I Am the light of the world. When He had thus spoken, He spat on the ground, and made clay of the spittle, and He anointed the eyes of the blind man with the clay, And said unto him, Go wash in the pool Siloam...He went his way therefore, and washed, and came seeing. (John 9:1-7)*

> *Then again called they the man that was blind, and said unto him, Give God the praise: we know that this man (Jesus) is a sinner. He answered and said, Whether He be a sinner or no, I know not: one thing I know, that, whereas I was blind, now I see...Since the world began was it not heard that any man opened the eyes of one that was born blind. (John 9:24-25, 32)*

A careful look

The preceding passages of scripture need to be looked at carefully. First, Greek manuscripts had accents above words for punctuation, a very different system than we use. I believe the scripture is incorrectly rendered in KJV. It reads: ...*but that the works of God should be made manifest in him. I must work the works...* This is inconsistent with the personality and character of Yahshua the Messiah. To make someone suffer all their life does not bring glory to the LORD. However, if we change this punctuation to: ...*but, that the works of God should be made manifest in him, I must work the works...* I added a comma after "but," and another comma after "him." With this new rendering, Jesus is detailing what He intends to do. It no longer reads that the man was born blind so Jesus could heal him. Instead, it shows WHAT JESUS WILL DO FOR THE MAN, revealing God had nothing to do with the man's blindness, but *everything* to do with His compassionate healing. The *Greek Interlinear* translation reads:

> ...*but that might be MANIFESTED the works—of God in him. Us it behooves to work the works of THE ONE having sent Me while day it is.*

Notice the dash after the word "works." This literal translation reveals that Jesus, in His compassion, desired to work the works of God in ALL men. The blind man was part of ALL men. The result indicates an OPPORTUNITY, rather than a DESTINY. This man's suffering is the OCCASION, not the APPOINTED PREPARATION for the miracle. It simply became an OPPORTUNITY for divine work.[1]

The word MANIFEST (*Vines*, phanero) means to make visible, clear, manifest, known. The root of this word, "phan," signifies shining. The works of Christ "shone forth" through this miracle and enraged the priests and Pharisees. A healing of this magnitude could only be ascribed to the anointed works of the Messiah.

And in that day...eyes of the blind shall see out of obscurity...rejoice in THE HOLY ONE of Israel. (Isaiah 29:18-19)

Note again the reference made to Yahshua as THE HOLY ONE in Isaiah, ties in with the *Greek Interlinear* above. The Pharisees were desperate to keep the formerly blind man from giving praise to Jesus, because otherwise, according to scripture, they would have had to acknowledge Him as Messiah. The Pharisees attempted to establish that Jesus was a sinner. *Give God the praise: we know that the man is a sinner.* Jesus, however, had already established Himself as the Messiah and made full proof of His ministry, according to the scriptures in Isaiah. *(Isaiah 61:1-2; Luke 4:18-19)*

It is of paramount interest to note the conditions under which Jesus healed this man. Right before the healing miracle occurred, the Jews had taken up stones to kill Jesus. *(John 8:59)* He hid Himself and was passing through the crowd when He saw the blind man. In the midst of a life-threatening crisis, compassion rose up in our Savior, and He stopped to heal the man. If God had made the man blind, then Jesus was going against His Father's will to heal the man, but we know this was not the case. At no other time did Jesus make anyone sick so He could heal him. Jesus simply redeemed the situation the devil had caused. This man was born blind *because of the devil.*

How God anointed Jesus of Nazareth with the Holy Ghost and with power: Who went about doing good, and healing ALL that were OPPRESSED OF THE DEVIL... (Acts 10:38)

It was not necessary that this man or his parents be guilty of a specific sin, because the Word of God reveals that ALL have sinned and come short of the glory of God. *(Romans 3:23)* The disciples inquired of Yahshua on the point of who sinned because of a common Jewish view that a mother's sinful thoughts while carrying her unborn child profoundly affected the child. Yahshua came to heal ALL who were OPPRESSED OF THE DEVIL. He states in John 9 that **regardless of the cause of this man's blindness, it is the work of God to heal him**. The disciples' question regarding the blind man gave rise to the Savior stopping to heal him. The blind man did not seek Jesus for healing which was unusual, therefore, Jesus told him to perform an act of faith (action) by sending him to the pool of Siloam to wash.

Later, the healed man showed great courage by standing up to the Pharisees in the synagogue, asking them if they, too, would like to be Jesus' disciples. *(John 9:27)* They reviled (*Strong's* 3058, loidoreo) him, meaning they abused, reproached, vilified and defamed him. Then, the man spoke great truth to them:

Well, this is astonishing! Here a Man has opened my eyes, and yet you do not know where He comes from---that is amazing!...Since the beginning of time it was never heard of that any one opened the eyes of a man born blind. If that Man were not from God, He would not be able to do anything like this. (John 9:30-33 Amplified)

The man was thrown out of the synagogue permanently for his declaration of faith. Once again, Yahshua demonstrated His love by finding the man after his ejection from the synagogue and securing the man's salvation. The man confessed Yahshua as LORD, and worshipped Him. *(John 9:38)* Yahshua demonstrated His power over the kingdom of darkness when He healed this man who was born blind.

And having spoiled principalities and powers, He made a show of them openly, triumphing over them in it. (Colossians 2:15)

Sickness comes from the enemy. YHWH, our God, is not your enemy. Jesus came to set us free, and constantly proved His intentions by always healing the sick, delivering them from the power of darkness, and translating us into the kingdom of God. *(Colossians 1:13)*

He sent His Word and healed us

God sent His Word to heal us. When Jesus was walking the earth He healed ALL who came to Him, including some who did not, such as the blind man in John 9. Get this down deep in your heart: There is none like our Wonderful Savior. Even when He was tired, compassion would move Him to heal the throngs that pursued Him in the wilderness. Persistence was a factor. They carried out His instructions and did not give up until they received their healing. The ones who cried out to Jesus were not ignored. They were healed. They had the faith to overcome their circumstances, or got someone to take them to see Jesus; they managed to find a way. We have no excuse. When we come to Jesus and cry out for His healing virtue and compassion, He is eager to meet us. He ever lives to make intercession for us. It is not our righteousness that qualifies us for healing, but belief in His Word.

He sent His Word, and healed them, and delivered them from their DESTRUCTIONS. (Psalm 107:20)

The word DESTRUCTIONS (*Strong's* 7825, shechiyth) means pit-fall, pit. Notice this word is plural. We face many pit-falls, yet God sent His Word (Jesus) and delivered us. We are to use the Word against the pit-falls and snares the devil sets in our paths.

Study Questions: Chapter 69
1. Who was Naaman?
2. Why did he come to Israel?
3. What caused him to want to leave before being healed?
4. Who was Hezekiah?
5. What were the circumstances of his healing?
6. What do the above instances show about God's love and mercy?
7. What were some of the unusual ways God raised the dead in the Old Testament?

Study Questions: Chapter 71
1. Who sent Jesus to heal us?
2. Who did Jesus heal when He walked the earth?
3. Is your own personal healing included in the stripes Jesus took on His back?
4. What was the true reason the man was born blind in John 9? Who made him blind?
5. Is there anything standing in the way of your healing? Unrepented sin? Fall on your face and repent, speak the Word over your body and receive your healing.

Chapter Seventy-Two
Humility: A Key to Healing

Pride and haughtiness can prevent healing

Do not let anything stand in the way of receiving your healing. When Naaman, the Syrian, came for his healing, he wanted to be honored. He wanted some great task that he could perform to make him feel important, but all Elisha said was to go and wash himself. *(2 Kings 5:11)* If we allow our pride to get in the way, then we have failed to acknowledge the greatness of God, and the completeness of Jesus' accomplishment on the cross. A spirit of haughtiness can prevent healing. If Jesus told us to do a small thing, we would be glad to do it!

Risking humiliation or death

The woman who begged Yahshua for her daughter's deliverance, humiliating herself even to the level of allowing herself to be alluded to as a dog eating crumbs from the Master's table, is a story of desperation. The wonderful end of the story is that her daughter was healed. *(Matthew 15:27)* There are so many heartbreaking times in my meetings when people who need a touch from the LORD will not come forward to receive it. They allow fear of man or a spirit of haughtiness to keep them from their healing.

I love the story of the woman with the issue of blood who risked her life and excommunication from her own people by going out in public with an issue of blood, just to touch the hem of His garment (tzit tzit). *(Matthew 9:20)* Healing belongs to you! Are you a child of the Most High God? Then healing, which is the children's bread, belongs to you.

Choose to believe the Word of God more than you believe the circumstances that surround you. Don't allow the circumstances to be big and the Word small. Make the Word big in your life, and the circumstance small. Oh, taste of the bread of life and see that it is good. He will even protect you in the valley of the shadow of death. *(Psalm 23)* Fear no evil! For God is truly with you in your time of trouble. He is an ever-present help in your time of need. *(Psalm 46:1)*

The humility factor

Faith comes by hearing, and hearing by the Word of God. *(Romans 10:17)* We know that Jesus was stirred to compassion over and over, and when He was stirred He would heal the multitudes. Compassion was the key. *(Mark 6:34)* He is the same Jesus now Who walked the earth two thousand years ago. His compassion is stirred toward you. Mercy, unfailing mercy, was always extended to those who asked for it, and our humility will cause us to be able to receive mercy.

Relentless pursuit of the prize

Blind Bartimeus ignored scorn and shame in order to receive his healing. As he relentlessly shouted for Jesus, others attempted to shut him up and shame him into silence, but he would not be silenced. He cried out even more until Jesus stopped. With an act of great faith he cast away his special begging garment and walked to Jesus by faith, a man *fully expecting* to receive his sight. *(Mark 10:46-52)*

We are not beggars but sons of God. How much more boldly can we ask, knowing Who He is and the power of the stripes He took for us, and go boldly as sons, not as beggars. True humility is in knowing that of yourself you are nothing, but through the Messiah you become a joint-heir to the promises of God. Come to Yahshua the Messiah in faith, trusting that He loves you and wants you to be healed.

Chapter Seventy-Three
Putting Action to Our Faith

Action is sign of faith

Action is often involved in healing. *Rise up! Stand forth! Stretch forth thine hand! (Luke 6:8-10) ...Arise, and take up thy bed, and go thy way... (Mark 2:11)* Sometimes it is necessary to elicit a positive verbal response from a person needing healing. *Believe ye that I am able to do this? (Mark 9:28) Wilt thou be made whole? (John 5:6)*

Frequently, Jesus said to people that as they acted on what they believed, it was being done unto them. *For this saying go thy way; the devil is gone out of thy daughter. (Mark 7:29)* Luke 6:10 reveals as the man stretched forth his hand he was healed. In the story of the ten lepers, the Bible says: *...AS THEY WENT, they were cleansed. (Luke 17:14)* Many times I will ask people I have just prayed for to do something they could not do before. There is a moment of truth that is the difference between simply being prayed for, and actually receiving and acting on your faith. At a meeting, where I was ministering, an elderly man came forward very slowly, hunched over a walker, asking for healing. I told him to stand up straight and walk. His faith surged and he began to walk normally, waving the walker as he went, praising the LORD. Recently, I ministered the "*Stripes*" song at a meeting, and the president of the meeting came forward as fast as she could, declaring she was getting healed of an enlarged heart. Healing virtue surged through her body, and one week later her doctor confirmed her heart had returned to normal.

Speak life

Your tongue is a little member, but in your tongue (what you say) resides the power of life and death. Speak life over your body, health to your flesh, healing to your bones. Call on God's ever present help in your time of need. Lean into God's compassion and His mercy. Hezekiah leaned into God's mercy. He cried out to God when he was dying, and God gave him fifteen more years.

Boldness brings results

When I minister, the LORD gives me great boldness. This is shocking to some, but a great blessing to those who receive their healing. I often go to prisons and alcohol and drug rehab centers where the people desperately need a touch from the LORD. I preach healing, deliverance and boldly minister to the sick and hurting, where they are used to hearing only salvation messages. The old joke about having a captive audience is completely false. These men and women have a choice about whether to come to the services. One woman at the rehab center was healed of severe arthritis, a cold and alcoholism. She wrote and told me how exciting it was to have someone minister healing to the group. Another woman in county jail, who I prayed for, was healed of a brain tumor, and extreme pain in her back. I have seen many other healings in the prisons, where men and women who are in for life weep like babies in the presence of the LORD. Let us be bold and take the whole gospel to these hurting men and women, and see them healed and delivered in Jesus' Name.

Smith Wigglesworth had such faith in God, he sometimes punched people in the stomach and they were healed. No one ever suffered ill effects from this treatment. Smith's answer to them was, "I don't hit people, I hit the devil...You can't deal gently with the devil, nor comfort him; he likes comfort." Smith drop-kicked a sick baby into the audience once and it was healed. Another time he chased down and tackled a demonized man who was trying to leave his meeting. He cast the devil out, and the man was gloriously saved. While I do not necessarily recommend these kinds of actions, I do heartily endorse the bold faith it took to do them. Like Smith, I would rather die acting on the true works of the LORD, than live disbelieving.[2]

Healing through word of knowledge

Sometimes, love and compassion come on me so strongly, I have to stop my concert and call out words of knowledge, and lay hands on the sick. People are blessed by ministers who follow the leading of the Holy Spirit, and a healed person will rejoice and glorify God, being filled with thankfulness. How can we, as Christians, do otherwise? Our God came to set the captives free. Can we walk away and not do the works of the ministry Jesus instructed us to do? *(Mark 16:15-20; Luke 4:18)*

A man asked me to pray for him after I had ministered the Word. I turned to him and said, "Honey!" He laughed. I told him if he would begin taking raw honey he would be healed of his ailment. This brought a surprised response, but he did it and was healed. Another woman showed me her head covered with pimples, which was aggravating her to no end. The LORD dropped the world shampoo in my heart. I told her to change her shampoo and sure enough the problem cleared up. Another woman came forward for healing, but I told her a terrible situation from childhood had to be dealt with first. She was slain in the Spirit. Later, she came forward again and said, "You're right! I was molested as a child and have had terrible unforgiveness and sickness ever since." I ministered to her, she repented and again she was slain in the Spirit. She was completely delivered after the third time I prayed for her. Another person came forward for healing in her back, but after deliverance from hatred, murder, jealousy and anger, her back was quickly healed. One word from God can change your life!

Speak to your body

Before my first son was born, I began speaking to my body, commanding it to function properly and normally, for the muscles to relax, and pain to be turned into pressure. I commanded my body to give birth quickly. No long, dragged-out labor. My first son was born within three hours of the onset of labor.

I believe this principle works in the realm of healing, as well. Begin speaking to your body. Command it to listen and pay attention. Then, command it to be healed. Bind scriptures to yourself and stand on them.

Them that believe

Signs should follow us if we are believers. A believer can and should heal the sick. Signs don't follow doubters, or those in unbelief. God is moved by the faith we put in His Word. An unbeliever has faith, but his faith is in his own ability, or luck, or fate. He has misplaced his faith. True faith in Jesus can bring salvation and healing.

> *And these signs shall follow them that believe; In My Name shall they cast out devils; they shall speak with new tongues. They shall take up serpents; and if they drink any deadly thing it shall not hurt them; they shall lay hands on the sick and they shall recover...the LORD working with them and confirming the Word with signs following...(Mark 16:16-20)*

In foreign countries, one of the easiest ways to win converts to Jesus is to heal the sick in His Name. They recognize authority when they see it. Tell them to bring their sick, and which ever (G)god heals them, that is the one we will all worship. Invariably, YHWH, the one true God, shows up. Bold faith gets bold results. I know of several missionaries who have done this in Mid-East countries, India and Africa. Signs will follow those who believe.

The faith factor

Our own faith is an important factor in receiving healing. *...thy FAITH hath made thee whole... (Luke 8:48)* This is a phrase repeated many times by Yahshua. He wanted us to clearly understand that the exercise of our own FAITH is vital. Even He could only heal a few sick folk when He was met with hardened hearts, and UNBELIEF.

> *And He could there do no mighty work, save that He laid His hands upon a few sick folk, and healed them. And He marveled because of their UNBELIEF... (Mark 6:5-6)*

Faith is like a sponge

My Dad was on a camping trip once when a skunk sprayed his car. He was wearing a suede jacket that took up the smell like a sponge, even though he was not sprayed directly. Some materials absorb odor very readily. Sometimes, when demons are cast out, the smell of sulfur will be present. On the opposite end of the spectrum, Jesus' love is like a fragrant perfume, and the anointing to heal is like a rose garden. There are times when I pray for people and I can sense the healing anointing going out of me, but sadly it returns because it was not met with faith. Faith is like a receiving sponge that absorbs the anointing. As it absorbs, eventually it will be saturated. Faith comes by hearing. Saturate your hearing with the Word of God. When faith goes in, then healing virtue will come out. Healing will manifest.

Growing out body parts

Jesus healed all who came to Him. The LORD told us to call those things that be not as though they were. *(Romans 4:17)* I have seen many feet, legs and arms grow out when one is shorter than the other. Often, when this occurs, the person's back will be healed, too. I have had reports from many people who have received new hearts, when they needed medicine or surgery. Kathryn Kuhlman tells of a man receiving a new heart, while the pace maker simply disappeared. All we need do is speak the Word over the person (or ourselves) and trust God to do the rest. In the cast of the man with the withered arm, Jesus told him to stretch it forth, and *as he obeyed*, it grew. *(Matthew 12:10; Mark 3:1; Luke 6:6)*

Chapter Seventy-Four
Bitterness Causes Sickness

Bitterness---a major cause of sickness and disease

After one of my concerts, I was praying for some people. When I got to one woman who had a long list of serious illnesses, the LORD did not let me pray for her. He spoke one word, "Bitterness." When I told her what He said she looked at me with consternation. She said she was not bitter. I told her to return to her seat where the LORD would begin speaking to her, and that she would be healed if she repented. Afterward, she grabbed me as I was leaving and said, "My mother was bitter, my grandmother was bitter, my children are bitter, my first husband was bitter. Do you think I could possibly be bitter?" I told her she was defiled by bitterness. I gave her some materials to help her get set free, she repented, and one week later she testified in front of the whole church that she was completely healed.

Bitterness can make you sick! It defiles your soul, your spirit and your body, eating away at your flesh until it destroys you. A root of bitterness will defile others around you, as well. Bitterness will prevent you from receiving your healing. When praying for someone with bitterness, it is like praying for a brick wall. The prayers just bounce back, like an echo of what might have been, repelled by the stench, the slime, and the hardened armor of bitterness.

> *We know that we have passed from death unto LIFE because we love the brethren. He that loveth not his brother abideth in DEATH. (1 John 3:14)*

Notice from this very instructive verse, that LIFE is gained through loving others, and that not loving others brings DEATH.

> *...lest any ROOT OF BITTERNESS springing up trouble you, and thereby many be defiled... (Hebrews 12:15)*

A partial list of diseases caused by bitterness: cancer, immune deficiency, heart disease, strokes, eating disorders, tumors, ovarian and breast cysts, leukemia, colon cancer. Bitterness against a mate can cause breast, ovarian, prostate cancer, and other maladies. Bitterness causes death, arthritis, and a host of other maladies. Sometimes self-hatred and self-bitterness can cause these same illnesses.[3]

Bitter-root judgments

Before I was born again, my brother and I had split up our band, and I had joined another band in Orlando. He took everything from me, tens of thousands of dollars worth of equipment we bought together over several years on the road. Everything was in his name and I was left with nothing. I was bitter and angry over a six month period. Ultimately, I became sick and unable to sing. In desperation I made the decision to get down on my knees and forgive my brother. Immediately, I felt a great weight lift off me, and I got well right away. About a week later he showed up in Orlando, and we enjoyed being together for the first time in years. Bitterness had destroyed our relationship and made me sick, but forgiveness set me free. (See section in *"Nails"* on *"Bitter-Root Judgments."*)

Our God says vengeance belongs to Him, alone. We must not make bitter-root judgments against others, no matter what they have done. If we judge another, then we will be judged. *(Matthew 7:1-2)* We must not harbor malice or anger in our souls, because it will manifest. *It has to manifest* because of the law of sowing and reaping. Once sown to the wind, bitterness reaps the whirlwind. Sowing always produces a much-increased result at harvest time, which is always larger than the material sown, good or bad. As you release others and yourself from these judgments, this will be a strong, positive step forward toward getting free from bondage, so that you can receive your healing.

> *Let all BITTERNESS, and ANGER, and CLAMOR, and EVIL SPEAKING, be put away from you, with all MALICE; And be ye kind one to another, tenderhearted, FORGIVING one another, even as God for Christ's sake hath FORGIVEN you. (Ephesians 4:31-32)*

Definitions for the scripture above

1. BITTERNESS: (*Strong's* 4088, pikria) meaning poison (literally or figuratively), acridity (like acid eating away at you).

(*Vines*) bitter hatred; a root producing bitter fruit; embitter, irritate.

(*Webster's*) sharp physical pain, grief or regret, caused by exhibiting strong animosity, severe grief, anguish or disappointment, resentfulness or rancor.

2. WRATH: (*Strong's* 2372, thumos) meaning passion, fierceness, indignation.

(*Vines*) an outburst of wrath; tends to quickly blaze up and quickly subsides.

(*Webster's*) violent, resentful anger, rage.

3. ANGER: (*Strong's* 3709, orge) meaning excitement of the mind, desire, violent passion, indignation, vengeance, wrath.

(*Vines*) anger, the strongest of all passions; a settled or abiding condition of mind, with a view to taking revenge, more lasting in nature than "thumos."

(*Webster's*) a feeling of great displeasure, hostility, indignation, exasperation, wrath.

4. CLAMOR: (*Strong's* 2906, krauge) meaning an outcry, tumult or grief, cry(ing).

(*Vines*) signifies a tumult of controversy.

(*Webster's*) loud outcry, hubbub; vehement expression of discontent or protest, public outcry; to make insistent demands or complaints; to drive or influence by clamor.

5. EVIL SPEAKING: (*Strong's* 988, blasphemia) meaning vilification, blasphemy, railing.

(*Vines*) slanderous. This is talking that promotes distress, sorrow, calamity, suffering, or misfortune; gossip, slander, complaining, or talebearing.

6. MALICE: (*Strong's* 2549, kakia) meaning depravity, malignity, evil, naughtiness, wickedness, trouble, badness.

(*Vines*) the vicious character generally; wickedness; malicious.

(*Webster's*) desire to harm others or to see others suffer; intent, without just cause, to commit an unlawful act injurious to another.

Deception prevents repentance

We are so DECEIVED. We actually believe we are getting away with holding grudges, unforgiveness, bitterness, malice, wrath and anger. God's Word tells us otherwise.

Be not DECEIVED; God is not mocked; for whatsoever a man soweth, that shall he also reap. (Galatians 6:7)

Look carefully at the list above, and search your heart. Many sicknesses are the result of God's law of sowing and reaping. Right now is a good time to repent! Take a moment to review your situation and relationships. Ask God to show you right now, the people you need to forgive. Let Him speak to your heart, and bring faces and names to your remembrance. Take a moment to pray. Whenever I think someone has gone too far, and I feel unable to forgive, I meditate on the perfect, sinless Son of God hanging on the cross for me, though He was innocent, and I am guilty. I dwell on how He asked God to forgive His murderers, even as He hung there, torn and bleeding. Then, it becomes easy for me to forgive others. My sin, in God's eyes, is probably far greater than Jesus' murderers, for withholding forgiveness from my offenders.

Offense prevents healing

Offense will keep you from receiving your healing. I ministered to a woman who took offense when the LORD prompted me to sing, "Oh, the blood of Jesus. It washes white as snow." She did not think she had any sin that needed washing. She went away offended, and still sick. Would you have been offended if Jesus spit on mud and put it in your eyes? Be ready for the unusual. That may be the way Jesus wants to heal you.

Word of none effect

Because of TRADITIONS in religious thinking, some people have come to the meetings where I am ministering and walked away not healed. The anointing was there, the faith was there, but they have been taught healing is not for today, and God wants them to suffer; or that through sickness they will bring glory to God. Please note that Jesus healed ALL who came to Him in faith. None were left to suffer who sought Him. *Jesus did not believe leaving people sick brought Him glory*, and neither should you.

...making the Word of God of none effect (useless) through your TRADITION, which ye have delivered (followed), and many such like things do ye. (Mark 7:13)

Getting free

1. Pray and ask God to show you the areas in your life, specifically, where you have made bitter-root judgments.
2. Repent for these judgments.
3. Forgive your offender; ask God to forgive you and your offender.
4. Break these bitter-root judgments in Jesus' Name.
5. Apply the blood of Jesus to the wounds.
6. Fill the holes left in your soulish realm with scripture.
7. Bless those who despitefully used you.
8. Fight your own tendencies to be bitter by welcoming the fruit of the Spirit, love, long-suffering and humility into your heart.

(See the chapter on *Bitter-Root Judgments*.)

Chapter Seventy-Five
Accuser of the Brethren

Your words have creative power, whether they are spoken for your good or to your detriment. No worse lie could have been foisted on us as children than the old rhyme, "Sticks and stones may break my bones, but words will never hurt me." I heard and said this so much as a child, I actually believed it. Imagine my surprise when I read the Word of God and discovered just the opposite to be true.

Terry Mize tells a story in his book, *More Than Conquerors*, that he was having trouble with his hearing since suffering a war injury. He started saying to his wife, "I think I am losing my hearing." She would agree with him. This went on and on, until he actually could not hear. When they realized how they had cursed his hearing, they repented, broke the power of the words and started making positive confessions about his hearing. Very soon his hearing was back to normal.

Your own words bless or curse

Could you be cursing yourself and others by speaking negative, evil words? Life and death are in the power of the tongue. *(Proverbs 18:21)* Is it common for you to talk about your own body in negative terms? Then you are cursing yourself. Satan is the accuser of the brethren, and he accuses us day and night. *(Revelation 12:10)* Our job is to stand against him, not join him in cursing ourselves. If you have cursed your own healing, then repent and ask God to forgive you. Break the power of every evil word spoken, in Jesus' Name. Then, command these words to be rendered null and void, and cancel their assignment against you. Pull down any structures or strongholds formed through the creative power of these words, in Jesus' Name. Resolve to speak only positive words about yourself, your body, your spouse and children, friends, job, church, etc.

Speaking the truth does not require you to curse yourself. This is convoluted foolishness. Stating the obvious is not a requirement. Yahshua would not even say Jairus' daughter was dead. *(Luke 8:41-56)* He said she was sleeping because He knew the secret of the power of His Word: that His faith-filled words would bring her back from the dead. The same was true with Lazarus. *(John 11:11)* God spoke the worlds into existence with the creative power of His Words. You, too, have creative power in your tongue. What if God had insisted on simply reporting the obvious problems: "Well, look at the earth. That sure is ugly nothingness. It's black, shapeless, formless and totally void. There is nothing I can do with this mess!" Instead, God used His creative ability to see the wonderful possibilities resident in the earth's shapeless mass. Likewise, we can use our God-given creative ability to see the positive, the possible, and the beauty in others.

Prayer of agreement

The prayer of agreement is an effectual way to receive your healing. Call someone you trust and speak forth your specific prayer requests and needs, asking them to AGREE with you. Pray in faith, and receive in faith. This releases your angels to go to work in your behalf. Faith moves the hand of God. Do not pray with someone who cannot agree with you, or who has no faith for what you are praying. Do not turn around and speak just the opposite after agreeing: "Well, do you think it worked?" This cancels your prayer! The angels have to fold their arms.

...if two of you shall AGREE on earth as touching anything that they shall ask, IT SHALL BE DONE for them of My Father which is in heaven. (Matthew 18:19)

Chapter Seventy-Six
Sickness from A Curse

My Aunt Melba

My Aunt Melba was well known in her small home town in Arkansas. She kept a minimum of fifteen cats at all times, some inside, some outside. My earliest childhood memories were of sitting in her wicker chair while her Siamese cats spiked me through the slats with their claws. Melba was feisty, like her cats, and a practical joker, but much beloved.

The battle begins

When my mom called and said Melba was dying and urgently wanted to see us, I felt the battle begin in the spirit realm. I was nursing my third son and knew it would be a long trip riding with my parents, but I spent the time reading my Bible and quietly praying. My dad kept saying things like, "You know she probably will not listen to you." I ignored him. Then he said, "You know she's a sinner and probably will not want to get saved." I just kept praying.

First things first

When I got there, she wanted to see me first. I went in alone, and immediately began to minister to her. I rebuked a spirit of death off her and bound 1 Peter 2:24 to her, commanding her body to be healed. She had not eaten for three days and was wasting away, almost unable to speak. I rebuked the spirit of infirmity off her and commanded her to eat a big breakfast the next morning. Then, I exhorted her to get up and go feed her cats.

The next morning she sat up and ate. The shocked doctor did some tests, found nothing wrong, and told her she was going home to feed her cats. The following day we had to return home, but I wanted to see her alone, once more. However, this time her sister-in-law would not leave the room. When I perceived an evil spirit was working through this relative to attack and kill Melba, I asked her to leave. Then, I prayed a salvation prayer with her, hugged her, and left with my folks. My mother cried when I told her Melba had prayed to be saved.

The battle is not over

Two weeks later, the hospital called my dad to say Melba had regressed. Later, that night, I got a call from the sister-in-law. I do not know how she got my number, but allegedly she had tried to call my dad and there was no answer. This was a lie because Dad insisted the phone never rang. Her voice had a hideous, gleeful tone as she related that she was tired of sitting in the hospital with Melba, and she had prayed for her to die. She left the room and when she returned, Melba was dead. The devil wanted to gloat over his triumph so he caused her to call me, instead of my dad.

What was my reaction? I rejoiced that Melba's name is written in the Lamb's Book of Life. I told the devil what he meant for evil had been turned for good. I thanked the LORD for opening the door for me to minister salvation to her, and for welcoming her into heaven, and praised God that someday I will see her again.

If you have been cursed

Satan and his minions hear a curse and go right to work. This gives them an open door to attack, and because they hate us they have no mercy, no pity. Our angels will not help us as long as our sovereign will has allowed, or in some cases invited in, demons. Whereas demons will attempt to gain power through lies, wiles and deception, God patiently waits until we act by speaking the Word over ourselves, others and our circumstances, and by resisting the devil. Our prayers release our angels and empower them to minister and war on our behalf.

Demons spend a lot of time analyzing us and formulating a plan for our demise. Our guardian angels will fight for us but will not interfere in our sovereign will. That is why demons work so hard on tearing down our will, enticing and enslaving us in evil and wicked thoughts, words and actions. If they can get us in this area, our angels cannot interfere. We must make a decision to work together with our angels for our own benefit. Our words and actions reflect our true will. Therefore, when we speak negative thoughts and perform negative actions, we are cursing ourselves and others, and our angels throw up their hands and say, "Apparently, she wants to be sick (poor, depressed). There is nothing we can do!"

Breaking curses

1. Break the evil words spoken by you or against you, in Jesus' (Yahshua Messiah) Name. Cancel their assignment against you and render them null and void. Stand strong in your God-given authority!
2. If you are having the same problems or sicknesses your mother, father, or other relatives have had, you are under a generational curse.
3. Break off generational curses to the fourth generation, and the curse of illegitimacy to the tenth generation.
4. Bind God's love and favor to yourself.
5. Bind scriptures to yourself involving protection, healing and deliverance.
6. If you have cursed yourself through words, deeds or actions, repent. Ask God's forgiveness.
7. Speak words of life over yourself, others and your circumstances.

Chapter Seventy-Seven
Sickness from Demonic Attack

Sickness is oppression

Sickness is oppression from the devil. It is *not* a good thing. I have heard people say such things as, "My angina is acting up." "My diabetes is…" They personalize a sickness and claim it as their own.

> *…God anointed Jesus of Nazareth with the Holy Ghost and with power: Who went about DOING GOOD, AND HEALING ALL THAT WERE OPPRESSED OF THE DEVIL; for God was with Him. (Acts 10:38)*

Jesus knew the source of sickness and disease was the devil, and His ministry was to SET THE CAPTIVES FREE.

> *…He hath sent Me to heal the broken-hearted, to preach DELIVERANCE TO THE CAPTIVES, and recovering of sight to the blind, to set at liberty them that are bruised… (Luke 4:18)*

The abundant life that Jesus gave us simply does not fit the profile of sickness, disease, and demonic oppression. Jesus gave us power (exousia, authority) to cast out the devil.

> *Behold, I give unto you power to tread on serpents and scorpions, and over ALL the power of the enemy: and nothing shall by any means hurt you. (Luke 10:19)*

The devil is the one who came to destroy your God-given right to abundant life: Sickness is not ABUNDANT life.

> *The thief cometh not, but for to steal, and to kill, and to destroy: I Am come that they might have life, and that they might have it MORE ABUNDANTLY. (John 10:10)*

YHWH, our God, gives GOOD GIFTS to His children. Sickness is definitely not a good gift.

> *Every GOOD GIFT and EVERY PERFECT GIFT IS FROM ABOVE, and cometh down from the Father of lights, with Whom is no variableness, neither shadow of turning. (James 1:17)*

Deuteronomy 28 examined

Deuteronomy 28:22 says, *The LORD shall smite thee with a consumption…* A more accurate translation of Deuteronomy 28:22 is: "The LORD will *allow* thee to be smitten…" He allows it because of *our* sin and disobedience, through which *we ourselves open the door* to sickness and disease. We remove *ourselves* from God's protection and covering. He wants to bless us. Just look at the multitudes of sick people who thronged Yahshua Messiah when He began His ministry. He healed them *all*. Through the stripes on Jesus' back, sickness and disease were dealt with. Through His death on the cross, sin was atoned for. Through His resurrection, you can receive eternal salvation. Being born again gives us a new spirit. Being healed gives us new flesh. BOTH SIN AND SICKNESS COME FROM SATAN, and neither applied to Adam and Eve *until* they failed during the temptation that came from Satan in the Garden of Eden.

A stubborn infection

After my third son was born, I began to have continuous bladder infections. It progressed into my kidneys and was continuously painful; it even hurt to move. I was trembling from fever and infection on and off for weeks. Antibiotics didn't help, though I took several kinds. The infection would subside temporarily, then return worse than before. Though I prayed, there was no manifestation of healing. Finally, I went to a specialist. After exhausting all possibilities, he threw his hands in the air and said, " I don't understand it. There's nothing wrong with you."

It was then that I realized I was dealing with a demonic attack. I could not wait to get home and begin a victory dance, singing and praising the LORD for opening my eyes. I took authority over the devil and resisted him with righteous anger, forcing him to flee from me. The demons that had caused the infection left immediately, and within two days my body was back to normal, free of pain. I have remained completely healed for twelve years. As a side benefit, I gave up caffeine. I am better, healthier and more alert without coffee and tea.

Mornings are much brighter and more cheerful without needing my caffeine fix. I drink fresh, clean water wherever I go these days, and I enjoy it with a lemon. I have read reports saying caffeine may actually contribute to some forms of disease such as breast cancer. Now, the Bible says you can drink any deadly thing and it will not harm you, but why subject your body to deadly things, and tempt God?

Deliverance clears path for healing

Deliverance does not heal anyone, but it clears a path for healing. Then, healing can take place. In the Star Trek series, the Borg (an evil enemy empire that forcibly assimilated all other civilizations in its destructive path) always say, "Resistance is futile!" This is just like the devil. He wants us to think there is nothing we can do to fight him. His greatest weapon is deception. When fighting Satan, continued *resistance* is the key to remaining free and healed.

Breaking the strongholds

1. Firmly, tell the wicked spirit plaguing you that it is not welcome, and you will no longer listen.
2. Cast out deception and every lying spirit in Jesus, the Messiah of Nazareth's, Name.
3. Ask God to forgive you for believing the lies of the devil over God's truth.
4. Break off a spirit of infirmity if this spirit is in operation, in Jesus' Name, and specifically rebuke the sickness and symptoms by name, commanding them to loose you and let you go.
5. Memorize healing scriptures and stand firmly on the solid rock, Jesus.
6. Symptoms are some of the lies of the devil. Refuse to believe them. Refuse to take them. Be sure you do not curse yourself by saying you have something you do not have, just because of a symptom. If the devil can get you to TAKE the symptoms and speak them out of your mouth, then he can defeat you with the words of your own mouth.
7. Resist the devil and he will flee from you.
8. Realize you have the victory in Jesus' Name.
9. Walk by faith and not by sight. Speak the truth, not your feelings about how you feel.

(See the chapter on the *Spirit of Infirmity* in the *Nails* section of this book.)

Study Questions: Chapter 73
1. Why did Jesus call for people to act on their faith?
2. What does it mean to speak to your body?
3. How is faith like a sponge?
4. What three things can you do today to act on your faith?
5. Why does Jesus often command action after a healing or miracle?

Study Questions: Chapter 74
1. How does a root of bitterness in your heart defile others? *(Hebrews 12:15)*
2. What does the scripture mean when it says if we do not love others we abide in death? *(1 John 3:14)*
3. What are people like who are eaten up with bitterness?
4. What is the law of sowing and reaping?
5. Do we ever get away with secretly holding grudges?

Study Questions: Chapter 77
1. Who came to give us abundant life?
2. What are God's good gifts?
3. From where do sin and sickness come?
4. Does deliverance heal you?

Chapter Seventy-Eight
Fear, Doubt, Unbelief

Keeping our mouths shut

Sometimes it is crucial to stand, and having done all to stand, stand therefore, believing for your miracle. Many times I cannot discuss either sickness or healing with relatives or friends because they call up and demand progress reports, which may involve cursing my own healing. It is often better to wait until receiving the manifestation before it is discussed with others. Otherwise, the door can be opened for the spirits of doubt, unbelief and fear to enter in.

Guarding your heart

Negative experiences do not invalidate the Word of God. The Word is true, and let every man be a liar. What people endure and allow in the realm of sickness has *no bearing* on God's ability to heal, any more than the existence of unsaved people in the world has any bearing on the reality and availability of salvation. Recently, I called up my hairdresser who is an old friend. I could barely talk because the devil was trying to get me to *take a cold*. I canceled my appointment so I could rest and pray. My hairdresser heard how I sounded and before I could quickly hang up, he insisted on telling me his son had a bad cold, and after two weeks, he still was not over it. Thoughts of doubt and unbelief began to flood my mind. I had to fight them off, as well as the symptoms, so it took longer than it should have to receive my healing. It would have been much better to have someone call for me, than to allow myself to hear that story. Faith comes by hearing, no matter whether it is positive or negative information.

Fear knocks down the hedge

Fear can bring sickness and other problems. A partial list of diseases caused by a root of fear, anxiety and stress is: multiple chemical sensitivities, allergies, asthma, high blood pressure, heart problems, angina, ulcers, colitis, irritable bowel syndrome, acne, fatigue, depression, shingles and hives, sinus infections, PMS, chronic fatigue syndrome, diabetes and hypoglycemia.[4] Our faith must outweigh our fear. FEAR removes our hedge of protection God has placed around us. Job unwittingly removed his hedge of protection through his FEAR.

> *For the thing which I greatly FEARED is come upon me, and that which I was AFRAID of is come unto me, I WAS NOT IN SAFETY, NEITHER HAD I REST, neither was I quiet; yet trouble came. (Job 3:25-26)*

Job knew, somehow, that his hedge of protection was down, but he did not understand the magnitude of God's peace and protection. He was FEARFUL and he could not even REST. God wants us to REST in Him. There is none like our God, YHWH. He is our Shalom, our PEACE. Yahshua the Messiah was the Prince of PEACE. We cannot earn His protection or peace because it is a free gift. Many of our physical ailments come from our failure to trust our God, which opens us up to the spirit of fear. Yahshua spoke powerful words of comfort to his disciples.

> *PEACE I leave with you, my PEACE I give unto you: not as the world giveth, give I unto you. Let not your heart be troubled, neither let it be afraid. (John 14:27)*

In Job 1:8 the LORD asks Satan, *Hast thou CONSIDERED my servant Job…?* The word CONSIDERED actually means "set thy heart against." God knew what Satan was thinking and plotting against Job. You see, Satan had his eye on Job, but he was not aware at that time that Job's hedge was already down though fear. If you have knocked down your hedge of protection through fear, repent quickly, and break the stronghold of fear off your life, in Jesus' Name.

A teenager shared with me that his father abused him physically and sexually when he was a child. One time, when his father came home in a rage, the child saw a hideous spirit with yellow, cat-like eyes, exit his father's mouth, and enter him. He whimpered in fear, but did not know how to get free. In the long term he developed asthma.

At a recent meeting, I had a word of knowledge that a woman would be delivered of asthma. I asked who had asthma. When a woman raised her hand I told her the root of asthma is fear, and that self-hatred and self-rejection played a part. I asked her to tell fear to leave because this spirit was not her friend. Then, I cast out a spirit of fear. Following that, she received her healing. Now, she can ride her bicycle outside with her husband. However, these wicked spirits have tried to return several times and she has had to resist. Jesus said, *...sin no more, lest a worse thing come unto thee. (John 5:14)* Doubt and unbelief are sin. When we fail to resist the temptation to sin we open ourselves back up to the enemy. He may be persistent, but we must be *more* persistent.

Sometimes an evil spirit comes, pretending to be a friend bringing comfort. This happens especially to children. This is a deception the person must realize and speak forth, followed by commanding the spirit to leave.

The land of unbelief

Our own strength cannot heal us or save us. We are WEAK and in need of a Savior. Part of the meaning of salvation is preservation, deliverance and healing. If you are AFRAID, speak these scriptures over yourself.

> *For God hath not given us the SPIRIT OF FEAR; but of power, and of love, and of a sound mind. (2 Timothy 1:7)*

> *...when I am WEAK, then am I strong. (2 Corinthians 12:10)*

Then you say, "Yeah, but I prayed before and nothing happened. What if that happens again?" You are deep in doubt and unbelief, and nothing will happen as long as you live in the land of unbelief.

The Word is true—sickness is the lie

Speak this Word over yourself: *LORD, I believe; help Thou mine unbelief. (Mark 9:24)* Begin to fill your heart up with God's Word. The Word is true. It is the sickness that is the lie. YHWH, our God, sent His Son Who suffered and died for us. A prophecy of the coming Messiah in Isaiah 53:5 states, *...and with His stripes we ARE healed.* This is Old Testament, and what Jesus was yet to do was being prophesied. In 1 Peter 2:24 it is written, *...by Whose stripes ye WERE healed.* Jesus has *already* healed you. Do not let the thief rob you of your healing through lies, fear, doubt and unbelief.

> *...let the WEAK say I am STRONG; (Joel 3:10)*

> *For though He was crucified through WEAKNESS, yet He liveth by the POWER OF GOD. For we also are weak in Him, but we shall live with Him by the power of God toward you. (2 Corinthians 13:4)*

How can you call on the LORD if you do not believe His Word?

The Word states, *How then shall they call on Him, in Whom they have not believed? (Romans 10:14)* There is a story in Acts 19:13-17 in which the seven sons of Sceva were attempting to cast out devils by the Name of Jesus. They were not only unsuccessful, they were beaten up for their trouble. Now, these men were not born again, they were just trying a new novelty they had seen Paul use, *hoping* it would work.

There is a principle here deserving further investigation. If you are born again, then you have authority over the devil. Why then, are so many of God's children sick and powerless? I believe it is because they are just *trying* out the Word to see *if* it will work, not using any real faith. David refused to wear armor against Goliath that he had not tested already against the lion and the bear. He wore a shield of faith which his adversary could not see. Faith is not something that appears, "poof." It requires integrity, endurance, standing in the face of all obstacles, learning to act like an overcomer, refusing to yield to doubt or back down no matter how things look. Faith requires standing, and declaring yourself victorious despite what others say. So what if you fail! I'd rather fail trusting God, than yield to the devil's lies. How about you?

Faith for miracles

I went to a visitation in a church for a friend who had died, suddenly. I had just been on the phone praising the LORD and praying with her a few days before. She had many friends and after the visitation I stayed until all had left except the people I brought with me. I went up and laid my hands on her and called the Spirit of Life back into her body. I rebuked the devil for taking her so young and rebuked the spirit of death off her. I know the LORD heard my prayer but she did not rise from the dead. An evangelist friend gave me a message from God: because I had stepped out in faith to raise her up, the LORD would now increase my faith and anointing. One day I would surely raise the dead. God has been faithful, and now I see more healings and anointing than ever before in my ministry.

Evangelist David Hogan, tells a story about driving his jeep when he spotted a man who had been run over by a train. The man was so smashed up he was unrecognizable. However, David laid hands on him and prayed for him to be raised up. Nothing happened, but a few months later a man told him he had accepted Jesus as his Savior. He said if God could give David faith to pray for such a hopeless case, he wanted to serve that God.

No guts—no glory

The previous two stories were told to let you know faith is a process. If nothing happens the first time, do it again. Never give up! The devil wants you to be embarrassed and defeated. He wants to produce failures, while God has already given you the victory. I am to the point that I really do not care what people think. After all, it is God Who gets the glory, and ultimately God Who must answer all the questions. God gets the increase. No one can tell me God does not heal today, because I have already seen miracles and healings with my own eyes and heard enough testimonies to build my faith up in YHWH Rapha, my healer. No negative reports, pessimistic people or depressing stories can ever take away my trust in the integrity of God and His Word! Do not unload that junk on me. You are too late! I have already seen the mighty power of the living God.

Revelation of the Word in our hearts

Often, if we can truly get a revelation of God's Word in our hearts, then the Word goes from being logos (words written on a page but not yet in our heart), to rhema (revelation of the Word, alive in our hearts), we will get healed. A scripture will jump off the page into our consciousness, suddenly opening our spirit to God's truth. This is revelation that will change our bodies, minds, affect our healing, and open the way for our miracle. This can only occur when we saturate our hearts with the Word and faith drops on us in a powerful way. Then, healing can occur. This is why preaching the Word before ministering to the sick is important. Faith comes by hearing.

Rebuking tornadoes

When I was a brand new Christian, I heard a sermon about a man of God who had rebuked a tornado headed straight for his picnic on the lake. I brashly charged out into a rainstorm that afternoon and commanded it to stop. It did not. In fact, it got worse. In time, I realized this was not God's failure, but my own lack of faith. I began to step out in small areas. When I was first married, all I had was my clothes and musical equipment from years of living on the road. First, I believed God would give us a refrigerator we badly needed, then I prayed for carpet. The old refrigerator we were given was so tiny it did not even have a freezer, so I prayed for a freezer. The next day a man called where my husband worked and told him if someone would haul away his deep freeze, he would give it away and pay them for hauling it. It still works after twenty years. Later, someone gave me a new refrigerator. I began to pray and believe for healing in my body. Building on each victory, I stepped out further and further, stretching my faith each time.

Weather will not stop God

One day, a few years later, we were getting ready for a concert in the park, and there were unbelievable problems with the equipment. We were hours late and Steve came down with a paralyzing headache. He could not move. I prayed for him and rebuked the devil off our concert. Steve's headache left. After we arrived and got set up, just before the concert, thunderclouds came barreling toward us. This would have wiped out our concert and ruined the equipment. I could literally see the rain pouring out of the ominous storm clouds in the distance, and heard on the radio there were flash floods in the suburbs west of us. I stood up in righteous anger, recognizing the devil was doing everything he could to stop the concert. I pointed my finger at the storm and said, "Thunderstorm, I rebuke you in the Name of Jesus, the Christ of Nazareth. I command you to turn and go around us. You will not rain on this concert, or prevent anyone from coming who is supposed to be here." To the amazement of everyone, the storm literally changed course, headed north, went around us, then resumed by dumping its fury on another town, due east. We had a wonderful time on that warm, clear evening. Several souls were saved.

Afterward, because the equipment was being hauled in an open trailer, the enemy tried to bring back some rain as we were packing up. I rebuked the storm again and ordered the rain not to start until every last piece of our equipment was safely back in the house. When this was accomplished, it began to pour.

The Word of God is not something we use in presumption. It is not something we use frivolously, or take lightly. We study the Word and build our faith by starting small, knowing the trying of our faith works patience. Someday, we will move mountains, but it is good to start with the molehills.

Different kinds of healing

The important thing to grasp about healing is that it is received by faith. Standing for your healing may be instant or gradual, but always behave as if you already have it. I have seen and experienced both. One time I prayed for a woman who had a large tumor on her shoulder. It disappeared instantly. Another time, a tumor on a woman's throat disappeared over a couple of weeks, and when she went to her doctor it was gone without her even noticing it. Another time, I prayed for blind eyes to be opened and it happened instantly. Once, I prayed for a man's blind eyes to be opened, but nothing happened; then I prayed again. We went outside and the healed man watched the sunset for the first time in many years. What a thrill!

In the healing of a blind man from Bethsaida *(Mark 8:22-26)*, notice that the first thing Jesus did was lead the man out of the city where unbelief and religious spirits controlled the people. Sometimes, people receive healing better when they are alone, than when they are with people with whom they are co-dependent. Jesus laid hands on the man twice. This town had a problem with negativity and unbelief. Jesus rebuked them in Luke 10. Lying, unbelief and religious negativity had to be separated from the man. Under ordinary circumstances it would insult a person to be spit on, but not this man. He wanted to be healed more than he wanted to keep his pride.

Imagine having the religious scales washed off your eyes by the spit of the One Who is the Living Water. Jesus knew the man was not fully restored, so He asked if he could see anything. Traditionally, we have wondered why the man responded that he saw men who looked like trees. However, this was great progress. You see, Jesus had taken the man out of the town, but He still had to get the town out of the man, so he could receive his healing. When those scales of deception were removed, Jesus healed him. Because of this man's vulnerability, Jesus instructed him not to tell anyone in the town. They would not have believed it and would have been all over him, telling him he really did not receive anything. He would have been pulled back into deception and unbelief, possibly losing his healing.

Avoid doubt and unbelief

Get away from doubters. They are like heavy, wet blankets. They will poison you and everyone they come into contact with, not just in the area of healing, but in every area. Hope and faith are built upon staying in the Word, hearing the Word preached, and associating with others who are like-minded. When I was first saved I wanted to reach out to musicians, agents, fans and friends I had known when I had my nightclub and concert act. The Lord would not allow me to do so because I was still vulnerable and weak, though I did not realize it. Temptation would have pulled me back into that lifestyle, because I knew nothing about spiritual warfare, or how to resist the devil. I could not have helped others, when I so desperately needed help myself? Though I got delivered from some things instantly at salvation, more a year later in a two day deliverance session with my pastor, there was still more. Deliverance was definitely a process for me. Overcoming self-rejection, and an initial tendency to judge myself too harshly, has taken time, as I got to know the loving forgiveness and patience of my heavenly Father. Things that were once temptations seem ridiculous to me, now.

Asa vs. Hezekiah

These two men were both kings of Judah, but in the end, when faced with death, they reacted in significantly different ways, and had dramatically different results. Both kings brought reforms to Judah and God spoke to both of them through His prophets. However, a significant statement to Asa reveals God's warning.

> *...The LORD is with you, while ye be with Him; and if ye seek Him, He will be found of you; but if ye forsake Him, He will forsake you. (2 Chronicles 15:2)*

Eventually, Asa began seeking treaties with ungodly nations and in the end, when he got sick, he sought the physicians instead of YHWH, his God. Hezekiah, on the other hand, turned to God when faced with death, and God gave him fifteen more years. *(2 Kings 15: 6)* Asa sought physicians and died; Hezekiah sought God and lived.

Disease clusters

Often, when I minister in a specific town or church there will be clusters of particular diseases, or physical ailments. For example, at one church where I ministered there was a plethora of back and neck problems. At another, an inordinate number of heart problems were present. When this kind of pattern emerges, I conclude that there is a conglomeration of active, wicked spirits of that specific kind gathered, operating through a person or group in that place.

For example, if a ruling spirit of fear is operating, then one could expect to see a number of people manifesting allergies, asthma, angina, etc. If the ruling spirit, that is, the spirit that is able to manifest most frequently is bitterness, then there might be a lot of cancer, leukemia, osteoporosis, arthritis, etc.

Spirits that set up strongholds in an area or church must have permission through the leaders, through unrepented sin, or through unbroken family curses. The curses of witches or Satanists may be behind some oppression or sickness that is manifesting. Discernment is necessary to expose the root. Warfare is imperative to break the strongholds. (See the *Nails* section of this book for steps to spiritual warfare.)

The gifts of healings, miracles and faith

The gift of healing and the gift of miracles are given as the Holy Spirit wills. They are two of the nine gifts of the Spirit. *(1 Corinthians 12:8-11)* When these gifts are in operation, healings and miracles will sometimes occur whether the person is saved, using faith, or not. These gifts sometimes override circumstances, and may include spontaneous healing in the audience, or be a surprise to the recipient. These gifts cannot be turned on and off at will. They are fully a manifestation of the power and mercy of the LORD. When the gift of faith manifests, all things are possible. A person can outrun a chariot such as Elijah did, walk on the water, or do creative miracles in Jesus' Name.

Jesus appears

I was doing a concert in the park on a lovely summer evening. At the end, I ministered "*Stripes.*" A cool fragrant breeze arose. The anointing was very strong as I called out words of knowledge, and many began to be healed. The next morning, the man who had put together the outreach called me and said his dad had video taped the whole concert. He said when I began ministering "*Stripes*" he saw on the video that Jesus walked in and stood beside me with arms outstretched. When I finished, He folded all the diseases in His arms and left.

Getting free

1. Repent of the sin of fear, doubt and unbelief.
2. Ask your loving, heavenly Father to forgive you for yielding to these spirits.
3. Tell fear, doubt and unbelief you do not want them anymore; that you recognize them for what they are.
4. Cast out the spirit of fear, doubt and unbelief.
5. Say, "LORD, I believe. Help Thou my unbelief."
6. Speak words of faith out loud. Faith comes by hearing.
7. Bind scriptures of faith to yourself, and write them on the tables of your heart.
8. Act healed. Act like a believer. Do the opposite of what the devil wants. Guard your mouth and your heart!

Study Questions: Chapter 78
1. What is the difference between doubt and unbelief?
2. How does fear work with these two spirits?
3. What are some positive steps you can take today to guard your heart from negative influences?
4. Explain how Job knocked down his hedge of protection.
5. What is the basic difference between Asa and Hezekiah?
6. Examine your heart. What is your true attitude toward God?

Chapter Seventy-Nine
Sickness for Attention

There are many people who will feign sickness for attention; others who actually want to be sick and helpless, because it is the only way anyone will notice them. My paternal grandmother disliked children. She was never very attentive to me, or her other grandchildren, because she was jealous of the attention children got. When we came to visit she would immediately start a progress report for us on her "roving pain." Every few minutes she would alert us that it had moved from her shoulder to her arm, to her stomach, then to her knee, and so on, throughout the visit. She was elderly, but the doctors told us there was *nothing* wrong with her.

In order to walk in the fullness of what God has for us, and to accomplish His perfect will, we need all our strength and endurance. If we expend our efforts on cultivating illness for attention, we miss out on God's best for us and His wonderful plan, we bring a pathetic witness to Jesus and shame on ourselves. In the movie *Jaws* there was a comical scene where two of the main characters on the boat in search of the shark begin comparing scars. Each one had a bigger and wilder story as they uncovered arms and legs, madly stacking them up to compete for attention and dominance. Immediately, the shark attacked them. When we give in to the devil's lies to gain attention, and curse ourselves with our words, then he launches a greater attack by permission out of our *own* mouths.

In a relative of mine's office, he told me of two people who claimed to be Christians. One would come in complaining of a hurt, pain or injury. Not to be outdone, the other one would complain of a worse pain or injury. Then, the first one would tell of another injury, or enlarge their story. My relative, who was unsaved, would scoff at them. They brought shame to the Name of Jesus. These people were supposed to be spreading the *good news* as ambassadors of the glory and goodness of God.

There is hardly a child who does not have a story of feigning illness in order to stay home from school. Once, I pretended to have pain in my stomach in order to avoid an IQ test in math. I spent the duration of the test in the restroom, not realizing how profoundly it would affect my life. When the results came back the teacher recommended that my mother stand over me and beat me until I understood math. This "method" caused me to have a mental block against *all* math which plagued me for years. My heavenly Father has delivered me, but it has taken a long time to recover in this area.

In the story "Pollyanna," there is a woman, typical of several people I have known. She was cranky and unpleasant, constantly demanding to be waited on hand and foot as she feigned illness. As soon as someone left her "sick" room, she would jump up and move around. When people came in, she would groan and complain. The true goal was to gain attention.

Why not gain attention through good words and deeds, and bring glory to the Name of Christ? If you have pretended sickness for attention, repent and ask God's forgiveness. Lying does not please YHWH, but He waits with open arms to forgive. He loves you and wants you to serve Him in perfect health. Walking in divine health is far preferable to always needing a healing. Confess daily that you are whole and full of healing and that you prosper and are in health, even as your soul prospers. *(3 John 2)*

Chapter Eighty
Healing in His Wings

The woman with the issue of blood suffered much at the hands of physicians. After many years, she was worse off than when she started, and broke as well. We can only imagine the nightmarish, primitive methods doctors used on her. The Bible says she suffered much, yet she was healed instantly when she encountered the power of Yahshua the Messiah. *(Mark 5:25-26)*

As a Jew, she was familiar with the scriptures. She was put outside the household of faith because of her issue of blood. The Torah forbid her to enter the city, contaminating everyone. Certainly she knew not to touch a kosher rabbi. At the end of all hope, in desperation, she broke the law, because she also knew that if Jesus was truly the Messiah, then there was healing in his WINGS (the tzit tzit that every Jewish man wore). The *tzit tzit* are fringes that hang down from a special garment worn by every Jewish man. It has a single blue thread woven into it, made to look like two threads with one end longer, to gaze on and always remember the commandments. Blue is the color of the throne room of God, reminding them that they are always in His presence.

> *But unto you that fear my Name shall the Sun of righteousness arise with healing in his WINGS (tzit tzit). (Malachi 4:2)*

If He proved not to be the Messiah, she was a dead woman. They would stone her on the spot. We are all in the same fix. If Yahshua (Jesus) is not the Messiah we are all dead in our sins. Yet, if we take hold of His *tzit tzit,* His wings, we too can be healed.

Medical science vs. YHWH Rapha

God is not limited, but medical science is. Medical science wants to treat the symptoms, rather than go to the root of the problem. Roots are painful to deal with, break, and repent of. It is so much easier to pop a pill than it is to STAND. *(Ephesians 6:13-14)* Medication simply covers up the real problem.

If you are on medication, do not throw it away. Too often people step out in presumption and suffer for it. Use wisdom in what you do with your medicine, and see a doctor for confirmation before taking rash action. Presumption and faith are like oil and water: they don't mix. There is a solid knowing in your "faith-O-meter" when you know that you know you are healed. A woman was healed of multiple sclerosis at one of my concerts last summer when her faith touched Jesus' healing virtue. Another man came with a sprained ankle. I laid hands on him and told him to walk on it. He jumped up and down, for YHWH Rapha healed him.

Dis-ease

I know of a woman who suffered for years with a "dis-ease" that caused her to be allergic to nearly everything, including most foods. She had many people praying for her, but was nearly unable to go out in public because of odors such as paint, cleaning products, perfume, etc. Her whole church took it upon themselves not to wear perfume or deodorant so she could attend services. Her husband was building a new house for her that would be entirely free from toxic products, because even her house was poisoning her. When an attack came she would choke and be unable to breathe, nearly dying each time.

One day she had a "knowing," a gift of faith unmistakably from God. Friends had been praying in shifts around the clock for a breakthrough. She called a friend over and asked to be taken to a fast food restaurant for a hamburger. Under ordinary circumstances this would have brought on an attack, but she had been suddenly and sovereignly healed. God gets all the glory! She remains healed to this day.

Help!

Don't be afraid to ask for help. Moses cried out in humility and others held up his arms. As the body of Messiah, we are to hold one another up. There have been so many times in the ministry when I have looked out across the crowd and seen people that God wanted to heal, but they would not come forward to receive it. I believe Jesus wants you to come forward and receive your healing. Reach out to Him. He is here for you. God loves you. He has gracious, compassionate, tender love and healing to give. He desires for us to prosper and be in health.

The LORD is gracious (disposed to show favors), and full of compassion (eager yearnings); slow to anger, and of great mercy. The LORD is good to all; and His tender mercies are over ALL HIS WORKS. (Psalm 145:8-9)

We are His WORKMANSHIP. *(Ephesians 2:10)* He longs to show us His love, His mercy and His healing power.

Cues from the redwood and the eagle

We can take our cue to help others from the redwood trees. When one redwood gets sick, the other healthy trees near it send out their roots and attach to the sick tree's roots, lending healing, nourishment and strength to the ailing tree. Thus, they can stand together, a great forest. If we would do the same, the body of Christ would be strong in the LORD, linking arms together for strength.

When an eagle is sick, it's beak grows over, and because it cannot eat it will die. So it sits on a mountain top and the other eagles come and pick off the overgrowth, so it may eat and live. The eagle beats its beak down on hard rock so it may be restored to proper shape and size. When we are sick emotionally, spiritually or physically we must seek the LORD first and allow Him to transform us with the wonderful life-giving power of the Word. We must beat down our pride by resisting the devil and renewing our minds, allowing other godly Christians to minister to us by breaking off the strongholds that prevent us from receiving the Word that will nourish us back to health. This process requires humility.

Be transformed

Be transformed by the renewing of your mind. That means to spend time reading God's Word and letting it build your faith and trust in Him.

I beseech you therefore, brethren, by the mercies of God, that ye present your bodies a living sacrifice, holy, acceptable unto God, which is your reasonable service. And be not conformed to this world: but BE YE TRANSFORMED by the renewing of your mind... (Romans 12:1-2)

So then faith cometh by hearing, and hearing by the Word of God. (Romans 10:17)

Webster's defines TRANSFORM as altering markedly the appearance or form of; to change the nature, function, or condition of. The word TRANSFORM used in Romans 12:2 (*Vine's*, metamorphoo) means to change into another form, the obligation being to undergo a complete change which, under the power of God, will find expression in character and conduct. This is where we derive the word metamorphosis. It is an apt expression of the changes the Father desires to work in us. We are to be transformed into the same image of our Messiah in all His moral excellence by the Holy Spirit.

But we all, with open face beholding as in a glass the glory of the LORD, are changed into the same image from glory to glory, even as by the Spirit of the LORD. (2 Corinthians 3:18)

This process of change, as led by the Holy Spirit, can sometimes be painful, but always brings a sweeter and closer relationship with the Father.

For though our outward man perish, yet the inward man is RENEWED day by day. (2 Corinthians 4:16)

RENEWED (*Strong's* 341, anakainoo) means restore, renovate, from the root (*Strong's* 2537, kainos) meaning freshness, new.

Study Questions: Chapter 80
1. Define "dis-ease."
2. By what process did the woman, with the issue of blood, receive her healing?
3. What lesson can we learn from the redwood trees?
4. Why does the LORD want to transform you?
5. What does He want you to renew? *(Romans 12:2)*
6. What is the process of renewal?

Chapter Eighty-One
Can You Lose Your Healing?

There is only one example of Jesus commanding a devil not to return. It is in the case of the father who had the sin of unbelief. The demon threw his son into the fire and the water. *(Mark 9:14-27)* It was the father's sin that caused the son to be possessed. After the father repented and Jesus cast the devil out, He ordered it not to return. The devil no longer had a legal right to the son. We can assume that demons did return to tempt people at other times when the person did not stand in faith, or refused to resist temptation to sin, or reopened the door to the evil one. Once the house is swept clean, if the victim does not fill his house with the Word of God, then it is an open invitation for the devil to return. The truth will set you free, but if you do not fill yourself with truth, then deception, a wicked, lying spirit, may try to reenter, and you will not know the difference.

> *When the unclean spirit is gone out of a man, he walketh through dry places, seeking rest, and findeth none. Then he saith, I will return into my house from whence I came out: and when he is come, he findeth it EMPTY, swept and garnished. Then goeth he and taketh with himself seven other spirits more wicked than himself, and they enter in and dwell there: and the LAST STATE OF THAT MAN is WORSE THAN THE FIRST. (Matthew 12:43-45)*

Demons look for gaps and chinks in our armor. If we open the door through sin, we are inviting demons to enter. If we fail to fill ourselves with the Word, the demons may be cast out but they are attracted to EMPTY vessels. This is why eastern religions that teach a person to empty themselves through meditation are so dangerous. Jesus was so concerned about this happening He sought out a man He had healed and warned him not to fall back into sin.

> *Afterward Jesus findeth him in the temple, and said unto him, Behold, thou art made whole: SIN NO MORE, LEST A WORSE THING COME UNTO THEE. (John 5:14)*

If a worse demon came on this man, he could not have made it. He was already unable to lift himself and had been in this state for thirty-eight years.

Began to sink
Peter began to sink; his faith wavered when he saw the storm. Is it easier to walk on stormy water or on still water? I have seen people either start to get healed or get fully healed, and lose their healing before they hit the back doors. Once a woman I prayed for received her healing. She got up from her wheelchair and walked a few steps. Then, she turned and looked at her doubt-ridden husband. He shook his head in blatant unbelief and pursed his lips in disgust. Though she had stood and walked, she now sat and stubbornly refused to try again. An unhealthy, co-dependent relationship, involving a controlling spirit manifesting through the husband, and fear that operated through her, manifested. Doubt and unbelief killed her hope and defeated her faith. She left in the same wheelchair in which she arrived.

Keeping your healing
Our faith is just as much involved in *keeping* our healing as when we receive our healing. We keep our healing by faith. Wavering can cause us to lose our healing. *(James 1:6-7)* Stand fast on the promises of God, resisting the temptation to take back the sickness. The devil thinks if he can wear you down long enough, you will stop resisting. In many cases, he is right. That is why doctors will not say a person is healed but that he is in remission. They see too many cases where a person who was perfectly well comes back in a few months or years with the same symptoms, or worse ones.

Getting free
1. Command doubt and unbelief to come to attention. Inform them you are now aware of their presence. Tell them they are no longer welcome in your house.
2. Cast out doubt and unbelief. Repent of the sin of entertaining them in Jesus' Name.
3. Ask forgiveness.
4. When lying symptoms manifest, firmly say, "No, in Jesus' Name!"
5. Staying in the Word is a key.
6. Trusting the LORD while you stand in your healing is just as important as trusting Him to receive your healing. Speak only faith-filled words.

Chapter Eighty-Two
The Thorn in the Flesh

Suffering for Jesus? Jesus warned we would be **persecuted** (*Strong's* 1377, dioko) for Him if we walked in righteousness. *(Matthew 5:10)* This word means ensue, follow after, given to, press toward. In Acts 9:16, Paul was shown what great things he must **suffer** (*Strong's* 3958, pascho). This word is translated: to experience a sensation or impression, feel passion, vex. These two words, persecuted and suffer, do not mean sickness, infirmity or disease. Rather, the Greek word *pascho* is where we derive the word passion or suffering of Christ. Paul's thorn in the flesh was the divinely permitted, constant persecution from Satan. The Bible is very clear on this point. It was given to Paul so he would not be overly lifted up in men's eyes.

> And LEST I SHOULD BE EXALTED above measure through the abundance of the revelations, there was given to me a THORN in the flesh, the messenger of Satan to BUFFET me, lest I should be exalted above measure. (2 Corinthians 12:7)

The word THORN (skolops) is a word meaning anything pointed, a stake. This was no ordinary stake. According to *Vines*, "What is stressed is not the metaphorical size, but the acuteness of the SUFFERING and its effects." [5] The word BUFFET (*Strong's* 2852, kolaphizo) is the same in every single reference in the Bible. It means to rap with the fist. It does not have anything to do with sickness. The Bible states that people are destroyed for a lack of knowledge. *(Hosea 4:6)* Sickness simply does not bring glory to God. If you believe it does, then stop going to doctors and buying medicine. Lay in your bed and stay sick. Jesus came and healed people in sick beds, and your sickness would have grieved and moved Him with compassion. He would not have applauded your accusation that God put sickness on you to teach you something. He would have said, "Learn of Me. I healed *all* that came to Me."

Afflictions of the righteous

The word AFFLICTIONS (*Strong's* 7451, ra') in the following scripture means trials, hardships, persecution, temptations, calamity, adversity, vexing, trouble. Please note that it does not indicate sickness or disease as traditionally taught, but rather adversity through trials. It is amazing that for every one Christian killed in Rome's circus, approximately eight Romans converted to Christianity because they were so moved by the faithfulness they witnessed.

> Many are the AFFLICTIONS of the righteous: but the LORD delivereth him out of them all. (Psalm 34:19)

Suffering

SUFFERED (*Vines*, pathema) is also translated AFFLICTION, and is where we derive the word pathos. It means suffering because of evil, external influences, also those exerted on the mind. Additionally, it denotes Christ's sufferings and those shared by believers. This scripture does not indicate sickness as some teach, but affliction and persecution for the gospel's sake.

> ...after ye have SUFFERED a while, make you perfect... (1 Peter 5:9)

Chastening

CHASTENETH (*Vine's*, paideuo) is used to denote the training of children, education, instruction, chastisement, correction with words, scourging, blows, reproving, and admonishing by the infliction of calamities. This word has nothing to do with sickness or disease as some have taught.

> ...for whom the LORD loveth He CHASTENETH... (Hebrews 12:5-8)

Chapter Eighty-Three
Overwork and Stress

Overwork can bring sickness

We must use common sense when doing the LORD's work. Often, ministers burn out, exhausting themselves long before their time. Many great men of God have pushed themselves, not resting enough, or eating properly, not caring how they are holding up under the strain and pressure. Holding the work above physical needs is admirable, but will inevitably result in sickness or death. Some great men of God who did not heed the warning their bodies gave them and died are: Jack Coe at 38, A. A. Allen at 59, William Branham at 56, Aimee Semple McPherson at 54, William Seymour at 52, Charles F. Parham at 56, John Alexander Dowie at 60.[6] There are many others. These great men and women of God often died of symptoms brought on by exhaustion. They could have continued God's work for many more years had they taken care of themselves.

Stress in the Bible

Epaphroditus, Paul's assistant, was sick and nigh unto death from trying to help Paul, without any assistance from others. He went far beyond his own strength. *(Philippians 2:25-30)* It is important to call on others to help if there is a need, rather than take the whole burden on yourself. If no one steps forward to take up the slack, then wait and pray until they do. One person cannot carry the entire burden of a ministry. Doing so may cause stress and sickness.

Stress brings sickness

God really loves you. He does not love anyone more than He loves you. His mercy is so rich toward you. His love is so intense toward you that He longs for intimacy with you, to spend private time with you, to show you the exceeding riches of His grace. *(Ephesians 2:4-7)* He wants you to lean on Him and trust Him with your love. He is the lover with His locks soaked with dew. *(Song of Solomon 5:2)*

Learn to lean on Him as John, the beloved disciple did. Just as the bride leaned on her beloved. *(Song of Solomon 8:5)* There is an impartation that He has for those who trust in Him: Peace. Without trust in Him there is no peace. Many sicknesses are caused by stress. Stress is a manifestation of fear; fretting and worry bring stress and sickness, and a lack of peace.

Opposite of fear

The opposite of fear is faith: trusting in God's love for you and His ability to care for you. If you are stressed, then repent and learn to lean on Jesus, that He may care for you. His wonderful plan is for you to live the good life *(Ephesians 2:10 Amp.)* worshiping Him, walking in divine health with all our needs met, to prosper in our lives and service to Him.

Deliverance

1. Stress means lack of trust in God to deliver us.
2. Repent of fear, doubt and unbelief, and ask God's forgiveness.
3. Cast out fear, doubt, unbelief and faithlessness. Cast out stress and strife.
4. If you are overworked and stressed, ask for God's grace and mercy in your situation. You may need deliverance out of your circumstances. If this is the case, ask your loving, heavenly Father for a solution that resolves the problem in a godly manner, and fulfills His plan for your life, but not one bringing escape from your God-given responsibilities, or manipulating others in an ungodly way. This is witchcraft. We must never pray to control others, but to see YHWH, our God's, will be done.
5. Bind faith and trust to yourself. Fight against the devil's plan to destroy you using the fruit of the Spirit, self-control.
6. Speak these words, "Peace, be still!" to your mind, emotions, circumstances and your body. Bind peace to yourself and speak peace over your body, your mind and your circumstances.

Confess your faults

If you have not confessed your faults to another person lately, this is a very uplifting and cleansing experience.

CONFESS YOUR FAULTS one to another, and pray for another, THAT YE MAY BE HEALED. (James 5:16)

The truth is that holding an unrepented sin causes guilt, guilt causes anguish and fretting, which causes worry and stress, all of which can cause sickness.

On national news a man came forward to confess the murder of a girl fifteen years before. He had become a Christian and stated he simply could not live with himself, or try to teach his son right from wrong, knowing what he had done. There is a great Russian novel, *Crime and Punishment*, in which a young man murders two innocent people. He is so obsessed with guilt he becomes gravely ill, finally confessing to the chief of police to get relief. He is sent to Siberia where he finds redemption through loving an unlovable girl, paying for his crime, and receiving Christ.

I minister to men and women in prison all the time. The ones who succeed in that environment are the ones who face up to what they have done and truly repent. The ones in denial never have that freedom. Accepting Christ is a positive step toward changing the character traits and sins that put them there in the first place. Many people I meet put themselves in prisons of their own making through guilt, shame and unforgiveness. A woman I know of had been fearfully abused as a child and had married a man who kept her locked and barred in a motor home, beating and abusing her for years. He moved from place to place to keep his abuse a secret. While he was gone one day, a couple of Christians broke through the bars on the window when they saw her crying out, pounding on the glass. She is now in Bible college, being delivered and working on a degree.

God does not want you to live like that. He came to set the captives free. I have seen men in prison who were more free than some on the outside, simply because of the quality of their relationship with Jesus Christ, and their humble acknowledgement of their desperate need for His cleansing. Humility is definitely a key. Conversely, I have seen men in prison full of pride, sometimes pride in their knowledge of the Bible; but this is head knowledge, not heart knowledge. True heart knowledge reveals to sinful man his continuing need to be cleansed by Jesus' blood and YHWH, our God's, mercy.

Abortion

Many women who have had abortions live in constant torment from their own conscience, and from the devil. Abortion is the murder of innocent life, and one will never have peace until dealing with this issue. Among the seven deadly sins, the LORD reveals that He hates *...hands that shed innocent blood... (Proverbs 6:16-17)* This sin, surrounded by a stronghold of guilt and shame, must be repented of and broken in Jesus' Name. If your abortion was a secret sin, then find someone to whom you can confess. A weight will lift off you as you confess and repent. Weep before the Father and repent for the murder of innocent life. Ask forgiveness and cleansing through Jesus' blood.

Breaking Free

1. Find someone you trust to confess to, or go directly to God. You will sense a great burden lifting off you.
2. Repent and allow God to cleanse you.
3. Break off the spirit of murder, hatred and anger in Jesus' Name.
4. Bind life, the Spirit of adoption and God's love to you.
5. Now ask God for your healing. This unrepented sin and the resultant guilt may have been the very thing preventing your healing.
6. Now, press into God for your healing.

Chapter Eighty-Four
Receiving Healing

Slain in the Spirit

It is not necessary to be slain in the Spirit to receive a healing. I have seen many dramatic healings occur with and without being slain in the Spirit. However, a deeper work often results in the spirit and soulish realm when one is "out under God's power."

Spirit of death

If a spirit of death is present its power must be broken. It must be cast out. This wicked spirit comes to steal, kill and destroy a life before the time. Terminal and incurable diseases are almost certainly a spirit of death. Vigilance must be maintained to keep it away. Pray for wisdom to discover what the open door is that allowed this spirit access to the victim, and minister accordingly. Bind a Spirit of Life to the person.

For the law of the SPIRIT OF LIFE in Christ Jesus hath made me free from the LAW OF SIN AND DEATH. (Romans 8:2)

Blockages

When I pray for people I admonish them not to speak, pray, or praise until the healing is received. There should only be one person praying at a time, speaking or ministering healing. Others around the person receiving prayer should intercede quietly. Otherwise, confusion can result because it is only possible to hear one person speak at a time. This is important in deliverance, too. The demons cannot get in or out if the person is talking. Demons will obey if one person is in authority. If several people are casting them out, it dilutes the deliverance and the demon often will not budge.

Prayer cloths *(Acts 19:11)*

I believe in prayer cloths and know of people healed with them. It is a great way to get the healing power of God to someone who is not present. As with everything in the kingdom, prayer cloths must be received with faith in God, not with faith in the person who sent them. As you exercise your faith, lay the prayer cloth on the sick person or put them under the pillow of someone who needs healing or deliverance.

And God wrought special miracles by the hands of Paul: So that from his body were brought unto the sick handkerchiefs or aprons, and the diseases departed from them, and the evil spirits went out of them. (Acts 19:11-12)

Intercessory prayer

Interceding for the sick is an important part of our Christian walk. We give ourselves to prayer because of our compassion, and when we mix it with love we see the results.

...the effectual fervent prayer of a righteous man availeth much. (James 5:16)

I received a call to pray for the daughter of a traveling evangelist who was dying of cholera. I told him I would fast and pray until I sensed a breakthrough. The next day I fasted and prayed intensely. About three PM the burden lifted and I knew she was healed. I heard a few days later she was healed that same afternoon. There is no distance in prayer. Fasting and praying for someone is very effectual.

Eye of the beholder

Some people think they are too insignificant for God to take notice of them, but Jesus never behaved this way. Throw down religious tradition that teaches you are a lowly worm. Jesus loves to take nobodies and make them somebodies. If we humble ourselves under God's mighty hand, He will exalt us in due season. Jesus' response to our cry for help is, *I will come and heal him. (Matthew 8:7)* Keep your confession positive, "I am healed by His stripes! Jesus took my sickness and carried my disease. He came that I might have abundant life, and this is my heritage as a child of the most high God."

Chapter Eighty-Five
Salvation Means Healing

Salvation includes healing—the good life

Salvation (sozo) is a wonderful word that embraces everything Jesus accomplished on the cross. Salvation is a mighty weapon. It includes our healing, our health and prosperity, rescue, safety, preservation, freedom, liberty, peace, righteousness, victory from fear of danger, material and temporal deliverance from danger and apprehension. This certainly sounds like the good life. But it does not stop there. Through salvation we are pardoned, recreated, healed, restored, made strong in our whole person: mentally, physically, materially, and spiritually.

We have a right to claim our healing based on salvation. This is the simple truth. The moment you were saved, you were healed. It is part of your God-given right to walk around completely well. Salvation is not carnal, or destructive, but mighty through God. *(2 Corinthians 10:4-5)* The devil attacks us through our thoughts, and feelings. "How do you *feel*, Bertha?" She answers, "Oh, I think I'm *taking* a cold. My back hurts, and I think need to go and see a doctor." Bertha passed up a perfectly good opportunity to praise the LORD. Instead, she cursed herself several times. When people ask me how I am I try to answer with something positive like, "Wonderful." The devil may constantly offer us sickness, but *we don't have to take it*!

Born again

If you are not born again, then you really have no covenant with God, and you cannot expect Him to heal you, though He may do so anyway in His compassion. Pray this prayer out loud right now: God, I am a sinner. I repent of all my sins right now in Jesus' Name. Jesus (Yahshua Messiah), I believe you are the Son of God. I believe God raised You from the dead and that You now sit at His right hand. I believe this in my heart and speak it out of my mouth. I repent of all my sins and ask You to forgive me and wash me clean of my sins in Your precious blood which You shed for me. Now, by faith, I receive salvation, healing and deliverance through Your shed blood, Your stripes, Your death, and Your resurrection, the finished work of the cross. Now, by faith I believe I am born again. Amen.

That if thou shalt confess with thy mouth the LORD Jesus, and shalt believe in thine heart that God hath raised Him from the dead, thou shalt be saved. For with the heart man believeth unto righteousness; and with the mouth confession is made unto salvation. (Romans 10:9-10)

Healing before salvation

When I was an entertainer, I was on stage one night, screaming a Janis Joplin song, and my throat tore, blood gushed out, and I fell forward on the audience. I was told I would never sing again. A back-slidden Christian friend said, "Why don't you just ask Jesus to heal you?" I waited until everyone left the house and I got down on my knees and silently mouthed the words, "God, if You are really there, heal my voice and I will give it to You." I got up off the floor completely healed. That summer I joined a repertory summer stock company and sang the part of Eve in "The Apple Tree." I always thought this was God's way of saying, "You work for Me, now."

However, it was several years, after this healing, before I was born again. No one ever personally witnessed about Jesus to me, though deep in my heart I was longing for answers. Under my polished entertainer's exterior was a miserable person. Do not hesitate to share Jesus with the hurting. Assume that if someone does not have Jesus in their heart, then they *are* in desperate need.

Begin to pray for divine appointments and the LORD will surely provide them. There is no more fulfilling life than one wholly submitted to God's direction. When Maria Woodworth-Etter (a great healing evangelist around the turn of the 20th century) would pray, whole cities would come to Jesus. People would suddenly fall down under the power of God, slain in the Spirit in their homes or on the streets, up to one hundred miles away. While lying as dead for hours or days at a time, these people would have visions of heaven or hell and awake begging to be saved.[7] As children of God, we must have the same desire to see souls won to Jesus, Yahshua the Messiah, as she did. Today is the day of salvation!

Chapter Eighty-Six
The Word, the Name, the Blood

The Name

We have mighty weapons to pull down strongholds: the Word (sword of the Spirit), the Name (of Jesus) and the blood (that He shed for us). Sickness is a stronghold. Whatever sickness you are suffering from, it has a name, and every knee must bow to the Name of Jesus.

> *That at the NAME of Jesus EVERY KNEE SHOULD BOW, of things in heaven, and things in earth, and things under the earth. (Philippians 2:10)*

This scripture covers every possible knee. There is not any creature or sickness that does not have to bow its knee before Jesus' Name. There is no special disease or affliction exempt from the power of THE NAME. "Every" knee must bow: Every sickness must go and every demon must flee.

The Blood

The blood of Jesus is a mighty weapon against the devil. *And they overcame him (Satan) by the blood of the Lamb... (Revelation 12:11)* His blood cleanses us from all unrighteousness. "*...and washed us from our sins in His own BLOOD.*" *(Revelation 1:5)* If we will repent, then He is faithful and just to forgive. *But if we will WALK IN THE LIGHT, as He is in the light, we have fellowship one with another, and the BLOOD of Jesus Christ His Son cleanseth us from all sin... (1 John 1:7-9)* Notice the requirement that we WALK IN THE LIGHT. When we keep ourselves pure through repentance, then the devil has no right (if we keep our hearts and minds pure) to condemn us. If you have opened a door through sin, repent quickly. Then stand on God's Word for your healing, and apply the BLOOD of Jesus to your body.

The Word

The Word is more powerful than any two-edged sword. It washes us in the pure water of truth *(James 1:18)*, it is the sword of the Spirit *(Ephesians 6:17)*, the Word is life *(Philippians 2:16)*, this very world was framed by the Word. *(Hebrews 11:3)*

> *For the WORD of God is quick, and powerful, and sharper than any two-edged sword, piercing even to the dividing asunder of soul and spirit, and of the joints and marrow, and is a discerner of the thoughts and intents of the heart. (Hebrews 4:12)*

Memorize healing scriptures and have them on the tip of your tongue. Nothing but the Word should come out of your mouth concerning your situation. No matter what questions people ask you, no matter what the devil tries to slap you with, speak the Word only. Jesus defeated the devil during His temptation by speaking the Word only, and so can you. What if Jesus had said, "I really feel weak and sick. After all, I haven't eaten in forty days. I can barely stand up, much less resist the devil." Instead, He spoke the Word over His situation: *It is written, That man shall not live by bread alone, but by every Word of God. (Luke 4:4)* Learn to fight the devil by using the powerful Word of God through speaking it out of your mouth.

Three witnesses

There are three witnesses in the earth: The Spirit, the blood and the water.

> *...there are three that bear witness in earth, the spirit, and the water, and the blood: and these three agree in one. (1 John 5:8)*

The Spirit, the water and the blood all resided within Jesus before His death. They all flowed out of Jesus at His death and were released for believers to receive after His resurrection to wash, cleanse, anoint and empower us. As born again believers these three should flow through us continuously, as they did Jesus.

> *For whatsoever is born of God overcometh the world: and this is the victory that overcometh the world...our faith. (1 John 5:4)*

Weapons	*Witnesses*
1. The Word	1. The Spirit (Word becomes the sword of the Spirit when we put it in our mouth).
2. The Name	2. The water (Jesus is the Word; we're washed by the water of the Word).
3. The Blood	3. The Blood (the blood cleanses our sin; it is both a weapon and a witness).

Do not let the enemy tell you that you are never going to get your healing. He is baiting his hook to catch you. Cast down every imagination attempting to exalt itself against the knowledge of God. *(2 Corinthians 10:4-5)* Do not let the devil tell you that you are not worthy enough for God to bother with you, that you are nobody, that you have sinned too much and God cannot forgive you, that your sickness is too big for God to handle. Do not believe it! The Word says to cast down those imaginations. What is the knowledge of God? You have the right, through salvation, to your healing. You are to bring every thought captive to the obedience of Christ. Say no to the devil's evil thoughts in Jesus' Name. Make them flee. You are already healed. Claim it! Stand on it! Trust God.

The Way, the Truth and the Life

When Jesus referred to Himself as "the way, the truth and the life," *(John 14:6)* the Jews were enraged. They understood this was a reference to the temple where they worshipped. The gate into the outer court was referred to as "the way." Jesus is truly the way, the actual door we must walk through to enter into the presence of God. In this outer court, they sacrificed animals, shedding blood for the remission of sins. Jesus shed His blood for us on the cross. Beyond this, there was a laver of water where the priests would cleanse themselves, washing their hands and feet (symbolic of the Word of God). By the washing of the water of the Word, they could see their image reflected and know they had fallen short of perfection (symbolic of the cleansing Word—Jesus). The Word leads us to the truth.

The second door into the inner sanctuary called the holy place, was known as "the truth." Inside this room was a lampstand that gave light, representing revelation knowledge from the Holy Spirit. Beyond the light was the shewbread, representing knowledge through eating the Word of God. The shewbread was sprinkled with frankincense, which had a sweet fragrance but a bitter taste. The bitter taste was symbolic of persecution. Persecution leads us to fervently seek God through worship. When a person gets revelation knowledge and anointing, the persecution begins. The next area was the altar of incense. There was incense burning and smoke continually rising from the altar, which represented worship. When the high priest entered the Holy of Holies, the smoke of the incense would go in before him, just as our worship should precede us as we enter into God's holy presence. His presence leads us to life.

The veil was the entrance into the Holy of Holies called "the life." [8] Jesus shed His blood so we may enter boldly into the Holy of Holies without fear of death. The high priest had fear and trembling when he entered once a year into the presence of God with the sacrificial blood, which he poured on the mercy seat of the Ark of the Covenant for the remission of sins. Jesus entered once for all into the Holy of Holies, and His perfect sacrifice was accepted. When we enter into the Holy presence of God we die to self. The blood of Jesus continuously cleanses us.

Jesus said unto him, I Am the WAY, the TRUTH, and the LIFE: no man cometh unto the Father, but by Me. (John 14:6)

1. Gate—gets you inside the outer court (The Way).
2. Door—gets you into Holy Place (The Truth).
3. Veil—entrance to Holy of Holies (The Life).

Chapter Eighty-Seven
Little Faith Vs. Great Faith

Our God has given each of us "the measure of faith." *(Romans 12:3)* How is it then that some have little faith, and some have tremendous faith? Jesus often admonished His disciples because they displayed such little faith. He was astonished at their lack of faith. Because He exercised His faith often, it was natural for Him to do so. If one rarely exercises faith, then faith is small. Because of little faith, the disciples nearly drowned, even with Jesus right there in the boat. When Peter walked on the water he would have drowned if not for Jesus holding him up. The disciples immediately forgot the feeding of the five thousand, behaving as if they had no food when faced with the *same* situation again. They even failed to believe Jesus had risen from the dead, though He had appeared to some of them. These failures were because of the hardness of their hearts. *(Matthew 19:8; Mark 3:5; 16:14)*

Great faith was evidenced by the woman from Canaan who would not stop crying out to Jesus until her daughter was delivered. *(Matthew 15:28)* The centurion is recognized by Jesus as a man of great faith. *(Matthew 8:10)* The two instances of great faith cited by Jesus were both non-Jews. These two people exercised their faith, and they were not even under God's covenant. Yet they moved Jesus to the point that He marveled at their faith. It is a well known fact when missionaries go to foreign countries they see many miracles. Yet, when the same missionaries come to the United States, they rarely see the same level of faith or miracles here.

Two ladies came to one of my concerts after being in a women's meeting. Their faith level was high *when they arrived*. One was slain in the Spirit and healed while God gave her a complete overhaul. The other was healed and delivered. This came quickly because they had been soaking in the anointing, and God's presence was there to heal. If a person is seeking a healing, it is important to spend time preparing by building up faith, soaking in scriptures about healing, praying, standing and trusting God.

There is a story about a tourist who was on the Santa Monica peer. He noticed a man fishing on the shore below. The man would catch a fish and measure it. If it was small he would put it in his bag, but if it was large, he would throw it back. Finally, the tourist asked the fisherman why he was throwing back all the big fish. The man replied that he only had a ten-inch pan.

How much oil can you pour? The widow's oil poured until she ran out of vessels to pour into. She could have poured forever if her sons had believed enough to gather more vessels. *(2 Kings 4:1-6)* How many vessels can you gather?

There is a treasure in our measure of faith. Do we have enough faith to fill a big frying pan or a small one? Can we feed the five thousand, or do we just have enough for a small boy's lunch. A missionary from Hong Kong spoke about how she fed a multitude of people. Once, they did not have enough food for the throngs that came, so they prayed over the small amount left. She attested that they continued to dip in the pot and fed hundreds of people after that, for God multiplied what they had. *...He (Jesus) said unto Simon, Launch out into the deep, and let down your NETS for a draught. And Simon answering said unto Him, Master, we have toiled all the night, and have taken nothing: nevertheless at Thy Word I will let down the NET. And when they had this done, they enclosed a great multitude of fishes: and their NET brake...they BEGAN TO SINK. (Luke 5:4-7)*

Notice that Jesus instructed them to let down NETS, plural. Peter answered with an excuse because he, like many of us, was a man who looked at the circumstances, rather than the bigness of God. He relented, but only let down one NET. Jesus had a huge miracle in mind, but Peter's thinking was too small. Because of this his one net broke and his boat nearly sank. When a person limits God, they limit the blessing. How many nets would you let down? When Jesus invited Peter to walk on the water, once again his faith was too small. *...BEGINNING TO SINK, he cried, saying, LORD, save me. (Matthew 14:30)* Without faith in God's Word we will all SINK!!!

The great evangelist, Smith Wigglesworth, said, "God has no favorites. He works through those who believe Him." David Hogan, a missionary to Central and South America has raised over 250 people from the dead through his ministry. He tells many awesome stories. A baby had died in a village where he was ministering on the power of God. The parents and grandparents brought the baby to him and he held it in his arms. He prayed for the baby and commanded life to come back into it. As he handed him to his father, David said, "The child is alive!" The father handed him to his mother and said, "The child is alive." She handed him to his grandmother who said the same thing and handed him to the grandfather. When the grandfather said, "The child is alive," the baby began to cry and they handed him back to his mother, alive and well. God is definitely still in the miracle working business.

Once David was ministering in a small village and he saw a heap of filthy clothes in the corner. He asked someone what it was. They told him it was a man filled with leprosy. The man was covered in a gooey slime but David stuck his hand on the man and prayed for him. Afterward, he stressed that all he could think about was how badly he wanted to wash his hand. When he came back to the village a few weeks later, a man with beautiful new baby-like skin, clean and dressed, came up to him. He asked, "Do you remember me?" David said, "I have never seen you before in my life." The man stated he was the one with leprosy who God had miraculously healed.

The prayer of faith

God's promise to us is: *...the prayer of faith shall save the sick. (James 5:15)* This promise is about faith, not feelings. Anointing with oil is effectual, and we can do this or trust the oil of the Holy Spirit Who lives in us to flow through us.

Feeling born again has nothing to do with actually being saved, any more than feeling healed has anything to do with actually being healed. Salvation and healing are both contingent upon faith. Moses lifted up the serpent in the wilderness (symbolic of the Messiah on the cross) and they were healed. *(Numbers 21:9)* When we lift up Jesus the Messiah, the Anointed One, we, too, are healed. *(John 3:14)*

Chapter Eighty-Eight
Discerning the LORD's Body

Sickness through taking the LORD's supper in an unworthy manner

Taking the LORD's supper in an unworthy manner can bring sickness, even death. I have seen many people take the LORD's supper in a very nonchalant manner, and offer it to their children like a snack. Before taking the LORD's supper, there should be a time of soul searching, repenting for any sins, and asking for forgiveness. Some time and solemnity should be part of the process. It is not to be taken lightly or rushed through. Read this scripture carefully and weigh the words in your heart. Could this be one of the reasons for sickness and premature death in the body of Christ? If you've missed God in this area, repent, ask God to forgive you and then pray for your healing.

> *For as often as ye eat this bread, and drink this cup, ye do show the LORD's death 'till He come. Wherefore whosoever shall eat this bread, and drink this cup of the LORD, unworthily, SHALL BE GUILTY of the body and blood of the LORD. But let a man EXAMINE HIMSELF, and so let him eat of that bread, and drink of that cup. For he that eateth and drinketh unworthily, eateth and drinketh DAMNATION to himself, NOT DISCERNING THE LORD'S BODY. For this cause MANY ARE WEAK AND SICKLY among you, and MANY SLEEP* (are dead). *(1 Corinthians 11:26-30)*

Discerning the LORD's body

When we take the LORD's supper, we are receiving into ourselves, symbolically, His body and His blood. One was for saving us and one was for healing us. Most people have no trouble believing His blood was shed for our sins. Being saved entails receiving that sacrifice as a free gift. Yet, when it comes to His blood being shed so that we might be healed (the stripes, the nails, the beating, the spear in the side and His death) they have trouble receiving their healing. In other words, they have trouble discerning the LORD's body. Jesus taught the disciples to receive not just the wine, but also the bread. Grapes must be crushed and pressed beyond measure to produce wine, and wheat must first be beaten, threshed and ground to powder to produce bread. Jesus suffered all this for us.

The type and shadow of Jesus' complete atonement for our sin-sick souls and bodies was in Egypt. God told the Hebrew children to kill the Passover lamb. The lamb was to have its entrails wrapped around its head, and be roasted in the shape of a cross. It was to be eaten completely, nothing wasted, so that all could walk out of Egypt healed and strong. Its blood was to be put on their doorposts so that death would pass over them. Later, in great strength of numbers, they were to possess the Promised Land. *(Exodus 12:3-14)*

Jesus was our Passover Lamb. He hung on a cross, giving His life to nourish us. We receive the blood that saves our souls when we apply it over the door of our hearts through salvation, and we must receive the bread that represents His body, as the flesh of the Passover lamb, taking the whole gospel, not just the parts we like, so we may walk out of the land of wickedness, sickness and idolatry, into the land of promise and provision, health and healing, walking in God's complete plan of redemption. Jesus' blood was shed to save us from death, His body tortured and killed for healing and deliverance. *...the blood of Jesus Christ His Son cleanseth us from all sin. (1 John 1:7) ...thy sins be forgiven thee. (Mark 2:5)*

Often, Jesus would forgive sins and heal the people. When asked how He dared to say these words He replied, *Whether it is easier to say to the sick of the palsy, Thy sins be forgiven thee; or to say, Arise, and take up thy bed, and walk? (Mark 2:9)* To Jesus, healing and salvation were one and the same. It is a travesty to separate the gospel into a "then and now doctrine (dispensationalism)," filled with unbelief and legalism. This separation of the properties of the gospel is the cause of much unbelief, robbing us of our faith that healing is for us, now. The old covenant included the right to receive healing, and our new covenant is even better. Jesus fulfilled the law perfectly for us. All we have to do is believe. Salvation and healing go together like the bread and the wine.

1. **Be saved:** *But as many as received Him...gave He power to become the sons of God, even to them that believe on His Name. (John 1:12)*
2. **Be healed:** *...as many as touched Him were made whole. (Mark 6:56)*

The great commission

When Jesus commissioned the disciples, He always told them both to preach, and to heal the sick. We must never separate one from the other. Jesus sent out the seventy to preach the gospel, giving them specific instructions on their journey: *And heal the sick that are therein, and say unto them, The kingdom of God is come nigh unto you. (Luke 10:9)* In other words, when the gospel is preached, one can be saved, healed and delivered all at the same time. The seventy came back with joy saying that even the devils were subject to them. It brings great joy to go in

Jesus' Name, because we can heal the sick and cast out devils, not just win souls. The last thing Jesus said before being taken up into heaven is known as the great commission, yet so few act on these instructions and promises, let alone, believe them. *Go ye into all the world, and preach the gospel to every creature. He that believeth and is baptized shall be saved…they shall lay hands on the sick, and they shall recover. (Mark 16:15-18)* In the book of Acts, when the apostles were threatened by the high priest and the council, they prayed.

And now, LORD, behold their threatenings: and grant unto Thy servants, that with all boldness they may speak Thy Word, by stretching forth Thine hand to heal; and that signs and wonders may be done by the Name of Thy holy child Jesus. (Acts 4:29-30)

They prayed to do two things: to have freedom to preach the Word and to heal the sick. These two things went together when Jesus walked the earth, and nothing changed during the apostle's ministry. It is the same for us today.

Chapter Eighty-Nine
Regeneration

Smith Wigglesworth attended a large outdoor meeting where men were questioning God. After a short time, he could take it no more. He leaped up and shouted, "LORD, stop their mouths. They're charging the air with unbelief!" Unbelief is the greatest obstacle to miracles. Jesus, Himself, could do no mighty works in a town filled with unbelief. *(Matthew 13:58)* He would often question people, ***"Believe ye that I am able to do this?"*** *(Matthew 9:28)*

Growing missing parts

Jesus healed all who came to Him, and that sometimes meant the regeneration of missing parts. Leprosy is a disease that eats away fingers and toes, yet the Bible states that Jesus healed them. If the LORD can make an ax head float *(2 Kings 6:5)*, He can create a new part for a human. Kathryn Kuhlman's ministry had many testimonies of new parts being created. According to your faith be it unto you! If the dead can be raised, then a person can receive a new arm or leg, or a new eye. It is a matter of calling those things that be not as though they were. *(Romans 4:17)* Jesus restored the crippled and the maimed, both *then* and *now*.

Regeneration, according to *Webster's*, means to reproduce, to beget; to reform spiritually or morally; to form, construct or create anew; TO REPLACE A LOST OR DAMAGED ORGAN OR PART BY FORMATION OF NEW TISSUE; revitalized, restored; renewed; revival or rebirth.

Regeneration (*Vine's*, paligenesia) means new birth: palin means again, and genesis means birth. "Paligenesia" involves a new life. According to *Vine's*, the two operating powers to produce this new life are:

1. The Word of truth (we speak the Word).
2. The Holy Spirit (He moves).

We speak the Word and the Holy Spirit moves. New birth (regeneration) takes place as we synergistically cooperate with the Holy Spirit. Synergism is effected by a combination of human will and divine grace (*Webster's*). We, as Christians, have the creative power of life, regeneration and renewal in our tongues.

*...according to His mercy He saved us, by the washing of **REGENERATION**, and **RENEWING** of the Holy Ghost. (Titus 3:5)*

Always remember faith activates the hand of YHWH, our God. Miracles are possible to them who believe. *(Mark 9:23)* Medical science had recently had breakthrough technology in taking a cow's cell, extracting the nucleus, and adding human DNA for the purpose of regenerating human body parts. Dr. Jesus has been doing this from the beginning, and much more efficiently.

Receiving your miracle

1. Cast out all doubt and unbelief. Miracles do not happen when unbelief is present.
2. Curse the disease or deformity at the root.
3. Call on the miracle power of YHWH Rapha, and His Son Yahshua Messiah (Jesus Christ) our healer, to create the new part.
4. Command new DNA to form.
5. Speak new body parts into existence.
6. Speak life to the person.
7. Bind Titus 3:5 and 1 Peter 2:24 to the person.
8. Command the new part to grow in Jesus' Name.
9. Trust God to restore and regenerate.

Chapter Ninety
The Weapon of Praise

Begin to praise your heavenly Father for your healing. Praise is a powerful weapon against the enemy. After I first got saved the devil would come and attempt to put depression on me, which used to lead to thoughts of rejection and suicide. The LORD mercifully intervened by showing me how to jump up and loudly say, "No, in Jesus' Name!" I would begin leaping and dancing and praising the LORD. Very quickly, the devil would leave because he could not stand to be in the midst of praise to the Father. Resist the devil through praise and he will flee. *(James 4:7)*

The hand of God

The hand of God is not moved by needs, but by faith. Faith grows as it is exercised, like a muscle. Each man is given THE measure of faith. We are free in Christ Jesus; FREE to receive our healing. Hallelujah!

For the law of the Spirit of life in Christ Jesus hath made me FREE from the law of sin and death. (Romans 8:2)

Let us sow faith and let us reap healing. Someone said, "Your expectation is the magnetism that pulls your miracle to you." Expect a miracle today! Believe God's Word far above the circumstances. Faith-filled words dominate the law of sin and death. The power of life and death is in your tongue.

Let us pray

Jesus, I praise You for what You have already done for me through the stripes You took and Your death on the cross. I repent for any doubt, unbelief, fear or faithlessness that I am harboring in my soul. I break the stronghold of guilt, shame and sin by asking Your forgiveness in every area of my life. Forgive me for every sin I've committed of thought, word, and deed, and every sin of omission and commission in Jesus' Name (take time here to let the Holy Spirit speak to your heart). Forgive me for listening to lying spirits instead of believing Your Word. I rebuke the spirit of infirmity off me. Infirmity, I do not want you. Loose me and leave me now; never come back, in Jesus' Name! You have no authority or right to attack me from this moment forward, for my body is the temple of the Holy Ghost.

I bind faith and trust, belief and peace to my heart. Today, I receive my miracle. I fully expect to receive great things from my heavenly Father Who yearns for me. YHWH, my LORD and my God, I choose the abundant life. I believe and receive my healing today. Thank You, Father, for setting me free. I have great hope and expectation and I will not give up, but I will continue to believe Your Word more than I believe what I see. All the praise and glory and honor belong to You. Thank You, Yahshua Messiah, LORD Jesus, for my healing. Thanks be to God Who ALWAYS causes me to triumph in the Messiah. Amen.

Study Questions: Chapter 87
1. What are the three elements of the prayer of faith?
2. What is THE measure of faith?
3. Why do some have great faith while others seem to have no faith?
4. What is the gift of faith? *(1 Corinthians 12:8-10)*
5. How does this differ from the measure of faith?
6. How does faith come?

Study Questions: Chapter 88
1. How are salvation and healing related?
2. Discuss the bread and the wine.
3. How are they related to salvation and healing?
4. Explain Jesus' instructions to the disciples in Luke 10:9.
5. How has this seminal issue affected YHWH's people from the original Passover to the present?
6. What is the "great commission?"

Chapter Ninety-One
How to Walk in Divine Health

It is wonderful to receive your healing, and glorious to have a miracle happen to you, but it is even better to walk in divine health all the time. This means you do not have to run to someone for prayer every time you get sick. Rather, you walk in divine health as a lifestyle: Knowing who you are in Christ, the authority of His Word, and believing and acting on God's promises at all times, are all important ingredients for walking in divine health.

To walk in divine health means putting the Word in your heart constantly, and speaking it out of your mouth, ceaselessly. Faith comes by hearing and it will come to your heart as you speak the Word. *(Romans 10:17)* When the devil tries to attack you with sickness, be ready! Remember that trusting in YHWH, our God, with all your heart, nothing wavering *(James 1:6)*, is part of your privilege and the secret to your success.

A lifestyle centered on godly purposes will promote healthy thinking and healthy living. Remember the saying, "Garbage in—garbage out!" The quality of what you put in your mind and heart will be reflected in your conversation, thought life and lifestyle.

> *...for out of the abundance of the heart the mouth speaks. A good man out of the good treasure of the heart bringeth forth good things. (Matthew 12:34-35)*

Did you catch that? By putting God's Words in your mouth, you will bring forth good things; abundant life and health from El Shaddai, the God Who is more than enough. You can have whatsoever you SAY! Jesus said it best:

> *...whosoever shall SAY unto this mountain, Be thou removed, and be thou cast into the sea; and SHALL NOT DOUBT in his heart, but shall believe that those things which he SAYETH shall come to pass; HE SHALL HAVE WHATSOEVER HE SAITH. (Mark 11:23)*

Skeptics hate this verse, but faith-filled words *do* dominate and take precedence over the law of sin and death. The Spirit of life has made us free from sin and death. *(Romans 8:2)* It is the devil who has come to steal good health and destroy your life. Defeat him as Jesus did, by speaking the life producing Word of God.

Health professionals tell us we are what we eat. It also bears saying we can have what we say.

> *If ye ABIDE in Me, and My Words ABIDE in you, ye shall ASK WHAT YE WILL, and it shall be DONE unto you. (John 15:7)*

ABIDE (*Strong's* 3306, meno) means to stay in a given place, relationship or expectancy; continue, dwell, endure, remain. The word DONE (*Strong's* 1096, ginomai) is where we derive the word GENERATE. It means to be created, produced, established, born, appointed, come into existence, come to pass. When the Word of God lives in us, that is, when it takes up residence in our hearts, it creates an expectancy in us: it GENERATES abundant life and health. That is our God's promise, if we dwell, endure and abide in His Word! Your mouth can be your greatest enemy or your best friend. Your mouth is a WELLSPRING OF LIFE.

> *Understanding is a WELLSPRING OF LIFE...The heart of the wise TEACHETH HIS MOUTH... (Proverbs 16:22-23)*

> *The MOUTH of a righteous man is a WELL OF LIFE. (Proverbs 10:11)*

Speaking the Word creates a rich foundation of faith, trust and wellness that promotes an environment of health. Let us review the earlier example of the fruitful tree. *A wholesome tongue is a tree of life...(Proverbs 15:4)* To grow as a healthy tree, produce good fruit, and walk in divine health, we must constantly receive the living water (the Word), have fertile soil (be enriched by and deeply rooted in the Word), and let the "Son light" shine in our hearts to continue to grow. Then we can joyfully produce the good fruit of divine health. Speak life to your body (not words that curse it) by speaking God's Word in faith. *...the Words that I speak unto you, they are Spirit, and they are life. (John 6:63)* It is definitely God's will for you to walk in divine health, but you must cooperate by living a healthy lifestyle, as well. Eat healthy live food such as raw fruit, vegetables and nuts; drink plenty of pure water. Use good sense in the type and quantity of exercise, and always try to rest and get sufficient sleep. Do not go beyond what you can handle physically. Some of God's greatest healing ministers ignored this simple wisdom and died before their time.

Live a life of peace and seek wisdom from God, daily. Stress and strife will kill you. Eliminate them. Make the necessary changes in your lifestyle to spend time seeking the LORD and His Word every single day. Learn to abide in His secret place and do not let circumstances drag you out of the center of His will, which brings perfect peace. Forgive everyone you know: wipe that scorecard of offenses you are keeping, completely clean. Humble yourself under YHWH, our God's, mighty hand and stay in an attitude of humility. Learn to stand on God's Word!

If you are sick now, do not be discouraged or condemned. Read this book and your Bible and be healed. Get my 100 minute *"Healing Scriptures"* tape, and the *"Heart & Soul Surrender"* CD or cassette. Listen to the song *"Stripes."* Many have been healed just listening to these materials. When you are well, learn to maintain your health God's way, which is to walk in divine health all the time.

Bibliography for *Stripes*

1. Tenny, *The Gospel of Belief*, p. 153
2. Hibbert, *Smith Wigglesworth: The Secret of His Power*, Harrison House, 1982, pp. 18-19, 91, 94
3. Wright, *A More Excellent Way*, Pleasant Valley Publications, 2000
4. Ibid.
5. *Vine's*, p. 1143
6. Lairdon, *God's Generals*, Albury Publishing 1996
7. Etter, *Signs & Wonders*, Harrison House 1916
8. Hinn, *Seven Keys To the Anointing* (video)

Other Materials Available
Through This Ministry

Jezebel VS. Elijah – The Great End Time Clash (book) $12.95 Anointed revelationary teaching on the great struggle for the souls of men. Jezebel is trying to take over the church, our country and the home. Elijah is arising to overcome her. Put on your seat belts. This one packs a wallop! (An accredited college course. Available by arrangement.)

Heart & Soul Surrender (music) CD $15.95; cassette $12.95 (price includes a study guide) Received nationwide airplay for three years. Anointed music to lead the listener into the presence of God, bringing salvation, healing, deliverance and worship. Includes four electrifying dramatic works, *"Stripes," "Nails," "Thorns"* and *"The Blood."*

Healing Scriptures (cassette) $10.00 One hundred minutes of healing scriptures, exhortation and music; the most riveting and complete healing tape of its kind.

Bitter-Root Judgments, Soul Ties and Inner Vows (cassette) $10.00 We have all made them—they are destroying our lives—get set free with this insightful teaching cassette that has already helped so many.

Advanced Spiritual Warfare (12 teachings on cassette) $40.00 Potent and compelling, powerful preparation for prayer warriors and for ministries. (An accredited college course: Available by arrangement.)

Victorious Scriptures (book) $10.00 A strategic and forceful new book; includes complete victorious scriptures, names of God and their significance, exhortation and prayers.

Victorious Scriptures (two 90 minute cassettes) $12.00 For the overcomer; powerful, uplifting scriptures, exhortation and music throughout; indispensable.

For the Bride: Song of Solomon, Esther & Ruth (two 90 minute cassettes) $12.00 Vibrant and profound, eye-opening, end-time message; calling forth the Bride. A four part series.

America—Repent or Perish (book) $5.95 An urgent call to repentance, prayer and fasting for the leaders and people of America.

Freemasonry (cassette) $10.00 Exposing Freemasonry.

About the Author

Dr. Bree M. Keyton is the author of several books. She is an ordained minister holding two teaching certificates in English and in Speech and Theater, with certification in Missouri. She holds doctorates in Theology and in Administration and Education. She is a professor at a Bible college where she designs curriculum and serves on the board as head of research.

Bree ministers in power evangelism, brandishing a sword of steel while exercising the sword of the Spirit. Thousands have been saved, delivered and received physical and emotional healing by the awesome power of God. Bree's mandate from the LORD is to *SET THE CAPTIVES FREE!*

Bree has a CD that received nationwide airplay for three years, and she travels preaching the gospel. She teaches the Word and leads her own family worship team, which performs where she ministers upon request. She has a zeal for soul winning, healing the sick and setting the captives free. She has hosted a national TV talk show and served as a worship leader. Before being born again, Bree traveled as a warm-up act for rock stars and had her own nightclub act. She was shot in the head, and through the miraculous intervention of the living God, she lived to tell the story and share God's great healing power with others.

Bree has appeared on *"The 700 Club,"* TBN, the National Right to Life Convention, the International Counter-Cult Conference, the National Full Gospel Business Men's Convention, and appeared on the international TV program *"It's Supernatural"* with Sid Roth. Bree has performed in arenas, churches, music halls, prisons, malls, parks, high schools, colleges, retreats, crusades, coffee houses, and outdoor festivals.

This book serves as a textbook for a college course, *Advanced Spiritual Warfare*, and college credit is available by arrangement.

To contact Bree Keyton's ministry:

Bree & Steve Keyton Ministries
PO Box 17802
Kansas City, Missouri 64134

www.breekeytonministries.com